D0464534

CHILDREN'S THINKING: WHAT DEVELOPS?

Edited by

ROBERT S. SIEGLER

CARNEGIE-MELLON UNIVERSITY

LAWRENCE ERLBAUM ASSOCIATES, PUBLISHERS
1978   Hillsdale, New Jersey

DISTRIBUTED BY THE HALSTED PRESS DIVISION OF
JOHN WILEY & SONS
New York   Toronto   London   Sydney

*In questions of science, the authority of
a thousand is not worth the humble
reasoning of a single individual.*

GALILEO GALLILEI

Lawrence Erlbaum Associates, Inc., Publishers
62 Maria Drive
Hillsdale, New Jersey 07642

Distributed solely by Halsted Press Division
John Wiley & Sons, Inc., New York

Library of Congress Cataloging in Publication Data

Main entry under title:

Children's thinking.

  Includes bibliographies.
  1. Cognition in children.   I. Siegler, Robert S.
BF723.C5C5   155.4′13   78-13119
ISBN 0-470-26520-5

Printed in the United States of America

Contents

Preface   VII

PART I: MEMORY DEVELOPMENT

1. Skills, Plans, and Self-Regulation
Ann L. Brown and Judy S. DeLoache **3**

    I.   Introduction   3
    II.   Differences Between the Memory
         Development and Problem-Solving
         Approaches to Cognitive Development   4
    III. Commonalities Between Memory Development
         and Problem-Solving Literature   12
    IV. Alternate Methods for Asking
         What Develops   17
    V.   Summary   30
         References   31

2. Intellectual Development from Birth to Adulthood:
A Neo-Piagetian Interpretation
Robbie Case **37**

    Intellectual Development During the
      First Three Stages of Life   37
    The Underlying Mechanism of Development:
      Long-Term Changes in the
      Human Psychological System   58
    Developmental Changes After Age Twelve   62
    Summary and Conclusions   64
    References   67

3. **Knowledge Structures and Memory Development**
Michelene T. H. Chi **73**

Factors in Memory Development   73
Memory Span for Faces   76
Memory for Chess Positions   80
Knowledge and Metamemory   87
General Discussion   94
References   95

4. **Comments**
John H. Flavell **97**

Comments on Brown and DeLoache's Paper   97
Comments on Case's Paper   99
Comments on Chi's Paper   102
References   105

PART II: PROBLEM SOLVING

5. **The Origins of Scientific Reasoning**
Robert S. Siegler **109**

Scientific Reasoning in Childhood
   and Adolescence   109
The Origins of Scientific Reasoning   118
What Develops in Scientific Reasoning   142
Epilogue   147
References   147

6. **How Do Children Solve Class-Inclusion Problems?**
Tom Trabasso, Alice M. Isen, Phyllis Dolecki,
Alexander G. McLanahan, Christine A. Riley and
Teressa Tucker **151**

Introduction   151
A Task Analysis   154
Discussion   177
References   179

7. **Goal Formation, Planning, and Learning by Pre-School**
Problem Solvers or: "My Socks are in the Dryer"
David Klahr **181**

Introduction   181
The Tower of Hanoi   183
Solution Strategies   187
A Study of Children's Performance   197

Concluding Comments   209
References   211

8. **Counting in the Preschooler:
What Does and Does Not Develop**
Rochel Gelman **213**

The Counting Model   213
The Data for Evidence on Ability to Use
   How-to-Count Principles   219
The Evidence   223
What Develops?   238
References   240

9. **A Discussion of the Chapters by Siegler, Trabasso,
Klahr, and Gelman**
James G. Greeno **243**

Author's Note   243
Dramatis Personae   243
References   251

PART III: REPRESENTATIONAL PROCESSES

10. **How Children Represent Knowledge of Their World
In and Out of Language: A Preliminary Report**
Katherine Nelson **255**

Study I   258
Study II   264
Implications   271
References   273

11. **Spatial Concepts, Spatial Names, and the Development
of Exocentric Representations**
Lee W. Gregg **275**

Method   276
Results   279
Comprehending the Symbolic Functions of Buttons   283
Are There Alternative Stages?   285
An Information-Processing Analysis   285
Mental Rotations and Exocentric Representations   287
Conclusion: Egocentric Children and
   Exocentric Representations   289
References   289

12. Imagery and Cognitive Development: A Teleological Approach
Stephen Michael Kosslyn **291**

    1.0 Overview 292
    2.0 Phase I: Discriminating Among Competing
         Hypotheses About Key Issues 294
    3.0 Phase II: Constructing a Process Model 306
    4.0 Extrapolating Backward: The Teleological
         Function of the Model 313
    5.0 Conclusions 320
         References 321

13. Individual Differences in Solving Physics Problems
Dorothea P. Simon and Herbert A. Simon **325**

    The Task Content 326
    Solution Times and Paths 327
    A More Difficult Problem 339
    Implications for Learning 344
    Conclusion 345
    References 347

14. Representing Knowledge Development
Gordon H. Bower **349**

    Commentary on Nelson's Chapter 349
    Commentary on Gregg's Chapter 352
    Comments on Kosslyn's Chapter 354
    Comments on the Chapter by Dorothea and
       Herbert Simon 357
    Final Comments 361
    References 362

Author Index   **363**

Subject Index   **369**

Preface

In 1963, John Flavell posed one of the truly basic questions underlying the study of chldren's thinking; his question was simply "What develops?" The 13th Annual Carnegie Cognition Symposium, held in May 1977, seemed to me an appropriate forum for considering what progress had been made toward answering this question in the past 15 years. Therefore, when I invited participants for the Symposium, I asked them to explicitly consider the issue as it applied to their areas of greatest current interest. Both the range of the answers they produced and the quality of the evidence they marshalled to support their views attest to the continuing importance of Flavell's original question; they also attest to the vitality of the field of cognitive development.

I have arranged the chapters within the book into three sections: memory development, development of problem solving skills, and development of representational processes. The first section concentrates on the area of memory development. In Chapter 1, Brown and DeLoache present an overview of current research in this field. Of particular interest is their contrast of memory development research with research on problem solving; they argue strongly that the two areas have exactly opposite sets of strengths and weaknesses. Brown and DeLoache also review Soviet research indicating that young children may have far greater memorial capacities than they usually are given credit for. Finally, they nominate their prime candidate for what develops: metacognition.

In Chapter 2, Case presents a new general theory of memory development. The theory is applied to a very broad range of childhood, from the first years of life through adolescence. Ideas of Piaget, Pascual-Leone, and Newell and Simon are given prime roles within it. M–space and executive strategies emerge as especially important sources of development within Case's theory.

In Chapter 3, Chi addresses directly the question of what causes developmental differences in memory. She indicates that there are three likely possibilities: changes in capacity, changes in strategies, and changes in knowledge about the material that is being memorized. In one of the most dramatic experiments reported in the volume, Chi demonstrates that 10-year-olds who are knowledgeable about chess outperform mildly knowledgeable adults on both mnemonic and metamnemonic tasks involving chess configurations. This was not due to the children having better memories in absolute terms—when tested on standard digit span tasks, the adults showed the usual superiority over the children. Thus, it is not surprising that Chi emphasizes sheer amount of knowledge as an important component of development.

Flavell discusses the three memory development articles in Chapter 4. As with all of the discussions, his comments are too diverse and demand too much understanding of the articles to be easily summarized here. They definitely should be read carefully, though; "What develops?" is his question, after all.

The next section of the book concerns the development of problem-solving skills. In the first chapter in this section, Chapter 5, I explore the origins of scientific reasoning. Children seem to acquire initial systematic strategies on a wide variety of scientific problems during the period between age three and age five. Their ability to learn systematic strategies that they do not already possess also improves dramatically during this period. The question is how we can explain these developments. Within the research that I present, improved encoding emerges as an especially important explanatory factor.

In Chapter 6, Trabasso, Isen, Dolecki, McClanahan, Riley, and Tucker review what is known about children's understanding of class inclusion; they also present a large number of new experiments of their own. The chapter is organized around a task analysis of what children would need to know to comprehend the class inclusion concept. This analysis indicates eight separate components. Represented among these are the physical display, interpreting the question, finding referents for the subordinate and superordinate classes, quantifying them, comparing the quantified symbols, and deciding on the correct amounts. Interestingly, when all the evidence is in, Trabasso et al. conclude that all eight components may be important sources of developmental change.

Klahr, in Chapter 7, examines three- to five-year-olds' ability to plan ahead. The task he uses is a variant of the familiar Tower of Hanoi, beloved to all students of problem solving. Klahr finds that children pass through a number of knowledge states on their way to understanding how to solve such problems. These knowledge states are reflected not so much in how many moves children can make without erring as in the types of moves they can make. Klahr also finds that at least some young children are capable of planning surprisingly long and complex sequences of activities. He nominates procedural knowledge as an especially important source of development.

In the final chapter in the problem-solving section, Gelman analyzes the development of counting skills. Her focus is on very young children, two- to four-year-olds. She ingeniously demonstrates that even before their performance is entirely accurate, such children often have considerable understanding of the principles underlying counting. Gelman sees development as occurring primarily in the range of situations in which these counting principles are correctly applied.

After Greeno's discussion, in which he considers what Piaget, Binet, Thorndike, Wertheimer, and Dewey might have to say about the problem-solving papers, we turn to the third and final section of the book, the development of representational processes. In Chapter 10, Nelson considers one type of representational development, the development of language skills. Nelson uses the script formalism to examine children's understanding of mealtime routines in three situations: home, the daycare center, and McDonald's. She finds that children as young as three and four years understand what is constant and what is variable within each setting. Elaboration of scripts emerges as an important aspect of development in this report.

Gregg, in Chapter 11, examines children's exocentric representations, their ability to take perspectives other than their own. The experimental situation involves three- to five-year-olds in guiding the Turtle, a computer-controlled robot, through a maze known as Turtle Town. The child always sits in the same place and uses a button box to make the Turtle turn left or right or go straight ahead; thus, he is forced to adjust his spatial perspective to that of the Turtle. Gregg suggests that development on this task is dependent on increasingly elaborated frames. This formalism emerges as quite similar to the scripts Nelson speaks of.

In Chapter 12, Kosslyn examines the development of another representational process, visual imagery. Taking seriously the metaphor that the child is father to the man, Kosslyn describes how he has worked back and forth between research with children and research with adults to derive theories of both mature and developing imagery systems. Among other accomplishments, Kosslyn has written a running computer simulation of how people form images and how they use them. The article includes both descriptions and prescriptions concerning how to develop psychological theories.

In Chapter 13, Dorothea and Herb Simon use protocol analysis and computer simulation techniques to analyze the transition from unskilled to skilled problem solving in physics. Their article focuses on the performance of two individuals on high school level kinematics problems. One of the subjects is a novice at such tasks, the other a relative expert. The contrast in the equations they use on different problems points to the importance of physical intuition in this domain. Physicists and others have often spoken of such intuition as crucial to skilled performance, but few attempts have been made to specify exactly what the term might mean. The Simons' chapter is a step toward this goal.

Finally, in the last discussion of the book, Bower critiques each of the representational development articles in turn, and then suggests that rather than playing the role of Grand Inquisitor, he would prefer to have been the Grand Cheerleader for the Symposium.

Scanning over all of the articles, several themes emerge; I think that these are quite revealing about current directions within cognitive development. One of the themes concerns the increasing age range that is coming under scientific scrutiny. Numerous investigators (e.g., Gelman, 1978; Neimark, 1975) have commented that cognitive developmentalists have concentrated their attention disproportionately on the age range between five and ten years. This situation appears to be changing rapidly. No less than six of the 11 articles in the volume (Brown and DeLoache, Gelman, Gregg, Klahr, Nelson, and Siegler) focus primarily or exclusively on children below the age of five. At the other end of the spectrum, there is also increasing appreciation of the relevance of research with adults to the study of development. This is most directly manifested within the chapters written by Chi, Kosslyn, and the Simons, but to varying degrees it is seen in almost all of the contributions.

Another apparent trend is the increasing focus on what children of given ages *can* do rather than on what they cannot do. This is especially evident in the work with very young children. Traditionally, children below age seven seem to have been included in cognitive development experiments primarily to provide a baseline against which cognitive growth could be measured. Yet, in the present volume, we hear Gelman speaking of the counting principles three- and four-year-olds understand, Nelson speaking of the scripts they know, Klahr describing the plans five-year-olds can formulate, Gregg indicating the nonegocentric perspectives they can take, and me describing the systematic rules they can use. Brown and DeLoache point out in Chapter 1 that it is much more informative to be told what children of any age are doing than to be told what they are not doing; the subsequent chapters in the book indicate how right they are.

Another trend evident in this volume is an emphasis on using more natural, nonlaboratory-oriented tasks. There have been many recent calls for more ecologically valid investigations in all domains of psychology (e.g., Charlesworth, 1976; Neisser, 1976). These calls seem to be having a substantial influence on students of cognitive development. Some of the tasks described in this collection are taken directly from the day-to-day lives of children: remembering a grocery list (Brown and DeLoache), counting (Gelman), and mealtime routines (Nelson). Others are tasks that many children encounter in school: balance scales, projection of shadows, probability problems (Siegler), and kinematics problems (Simon and Simon). The game of chess (Chi) would also seem to qualify for the ecologically valid seal of approval.

A final direction in which the field seems to be going is toward increasing use of formalisms to represent what children know. The formalisms are quite diverse, ranging from computer simulations (Klahr, Kosslyn, Simon and Simon), to frames and scripts (Gregg and Nelson), to principles, rule models, and flow charts (Gelman, Siegler, and Trabasso et al.) and to M–space models (Case). In all instances, there seems to be a recognition that verbal descriptions are often vague and ambiguous and that more explicit languages are necessary if we are to build rigorous and testable theories; it therefore seems that the representation of knowledge will become an increasingly important issue in the coming years.

I would like to thank a number of people for their work on this Symposium. Elaine Shelton contributed greatly to the editing of the book and took care of a million and one details that arose during its preparation; without her help, putting together the book would have been far more difficult. Ed Sieger did the bulk of the typing and did it extremely well. Greg Long took care of arrangements during the Symposium itself, and made everything run more smoothly. Finally, Betty Boal, who has shepherded through all 12 of the previous Symposia, contributed her considerable experience and expertise to this one as well. I owe her a considerable debt of gratitude.

A different type of contribution was made by my wife Alice and my children Beth and Todd. Alice took over many responsibilities while I was working on the book, gave me good advice, listened patiently, and, in general, helped keep me on an even keel. Beth and Todd never hesitated to remind me that from some perspectives, at least, whether Daddy will play horsie is more important than whether a manuscript gets sent off on Thursday or Friday. It is difficult to argue with them.

Robert S. Siegler

To My Mother and Father

MEMORY
DEVELOPMENT

1 Skills, Plans, and Self-Regulation

Ann L. Brown
Judy S. DeLoache
University of Illinois

I. INTRODUCTION

In thinking about memory development, we have rarely questioned the essential similarity of the processes studied under the rubrics "problem-solving skills" and "memory strategies" (Brown, 1975a, 1977, in press a). A general class of information-processing models, with their emphasis on routines controlled and regulated by an executive, seems suitable for describing the major psychological processes of interest in both domains. However, because our charge is to function under the memory development heading, we have decided to refocus our thinking from our usual position of regarding the problem-solving and memory people as those who study the same processes on different tasks. Instead, we have begun by looking for any interesting differences between the major emphases and accomplishments in one field that could intelligently aid the development of the other. There do appear to be some psychologically interesting differences, not only in the tasks and skills studied but in the depth of the analyses of those tasks and skills and in the commitment to addressing instructional goals. In the first part of this chapter we highlight some of these differences between the two approaches and try to illustrate a weakness in the current mainstream of memory-development research. In the second part we concentrate on an area of concern to both the problem-solving and memory-development literatures: self-regulation and control, our candidate for the most fundamental difference between the experienced and the naive. In the final section we indicate new problem areas and new ways of considering what it is that develops with age and experience.

II. DIFFERENCES BETWEEN THE MEMORY DEVELOPMENT AND PROBLEM-SOLVING APPROACHES TO COGNITIVE DEVELOPMENT

Because our task is to consider what memory theorists have to say about development, we approach the issue from the perspective of the memory-development literature. Studies of a few aspects of memory dominate the field at this time, at least in number if not in content. Before we address the issues central to such research, a brief history of the way developmental psychologists interested in memory have approached the question of "What develops?" is illustrative.

A. Early Studies

Prior to the 1960s, the question "What develops?" would not have been raised. Obviously, memory develops. Lacking a fine-grained analysis of memory processes, early researchers selected tasks and age groups somewhat randomly. They found that on most tasks older children remembered more than younger ones, and slow learners had more difficulty remembering than those of average ability! The predominant explanation, when one was offered at all, was that immature learners have a limited memory "capacity." As they mature, this capacity increases, allowing them to retain more. The underlying metaphor, whether implicitly or explicitly stated, was of the mind as a container: Little people have little boxes or jars in their heads, and bigger people have bigger ones. Any demonstration of inferior performance on the part of the smaller person proved the capacity limitation "theory," not surprisingly since such a theory was merely a restatement of the data (Chi, 1976). The same general state of affairs also characterized the problem-solving literature, where early studies also showed poor performance by young children on a variety of tasks. Explanations of why the young did poorly were either not forthcoming or involved a circular argument: Little people have little problem-solving capacity, a restatement of the data masquerading as a theoretical explanation.

More sophisticated, or simply more adventurous, theorists subdivided the metaphorical containers. They attributed the deficits in memory or problem-solving performance to a limitation in the space available in one of the main architectural structures of the information-processing system, with space defined in terms of the number of slots, spaces, or buffer units available to the system at any one time. It was thought that as a child matured, his available space increased. The correlation of digit span with age, intelligence, and general problem-solving efficiency was taken as firm support for this notion of increasing space with increasing age, and short-term memory was cited as the most likely culprit in the young child's mental overpopulation problem. It should be noted, however, that most developmental psychologists avoided the issue of architectural systems and capacity limitations, thanks to two important influences on the field: the pioneering work of John Flavell (1970) on memory strategies in the young and the widespread dissemination of levels-of-processing approaches (Craik & Lockhart, 1972) with their de-emphasis on capacity, coding, and flow in and between containers.

B. The Production-Deficiency Hypothesis

The guiding hypothesis of developmental memory research, initiated by Flavell in the 1960s and still popular today, is that the main difference between young children and mature memorizers is the tendency to employ a variety of mnemonic strategies whenever feasible. Borrowing from mediational theories of learning, Flavell introduced the terminology of production and mediational deficiencies to describe this difference. A production deficiency is said to exist when the child does not spontaneously produce a task-suitable mnemonic but if trained to do so can use the mnemonic to improve performance. A mediational deficiency exists when a child produces a necessary mnemonic, either spontaneously or under instruction, but the mnemonic fails to enhance performance. Probably owing to the paucity of strategies selected for study, mediational deficiencies have rarely been documented, and therefore the central issue in the memory-development research has been the spontaneous production of appropriate mediation.

Simply stated, the theory consists of three propositions: (1) Young children do poorly on a variety of memory tasks because they fail to introduce the necessary mnemonic intervention; (2) if they are trained to use a suitable strategy, their performance improves, at least temporarily; (3) if the memory task does not demand mnemonic intervention, developmental differences will be minimal. To prove or disprove one or the other of these hypotheses is still the goal of the majority of developmental memory studies.

To date, the field has been remarkably limited in the tasks selected for examination. When seeking to prove or disprove proposition 1 or 2, investigators almost invariably choose some rote memorization situation, such as list learning, in which rehearsal or taxonomic categorization is the strategy of choice. When seeking to prove or disprove proposition 3, they select some sort of recognition memory task. We have objections to both approaches. We believe that the strategy—no-strategy distinction served a valuable function in its time by organizing a chaotic field and by attempting to distinguish when and where the limitations of youth, lack of experience, or low IQ would be most debilitating. However, the two main lines of research now following this tradition have such severe built-in limitations that future proliferation should be discouraged. The main problems center around the study of tasks rather than processes and the paucity of developmental information provided by the particular tasks selected.

1. *Nonstrategic Tasks.*   The first of these two lines of research currently generating a spate of studies is one for which we feel personally responsible. These studies focus on proposition 3, which we were rash enough to make explicit (Brown, 1973a, 1974, 1975a) rather than implicit as Flavell had done (1970). The proposition asserts that if a situation exists in which deliberate mnemonic intervention is not a prerequisite for efficient performance, developmental differences will be minimized. Obviously, it would be futile to seek tasks where no developmental differences occur. Not only must such tasks be impervious to mnemonic efforts, but they must also be uncontaminated by any other developmentally sensitive factor. The point of the original statement was not to prove the absence of developmental trends but merely to demonstrate that the magnitude of any developmental effect is sensitive to the degree that sophisticated plans and strategies can be used. In general, the hypothesis is well supported, whether the comparison involves intentional versus incidental learning instructions in adults or cross-age comparisons (Brown & Smiley, 1977b). Situations do differ in the degree to which intentional mnemonics can enhance performance, and some recognition memory and recency tasks are less sensitive to strategic intervention than are many other memory tasks that require rote recall (Brown, 1975a).

This does not seem to be the point that the current set of studies seeks to prove. Interest has shifted from processes to tasks per se, and the game has become one of trying to show developmental differences in recognition memory tasks. In general, such attempts are successful, but their success is not surprising. Recognition memory *as a task* is clearly not impervious to developmental differences. True, with distinct target and distractor items, excellent levels of performance have been found for very young children as well as for adults, a ceiling effect that often clouds interpretation of age effects. However, with careful choice of distractors, one could easily produce a floor effect across all ages. Matching-to-sample tests have been devised so that choice of the correct alternative is extremely difficult even without any memory load. Floor or ceiling effects can completely obscure developmental differences, and it was for this reason that we selected variants of a recency problem for our earlier studies of the strategy—no-strategy distinction (Brown, 1973a, 1973b, 1973c).

If the question of interest is whether or not age differences will be found in a recognition memory task, the distractor items are crucial. Even the simple manipulation of increasing the number of distractors on a choice trial increases the likelihood of finding a developmental trend because young children's performance is disrupted by this manipulation (Brown, 1975b). If, however, one would like to show that young children perform better than older children, then a more subtle manipulation might be needed. For example, one could vary the similarity of the distractor and target items along some scale of physical or semantic similarity not yet salient to the young but distracting to the old. The less mature child would not be snared by the "related" distractor and should outperform the confused older participant. If we knew enough about the development of conceptual systems, we would be able to produce any possible pattern of age effects in recognition tasks by varying the target-distractor similarity on dimensions differentially salient to the ages under investigation.

Such an endeavor, however useful for testing hypotheses concerning conceptual development, is not relevant to the original discussion of whether some situations exist in which young children perform well on memory tasks. Our position is that in order to understand what memory development is, it is essential to identify areas of strength as well as areas of weakness (Brown, 1974, 1975a). Furthermore, if we wish to devise remedial help for the inexperienced, we need to capitalize on naturally occurring strengths as well as to identify major areas of weakness. Finally, as Chi (1976) has argued persuasively, it is only by eliminating candidates for what develops that we can identify the true areas of developmental change.

2. *The Modal Memory Strategy Experiment.* The second line of research currently dominating the field is a proliferation of replication studies demonstrating the developmental sensitivity of strategy-susceptible tasks. The typical experiment in this area consists of crude assessments of the presence or absence of strategic intervention. Children are then divided into those who produce and those who do not; those who do produce almost invariably outperform those who do not. We rarely have evidence of intermediate stages of production.

One problem with these studies is overkill — they long ago provided ample documentation of young children's mnemonic ineptitude. Another problem stems from undue concentration on a limited subset of tasks and strategies. Almost all studies concerned with the mnemonic production deficiency hypothesis have centered on list-learning tasks and the strategies of taxonomic categorization and rehearsal. Apart from the obvious undesirability of such a restricted focus and the oft-lamented lack of ecological validity of such tasks (Brown, in press a), there are some interesting limitations imposed by this particular approach. First, these two strategies tend to emerge between the ages of five and seven years and, under the conditions usually studied, do not undergo much refinement after the grade school years. Thus, we are left with an almost total lack of information concerning what develops before 5 and after 8 or 9 years of age. The second problem is that we lack detailed models of the gradual emergence of even these simple strategies; indeed, they may not be susceptible to detailed task analyses.

Probably the most important deficiency of this approach, though, is that the tasks are set up in such a way that we cannot say anything about nonproducers. If children are not rehearsing on our task, we have no way of knowing what they are doing. They perform poorly, and therefore they highlight the improvement with age that we wish to demonstrate. However, we know nothing about their state of understanding. They are characterized as *not* being at a certain level, as *not* having a certain attribute; they are nonproducers, nonmediators; they are not strategic or not planful. They are sometimes described as passive, even though the tasks are designed so that the only way to be characterized as active is to produce the desired strategy. All these descriptions are based on what young children do not do compared with older children, for we have no way of observing what they *can* do in the confines of these tasks.

In the memory development area, the dominance of the modal experimental design aimed at list-learning strategies has led to two veritable wastelands in our knowledge: We know next to nothing about memory development in the preschool period and even less about how the process evolves during adolescence. The major forays into these territories have been the attempts to clever investigators to push down the age at which production of common strategies occurs (Wellman, 1977). There have been very few attempts to look at the emergence of more ingenious strategies in the high school population (Brown & Smiley, 1977b).

This description of the modal production deficiency experiment is overly harsh, but it is intended to indict the pedestrian nature of most of the current literature rather than the creativity of the original investigations in the area. And we should not ignore a major strength of this research area; the sheer bulk of data does provide impressive support for the generality of the strategic-deficit hypothesis. However, there are also the attendant weaknesses we have mentioned: (1) an undue concentration on a few standard tasks of limited ecological validity; (2) the lack of precise developmental models of emergent skills; (3) the concentration on a very narrow age range; and (4) the lack of information about nonproducers.

C. Task Analyses

Many of the major investigators in the problem-solving area share a common approach of providing detailed task analyses of the processes they study. They also share a common location, Carnegie—Mellon and Pittsburgh. Not surprisingly, therefore, their approach is well represented in this book. Therefore, we will concentrate on just a few main facets of this work, which contrast sharply with the modal production deficiency experiment of developmental memory research.

The main emphasis is on providing detailed explicit models of cognitive development within a limited task domain. The aim is to provide precise descriptions of the initial and final forms of the cognitive process under investigation and to delineate important intermediate stages. The area is characterized by the principle of developmental tractability, that is, the charge that developmental models should, according to Klahr and Siegler (1978), "allow us to state both early and later forms of competence and provide an easy interpretation of each model as both a precursor and successor of other models in a developmental sequence [p. 65]." With a well-designed task analysis it should be possible to detect not only the presence or absence of a desired piece of knowledge or skill but starting and intermediate stages as well. One important feature of the experimental designs in this area is that the problems selected are sensitive to the gradual emergence of the knowledge studied. Errors produced by the novice are as informative as correct responses produced by the proficient, thus providing as rich a picture of the "nonproducer's" strategy as of the producer's.

One of our main criticisms of developmental memory research is that such detailed task analyses have rarely been performed. Notable exceptions are the work of Ornstein and Naus (in press) and Belmont and Butterfield (1977) on the emergence of sophisticated rehearsal strategies. Ornstein and Naus have shown an interesting developmental progression from no production, to an intermediate stage of repeating single items, to an efficient strategy of cumulative rehearsal. The cumulative rehearsal stage is also subject to gradual refinement as the size and stability of the chunks selected become more uniform. Butterfield, Wambold, and Belmont (1973) have shown that adequate encoding and retrieval, and a coordination of the two, are necessary for efficient performance on their circular recall task. Immature memorizers perform inadequately because of a failure on any one or all of these activities. Such attention to intermediate stages of competence, however, is rare.

In contrast to the memory research, consider two experimental programs from the problem-solving literature — Gelman's analysis (this volume) of the emergence of counting principles in very young children and Siegler's (1976, and this volume) detailed developmental description of children's strategies for solving the problem of the balance scale. These programs share two important features that are not commonly found in studies of the development of memory strategies. First, the knowledge under investigation emerges gradually, with several readily identifiable substages. This is particularly true of Siegler's work, for the balance task has provided interesting information about the levels of competence of children from five to 17 years. Second, both programs specify in detail the feasible rules for solution, and the tasks are engineered so that the particular rule used (or not used) by the child can be detected. Thus, both programs provide optimal information for those who would attempt instructional intervention. Systematic error patterns can be used to diagnose the child's pretraining competencies and areas of weakness, so that instructional routines can be tailored to fit the diagnosis.

To illustrate, we will use the balance scale problem because of its detailed description of stages and because the instructional relevance of the task analysis has already been demonstrated (Klahr & Siegler, in press; Siegler, 1976). The apparatus is a balance scale with four equidistant pegs on each side of a fulcrum. Small circular discs, all of equal weight, can be placed on the pegs in various configurations. The arm of the balance can tip left or right or remain level, depending on how the weights are arranged. The arm is prevented from tilting, however, until the child predicts which side (if either) will go down. Siegler identified four systematic rules that children can employ to solve this task, rules that fall into a nice hierarchy of increasing maturity. A child using Rule 1 attends only to weight — the number of circular discs on each side of the fulcrum. If they are the same, the child predicts balance; otherwise, the child predicts that the side with the greater weight will go down. A child following Rule 2 is more advanced, for he considers both amount of weight and, whenever the weight on the two sides is equal, distance from the fulcrum. Children using Rule 3 always consider both weight and distance, but when the cues conflict they lack a rule for conflict resolution and must guess. Rule 4 represents "mature" knowledge or the "end state," and solution is based on the sum-of-products calculation. Although most 5-year-olds can operate systematically with Rule 1, most 16-year-olds still have problems with Rule 4, a nice developmental spectrum for description.

Siegler's task analysis is successful because he can detect not only when mature knowledge of the torque principle is reached but also significant milestones along the route. Similarly, by considering the errors produced by 2- to 4-year-olds in a counting task, Gelman (this volume) can diagnose which counting principle the child lacks — whether one-to-one correspondence, stable ordering, cardinality, or whatever. In both cases the key word is diagnosis, not only of end-state activity but of starting and intermediate levels as well.

D. Instructional Relevance and Training Studies

Training studies have become a characteristic feature of both the memory development and problem-solving literatures, although such endeavors are initiated for different reasons. Training studies in the memory development literature are by-products of the production deficiency modal experiment and are usually designed to answer a question of theoretical rather than practical interest. Having demonstrated that young children do not use a particular strategy effectively on their own volition, the researcher moves on to the next step in the modal experiment — determining whether the deficiency is one of production or mediation. Training is instigated. If performance now improves, the original problem is deemed to be one of production; if not, a deficit in mediation is inferred. These studies are, in general, successful in providing answers to the original question of whether production or mediation deficits underlie poor performance. The matter rests here, and the modal experiment is judged complete.

Because instructional relevance was not a guiding concern in the area, the proponents can scarcely be blamed for falling short of some criteria of accountability. The outcomes of such studies, however, have little practical utility. The fact that 5-year-olds can be trained to rote rehearse like 7-year-olds may answer a theoretical question, but it is of questionable practical significance. Indeed, it is interesting that the only programs in the area of memory development in which practical application has been a major issue are those aimed at inducing strategic behavior in aberrant populations (Brown, 1974; Brown & Campione, in press; Butterfield & Belmont, 1977; Campione & Brown, 1977).

One must doubt the practical utility of training memory strategies because at best the result is durable improvement on the training task itself; there is little evidence for general improvement in performance on similar tasks (Brown, 1974, in press a). To borrow from Greeno (1976), we can satisfy *behavioral* objectives in that the subjects do perform the trained behaviors, but we certainly have not satisfied *cognitive* objectives of changing the subject's underlying cognitive processes or the way he views memory problems in the future. Without evidence of transfer, of a genuine improvement in the subject's understanding of the processes involved, one must ask whether improvement on the training task itself is a desirable end product. Because the majority of memory training studies have focused on inculcating specialized skills of rote learning of lists, the instructional relevance is questionable.

Given the cost of the detailed task analyses necessary for informed instruction (Brown, in press a; Butterfield & Belmont, 1977; Klahr & Siegler, 1978), it seems reasonable to suggest that instructional relevance be the guiding force in the initial choice of training tasks (Resnick, 1976). We should consider tasks in which improvement would be a desirable outcome even without generalization from the training situation. For example, most training attempts in the problem-solving literature have focused on elementary arithmetic, counting, reading subprocesses, scientific reasoning, and the like. The major investigators in this area have taken the instructional relevance principle seriously, although this has not been a main purpose of memory-training studies.

A second feature of memory-training studies is that the training itself is somewhat cursory. Some of the better procedures consist of the experimenter's briefly modeling what is determined (intuitively) to be the desired strategy. Some of the worst procedures consist of the experimenter's restructuring the material to be remembered (e.g., by blocking categories), presumably in the hope that the trainee will derive the implicit strategy for himself. The superiority of explicit intervention has been amply documented (Brown & Campione, 1977, in press; Butterfield & Belmont, 1977; Campione & Brown, 1977). However, even the better attempts at explicit instruction are not based on sophisticated task analyses and do not take into consideration the particular needs of the trainee. The one notable exception to this rule is the program of Butterfield and Belmont (1977).

In contrast, detailed task analysis is a characteristic feature of training studies in the problem-solving area. The benefits of this approach for tailoring individual instruction can be illustrated by again considering the balance-scale problem. Having established the psychological reality of the four-rule hierarchy, Siegler (1976) proceeded to provide training relative to the starting level of the trainee. Groups of 5- and 8-year-old children who were operating with Rule 1 were presented with one of two types of training: distance problem training or conflict problem training. Distance problem training provides the child with experience with the type of problems mastered in Rule 2, whereas conflict problem training provides experience with the type mastered in Rule 3. Thus, training with distance problems was geared one step above the child's starting point, and conflict training was aimed two (or more) steps ahead.

The stage was set to test a widespread assumption concerning training — that the distance between the child's existing knowledge and new information is a critical determinant of how successful that training will be (Brown, 1975a, in press; Inhelder, Sinclair, & Bovet, 1974; Kuhn, 1974). This was confirmed because both age groups benefitted from training only one level beyond their initial competence. When training was geared two levels beyond pretest levels, only the older children showed improvement. In subsequent studies it was determined that the 5-year-olds' difficulty was one of encoding; they failed to encode distance information, concentrating their attention solely on weight. After training in encoding distance, they too could benefit from the conflict problems. Of main interest, though, is that detailed task analyses were the foundation of intelligent instruction. As a result of his task decomposition, Siegler was able to determine the initial level of the trainee and what would constitute near or far training for the child. Training could therefore be aimed at the child's present level, and entering ability was the determinant of what type of training was needed, rather than age or pretest failure as is the case in memory studies.

In this section we have emphasized differences in current approaches to memory development and problem solving. These differences are most apparent when one considers task analyses and instructional relevance. Notice, however, that although there is a clear difference in emphasis, both literatures have followed a similar evolution, progressing from a concentration on demonstration studies, through a period of production deficiency examinations, to a concern with training (Kuhn, 1974). By emphasizing recent advances in the problem-solving literature, we hoped to illustrate a weakness in the current state of the art concerning memory development.

III. COMMONALITIES BETWEEN MEMORY DEVELOPMENT AND PROBLEM-SOLVING LITERATURE

In the previous sections we have emphasized divergence between cognitive psychologists in the mainstream of memory development research and those interested in problem solving. Here we emphasize convergence because investigators in both areas are becoming increasingly concerned with the child's knowledge *about* the rules, strategies, or goals needed for efficient performance. In the problem-solving area, Klahr (1974) distinguished between knowledge and the understanding of that knowledge. For memory theorists, the division is between memory skills and metamemory, the knowledge one has about those skills (Flavell & Wellman, 1977). Most theories of human cognition and artificial intelligence also make a distinction between the knowledge and routines available to the system and the executive that monitors and controls the use of these data. Although we appreciate that there are serious problem with this simple dichotomy (Brown, 1977, in press a; Klahr, 1974; Winograd, 1975; Woods, in press), in the interest of brevity we accept the division here and ignore the theoretical complications. Also in the interest of brevity, we will not review the literature on metacognitive development, as there are now available several reviews of the gradual emergence of self-interrogation and regulation over a wide range of situations (Brown, 1977, in press a, in press b; Flavell, 1976; Flavell & Wellman, 1977).

A. Self-Interrogation and Self-Regulation

The main premise we discuss is that when faced with a new type of problem, anyone is a novice to a certain extent. Novices often fail to perform efficiently, not only because they may lack certain skills but because they are deficient in terms of self-conscious participation and intelligent self-regulation of their actions. The novice tends not to know much about either his capabilities on a new task or the techniques necessary to perform efficiently; he may even have difficulty determining what goals are desirable, let alone what steps are required to get there. Note that this innocence is not necessarily related to age (Chi, this volume) but is more a function of inexperience in a new problem situation. Adults and children display similar confusion when confronted with a new problem: A novice chess player (Chi, 1977) has many of the same problems of metacognition that the very young card player experiences (Markman, 1977). For both, the situation is relatively new and difficult. Barring significant transfer from prior experience, the beginner in any problem-solving situation has not developed the necessary knowledge about how and what to think under the new circumstances.

The point we wish to emphasize is that children find themselves in this situation more often than do adults, and very young children may be neophytes in almost all problem situations. Thus, an explanation of why young children have such generalized metacognitive deficits (Brown, in press a; Flavell & Wellman, 1977) is that most of our experimental tasks are both new and difficult for them. It is this lack of familiarity with the game at hand that leads to a concomitant lack of self-interrogation about the current state of knowledge and to inadequate selection and monitoring of necessary steps between starting levels and desired goals. The child's initial "passivity" in many memory and problem-solving tasks, his failure to check and monitor his ongoing activities, and his failure to make his own task analysis could be the direct result of gross inexperience on such tasks. This does not mean that young children are incapable of self-regulation, only that they tend not to bring such procedures to bear immediately on new problems. Children are universal novices; it takes experience before they build up the knowledge and confidence that would enable them to adopt routinely the self-interrogation mode of the expert (Bransford, Nitsch, & Franks, 1977).

Although absolute novices tend not to incorporate effective metacognitive activities into their initial attempts to solve problems, it is not simply the case that experts do and novices do not engage in effective self-regulation. As Simon and Simon (this volume) have pointed out in their study of physics problem solvers, the expert engaged in less observable self-questioning than did the relative novice, for the processes of problem solving in this domain had become relatively automatic for the expert. The relative novice, on the other hand, showed many instances of overt self-questioning and checking. Notice that Simon and Simon's novice had received sufficient background instruction so that the basic rules for solution were known to her. We would characterize her state of knowing as being typical of the learner: acquainted with the rules of the game and beginning to acquire expertise.

We would not be surprised to find that the following pattern is typical. First, the absolute novices show little or no intelligent self-regulation. Then, as the problem solver becomes familiar with the necessary rules and subprocesses, he enters into an increasingly active period of deliberate self-regulation. Finally, the performance of the expert would run smoothly as the necessary subprocesses and their coordination have all been overlearned to the point where they are relatively automatic.

We have as yet little developmental data to suggest that such a pattern is a characteristic feature of growth during problem solving, but we predict that such a progression may be a common feature of learning in many domains. Furthermore, although age and experience are obviously intimately related, we do not believe that the growth pattern is necessarily related to age. Young children may show the same progression of naïveté to competence within simpler task domains. Evidence such as that provided by Chi's (this volume) young chess experts is exactly the kind needed to support this conjecture. If we wish to understand how much of the young child's ineptitude is due to lack of expertise, rather than age per se, we must look at behavior in areas in which the child is competent as well as those in which he is inefficient.

There is one other factor that might contribute to the young child's general metacognitive problem. In addition to being hampered by the novelty of most experimental situations, young children may simply not realize that certain metacognitive operations are useful in practically any situation. These general metacognitive skills are discussed at length in another paper (Brown, in press a), and we only briefly summarize them here. The basic skills of metacognition include *predicting* the consequences of an action or event, *checking* the results of one's own actions (did it work?), *monitoring* one's ongoing activity (how am I doing?), *reality testing* (does this make sense?), and a variety of other behaviors for *coordinating* and *controlling* deliberate attempts to learn and solve problems. These skills are the basic characteristics of efficient thought, and one of their most important properties is that they are transsituational. They apply to the whole range of problem-solving activities, from artificially structured experimental settings to what we psychologists defensively refer to as "real world, everyday life" situations. It is important to check the results of an operation against some criterion of acceptability, whether one is memorizing a prose passage, reading a textbook, or following instructions in a laboratory experiment, a classroom, or on the street. A child has to learn these various skills, but perhaps of equal importance, he has to learn that they are almost universally applicable, that whenever he is faced with a new task, it will be to his advantage to apply his general knowledge about how to learn and solve problems.

Not only does interest in metacognition characterize both the problem-solving and memory-development literatures of American developmental psychology, but traditionally this has been a prime concern of Soviet studies of cognitive development. Vygotsky (1962) was one of the first to describe the two phases in the development of knowledge: first its automatic unconscious acquisition, followed by a gradual increase in active, conscious control over that knowledge. Recent translations of previously unknown work of Vygotsky's attest to his lifelong interest in what we now call metacognition (Wertsch, personal communication). The ingenious studies of Istomina in tracing the goal-directed, conscious control of early memory strategies (Istomina, 1975) and later study skills (Smirnov, Istomina, Mal'tseva, & Samokhvalova, 1971) are also notable. Thus, there is considerable agreement among American and Soviet psychologists that one thing that develops in a variety of problem-solving situations is the increasingly conscious control and regulation of goal-oriented strategies.

B. Invention and Generalization

Given their common interests in training strategies and metacognitive development, it is not surprising that in both the problem-solving and memory-development fields there is growing interest in whether metacognitive development can be fostered or accelerated by direct intervention. The position has been nicely stated by Norman, Gentner, and Stevens (1976):

> The skills of debugging are clearly important ones. Papert believes it is perhaps even more important to teach a child how to debug his own knowledge than to teach him the knowledge itself. The implication is that if a child knows how to learn, then he can get the knowledge by himself. We find that this philosophy strikes a sympathetic chord: Why do we not attempt to teach some basic cognitive skills such as how to organize one's

knowledge, how to learn, how to solve problems, how to correct errors in understanding. These strike us as basic components which ought to be taught along with the content matter [p. 194].

The question of whether direct intervention can bring about improvement in metacognitive functions is only just beginning to be the subject of intensive research activity. It is easy to suggest that training should be aimed at showing children "how to organize their knowledge," "how to learn," and "how to solve problems," but it is considerably more difficult to incorporate these suggestions in concrete training programs. Some advances have been made, however. Resnick (1976) has had some success in the area of elementary mathematical reasoning in instructing "routines that put the learner in a good position to discover or invent efficient strategies for themselves [p. 72]." Similarly, our initial attempts at inculcating simple checking and monitoring strategies have been quite successful and, indeed, are our only evidence of generalization in educable retarded children (Brown & Campione, in press). For example, children trained to estimate their recall readiness prior to a test of ordered rote recall of a list of picture names became more efficient and maintained their efficiency for at least a year. Furthermore, the effects of training generalized to a somewhat different task on which the children were required to indicate their readiness to reproduce the gist of simple stories. Training children to stop, check, and self-question before responding does seem to be effective.

As a further illustration of the convergence of the problem-solving and memory-development fields, Resnick (Resnick & Beck, in press) and Brown (in press b) have independently extended the notion of self-regulation as a general characteristic of successful learning to the problem of reading comprehension. Both suggest that instruction in conscious use of self-interrogation and self-monitoring strategies might enhance comprehension skills of poor readers.

These preliminary successes with training children in self-monitoring are most encouraging. Also encouraging is the outcome of an intensive course in problem-solving skills for college students (Hayes, 1976). Self-reports at the end of the semester-long training program indicated that the main areas of improvement were ones we would term metacognitive. The students reported increased awareness of their own cognitive processes, improvement in planning and organizing, increased diagnostic skills (or personal task analyses), and improvement in generalized problem-solving skills. Attempts to develop intensive training programs aimed at young and slow-learning children are currently under way in our laboratory (Brown, in press a).

C. Strengths and Weakness of Both Approaches

The two major bodies of knowledge concerning cognitive development, the problem-solving and memory-development literatures, have been compared and contrasted. We have emphasized the major differences in approach and indicated that the one topic of current concern in both areas is metacognition. This merging of interest from two distinct fields is exciting, and it is because of this convergence that we select the metacognitive skills of self-interrogation and self-regulation as prime candidates for what develops. In emphasizing the differences of evolution in the two research areas, we have also highlighted the strengths and weaknesses of each approach, for the strengths of one are the weaknesses of the other. The large body of memory-development literature has provided us with impressive evidence of the generality of the strategy-deficit problem in young children's thinking. There are literally hundreds of examples of the young child's failure to employ common mnemonics on laboratory rote-learning tasks. We also know a considerable amount about what does not develop in memory. We can predict fairly accurately not only that the young will perform poorly on memory tasks but where or when their difficulties will be most apparent. We also are beginning to identify the underlying processes responsible for inadequate performance (Chi, 1976; Huttenlocher & Burke, 1976). These are real and important advances. Researchers in the problem-solving areas, because of the need for expensive, detailed task analyses, do not have a similar mass of data to support their conclusion. Their concentration on a very limited set of problems, with the fortunate properties of easy discomposition into steps, is inevitable.

The major weaknesses in the memory-development literature are the strengths of the problem-solving area. Whereas the memory studies generally lack detailed explicit models of varying states of competence, the problem-solving literature has several good examples of detailed models. Similarly, a concern for instructional relevance is a notable feature of the problem-solving area, but memory-training studies have not been designed to answer questions of instructional relevance.

What is needed at this point is a merging of the two disciplines, a convergence that can most readily be achieved by considering new tasks and processes in which a dichotomization between strictly memory versus problem-solving tasks would not be made. In the next section we introduce some of our favorite candidates.

IV. ALTERNATE METHODS FOR ASKING WHAT DEVELOPS

To answer the question "What develops?," it may be necessary for us to expand the repertoire of tasks and strategies we select for intensive examination. If such an expansion is warranted, it might be wise, before embarking, to consider critically the criteria by which we select new tasks. Ideally, we would like to harness the strengths of both the traditional memory and problem-solving literatures. In this section we (1) indulge in speculation about ideal criteria for task selection, (2) introduce a subset of tasks for which we have some initial data and which we believe tap important psychological processes, and (3) suggest alternate methods of observing cognitive growth.

A. Criteria for Selecting Tasks and Strategies

Extrapolating from the previous sections, we believe that an ideal strategy to study would be one that is within the repertoire of children across a wide age range and one that can fairly be said to represent an important cognitive activity. Furthermore, starting, intermediate, and ending states should all be traceable. Ideally, the process should be describable by means of detailed, explicit models that can map its developmental progression. The types of activity we have been looking for, therefore, are those that show interesting early precursors and are activities engaged in during problem solving by both young and old.

In addition to a broad age range in which the processes of interest are undergoing change, a broad task range should also be a selection criterion. By this we mean that the process under investigation should be involved in a wide variety of tasks. If we are to invest considerable effort in mapping a developmental progression in some cognitive domain, we should focus on a cognitive process of widespread generality. And, in the same vein, if we are prepared to embark on training attempts, whether for basic or applied reasons, the process we wish to inculcate should have reasonable instructional relevance. Furthermore, training preferably should result in cognitive gains as well as behavioral gains (Greeno, 1976). Finally, we should select a task through which we can consider not only the activity of interest but the growing knowledge that the child has about the activity. This knowledge should be measurable by means other than self-report; that is, there should be some method of externalizing the flexibility with which the child controls and governs his own behavioral repertoire.

Of course, various criteria become differentially important depending on the particular goal of a research program. For example, for those interested in training, the criteria of instructional relevance and a broad range of applicability are paramount. However, these criteria would not be so important for those concerned with, for example, the earliest signs of strategic planning. We have included the set of criteria here merely to illustrate some of the general concerns that should be considered when embarking on a program of developmental research. The ones we have chosen are no doubt important, but there are clearly others we have overlooked. In addition, we would not pretend that the tasks we have selected successfully meet even our own criteria. Rather, we have introduced a few idiosyncratic candidates that we favor and that we believe have the potential of eventually satisfying a subset of the criteria.

B. Selected Tasks and Strategies

1. *Extracting the Main Idea.* Getting the gist of a message, whether it is oral or written, is an essential communicative as well as information-gathering activity. Without this ability, children would never learn a language and would certainly never come to use that language to communicate. The ability to extract

the main idea to the exclusion of nonessential detail may be a naturally occurring proclivity given, of course, a reasonable match between the complexity of the message and the receiver's current cognitive status (Brown, 1975a).

In a recent series of studies (Brown & Smiley, 1977a, 1977b), we have been considering the situation in which children must extract the main theme of a prose passage, a story. Our subject population has ranged from preschoolers as young as three years of age to college students, and the stories are adapted to suit the different age groups. We find the same pattern across age: With or without conscious intent to do so, subjects extract the main theme of a story and ignore trivia. Older children have more highly developed scripts (Nelson, 1977; Nelson & Brown, in press) for storytelling, but even very young children apprehend the essential gist of a story plot (Brown, 1976).

Children are misled in their comprehension of stories by the same snares that trap adults (Brown, Smiley, Day, Townsend, & Lawton, 1977). Led to believe certain "facts" concerning a main character or the location of an action, facts that never appear in the original story, children disambiguate and elaborate in the same way as adults. They falsely recognize theme-congruent distractors in recognition tests and include their pre-existing knowledge when recalling. In addition, they have difficulty distinguishing between their own elaborations and the actual story content.

If there is such essential similarity across ages in the way children construct a message from prose passages, what then is the interesting developmental trend? Not surprisingly, given the theme of this chapter, we believe that what develops in an increasingly conscious control of the naturally occurring tendency, a control that allows more efficient gathering of information.

As children mature they begin to predict the essential organizing features and crucial elements of texts (Brown & Smiley, 1977a, 1977b). Thanks to this fore-knowledge, they make better use of extended study time. If given an extra period for study (equal to three times their reading rate), children from the seventh grade up improve considerably their recall for important elements of text; recall of less important details does not improve. Children below the seventh grade do not usually show such effective use of additional study time; their recall improves, if at all, evenly across all levels of importance. As a result, older students' recall protocols following study include all the essential elements and little trivia. Younger children's recall, though still favoring important elements, has many important elements missing.

To substantiate our belief that metacognitive control governs this developmental trend, we have observed the study actions of our subjects. In particular, we have examined their physical records that can be scored objectively — notes and underlining of texts. A certain proportion of children from the fifth grade and up spontaneously underline or take notes during study. At all ages, the physical records of spontaneous subjects favored the important elements, that is, the notes or underlined sections concentrated on elements previously rated as crucial to the theme. Students induced to adopt one of these strategies did not show a similar sensitivity to importance; they took notes or underlined more randomly. Some of the very young children underlined all the text when told to underline. Although the efficiency of physical record keeping in induced subjects did improve with age, it never reached the standard set by spontaneous users of the strategy. Furthermore, the recall scores of spontaneous producers were much superior. Even fifth graders who spontaneously underlined showed an adult-like pattern and used extra study to improve differentially their recall of important elements. When we combined all fifth graders, the efficient pattern of the spontaneous children was masked.

It should be pointed out that we do not believe there is a magical age at which children become able to detect the important elements of a text. This is obviously a case of headfitting (Brown, 1975a, in press, a) — that is, the intimate relation of the child's current knowledge to the complexity of the stimulus materials. We have found that children can pick out the main ideas of much simpler texts at much earlier ages. We are currently examining whether, given this foresight, they show a concomitant decrease in the age of onset of simple strategies.

In short, knowledge about texts (or any message source for that matter) must consist of general knowledge about consistent features of all texts and specific knowledge about the particular example at hand, a specific knowledge that must be influenced by idiosyncratic characteristics such as complexity. Similarly, we would expect that strategies for learning from a text would depend on general strategic knowledge about suitable activities, but these would have to be triggered by certain specific features of the text being studied. Quite simply, if the text is so complicated that the reader cannot identify the main points, he can scarcely be expected to select them for extra study, even if he possesses the prerequisite strategic knowledge that this would be a good study ploy. Thus, we would predict that even the sophisticated college student may behave immaturely when studying a difficult text.

This brief summary of some of our ongoing research (for details see Brown & Smiley, 1977b) illustrates what we believe to be a repetitive pattern in cognitive development. What develops is often an increasingly conscious control over an early emerging process. Even young children extract the essential gist of messages if they are not misled by red herrings, such as artificially increased salience of nonessential detail (Brown, in press b). All our subjects have shown this ability to a lesser or greater extent — even preschool children (Brown, 1976), poor readers (Smiley, Oakley, Worthen, Campione, & Brown, 1977), and slow learners (Brown & Campione, in press). What develops with age are strategies and control over these strategies. Using knowledge about elements of texts, knowledge about how to study, and the interface of these two factors, the older student can become much more efficient at processing information presented in texts.

2. *Visual Scanning.*   Our next selection of a naturally occurring ability that shows interesting refinement and increasingly conscious control with age and experience is visual scanning, the process by which one, as Day (1975) says, "actively, selectively, and sequentially acquires information from the visual environment (p. 154)." Effective and efficient visual scanning requires a high degree of executive control, directing fixations and sequencing eye movements from one point of the visual array to another.

Visual scanning begins in the first hours of life. Even newborn infants scan visual stimuli (Salapatek, 1975) but in a very restricted fashion; the young infant is likely to limit his fixations to only one corner of a simple geometric figure (Salapatek, 1968) or to just one feature of a face (Maurer & Salapatek, 1976). The young infant's attention is drawn, almost compelled, to small areas of high contrast. He seems to have very limited voluntary control over his looking and has been characterized as being "captured" by visual stimuli (Ames & Silfen, 1966; Stechler & Latz, 1966).

This involuntary looking gradually gives way during the first few months to much more voluntary control. By three or four months a baby scans the entire pattern, not just a single feature (Gibson, 1969), and thus becomes capable of extracting more and higher-level information. In addition, active stimulus comparison is performed (Ruff, 1975): When presented with two visual patterns, a baby looked back and forth between the two. The degree of shifting increases with age. The more similar the stimuli, the more looking back and forth the infant does, suggesting that even for infants, deployment of a strategy depends on the difficulty of the task. Thus, in the first few months of life we can see important refinements in visual scanning. The behavior comes more and more under voluntary control and produces an ever-increasing amount of information.

The later development of visual scanning parallels the changes that occur during infancy. Many aspects of development can be attributed to the expanding role of internal, planful, self-regulation of scanning and the concomitant decreasing importance of external variables. Although the young infant gradually stops being "captured" by simple stimuli, we see repeated examples of this same problem in older children attempting to cope with more complex tasks. The exact manifestation varies according to the situation. For example, when studying an unfamiliar irregular shape, 3-year-old subjects made fewer eye movements than did 6-year-olds (Zinchenko, Chzhi-tsin, & Tarakanov, 1963). Furthermore, the younger children fixated primarily in the center of the figure, whereas the older children's fixations covered its more informative contours.

Although 6-year-olds in the Zinchenko et al. study showed relatively mature scanning, if a more complex stimulus had been presented, they might have displayed immature scanning. Mackworth and Bruner (1970) showed to adults and 6-year-old children sharply focused photographs containing much detailed information. The 6-year-olds often became "so hooked by the details" that they failed to scan broadly over the rest of the stimulus: "Having arrived at a 'good place' on which to rest their gaze, they seem to feel 'disinclined' to leap into the unknown areas of the sharp pictures [p. 165]." Mackworth and Bruner concluded that adults possess an effective visual search program that enables them to *coordinate* central and peripheral vision together but that children do not. Children can extract detail information centrally, and they can detect peripheral stimuli. However, they cannot execute the two operations *simultaneously*. Thus, the main problem is one of coordination and control, not the presence or absence of specific skills.

Increased cognitive control is also reflected in other important developmental changes in visual scanning. For example, children's scanning gradually becomes more systematic, indicating the presence of higher-order organization. Vurpillot (1968) filmed the eye movements of 4- to 9-year-old children as they were deciding if two houses were identical. Unlike the older subjects, the youngest children rarely made the systematic paired comparisons of comparably located windows that are necessary for successful performance. Furthermore, the young children's scanning was less exhaustive. When two identical houses were shown, they often failed to look at all the windows before pronouncing the houses the same.

Another important developmental change is in focusing on the more informative areas of a visual stimulus. The older the child, the more likely he is to fixate those distinctive features that give him the greatest amount of relevant information for the task at hand (Mackworth & Bruner, 1970; Olson, 1970; Zinchenko et al., 1963). Conversely, young children find it more difficult to ignore irrelevant information. Just as in incidental memory studies and in prose-studying experiments, the younger the child, the more attention he is likely to devote to stimuli that are irrelevant to the task he is performing (Pushkina, 1971).

Although by adulthood scanning has usually developed into quite an efficient, individualized process (Noton & Stark, 1971), adults are by no means immune to the metacognitive problems children experience so frequently. If required to perform a difficult scanning task, such as inspecting chest x-rays for signs of pathology (Thomas, 1968), adults (relative novices) often suffer some of the same deficiencies seen in children, e.g., failing to scan as exhaustively as necessary or failing to focus on the most informative areas.

Scanning tasks thus reveal the same general pattern illustrated by the gist-recall procedure. Scanning a visual array, like extracting the main idea, is a naturally occurring response necessary for a wide variety of tasks and for survival. As the child matures, he develops the ability to control and coordinate scanning, to make scanning a strategic action tailored to changing task demands.

3. *Retrieval Processes.*   For our third example we have selected retrieval, considered broadly to encompass finding objects hidden in the external environment as well as retrieving information temporarily lost in memory. In both cases the subject often must use some other information to help him track down the

desired object or thought. Although children use external cues to search the environment before they use internal cues to search their own memories, many of the same strategies are relevant to both activities. Furthermore, in both activities the child is increasingly able to direct and control his search procedures, that is, he achieves increasing metacognitive control, including planning ahead to facilitate later retrieval and executing a search according to a logical plan. Our discussion here will draw heavily on the work of John Flavell and his colleagues, for they have been by far the most active and creative investigators in this area.

Retrieval activities occur naturally at an early age and continue to develop over a long period of time. Even infants are capable of organizing a sequence of behaviors into a search, but their initial efforts are very limited. The earliest information we have about the development of retrieval comes from object-permanence tasks. When 6- or 7-month-old infants first start searching for hidden objects, they often do something very interesting from the point of view of self-regulation. A child may initiate what appears to be an attempt to remove the cloth concealing a desired object, only to become distracted by the cloth itself. We can characterize this as a failure to maintain executive control: In the midst of conducting a search, the child appears to forget the goal and subsequently ceases those behaviors originally directed toward achieving it. A minimal requirement for the coordination and control of retrieval efforts is the ability to keep the goal in mind for a sufficient period of time and in the face of distractions.

Another interesting aspect of early retrieval activities is that even toddlers employ rudimentary search strategies, as revealed by the regular errors they make in object-permanence tasks (the Stage IV error). Beginning at about 8 months, an infant who has previously found an object hidden at one place (A) is likely to search for it again at A, even though he has just witnessed the object being hidden at a second location (B). We would say with Harris (1973) that the infant seems to employ a strategy of looking for an object in the place where he found it before. Although this strategy has obvious limitations and often causes the infant to fail in object-permanence tasks, it seems reasonable that looking for an object where he found it before would serve the child relatively well in his everyday environment. Interestingly, children as old as 2 years have been found to rely on this same strategy (Loughlin & Daehler, 1973; Webb, Masur, & Nadolny, 1972).

We have characterized the toddler's search as strategic because it suggests the systematic execution of a plan. The degree of self-conscious participation involved, however, is probably minimal. As with the other areas we have reviewed, children's retrieval processes become increasingly sophisticated as conscious, voluntary control over them intensifies. In the case of retrieval, this sophistication is clearly reflected in at least two characteristics of performance: Children become more likely to do something deliberate *at the time of storage* to facilitate later retrieval, and their attempts at retrieval become more *systematic* and efficient.

Even very young children engage in relatively simple behaviors whose sole function is to help them remember. Children as young as 3 years, informed that they will later have to recall the location of an object (Wellman, Ritter, & Flavell, 1975) or an event (Acredolo, Pick, & Olsen, 1975), show better memory than children not so informed. Thus, the children must do something to help them remember during the delay. Wellman et al. (1975) observed their subjects and reported that while they waited, the children in the instructed memory condition looked at and touched the location they were supposed to remember. Preschool children are also able to use a specific cue provided for them. When an external cue marking the location of an object is made available, they can use it to help retrieve the object (Ritter, Kaprove, Fitch, & Flavell, 1973). In addition, they are sometimes capable of arranging a cue themselves to aid their later retrieval (Ryan, Hegion, & Flavell, 1970).

Not surprisingly, the tendency to use such cues improves with age. However, even when they think to use a retrieval cue, younger children may fail to use it as effectively as older children. In a study by Kobasigawa (1974), first graders who spontaneously used an available category cue still recalled fewer items per category than did third graders. In other words, even when they thought to use the retrieval cues, the younger children failed to conduct an exhaustive search for the items associated with each cue. Istomina (1975) also noted the tendency of younger children not to execute an exhaustive search of their memories. Although some of her 4- and 5-year-old subjects actively attempted to recall a list of items, they did not try to retrieve items not immediately recalled. Older children, however, often showed signs of conducting an active internal search (Istomina, 1975): "In some cases the child recalled what he had forgotten only with long pauses, during which he would try not to look at those around him, i.e., he would direct his gaze downward, to the side or screw up his eyes [p. 31]." The nonexhaustive search could result from several possible factors. The child may not check his output against a criterion of acceptability, or, alternatively, he may have a different criterion from that of the experimenter's (Kobiasigawa, 1974). Or his monitoring of his own memory may be inadequate to inform him that there are items yet to be recalled. In any case, these all represent metacognition problems of one sort or another. The essential similarity of nonexhaustiveness in both visual scanning and retrieval is obvious.

We have argued that there are some essential similarities between the retrieval of objects from the environment and the retrieval of information from memory and that many of the same strategies are relevant in both cases — for example, conducting an exhaustive search. However, it is clear that external retrieval is an easier task than memory scanning. Object retrieval studies show evidence of intentional efforts to remember and the use of strategies in children as young as 3 years, a much younger age than that at which Istomina's (1975) children could deliberately adopt the goal of remembering and recalling a list of words. In object-retrieval situations the cues available to aid memory are external and physically present; all the child must do is think to use them or orient to them. Thus, the problem is much simpler than one in which the child must initiate and maintain a purely internal, cognitive orientation to information in memory. The latter requires a greater degree of metacognitive control: The child must use internal processes, cognitions, to control other internal processes.

There is some additional similarity among visual scanning, retrieval, and story recall. When structure is provided by the external environment, a young child will perform much better than when he must provide that structure for himself (Day, 1975). A similar dependence on structure in story recall has been reported by Mandler and DeForest (1977). Young children are even more dependent than their elders on the fact that the structure of stories conforms to an idealized schema. Disturb this familiar structure and the young child is lost, but the older learner can use strategies to recover to some extent from the violation of the normal story structure.

Another interesting aspect is the growing knowledge children have about retrieval processes. Although young children can use external cues provided for them, they have at best very limited knowledge about why such cues are useful or what types of cues would be most effective (Gordon & Flavell, 1977; Kreutzer, Leonard, & Flavell, 1975). Such metamnemonic knowledge, which permits intelligent direction of memory activities, develops gradually. For example, not until the age of 7 or 8 years do most children understand that the search for a lost object should be limited to the area in which the object could logically be, that is, the area between where one first discovers its absence and where one last remembers having it (Drozdal & Flavell, 1975). Nine - to 14-year-old children realize that an external retrieval task, finding a jacket lost at school, would be easier than a purely internal one, remembering a great idea one had for a birthday present (Yussen & Levy, 1977). Better informed about retrieval processes in general, the older child can become more flexible in generating strategies appropriate to the solution of a given problem.

Our three selected tasks — extracting the gist, visual scanning, and retrieval — cannot be claimed to satisfy all the criteria set out at the beginning of this section, but they approach this goal. The processes examined are clearly important cognitive activities relevant to a broad range of tasks. They develop over a wide age range during which starting, intermediate, and end states can be identified and reidentified at several developmental stages depending on the difficulty of the task and the match between the task demands and the child's current cognitive status. We know that extracting the gist and retrieval have reasonable instructional relevance. Visual scanning has received little attention as to its relevance for instructive purposes, but training in scanning strategies has been found to modify the behavior of impulsive children who tend not to focus on the more important areas of a stimulus (Egeland, 1974). Finally, the knowledge that children possess has been shown to augment experiences in retrieval and getting the gist; both self-reports and observed behaviors confirm the notion of increasing self-regulation. Although scanning also shows increasing self-regulation, we know of no investigations aimed at the child's conscious knowledge of his own visual-scanning behavior. This would be an interesting area of inquiry, although we hope it will not be dubbed "metascanning." The main criterion left unsatisfied by all our tasks is that none of the processes have been described by detailed, explicit developmental models of the type formulated by Klahr & Siegler (in press). This unfortunately does not distinguish them from most other processes under investigation by developmental psychologists, and it suggests what our future goals should be. The possibility of formulating such models, we believe, depends on first selecting a task meeting at least the criteria of development over a broad age range with identifiable states.

In summary, we believe that one main aspect of "what develops" is metacognition — the voluntary control an individual has over his own cognitive processes. This is certainly not to say that metacognition is the only thing that develops; however, we have tried to illustrate our belief that the growth of metacognitive abilities underlies many of the behavioral changes that take place with development. When we examine a naturally occurring behavior, a behavior that begins very early in life without tutelage, what develops is often not so much the process itself but increasing sophistication and refinement in its exercise. We have seen various aspects of this gradual refinement in all three processes examined. Children become increasingly efficient at extracting information, whether from a story, a picture, or their own memories. They come to rely less on externally provided structure because they become able to generate their own structure internally. This efficiency seems to be traceable in part to the development of more efficient and effective strategies to help organize the extraction process and to a growing tendency to monitor it. These strategies include making more exhaustive attempts, whether at recalling or scanning; the spontaneous adoption of skills, such as note taking, underlining texts, or using a cue for retrieval; and greater reliance on internal control, whether scanning a picture, comprehending a story, or retrieving ideas. By examining a variety of apparently unrelated processes that develop over a wide age range, these commonalities in "what develops" become quite striking.

C. Methods for Observing Developmental Change

As our last general point, we would like to emphasize that in order to construct a realistic picture of the child's competencies, it is sometimes necessary to use methods other than traditional experimentation. We sometimes gain our most interesting information from informally observing, questioning, and playing with children, particularly the very young. Indeed, without these methods we would have even less information about cognitive development below 5 years of age than we now do. We do not wish to denigrate experimentation. In fact, it is our bias that to confirm a hypothesized developmental trend, it is almost always necessary to devise a tightly controlled experimental test. However, we plead for other approaches because of the predominance of laboratory experimental methods in our field.

Although we realize that calls for an increased concern with ecological validity are becoming commonplace, and to some wearisome, we support the movement in the area of the development of cognitive skills. Our estimate of a child's competencies are sometimes dramatically changed if we consider them in naturally occurring situations. If, therefore, we are in the business of delineating the cognitive competencies of the 4-year-old, we will have a distorted picture if we see the 4-year-old only in a laboratory setting. Of course, the 4-year-old's laboratory performance is informative, but it is only one side of the picture. We also need to consider the other side, how our 4-year-old functions in the world around him, outside the confines of the laboratory. This argument probably holds for any population, including the rat, but it gains more credence the younger and less compliant the laboratory game player.

For these reasons we advocate a three-pronged research plan similar to that described by Cole and Scribner (1975) for cross-cultural research comparisons. The basic theme is an interweaving of experimental and ethnographic research to investigate a particular activity in a range of situations, from the naturally occurring to the experimental. Such a strategy seems ideally suited for comparative research with groups that differ not in terms of national origin or degree of formal schooling but in age or school success within our society.

First, one should investigate the subject's understanding of the experiment or task and his role as subject. Before reaching any conclusions about competency one should become thoroughly familiar with the task demands and how these appear to the child. We must know whether the child is familiar with the materials and the response demands, whether he can understand the instructions, and whether the point of the experiment seems reasonable to him. In short, is the leading activity that is envisaged by the experimenter (e.g., deliberate retention as goal) also countenanced by the child? As a second approach, Cole and Scribner (1975) suggest that we should "experiment with the experiment." Instead of repeating one fixed paradigm across ages, we should work with many different variations of a paradigm, variations suited to the interests and abilities of the children studied. The third strategy is to investigate the same process in a range of situations, including the naturally occurring context of the culture — for example, early childhood.

Cole and Scribner's plea is similar to that made by Soviet developmental psychologists (Brown, in press, c; Meacham, 1977). They emphasize that cognitive activities develop and change within a sociohistorical cultural context and that the nature of these acculturation processes influences the activities, motives, focus, and types of cognitive competence displayed by the individual. Therefore, it must be profitable to view the memory of the developing child in relation to the ecology of childhood.

We know of few studies that exemplify this approach; in fact, to illustrate it we turn to some research conducted "long ago and far away." Almost 30 years ago Istomina (1975) published a study in the Soviet Union on the development of voluntary memory in children between three and seven years. We describe this experiment in some detail because it is an excellent example of our argument that assessment of children's memory capacity and metacognitive skills is influenced by the artificiality of many laboratory tasks, which the child may not fully understand or be fully engaged in.

One of the most interesting features of Istomina's experiment was a comparison between children's memory for lists of words in a relatively standard list-learning situation versus their memory for comparable lists embedded in a meaningful (to the child) activity. Isotamina's reason for contrasting these two conditions was "that the development of retention and recall as internal, purposeful acts takes place initially as part of a broader, articulated, and meaningful activity (since it is only within the context of such activity that the specific acts of remembering and recall can have any meaning for a child) [pp. 8–9]." A game that made sense to the child and aroused a desire to participate should provide motivation for the child to set memory goals for himself and to discover various mnemonics. The child should be more likely to adopt the goal of remembering and to seek strategies to help him remember if he is highly motivated to perform some task in which memory plays an essential role.

Istomina set children the task of remembering a list of items to be bought at a play store. The store was set up in their preschool and equipped with a cash register, scale, play money, and a variety of items "for sale," including toys, food, clothing, and the like. One at a time, the children were recruited to go on a shopping errand. The teacher would slowly name five items for the child to buy and send him to the store in the next room. An assistant at the store recorded how many items the child recalled and observed the accompanying activity. In an control condition, the experimenter called each child for a "lesson," and instructed him to listen attentively so he could later recall all the words. The list of words was of comparable length, meaning, and difficulty to the list of store items. In both situations, the experimenter prompted the child to remember as much as he could, asking if he could remember any more if he had forgotten anything. Recall was clearly superior in the game situation, indeed almost twice as high at the younger ages. When remembering is an intrinsic part of some meaningful activity, we obtain a higher estimate of young children's memory capabilities (Murphy & Brown, 1975).

We do not know exactly why recall is higher in a meaningful activity, but Istomina (1975) suggests several possibilities. For one thing, the children are more motivated to remember: They want to play the game properly, and at some point most of the older children realize that this means remembering their shopping lists. Istomina argues that although the youngest children know what it means to remember "...this is not enough: they must not only know what remembering is by itself but also be able to see it as an end result, an objective to which activity must be directed, i.e., to grasp it as a goal [p. 59]." The goal of remembering is more salient in the game situation, so children are more likely to adopt it as their own goal. This is in contrast to the typical learning situation in which we are often uncertain that the child shares the experimenter's goal.

Once the child can set remembering as a conscious goal, he then starts searching for more effective ways to carry it out. Istomina's naturalistic situation produced a delightful set of protocols detailing individual children's emergent procedures for remembering. Many of her subjects seem to have discovered spontaneously most of the mnemonic strategies developmental psychologists have identified. The strategies adopted and the way in which they are used become increasingly complex and sophisticated with age.

Three-year-old Valerik barely waited for the list of items to be read before rushing off to the store. The 3-year-old's view of the game seemed to be limited to going to the store and returning with items but did not seem to include the notion of bringing back the specific items on the list. Four-year-old Igor listened attentively to the shopping list and then tried to carry out his errand as quickly as possible. He even seemed to try to avoid distractions, refusing to stop and talk when on his way to the store. Very few 4-year-olds showed more specific mnemonic behaviors, but between four and five a qualitative shift seemed to occur, and all the older subjects seemed to make active attempts to remember. Many 5- and 6-year-olds actively rehearsed: They were often observed moving their lips, repeating the words over to themselves as the experimenter read them and as they walked to the store.

Many of the older children showed strong executive control and seemed to be monitoring their own memory states and even checking themselves to determine how well they remembered.

Slava M. (five years, six months) listened silently as the list was read, looking at the experimenter tensely, and after a slight pause asked him to repeat the list one more time. He did not recall the list immediately, frowning, shrugging his shoulders, and saying: "Wait a minute, I'll get it, hold on. . . ." [p. 26].

Dima F. (six years, six months) listened to the list, muttering silently, and then repeated it almost as if to himself. He quickly recalled three items, then paused, screwed up his eyes, and said, with concern: "Oh! What else was there? Nope, I can't remember what else I have to buy. . . ." [p. 26].

Alik K. (five years, eight months) listened to the message to the end and then quickly went off to the store. However, halfway there he turned back. "I can only remember endive. What else was there?" he asked the experimenter [p. 27].

Alochka also returned from the store to ask the experimenter for the items she had forgotten. Clearly, these children must have been testing themselves on their way to the store. Finally, the oldest children (6 to 7 years old) displayed more sophisticated strategies such as trying to form logical connections between the items on their lists, often rearranging the order of the words based on their meaning.

Istomina's (1975) work is fascinating not only for the information it provides about young children's memory processes but also for the methodological point it emphasizes. The best situation in which to study very early memory development is in a natural context in which the child is likely to understand the task and be motivated to perform it. The young child's performance on laboratory tasks is often markedly inferior to his performance in a game setting. Although this variable is crucially important when studying very young children, the same general point is applicable to other ages as well. Subjects of any age, even adults, are likely to perform better in a meaningful task in which they are actively engaged. Thus, if we want accurate, generalizable information about development, we should extend the realm of our investigations from the laboratory into the real world. However, a vital aspect of this approach is that we must investigate the same process in both situations; we must look at the process in a natural activity that is meaningful to the subject and suited to his abilities, and we must also use well-controlled experiments to test particular hypotheses about the process. Experiments themselves can be engineered to provide controlled observations and exciting activities for children.

V. SUMMARY

The first section of this chapter was devoted to traditional memory studies that have provided us with much of our information about what develops. Major strengths and weaknesses of memory-development studies were illustrated by comparison with recent research into children's problem-solving skills. In the second part we concentrated on alternate methods and procedures for attacking the problem of important developments in the ability to think, reason, and solve problems.

A common theme throughout was the gradual emergence of finely tailored skills adapted to meet specialized task demands. We attributed the heightened sensitivity to fine gradations of the task and strategy interface to enhanced metacognitive insights, that is, the thinker's knowledge, control, and coordination of his own cognitions. This accumulation of knowledge about how to think in an increasing array of problem situations is an outcome of experience with more and more complex problems. Young children's insensitivity to their problem-solving potential is the result of lack of exposure to such situations, rather than age per se, for the same problems that beset the very small problem solver can often impede effective thinking in the adult novice.

To illustrate the emergence of increasingly strategic action we concentrated on three main tasks: extracting the gist of a message, scanning the visual environment, and retrieving lost information from the external world or from the mind. These three tasks share several interesting similarities in development. Examination of cognitive growth in these domains, from infancy to maturity, provided the principal support for our conceptualization of "what develops." Our candidate for a primary developmental agent is an expanding knowledge of how to think and the ability to monitor and coordinate the activities displayed in effective thinking.

As a final point, we concentrated on "what develops" in keeping with the title of the volume. However, we would like to point out that an equally important question is how development occurs (Brown, in press, a). Considerable progress has been made in mapping what develops, but there has been far less attention paid to what mechanisms underlie this progression. The problems of growth and change are quintessential developmental questions and are of fundamental importance no less to the instructional psychologist who wishes to accelerate growth than to the theorist who seeks to understand development. Therefore, in conjunction with descriptions of the steps along the route from naïveté to expertise, we would like to see extended discussion of the conditions fostering this growth in competence.

ACKNOWLEDGMENTS

The preparation of this manuscript was supported in part by Grants HD 06864 and HD 05951 and a Research Career Development Award HD 00111 from the National Institutes of Child Health and Human Development and in part by the National Institute of Education under Contract No. MS–NIE–C–400–76–0116.

REFERENCES

Acredolo, L. P., Pick, H. L., & Olsen, M. G. Environmental differentiation and familiarity as determinants of children's memory for spatial location. *Developmental Psychology*, 1975, *11*, 495–501.

Ames, E. W., & Silfen, C. K. *Methodological issues in the study of age differences in infants' attention to stimuli varying in movement and complexity*. Paper presented at the meeting of the Society for Research in Child Development, Minneapolis, March 1966.

Bransford, J. D., Nitsch, K. W., & Franks, J. J. Schooling and the facilitation of knowing. In R. C. Anderson, R. J. Spiro, & W. E. Montague (Eds.), *Schooling and the acquisition of knowledge*. Hillsdale, N.J.: Lawrence Erlbaum Associates, 1977.

Brown, A. L. Judgments of recency for long sequences of pictures: The absence of a developmental trend. *Journal of Experimental Child Psychology,* 1973, *15,* 473–481. (a)

Brown, A. L. Mnemonic elaboration and recency judgments in children. *Cognitive Psychology,* 1973, *5,* 233–248. (b)

Brown, A. L. Temporal and contextual cues as discriminative attributes in retardates' recognition memory. *Journal of Experimental Psychology,* 1973, *98,* 1–13. (c)

Brown, A. L. The role of strategic behavior in retardate memory. In N. R. Ellis (Ed.), *International review of research in mental retardation* (Vol. 1). New York: Academic Press, 1974.

Brown, A. L. The development of memory: Knowing, knowing about knowing, and knowing how to know. In H. W. Reese (Ed.), *Advances in child development and behavior* (Vol. 10). New York: Academic Press, 1975. (a)

Brown, A. L. Recognition, reconstruction, and recall of narrative sequences by preoperational children. *Child Development,* 1975, *46,* 156–166. (b)

Brown, A. L. The construction of temporal succession by preoperational children. In A. D. Pick (Ed.), *Minnesota symposia on child psychology* (Vol. 10). Minneapolis: University of Minnesota, 1976.

Brown, A. L. Development, schooling and the acquisition of knowledge about knowledge. In R. C. Anderson, R. J. Spiro, & W. E. Montague (Eds.), *Schooling and the acquisition of knowledge.* Hillsdale, N.J.: Lawrence Erlbaum Associates, 1977.

Brown, A. L. Knowing when, where, and how to remember: A problem of metacognition. In R. Glaser (Ed.), *Advances in instructional psychology.* Hillsdale, N.J.: Lawrence Erlbaum Associates, in press. (a)

Brown, A. L. Metacognitive development and reading. In R. J. Spiro, B. Bruce, & W. F. Brewer (Eds.), *Theoretical issues in reading comprehension.* Hillsdale, N.J.: Lawrence Erlbaum Associates, in press. (b)

Brown, A. L. Theories of memory and the problem of development: Growth, activity, and knowledge. In F. I. M. Craik & L. Cermak (Eds.), *Levels of analysis approaches to cognition.* Hillsdale, N.J.: Lawrence Erlbaum Associates, in press. (c)

Brown, A. L., & Campione, J. C. Training strategic study time apportionment in educable retarded children. *Intelligence,* 1977, *1,* 94–107. (a)

Brown, A. L., & Campione, J. C. Memory strategies in learning: Training children to study strategically. In H. Pick, H. Leibowitz, J. Singer, A. Steinschneider, & H. Stevenson (Eds.), *Application of basic research in psychology.* New York: Plenum Press, in press.

Brown, A. L., & Smiley, S. S. Rating the importance of structural units of prose passages: A problem of metacognitive development. *Child Development,* 1977, *48,* 1–8. (a)

Brown, A. L., & Smiley, S. S. *The development of strategies for studying prose passages.* Unpublished manuscript, University of Illinois, 1977. (b)

Brown, A. L., Smiley, S. S., Day, J. D., Townsend, M. A. R., & Lawton, S. C. Intrusion of a thematic idea in children's comprehension and retention of stories. *Child Development,* 1977, *48,* 1454–1466.

Butterfield, E. C., & Belmont, J. M. Assessing and improving the cognitive functions of mentally retarded people. In I. Bailer & M. Steinlicht (Eds.), *Psychological issues in mental retardation.* Chicago: Aldine Press, 1977.

Butterfield, E. C., Wambold, C., & Belmont, J. M. On the theory and practice of improving short-term memory. *American Journal of Mental Deficiency,* 1973, *77,* 654–669.

Campione, J. C., & Brown, A. L. Memory and metamemory development in educable retarded children. In R. V. Kail, Jr., & J. W. Hagen (Eds.), *Perspectives on the development of memory and cognition.* Hillsdale, N.J.: Lawrence Erlbaum Associates, 1977.

Chi, M. T. H. Short-term memory limitations in children: Capacity or processing deficits? *Memory and Cognition,* 1976, *4,* 559–572.

Chi, M. T. H. *Metamemory and chess skill.* Unpublished manuscript, University of Pittsburgh, 1977.

Cole, M., & Scribner, S. Theorizing about socialization of cognition. *Ethos,* 1975, *3,* 249–268.

Craik, F. I. M., & Lockhart, R. S. Levels of processing: A framework for memory research. *Journal of Verbal Learning and Verbal Behavior,* 1972, *11,* 671–684.

Day, M. C. Developmental trends in visual scanning. In H. W. Reese (Ed.), *Advances in child development and behavior* (Vol. 10). New York: Academic Press, 1975.

Drozdal, J. G., & Flavell, J. H. A developmental study of logical search behavior. *Child Development,* 1975, *46,* 389–393.

Egeland, B. Training impulsive children in the use of more efficient scanning techniques. *Child Development,* 1974, *45,* 165–171.

Flavell, J. H. Developmental studies of mediated memory. In H. W. Reese & L. P. Lipsitt (Eds.), *Advances in child development and behavior* (Vol. 5). New York: Academic Press, 1970.

Flavell, J. H. Metacognitive aspects of problem solving. In L. B. Resnick (Ed.), *The nature of intelligence.* Hillsdale, N.J.: Lawrence Erlbaum Associates, 1976.

Flavell, J. H., & Wellman, H. M. Metamemory. In R. V. Kail, Jr., & J. W. Hagen (Eds.), *Perspectives on the development of memory and cognition.* Hillsdale, N.J.: Lawrence Erlbaum Associates, 1977.

Gibson, E. J. *Principles of perceptual learning and development.* New York: Appleton-Century-Crofts, 1969.

Gordon, F. R., & Flavell, J. H. The development of intuitions about cognitive cueing. *Child Development,* 1977, *48,* 1027–1033.

Greeno, J. G. Cognitive objectives of instruction: Theory of knowledge for solving problems and answering questions. In D. Klahr (Ed.), *Cognition and instruction.* Hillsdale, N.J.: Lawrence Erlbaum Associates, 1976.

Harris, P. L. Perseverative errors in search by young infants. *Child Development,* 1973, *44,* 28–33.

Hayes, J. R. It's the thought that counts: New approaches to educational theory. In D. Klahr (Ed.), *Cognition and instruction.* Hillsdale, N.J.: Lawrence Erlbaum Associates, 1976.

Huttenlocher, J., & Burke, D. Why does memory span increase with age? *Cognitive Psychology,* 1976, *8,* 1–31.

Inhelder, B., Sinclair, H. & Bovet, M. *Learning and the development of cognition.* Cambridge, Mass.: Harvard University Press, 1974.

Istomina, Z. M. The development of voluntary memory in preschool-age children. *Soviet Psychology,* Summer 1975, *13,* 5–64.

Klahr, D. Understanding understanding systems. In L. W. Gregg (Ed.), *Knowledge and cognition.* Hillsdale, N.J.: Lawrence Erlbaum Associates, 1974.

Klahr, D., & Siegler, R. S. The representation of children's knowledge. In H. W. Reese (Ed.), (Ed.), *Advances in child development and behavior* (Vol. 12). New York: Academic Press, 1978.

Kobasigawa, A. Utilization of retrieval cues by children in recall. *Child Development,* 1974, *45,* 127–134.

Kreutzer, M. A., Leonard, C., & Flavell, J. H. An interview study of children's knowledge about memory. *Monographs of the Society for Research in Child Development,* 1975, *40*(1, Serial Number 159).

Kuhn, D. Including development experimentally: Comments on a research paradigm. *Developmental Psychology,* 1974, *10,* 590–600.

Loughlin, K. A., & Daehler, M. A. The effects of distraction and added perceptual cues on the delayed reaction of very young children. *Child Development,* 1973, *44,* 384–388.

Mackworth, N. H., & Bruner, J. S. How adults and children search and recognize pictures. *Human Development,* 1970, *13,* 149–177.

Mandler, J. M., & DeForest, M. *The code in the node: Developmental differences in the use of a story schema.* Paper presented at the Society for Research in Child Development Meetings, New Orleans, March 1977.

Markman, E. M. Realizing that you don't understand: A preliminary investigation. *Child Development,* 1977, *48,* 986–992.

Maurer, D., & Salapatek, P. Developmental changes in the scanning of faces by young infants. *Child Development,* 1976, *47,* 523–527.

Meacham, J. A. Soviet investigations of memory development. In R. V. Kail, Jr., & J. W. Hagen (Eds.), *Perspectives on the development of memory and cognition.* Hillsdale, N.J.: Lawrence Erlbaum Associates, 1977.

Murphy, M. D., & Brown, A. L. Incidental learning in preschool children as a function of level of cognitive analysis. *Journal of Experimental Child Psychology,* 1975, *19,* 509–523.

Nelson, K. Cognitive development and the acquisition of concepts. In R. C. Anderson, R. J. Spiro, & W. E. Montague (Eds.), *Schooling and the acquisition of knowledge.* Hillsdale, N.J.: Lawrence Erlbaum Associates, 1977.

Nelson, K., & Brown, A. L. The semantic-episodic distinction in memory development. In P. Ornstein (Ed.), *Memory development.* Hillsdale, N.J.: Lawrence Erlbaum Associates, in press.

Norman, D. A., Gentner, D. R., & Stevens, A. L. Comments on learning schemata and memory representation. In D. Klahr (Ed.), *Cognition and instruction.* Hillsdale, N.J.: Lawrence Erlbaum Associates, 1976.

Noton, D., & Stark, L. Eye movements and visual perception. *Scientific American,* 1971, *224,* 34–43.

Olson, D. R. *Cognitive development: The child's acquisition of diagonality.* New York: Academic Press, 1970.

Pushkina, A. G. Mechanisms of transposition of relations in preschool-age children. *Soviet Psychology,* 1971, *9,* 213–234.

Resnick, L. B. Task analysis in instructional design: Some cases from mathematics. In D. Klahr (Eds.), *Cognition and instruction.* Hillsdale, N.J.: Lawrence Erlbaum Associates, 1976.

Resnick, L. B., & Beck, I. L. Designing instruction in reading: Interaction of theory and practice. In J. T. Guthrie (Ed.), *Aspects of reading acquisition.* Baltimore, Md.: Johns Hopkins Press, in press.

Ritter, K., Kaprove, B. H., Fitch, J. P., & Flavell, J. H. *Cognitive Psychology,* 1973, *5,* 310–321.

Ruff, H. A. The function of shifting fixations in the visual perception of infants. *Child Development,* 1975, *46,* 857–865.

Ryan, S. M., Hegion, A. G., & Flavell, J. H. Nonverbal mnemonic mediation in preschool children. *Child Development,* 1970, *41,* 539–550.

Salapatek, P. Visual scanning of geometric figures by the human newborn. *Journal of Comparative and Physiological Psychology,* 1968, *66,* 247–258.

Salapatek, P. Pattern perception in early infancy. In L. B. Cohen & P. Salapatek (Eds.), *Infant perception* (Vol. 1). New York: Academic Press, 1975.

Siegler, R. S. Three aspects of cognitive development. *Cognitive Psychology,* 1976, *8,* 481–520.

Smiley, S. S., Oakley, D. D., Worthen, D., Campione, J. C., & Brown, A. L. Recall of thematically relevant material by adolescent good and poor readers as a function of written versus oral presentation. *Educational Psychology,* 1977, *69,* 381–387.

Smirnov, A. A., Istomina, Z. M., Mal'tseva, K. P., & Samokhvalova, V. I. The development of logical memorization techniques in the preschool and young school child. *Soviet Psychology*, Winter 1971–1972, *10*, 178–195.

Stechler, G., & Latz, E. Some observations on attention and arousal in the human infant. *Journal of the American Academy of Child Psychiatry*, 1966, *5*, 517–525.

Thomas, E. L. Movements of the eye. *Scientific American*, 1968, *219*(2), 88–95.

Vurpillot, E. The development of scanning strategies and their relation to visual differentiation. *Journal of Experimental Child Psychology*, 1968, *6*, 632–650.

Vygotsky, L. S. *Thought and language*. Cambridge, Mass.: MIT Press, 1962.

Webb, R. A., Masur, B., & Nadolny, T. Information and strategy in the young child's search for hidden objects. *Child Development*, 1972, *43*, 91–104.

Wellman, H. M. The early development of intentional memory behavior. *Human Development*, 1977, *20*, 86–101.

Wellman, H. M., Ritter, K., & Flavell, J. H. Deliberate memory behavior in the delayed reactions of very young children. *Developmental Psychology*, 1975, *11*, 780–787.

Winograd, T. Frame representations and the declarative/procedural controversy. In D. G. Bobrow & A. Collins (Eds.), *Representation and understanding: Studies in cognitive science*. New York: Academic Press, 1975.

Woods, W. A. Modeling comprehension: Multiple theory formation in high-level perception. In R. J. Spiro, B. C. Bruce, & W. F. Brewer (Eds.), *Theoretical issues in reading comprehension*. Hillsdale, N.J.: Lawrence Erlbaum Associates, in press.

Yussen, S. R., & Levy, V. M., Jr. Developmental changes in knowledge about different retrieval problems. *Developmental Psychology*, 1977, *13*, 114–120.

Zinchenko, V. F., Chzhi-tsin, B., & Tarakanov, V. V. The formation and development of perceptual activity. *Soviet Psychology and Psychiatry*, 1963, *2*, 3–12.

2 Intellectual Development from Birth to Adulthood: A Neo-Piagetian Interpretation

Robbie Case
The Ontario Institute for Studies in Education

This chapter is an attempt to provide a new theoretical account of intellectual development from birth to adulthood. It is divided into three sections. In the first section, I examine recurrent patterns of intellectual development. Following Piaget (e.g., 1970), each of three stages of development is considered separately: the sensorimotor stage (birth to 2 years), the preoperational stage (2 to 6 years), and the concrete operational stage (6 to 12 years). Following Simon (1962), the sequence of substages within each stage is characterized as a progression of increasingly complex and powerful executive strategies. Following Pascual–Leone (1969), two factors are suggested as being responsible for these progressions: experience with the strategy in question and an increase in the size of working memory. In the second section, I discuss long-term cognitive changes underlying the recurrent pattern of development. My hypothesis is that an increase in the automaticity of basic operations accounts for the increase in working memory within each stage. I also suggest that a certain minimum level of operational automaticity at one stage is prerequisite for transition to the next stage. Finally, in the third section, I predict the sequence of intellectual developments in adolescence and adulthood on the basis of the pattern and mechanism of development hypothesized to characterize the first three stages of life.

INTELLECTUAL DEVELOPMENT DURING THE FIRST THREE STAGES OF LIFE

Development During the Concrete Operational Stage

From ages 3 to 11 years, the child goes through a number of qualitatively distinct substages in which his thinking becomes progressively more systematic and logical. A major contribution of computer simulation to the study of develop-

TABLE 2.1
Sequence of Strategies Observed on Noelting's Juice Problem

Developmental Level	Age of Assession	Type of Item Passed	Global Description of Strategy
1	3 to 4		Isolated Centration
2	4 to 5		Unidimensional Comparison[a]
3	7 to 8		Bidimensional Comparison
4	9 to 10		Bidimensional Comarison, with Quantification[b]

[a]Noelting's data (1975) show the age of accession for this item as 4 years. Our data suggest that this is true only for very simple number comparisons, for example, 1 versus 3. Thus, I have listed the age of accession as 4 to 5 years.

[b]The strategy for this item has been induced from Noelting's (1975) error data. His own description is somewhat different.

ment has been the suggestion that this series of substages can be modeled as a series of increasingly complex and powerful executive strategies (cf. Simon, 1962). An excellent illustration of a developmental sequence that can be modeled in this fashion is provided by Noelting (1975). In Noelting's task, children are shown two large pitchers, *A* and *B*. The experimenter explains that he is going to dump several tumblers of orange juice and several tumblers of water into each. The child's task is to predict which pitcher will taste more strongly of orange juice. He may count the tumblers of each liquid that will be poured into each pitcher, but he may not pour the tumblers in to see if he is right. Table 2.1 presents several of the specific problems and the ages at which these problems are first passed.

Noelting has modeled children's reasoning at each substage both in terms of the executive strategies they use and the logical structures these strategies imply. His account of the executive strategies is especially interesting.

Strategy I (3 to 4½ Years): Isolated Centration.   At the earliest stage, children evaluate each array of tumblers in isolation, noticing only one global feature: the presence or absence of juice. They therefore succeed on problems where only one side receives juice, but they fail in all other instances.

Strategy II (4½ to 6 Years): Unidimensional Comparison.   By the age of 4½ to 5 years, children notice not only the presence or absence of juice on each side but also the quantity of juice. Their strategy thus becomes comparative rather than absolute. They succeed on all items that can be passed by picking the side with the greater number of juice tumblers.

Strategy III (7 to 8 Years): Bidimensional Comparison. By age 7 years or so, children notice the number of water tumblers on each side as well as the number of juice tumblers. They compare the number of water and juice tumblers on each side and pick the side having an excess of juice over water. However, if both sides have more juice, or more water, or if both sides are equal, the children simply guess.[1]

Strategy IV (9 to 10 Years): Bidimensional Comparison with Quantification. By age nine, children notice the extent of the excess or deficit of juice tumblers over water tumblers on each side. They therefore succeed on any item where the correct answer may be obtained by determining which side has the greater excess or lesser deficit. They continue to fail, however, on items where understanding of ratio is necessary.

The most striking characteristic of this sequence is that each strategy is a modified and more powerful version of the previous one. That is, each successive strategy works for a greater variety of problems because it takes into account some new and relevant aspect of the task. In Piagetian terms, each strategy is both more differentiated and more equilibrated than previous ones. Two broad classes of factors may influence this process. The first class is relatively specific and includes physical and social experience; the second is more general and includes maturation and internal coordination (Piaget, 1964).

Strategy Evolution: The Specific Experiential Hypothesis

At the earliest stage, children must be able to discriminate tastes and visual appearances and notice their covariation. This would lead to the most elementary strategy, namely, basing predictions on the presence or absence of the orange liquid. What about the transition to the second strategy? Following Piaget, one or both of the following processes might be at work: (1) The subject might encounter situations in which his expectations were not confirmed, that is, in which there was a clear difference in taste between two mixtures, both of which were orange and could be classified as "orange juice" (cf. Klahr & Wallace, 1973; Piaget, 1971). Because such situations would generate cognitive conflict, they would lead the subject to search for and discover an additional relevant feature of the situation (in this case, the numbers of orange juice tumblers). (2) Alternatively, and perhaps more probably, the child simply might come to

---

[1]Only qualitatively distinct strategies are described here. There are also a number of intermediate versions. For example, as with Siegler's problems (this volume), between Strategies II and III there is a stage where children consider the number of water glasses but only if the number of juice glasses are equal. For a more complete account, see Noelting (1975).

notice the dimension of numerousness with repeated exposure to situations in which numerousness varied (cf. Gibson, 1969; Piaget, 1957). In either case, once the critical dimension was isolated, the subject would again be in cognitive disequilibrium. He would know that his current basis for prediction worked sporadically and that some additional factor must be involved. His task would therefore be to experiment with modifications of his strategy until it was correct.

Given that strategy modification occurs by this sort of process, what environmental factors might influence the rate of modification? The first factor is simply exposure to situations in which liquids are mixed (cf. Gibson, 1969; Piaget, 1957). The second factor is exposure to situations where there is some clear indication that the current basis for predictions is inadequate (cf. Halford, 1970; Klahr & Wallace, 1973). The third factor is exposure to situations where the unattended feature is highlighted in some fashion (cf. Gelman, 1969). Finally, the fourth factor is exposure to models of how to incorporate this additional feature (cf. Gagné, 1968).

Traditional Piagetian theory makes a distinction between the first two kinds of factors and the second two. The first two are seen as involving only the opportunity to learn, whereas the second two are seen as involving direct instruction. According to Piaget and Inhelder, cue extraction and coordination are normally controlled by the subject's general operative structures, and when this control is taken over by an instructor, the type of learning and the pattern of transfer are different (cf. Inhelder, Bovet, Sinclair, & Smock, 1966). A clearer basis for this conclusion will be provided once a second major feature of the strategy sequence is described.

Strategy Evolution: The General Developmental Hypothesis

If one counts the number of items that must be held in working memory to execute Noelting's strategies, one notices a remarkable progression. For the simplest strategy, only one item must be considered: the presence or absence of juice. For the second strategy, two items must be considered: the number of orange juice tumblers poured into A and the number poured into B. For the third strategy, three items must be considered: the number of orange juice tumblers in B, the number of water tumblers in B, and the stored conclusion of the relative quantity in A. Finally, for the fourth strategy, four items must be considered, the additional item being the exact quantity of the difference between orange juice and water in A. A more detailed calculation of these values is presented in Table 2.2. As may be seen, the calculations are based not on the total number of items an external observer might count but rather on the total number of items the subject must hold in working memory at each step of his

TABLE 2.2

Working Memory Demands for Executing Noelting's Strategies

Strategy	Steps Involved	Items in Working Memory (i.e., items being attended to)	Memory Demand
I Isolated Centration (3 to 4 years)	Step 1 – Look for orange juice in A. If it is there, say it will taste of orange juice; if it is not there, say it won't taste of orange juice.	(1) color of tumblers in array A.	1
	Step 2 – Look for orange juice in B. If it is there, say it will taste of orange juice, too. If not, say it won't.	(i) Color of tumblers in array B.[a]	1
II Unidimensional Comparison (5 to 6 years)	Step 1 – Count the number of orange juice tumblers to be dumped into A. (Store)	(i) No. of orange juice (A).	1
	Step 2 – Count the number of orange juice tumblers to be dumped into B. (Store)	(i) No. of orange juice (A). (ii) No. of orange juice (B).	2
	Step 3 – Select larger number and predict that the side with that number will taste stronger. If the two numbers are equal, say they will taste the same.	(i) No. of orange juice (A). (ii) No. of orange juice (B).	2
III Bidimensional Comparison (7 to 8 years)	Step 1 – Count the number of orange juice tumblers to be dumped into A. (Store)	(i) No. of orange juice (A).	1
	Step 2 – Count the number of water tumblers to be dumped into A. (Store)	(i) No. of orange juice (A).[b] (ii) No. of water (A).	2

(continued)

TABLE 2.2 *(continued)*

Strategy	Steps Involved	Items in Working Memory (i.e., items being attended to)		Memory Demand
	Step 3 – Notice whether amount of orange juice is more or less than amount of water. (Store)	(i)	orange juice ⋛ water (A).	1
	Step 4 – Count number of orange juice tumblers to be dumped into B. (Store)	(i) (iii)	orange juice ⋛ water (A).[b] No. of orange juice (B).	2
	Step 5 – Count the number of water tumblers to be dumped into B. (Store)	(i) (ii) (iii)	No. of orange juice ⋛ water (A).[b] No. of orange juice (B).[b] No. of water (B).	3
	Step 6 – Notice whether amount of orange juice in B is more, less, or same as amount of water in B. (Store)	(i) (ii)	orange juice ⋛ water (A).[b] orange juice ⋛ water (B).[b]	2
	Step 7 – Pick side with more orange juice than water (as more) or side with less orange juice than water (as less). If relative amount on each side is in the same direction, say they have the same.	(i) (ii)	orange juice ⋛ water (A). orange juice ⋛ water (B).	2
IV Bidimensional Comparison, with Quantification (9 to 10 years)	*Step 1* – Count orange juice in A. (Store)	(i)	No. of orange juice (A).	1
	Step 2 – Count water in A. (Store)	(i) (ii)	No. of orange juice (A).[b] No. of water (A).	2
	Step 3 – Notice which has more and how much more. (Store)	(i) (ii)	orange juice ⋚ water. (A).[b] difference = X.	2

42

Step		Working memory items	
Step 4 – Count orange juice in B. (Store)	(i)	orange juice $\gtrless$ water (A).[b]	3
	(ii)	difference = X.[b]	
	(iii)	No. of orange juice (B).	
Step 5 – Count water in B. (Store)	(i)	orange juice $\gtrless$ water (A).[b]	4
	(ii)	difference = X^2.[b]	
	(iii)	No. of orange juice (B).[b]	
	(iv)	No. of water (B).	
Step 6 – Notice which has more and how much more.	(i)	orange juice $\gtrless$ water (A).	4
	(ii)	difference = X.	
	(iii)	orange juice $\gtrless$ water (B).	
	(iv)	difference = Y.	

Step 7 – Apply same decision rule as in Strategy III, unless relationship is the same on both sides, in which case say equal if difference is equal, or make judgment on basis of greater difference (e.g., if H_2O > OJ by 5 in A, and by 3 in B, pick A as weaker).

[a] The reason this is not listed as a second item in working memory is that the first item has already been responded to and no longer needs to be stored.

[b] This item, which was generated in a previous step, must be stored for use in a subsequent step.

thinking.[2] This step places the maximum load on the system and therefore is the point at which insufficient working memory will lead to failure.

Given that Noelting's sequence of strategies shows this progressively increasing demand on working memory, an obvious hypothesis is that the child's rate of progression through the sequence is determined not only by the quantity or quality of his specific experiences but also by the rate of growth of his working memory. A number of investigators have proposed such a hypothesis to account for the general organismic factor in development (cf. Bruner, 1966; Case, 1968; Halford & MacDonald, 1977; McLaughlin, 1963; Pascual–Leone, 1969; Piaget, 1920). However, my approach for computing the memory load is based on a modified version of the procedure proposed by Pascual–Leone (cf. Pascual–Leone, 1970, 1972; Case, 1974b).

Once the importance of this sort of general developmental factor is granted, the difference between the two classes of environmental events is clarified. A child provided simply with the opportunity to learn should move to a higher strategy only if his working memory is large enough to handle the additional cue or cues. By contrast, if the child is actively taught cue discovery and strategy reorganization, then the demands on his working memory should be reduced considerably, either by automization of certain operations or by chunking items that would normally be attended to separately (cf. Case, 1975). However, problems sufficiently different from the original problem that require the subject to work from first principles should demand more working memory than he has available.

So far, I have spoken of the sequence of strategies observed on a specific task — Noelting's juice-mixing problem. However, as Piaget originally noted (and as has been repeatedly confirmed since), a very similar progression of strategies is observed in many other domains. Table 2.3 illustrates a similar progression for three Piagetian tasks: quantification, seriation, and control of variables. A similar progression for three neo-Piagetian tasks may be found in the article by Siegler in this volume.

Given the remarkable parallels in the progression of strategies across tasks, it seems reasonable to generalize the account of the process underlying the progression as well. That is, it seems reasonable to propose that (1) the sequence of behaviors that emerges during the concrete operations period may be ascribed to the evolution of qualitatively distinct executive strategies; (2) progress through

---

[2]For a discussion of the relationship between the number of items an external observer might count (e.g., number of sets in an array) and the number of items that must be placed in working memory, see Case (1947a) or Scardamalia (1977a).

any given sequence of executive strategies can be influenced by practice, feedback, cue highlighting, and strategy modeling; and (3) the size of a child's working memory limits the complexity of the strategy he can acquire and utilize, particularly when his only experience is practice or practice with feedback.

Evidence for the Model of Concrete Operational Development

During the last 10 years, a good deal of empirical evidence has been accumulated for each of the foregoing general propositions. First of all, both Simon and Pascual–Leone (and their colleagues) have shown that performance on most of Piaget's tasks can be described as a series of increasingly complex executive strategies. The tasks analyzed in this fashion include the water-level test (Pascual–Leone, 1969), the cylinder test (Pascual–Leone, 1969), conservation (Pascual–Leone, 1972), class inclusion (Klahr & Wallace, 1973; Pascual–Leone & Smith, 1969), control of variables (Case, 1974b), ratio and proportion (Siegler, 1976), and combinatorial reasoning (Scardamalia, 1977b). For all these tasks, it has been shown that this sort of executive-strategy analysis increases the precision of predictions; an excellent example of the sorts of predictions that can be made is to be found in the article by Siegler in this volume.

Second, Piagetian, neo-Piagetian, and non-Piagetian psychologists alike have shown that specific experience can exert a considerable effect on the acquisition of these executive strategies. The effectiveness of simple practice has been demonstrated by Strauss & Langer (1970) and by Inhelder et al. (1974); the effectiveness of practice with feedback by Siegler (1976) and Bryant (1972); the effectiveness of practice with cue highlighting by Gelman (1969) and Lefebvre and Pinard (1972, 1974); and the effectiveness of modeling and/or rule provision by Sullivan (1967), Bucher and Schneider (1973), and Zimmerman and Rosenthal (1974). In addition, I have attempted to show first, that the first two sorts of experience are effective only when children have reached the normal level of general development for the acquisition of a strategy, and second, that the latter two types of experience are effective at lower levels of general development but may change the pattern of transfer (Case, 1974b; 1977a; 1977b).

Third, Pascual–Leone and his colleagues have shown a direct link between the growth of working memory and the ability to acquire and utilize increasingly complex executive strategies. Their evidence can be divided into four categories. The first type of evidence shows that working memory grows during the concrete operational period according to the same scale suggested by the analysis of the strategies. At least six tests of working memory have been designed and all have yielded approximately the same norms as those mentioned in Table 2.2 (cf. Biemiller, Boychuk, & Rochford, 1977; Case, 1972; Case & Kurland, 1978;

TABLE 2.3

Strategies Observed on Piagetian Tasks During the Period of Concrete Operations

Substage	Task		
Task	Pick beaker with more water.	Place stick of given size "in its place" in a previously constructed series.	Answer question: "Does the material of a rod affect how close it comes to water (when weight on each also differs)?"
	Strategies		
Isolated Centration (3 to 4 years)	Notice global appearance of water column. If it appears large, say it has more.	Decide whether stick is big or little; place it at big end or little end.	Check each rod to see if it is close to water.
Unidimensional Comparison (5 to 6 years)	Make careful comparison of height. Pick higher water column as having more.	Compare height of two sticks. Higher stick is one on right for each placement.	Compare the amount by which each rod extends from water. Say which one goes down further.

(continued)

TABLE 2.3 (continued)

Substage		Strategies	
Substage	Bidimensional Comparison (7 to 8 years)	Notice both height difference and diameter difference between beakers. Attempt qualitative compensation.	Compare height of stick to left and to right before placement. Pick spot where it is bigger than left, smaller than right.	Compare the material of rod, compare the amount of rod, compare the amount it bends. If both differ, conclude material →bending.
	Bidimensional Comparison with addition of third dimension (e.g., quantification)	Notice both height difference and diameter difference. Make quantification compensation.	No further response (i.e., bidimensional strategy is adequate for all versions of task).	Compare (a) weight on each rod, (b) material, (c) bending. If no difference in (a) and difference in (b) and (c), conclude material →bending.

Case & Serlin, in press; Diaz, 1974; Parkinson, 1976; Pascual—Leone, 1970).[3] In addition, substantial within-age correlations for the various tests have been demonstrated (cf. Case & Globerson, 1974).

The second type of evidence is also correlational. There is a positive correlation between tests of working memory and tests of executive functioning, after the common correlation with age is partialled out statistically. To date, this has been demonstrated for tests of conservation (Case, 1977b; DeAvila & Havassy, 1974; Parkinson, 1976), control of variables (Case, 1977c), and combinatorial reasoning (Dale, 1976).

The third type of evidence comes from studies in which children of the same age but different working memory capacities have been given the opportunity to learn new strategies. Those with larger working memories generally learn more efficiently, whereas those with working memories smaller than the hypothesized minimum for the task often fail to learn at all (cf. Case, 1977c).

The final type of evidence comes from studies in which the memory demand of a task or strategy is manipulated and the memory capacity at which the strategy is first observed is shifted by the appropriate number of units. Two studies manipulating the memory loads of tasks have recently been conducted by Scardamalia (1977a, 1977b). In both studies, subjects employing a relatively sophisticated strategy have fallen back on a more primitive approach when the memory demands of the more sophisticated strategy were increased by one unit. Similar results have also been shown for traditional Piagetian tasks by Pascual—Leone (1969) and Pascual—Leone and Smith (1969).

Taken together, this evidence suggests three conclusions: (1) As suggested by Simon (1962), Piaget's operational structures can be interpreted as sequences of increasingly complex and powerful executive structures; (2) as suggested by learning and attention theorists, simple practice, practice with feedback, cue highlighting, and modeling can affect the acquisition of these structures; (3) as suggested by Pascual—Leone, a subject's ability to profit from experience is limited by the size of his working memory. This memory develops from 1 unit at age 3 or 4 years to 5 units at age 11 or 12 years.

---

[3]In order to qualify as a measure of working memory, a task must meet the following requirements: (1) It must require some transformation of the input to ensure that it truly measures "working" memory and not simply "reproductive" or "short-term" memory (cf. Posner, 1967); (2) the task must be solvable by only one strategy or at most by a family of equivalently complex strategies to ensure that whatever developmental trends are obtained cannot be ascribed to increasing strategic sophistication; (3) the task must include a substantial training component to ensure that developmental differences cannot be ascribed to differences in the availability of the underlying strategies or operations; (4) the task must be constructed so that the experimenter can gradually increment the number of items that must be held in storage while the strategy is executed to determine the subject's highest level; (5) last, the task must employ items not amenable to any higher-order coding of relevance to the task.

Development During the Preoperational Stage

During the years from 1 to 5, the child passes through a series of substages in which his strategies also become more complex and powerful. The content of such "preoperational" strategies differs fundamentally from that of concrete operational approaches. In Piagetian terms, the content tends to be figurative rather than operative. That is, it tends to be representational or imitative rather than transformational. In spite of the difference in content, however, there is a remarkable similarity in both the sequence of substages and in the process regulating the transition from one substage to the next. Consider, for example, how children's performance changes on the task of encoding and reproducing a meaningful spoken sentence.

Substage I — Isolated Centration (1 year).   Somewhere between their first and second birthdays, children begin to isolate frequently heard and pragmatically relevant words from the stream of language. If an adult smiles and says one of these words, they will repeat it. If the adult utters several words, however, they will repeat only the one that is pragmatically or acoustically most salient.

Substage II — Unirelational Encoding (2 years).   As he approaches his second birthday, the child enters the "two-word" stage. If he is asked to repeat pairs of words such as "Daddy come," he can do so. However, if he is asked to repeat a sentence with subject, verb, and object, he will repeat only two of the three possible words.

Substage III — Birelational Encoding (3 years).   The two-word stage does not last long. Children soon master more differentiated patterns or "frames" that refer to objects or actions [e.g., (a big girl) (wanna go)] . By about age three, the child can repeat a sentence with a differentiated subject, verb, and object (e.g., The little girl wants to feed the puppies). As Bever (1970) has pointed out, this is also the age when the child starts misinterpreting more complex sentences by imposing a subject-verb-object pattern on them.

Substage IV — Birelational Encoding with Modification (4 to 5 years).   By age 4 or 5 years, children can encode and repeat sentences having several fully differentiated linguistic frames arranged in the conventional subject-verb-object pattern, even those with a modifier frame attached. A sentence repetition item on the Stanford Binet, for example, is "Jack likes to feed the little puppies in the barn."

There is a clear parallel between the sequence of substages in the sentence repetition task from ages 1 to 5 years and the sequence in Noelting's task from ages 3 to 11 years. Each successive pattern is more differentiated than the previous one and requires a greater coordination of elements. It includes all the information in its predecessor and some new feature as well. Given this parallel sequence, there may also be a parallel in the underlying process. First, specific experiences may affect the rate of progression. Practice, practice with feedback, accentuation of unencoded features, and explicit modeling should all have an effect. Second, it seems likely that a general developmental factor also affects the rate of progress. As a number of psycholinguists have noted, a certain minimum short-term memory size appears to be prerequisite for utilizing each of the linguistic constructions appearing in this period (cf. Bates, 1976; Bever & Langendoen, 1971; Slobin, 1973). Although there is no standard procedure for segmenting sentences and counting their memory demands, segmentation may proceed according to the frame analysis proposed by Halliday and utilized by Winograd in his computer simulation of natural language comprehension (Winograd, 1972). If this is the case and if 1 unit of short-term memory is necessary to store each frame, then the absolute numerical progression across stages is also the same as on Noelting's task. The demand for segmenting and reproducing at the first level is 1 unit; at the second level it is 2; at the third level 3; and at the fourth level 4.

The types of "figurative" strategies that children exhibit from 1 to 5 years have not been subjected to nearly as much scrutiny as the operative strategies

TABLE 2.4
Intelligence Scale (or Scale-like) Items for the Preoperational Period

Task	Sentence Repetition	Block Building	Commissions
Isolated Centration (1.0 to 1.9 years)	Say: – "Ball" – "Daddy" – "More"	[Gesell]	– Go get Micky Mouse [anecdotal]. – Put it on the table [Gesell].[a]
Unirelational Coding (2.0 to 2.5 years)	– (I'm) (a big girl). – (Judy) (is skipping).	[Gesell]	– Put the button in the box [Binet]. – Give me the dog [Binet].
Birelational Coding (3.0 to 3.9 years)	– (Jack) (likes to feed) (the little puppies). [Case, Kurland, & Daneman 1977].	[Gesell, Binet]	– Open the door. Then bring the box to me [interpolated from Binet].
Birelational Coding, with Modification (4.0 to 5.9 years)	– (Jack) (likes to feed) (the little puppies) (in the barn). [Stanford Binet].	[Gesell]	Put pencil on chair [1].[b] Open the door [1]. Bring the box to me [2]. [Binet]

[a]If the relationship is changed to a less typical one (e.g., under), the child fails. (c.f., Knobloch & Pasamanick, 1974)

[b]Pencil is placed in child's hand. If he must first locate it, he fails the item.

they exhibit from 3 to 11 years. Nevertheless, as shown in Table 2.4, such data as can be culled from preschool intelligence scales suggest that the progression on sentence imitation tasks may have close parallels on a variety of other tasks as well. This being the case, I hypothesize that the model of preoperational development applies to the whole range of tasks children master during the preoperational period. Specifically, I propose that (1) the sequence of behaviors in the preoperational period can be ascribed to the evolution of qualitatively distinct executive strategies or "frames,' (2) progress through any given sequence can be influenced by practice, feedback, cue highlighting, and modeling, and (3) the size of a child's short-term memory limits the complexity of the pattern or frame he can utilize, particularly when the only experience he receives is practice or practice with feedback.

Evidence for the Model of Preoperational Development

Although the data are much less extensive, the same general results obtained for the model of concrete operational development have been obtained for the preoperational model. First, a number of recent studies have analyzed children's performance on encoding and reproduction of linguistic or visual patterns (cf. Bever, 1970; Goodson & Greenfield, 1975). These studies suggest that the sorts of analyses I attempted in Table 2.4 may be extended to other domains and that development during this period may involve a sequence of executive strategies very similar to that which emerges on logical tasks during the concrete operational period.

Second, although the effects of experience on the evolution of these strategies have not been probed in much detail, it is clear that experience must exert a major effect, since the specific strategies children acquire vary as a function of the language to which they are exposed.

Third, the same four types of data mentioned in the previous section suggest a connection between children's ability to profit from specific experience and their ability to store the products of representational operations.

The first type of evidence is that short-term memory grows during the preoperational period according to the scale suggested by the analysis of children's linguistic strategies.[4] When appropriate controls are exercised, both digit span and word span show precisely the growth curve suggested by the linguistic analysis. They are 1 at 1 to 1½, 2 at 2 to 2½, 3 at 3 to 3½, and 4 at 4 to 5 years (cf. Bronner, Heart, Lowe, & Shimberg, 1927; Case, 1977a).

---

[4]To qualify as a measure of short-term or "representational" memory, a test must meet all the requirements mentioned for tests of working memory except the first. A test of representational memory must *not* require any input transformation. Rather, it must require the input to be reproduced in as similar a form to that in which it was presented as possible.

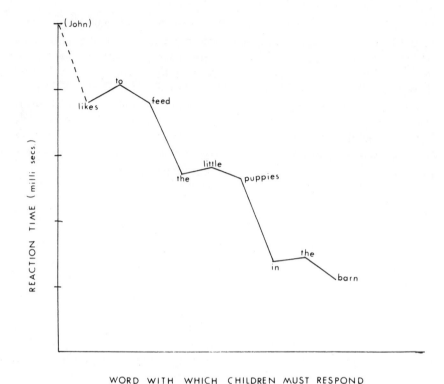

FIG. 2.1.   Children's reaction time to say the next word of a well known sentence, given that the sentence is interrupted.

The second type of evidence is correlational. Although little work has been done on this problem recently, the data from tests such as the Stanford Binet are highly supportive. At levels 2 to 4, there is a substantial correlation between performance on digit span and total IQ score. Averaged across forms L and M, the correlations are .59 at age 2.0 to 2.9, .71 at age 3.0 to 3.9, and .69 at age 4 to 4.9 years (McNemar, 1942).

The third type of evidence is an absolute matching between the size of short-term memory and the memory demands of performance. One such study was recently conducted in our laboratory in Toronto. In the first stage (Kurland, 1977), a sentence from the Stanford Binet was analyzed into simple noun and verb frames as follows: (Jack) (likes to feed) (the little puppies) (in the barn). The validity of this analysis was then established empirically by using a modified form of a technique proposed by Suci, Ammon, & Gamlin (1967). Five-year-olds were asked to memorize the sentence. Then the sentence was played over a tape recorder and interrupted at different points by a tone. The children's task was to say the word that came after the one they heard last. The results are shown graphically in Fig. 2.1; reaction time was a step function, with the steps corresponding to the hypothesized frames.

The second stage of the study examined the relationship between children's short-term memory and their ability to effect this four-frame organization (cf. Case, 1977a). Two groups of 4-year-olds were selected, one having a word span of 3 and the other of 4. Both groups came from language-rich environments and attended the same university preschool. In addition, both had extensive experience in the repetition paradigm. As predicted, children with spans of 4 repeated the sentences perfectly, whereas those with spans of 3 did not.

Clearly, this sort of study is only a beginning. In a sense, all it really shows is the functional equivalence of two different types of short-term memory tasks. However, if the results continue to hold across tasks more remote from digit span than sentence repetition, there will be strong support for the model. A small and informal pilot study of this sort was conducted by Fabian, Ammon, and myself (cf. Fabian, 1977). Using a facilitating rather than a misleading form of Carol Chomsky's (1969) sentence "The doll is hard for us to see," we found that children with a span of 4 could act out the sentence appropriately, but children of the same age with a span of 3 could not. Similar results were obtained in an artificial language-learning study conducted recently in our laboratory (Daneman, 1977).

The final type of evidence required to validate the general developmental hypothesis is evidence that when the memory demand of a preoperational task is manipulated, the capacity level at which the task is passed is shifted by the appropriate number of units. Once again, the evidence is not as extensive as for the operational period. However, the basic paradigm is illustrated in a follow-up to the sentence repetition study cited earlier. Having shown the appropriateness of the subject-verb-object + modifier frame pattern for children with a span of 4, this pattern was changed to form a variety of 5-item patterns (e.g., SV (SVO + modifier). Several 3-item patterns were also created. Sentence length was held constant by manipulating the size of the frames [e.g., Level 3 (My best friend John) (likes to feed) (the little puppies), Level 4 (John) (likes to feed) (the little puppies) (in the barn), Level 5 (John likes) (Gerry) (to feed) (the puppies) (in the barn)]. The results showed that the three-item patterns were within the capacity of children with a span of 3 and that the 4- and 5-item patterns were within the capacity of children with spans of 4 and 5, respectively.

In summary, although the analytic and empirical evidence is weaker for the preoperational period than for the concrete operational period, it is still broadly consistent with the following three propositions:

1. Children go through a series of at least four substages in the preoperational stage, and at each of these stages, they are capable of encoding and reproducing all features noticed in the immediately previous stage, plus one more.

2. Children's progress through these stages is affected by their specific experiences.

3. The growth of children's short-term memory plays an important role in regulating the rate at which the sequence progresses, and this memory grows from one unit at age 1 to 2 to five units at age 4 to 5 years.

Development During the Sensorimotor Stage

During the first 2 years of life, the child passes through a series of qualitatively distinct substages in which his strategies become increasingly complex and powerful. The content of these strategies is dramatically different from the content of the strategies of subsequent periods: The operations are motoric rather than representational or logical. Nevertheless, the progression parallels that observed in later periods. Consider the following sequence of developments taken from Piaget's description of the means-end scheme.

Substage 0 (Reactive Exercise).[5]   In the first few weeks of life, the child shows little evidence of any strategies for achieving desired ends. In the presence of certain stimuli, he will exercise his innately determined motor schemes. For example, if a small object is placed in his mouth, he will suck it. However, his motor competence extends little beyond the exercise of such patterns.

Substage 1 (Isolated Centration).   The first stage in the development of genuine strategies occurs somewhere between 1 and 4 months. During this period, the child becomes capable of isolating and repeating actions that lead to the exercise of a more basic scheme. Piaget gives the example of his son Laurant, whose hand happened to be placed near his mouth by his caretaker. Immediately following this, the child made 13 attempts in a row to put his hand in his mouth until he had perfected the movement. Piaget refers to such one-step strategies as *primary circular reactions.*

Substage 2 (Relational Centration).   Somewhere between 4 and 8 months, the child becomes capable of centering not only on one action of his own but on the relationship between his action and some consequence in the external world. For example, if a child happens to strike a mobile in a way that produces a particularly interesting movement, he will repeat that striking action again and again, delighted with the result produced. Because the strategies are now two-stage (i.e., action of subject + reaction of object → attainment of desired end), Piaget calls them *secondary circular reactions.*

---

[5]Piaget numbers the stages of the means–end scheme from 1 through 6 rather than 0 through 5. I have chosen the latter system to make the number of each stage correspond to its short-term memory demand and thus emphasize the parallel between development during the sensorimotor period and later periods.

Substage 3 (Birelational Centration).   Somewhere between 8 and 12 months, the child becomes capable of executing actions that only indirectly produce interesting results. For example, the child becomes capable of striking one object (Relation 1) so that he can act on a second object (Relation 2), which is the real focus of his interest. This strategy clearly incorporates one additional element beyond the previous stage. It can be characterized as: action 1 + action 2 + reaction of object → gratification.

Substage 4 (Birelational Centration with Particularization, or Trirelational Centration).   Between 12 and 18 months, the child becomes capable of using one object to move a second object so that he can act on it. For example, he may pull a towel so that the towel will move the object sitting on it so that he may act on the object. This may be represented as: action 1 (subject on object) + action 2 (object on object) + action 3 (subject on object 2) + reaction of object 2 → gratification.

The foregoing analysis is only preliminary. It is not yet grounded in a theoretically derived set of procedures for computing the load on immediate memory, nor does it have the support of a set of procedures for verifying the hypothesized segmentation of input. Nevertheless, it does show striking parallels to other sensorimotor developments (see Table 2.5) and to development in other periods. During the sensorimotor period, as during subsequent periods, the child considers one more feature at each substage than he did in the previous one. It therefore seems likely that the same general factors are responsible for producing the transition from one substage to the next.

On the specific-experiential side, it seems likely that a certain amount of motor practice in a given domain, coupled with feedback, is necessary for the substages to emerge at the normal points in development. It also seems likely that particular strategies can be induced at an earlier age than normal if relevant cues are highlighted or if the appropriate response to these cues is modeled. On the general-developmental side, it seems likely that the size of a child's sensorimotor memory sets a limitation on the complexity of the strategy he can assemble and thus that the growth of this memory sets a limit on the role of specific experience (cf. Bower, 1974; Pascual—Leone, 1975; Watson, 1967).

Empirical Evidence for the Model of Sensorimotor Development

Piaget's description of the sequence of behaviors that emerge during the sensorimotor period is quite close to the information theorists' language of strategies. Perhaps for this reason, the ordinal sequence of tasks children pass at different substages is also more clearly delineated (cf. Uzgiris & Hunt, 1975). Recent work in the area shows that the structures underlying these behaviors can be modeled as a sequence of increasingly complex rules or strategies and that

TABLE 2.5
Substages During the Sensorimotor Period

Substage	Means-End Scheme		Vanished Object Scheme (Object Permanence)	
	Behavior	Items to be Stored	Behavior	Items to be Stored
Isolated Centration (1 to 4 months)	Repeat action that produces satisfaction.	(i) Satisfying action.	Eyes continue to rest on or explore point at which object disappeared.	(i) "Image" or trace of object at point X.
Relational Centration (4 to 8 months)	Repeat action that produces interesting event.	(i) Action executed. (ii) Satisfying or interesting event that followed.	Eyes anticipate re-emergence of object that repeatedly disappears at point X and reappears at point Y.	(i) Image of object disappearing at point X. (ii) Image of object reappearing at point Y.
Birelational Centration (8 to 12 months)	Strike obstacle and obtain desired object.	(i) Action of removing barrier (ii) Action executed to obtain desired object. (iii) Satisfying event permitted	Child removes cover that is pulled over desired object.	(i) Image of object disappearing under cover. (ii) Action of reaching toward cover and pulling it off. (iii) Image of object reappearing.

| Birelational Centration with Particularization or Trirelational Centration (12 to 18 months) | Utilization of novel means to achieve goals (e.g., pull towel to obtain object resting on towel but out of reach). | (i) Action of pulling towel.
(ii) Movement of object that followed.
(iii) Action executed to obtain object.
(iv) Satisfying event permitted. | Child removes cover Y which is placed over desired object, after habit of removing cover X and finding object has been established. | (i) Image of object disappearing under cover.
(ii) Image of specific location or physical characteristics of cover Y.
(iii) Action of reaching toward location of cover in question.
(iv) Image of object reappearing. |

experience of the sort described for operational development can influence the rate at which these strategies or rules are acquired (cf. Bower, 1974; Jackson, Campos, & Fischer, 1977; Watson & Fischer, 1977; White, 1969). What remains to be done, then, is to develop measures of sensorimotor memory parallel to those for representational and operational memory and to determine whether they bear the same sort of relationship to strategic development.

To summarize: I have suggested that, although the content of intellectual development changes radically throughout the course of development, the form changes very little. During each stage, the sequence of substages stems from a series of qualitatively distinct executive strategies, each of which incorporates one more feature of the domain in question than did the previous stage. During each stage, at least four kinds of experience facilitate strategy evolution: practice, feedback regarding goal attainment, cue highlighting, and modeling. Finally, the pace of development is regulated by the gradual increase in the size of working memory.

The evidence I have presented in support of this general view is by no means conclusive. Nevertheless, as a heuristic device, I will assume for the balance of this chapter that the view is accurate and postulate long-term changes in the human cognitive system to explain this recurrent pattern.

THE UNDERLYING MECHANISM OF DEVELOPMENT: LONG-TERM CHANGES IN THE HUMAN PSYCHOLOGICAL SYSTEM

Developmental Changes in Attentional Capacity

As the reader will no doubt have noted, I have proposed three different quantitative scales, each of which shows a similar growth curve, and each of which is presumed to exert a similar influence on strategic development. The most satisfactory explanation I can think of for this cyclic pattern is the following: (1) There is one central working memory which can serve as a space for storing information or for operating on it (cf. Pascual-Leone, 1969); (2) the underlying capacity of this working memory does not change with age, at least after the age of two (cf. Case, 1976; Chi, 1975; Dempster, 1976; Simon, 1972); (3) the measured increase in capacity within each stage is due to a decrease in the capacity required to execute the operations which are characteristic of that stage. Symbolically, these three propositions may be represented as:

$$o + s = k$$

where o = functional operating capacity
s = functional storage capacity
k = a constant, equal to the total structural capacity of the system

To say that the *structural* capacity of the human organism does not change with development is not to belie the importance of the *functional* changes that occur: It simply pushes the chain of explanation back one step. Just as the increasing sophistication of children's executive strategies within a stage may be partially explained by increasing storage space, so the increasing storage space may be partially explained by the decreasing attentional control required to execute the basic operations the strategies entail.

Developmental Changes in Operational Automaticity

How can we explain the increase in automaticity? To say that operations become more automatic is simply to label the phenomenon, since an operation's automaticity is normally defined by the extent to which it can be executed without interfering with other activity. At a general level of analysis, at least three factors might be responsible. The first is specific experience. As children practice encoding numbers, for example, the automaticity of their encoding and retrieval might increase (perhaps as a function of "chunking"). The second factor is general experience. The increase in measured digit span, for example, might not be due to any particular experience, but rather to general experience in encoding and retrieving words. The final factor is maturation. Perhaps the increased automaticity of sensorimotor operations requires maturation of the part of the brain that directs motor activity.

Of the three alternatives, the first seems least likely. If specific experience caused the increase in span, then the observed cross-task constancy on tests of working memory would be very improbable. Tasks would show a common growth curve only to the extent that specific experiences on each were identical. A recent study conducted by Daneman and I further supports the conclusion that specific experience is not a sufficient explanation for the growth curves. A 2½-year-old child with a mental age of 4½ years was presented the standard Backward Digit Span test. As is the case with many children of this mental age, he could not perform the task at all, even though he had a Forward Digit Span of five items. After several days of training, he mastered the two-digit items, and after 17 more days of training he succeeded regularly on the three-digit items. Even after 34 more consecutive days of practice, however, he showed no further improvement. The original number of days required to improve from two to three items was almost exactly the same as that required to produce complete automaticity of a more complex skill in adults (cf. Spelke, Hirst, & Neisser, 1976). Thus, it seems that the child's span had reached a ceiling that could have been elevated only by massive general experience or by further maturation. In short, it seems that specific experience increases span by increasing operational automaticity to some degree but that general experience and/or maturation plays a greater role.

Developmental Changes in the Types of Operations Available

Another problem is how to account for the qualitative changes in underlying operations across stages. Throughout this chapter I have argued (following Piaget) that the operations that characterize each major period of development are qualitatively distinct. This raises two questions: (1) how best to characterize the qualitative differences among elementary operations, and (2) how to account for the sequence and approximate timing of their emergence being invariant.

In discussing the achievements of each stage, I have spoken as though the differences between the underlying operations (sensorimotor, representational, and transformational) were obvious. In fact, although their labels represent rather "natural" categories, they suffer from the same disadvantages as all such terms. The entities they represent are relatively easy to recognize but not to define, nor are they even easy to discriminate once the examples are nonprototypic. For the moment, the best formal definitions I can offer are the following: A sensorimotor operation is one whose releasing component is some sensory input and whose effecting component is a physical movement. A representational operation is one whose releasing component is some sensory input and whose effecting component is an abstract encoding of that input. Finally, a logical or "transformational" operation is one whose releasing component is an abstract coding of a situation and whose effecting component is some other coding of the same situation. Although these definitions capture some of the meaning I attribute to each type of operation, it remains to be seen whether they will adequately classify the full range of developmental phenomena.

What about the sequential relationship among the operations? Why does rapid growth in an operation seem to await a critical level of achievement in the previous one? The Piagetian position is clear: Higher-order operations build on and incorporate lower-corder operations. Bates (1976) provides a similar argument in the linguistic domain. She contends that the use of language to accomplish an end (i.e., the imperative use) depends on the realization that one object can be used to obtain another. It follows that the sensorimotor memory necessary for the first realization (I believe it is 3 or 4 units) is a prerequisite for entry into the next stage. A similar sort of contingency might be present at the next transition point at which a certain minimum representational memory might be necessary for executing an elementary concrete operation. Consider the basic operation underlying the strategies in Noelting's (1975) task — counting. Granted that even two-year-olds have some understanding of counting (as Gelman suggests in this volume), a certain functional storage space may still be necessary for counting in an adult fashion. One unit of space may be required to monitor the set of objects just counted, one to monitor the next object to be counted, one to monitor the number just said, and one to monitor the number about to be said. Because a functional storage space of 4 is not attained during the representational period until age 4 or 5 years, this would explain why accurate counting is also not consolidated until age 4 or 5 years. It would also explain why children do not progress through Noelting's series of strategies until then.

Developmental Changes in Learning

There is one final question that falls within the purview of this book and that is raised by the neo-Piagetian account of development I have presented: Is there any change in the child's capacity for learning across stages of development? Implicit in my account were the following assumptions: (1) that learning occurs very rapidly when the elements to be learned can be placed in working memory simultaneously, and (2) that the capability for learning certain content varies radically as a function of the strategies that are available and the size of the functional storage space in the domain in question. From these two assumptions it follows that there is no change in the *capacity* of the psychological system for learning over time, but there is a great change in the types of learning that can occur.

For many of the tasks that were considered, the necessary functional storage space was 3, 4, or 5 units. However, remember that most of these tasks were derived from Piaget's pioneering work in the area. Piaget's interest was not in children's knowledge per se but rather in the structure of their knowledge gathering activity, so the tasks he devised had two important properties. First, they were novel. Although the child might be highly familiar with the materials and the general situation, it was unlikely that he had heard the specific questions before. Second, the tasks were "misleading" (cf. Pascual–Leone & Bovet, 1966). That is, they suggested a solution by a simpler strategy than the one required for success. Unless the child already had the strategy of interest in his repertoire, he would be unlikely either to see the need for it or to assemble it even if he did see the need. The simpler and more natural strategy would constantly interfere with his efforts.

Although this sort of "misleading" task is well suited for showing the functional dependence of learning on general development, many tasks a child encounters in his everyday life are both familiar and facilitating. The child is exposed to the task repeatedly, and the task has no feature that suggests the application of an incorrect strategy. For these tasks (an example of which is provided in Nelson's chapter), it is not critical that the child bring a complex knowledge-gathering strategy to the situation. The only critical requirement is that the child have sufficient functional storage space to attend to two task elements at the same time and sufficient motivation to persist until these elements form one chunk (cf. Miller, 1956). Once these prerequisites are met, a great many familiar and facilitating tasks can be mastered in pieces, with each new element gradually being incorporated into the whole.

Thus, a critical learning stage for many everyday behaviors should be attained when the child's functional storage space reaches 2 units. This should occur at about 4 months for sensorimotor tasks, 20 months for representational tasks, and 5 or 6 years for concrete operational tasks.

The transition from the one- to two-word stage in language learning does, in fact, exhibit this sort of learning explosion. As mentioned earlier, children remain at the two-word stage for a relatively short time and are soon producing most of the elementary linguistic frames characteristic of their culture (although their sentences may remain at the two-chunk stage for about a year or so). A similar explosion in conceptual learning has often been reported during the years 5 to 7 (White, 1970). Because this is the time when operative memory shifts from one to two units, it seems likely that an identical process is at work. In a recent experiment designed in our laboratory, Fabian, Portnuff, and I obtained preliminary evidence on this possibility. First, we designed a facilitating operative task requiring children to learn 1-, 2-, or 3-unit patterns. We then divided the children into two groups having operative capacities of 1 and 2 units. As predicted, we found that the 1-unit children learned the 1-unit task very rapidly, and they learned the 2-unit task either very slowly or not at all.. In contrast, children of the same age with a capacity of 2 learned the 2-unit task very quickly, and they learned the 3-unit task with only a few extra trials. Although the evidence is by no means definitive, it is suggestive, If the hypothesis is correct, it should be possible to isolate a similar explosion in sensorimotor learning at 4 to 8 months.

In summary, to explain the three-stage pattern of development outlined in the first section, I suggest that the attentional capacity of the organism is fixed from birth (or at least from age 2 years) and that the apparent changes in capacity during each stage stem from a gradual automization of the operations characteristic of that stage. I also suggest that the operations of one substage are assembled in working memory from the components of the previous stage, once the operations are sufficiently automatized that the requisite working memory is available. Finally, I suggest that learning can occur rapidly only when the items to be learned can be placed in working memory simultaneously but that the capacity for such rapid learning is present virtually from birth.

Although there is as yet little empirical evidence for the foregoing propositions, I once again will assume as a heuristic device that they are valid, and consider the intellectual developments one would expect to find during adolescence and adulthood on this assumption.

DEVELOPMENTAL CHANGES AFTER AGE TWELVE

Development During the Formal Operations Stage

Consider first the developments during the stage Piaget has labeled *formal operations*. If the underlying developmental mechanism is as sketched in the previous three sections, it follows that:

1. Second-order operations, or "operations on operations" must be assembled in working memory from first order operations.

2. Until these second-order operations are automatized, functional storage space should be very restricted.

3. As these operations become automatized, functional storage space should increase.

4. As functional storage space increases, executive strategies should increase in sophistication and power (providing, of course, that children are exposed to appropriate experiences).

Because the formal operations period has not been subjected to the same sort of theoretical and empirical scrutiny as the period of concrete operations, the foregoing propositions are speculative. However, it is worthwhile to note that Noelting (1975) has described four further strategies that children employ on his task, culminating with the most sophisticated strategy of finding the lowest common denominator. He also suggests that the progression culminating in formal operations is directly parallel to the progression culminating in concrete operations. The major difference is that all the strategies in the first sequence involve operations directed at sets of the array (e.g., counting), whereas all the strategies in the second sequence involve operations directed at the relationships between arrays (e.g., division). It appears, then, that the aforementioned four hypotheses may be true and that development during the period of formal operations may proceed according to the same sequence and laws as development during earlier stages.

Development in Adulthood

What about development after the formal operations stage? To date, this sort of development has received even less attention than has the development of formal operations. When considered at all, it has been conceptualized as "problem finding" as opposed to "problem solving" (cf. Arlin, 1975). If the underlying developmental mechanism is as proposed in this chapter, this may prove to be an inappropriate way to conceptualize further intellectual development. The search for "development beyond formal operations" should instead concentrate on clarifying the nature of second-order intellectual operations and on searching for third-order operations. One possibility is that (in physics and mathematics, at least) the operations in calculus might constitute such third- (or fourth) order entities. If this is the case, subjects learning calculus should go through a series of substages similar to those observed at earlier ages. It also follows that further stages of intellectual development would have to await further cultural inventions — inventions of the magnitude and significance of counting, division, or calculus.[6]

---

[6]Notice, too, the implication that the development of knowledge in the individual must recapitulate the development of knowledge in the culture.

SUMMARY AND CONCLUSIONS

I conclude by summarizing my position and placing it in historical perspective.

Overview of the Theory

During each of the major stages of intellectual development, there is a succession of substages. The first postulate of my theory is that this succession of substages stems from a succession of qualitatively distinct control structures or executive strategies. The second postulate is that two sorts of factors explain the succession of strategies within any stage. The first is the child's responsiveness to the strategy-related experiences he encounters. In order of increasing power, one would expect practice, practice with feedback, cue highlighting, and modeling to affect the rate at which a child progresses through a given strategy sequence. The second factor is a gradual increase within each stage in the size of the child's working memory. As working memory increases, it becomes easier to acquire and utilize more complex executive strategies. The third major postulate is that the gradual increase in working memory does not stem from a structural increase in the attentional capacity of the organism but rather from an increase in the automaticity of the basic operations it is capable of executing. As these operations become more automatic, their execution requires a smaller proportion of total attentional capacity. The result is that more capacity is available for "storage" or "working." Exactly how the increase in automaticity occurs is unclear, but it seems likely that, if experiential input plays a role, it is general rather than specific. The fourth major postulate is that the executive strategies of each major stage involve qualitatively distinct underlying operations and that the operation at any given stage must be assembled in working memory from components available at the previous stage. It follows that the transition to any given stage depends on the attainment of a certain degree of automaticity during the previous stage. Finally, implicit in the above postulates is an assumption about the type of learning that causes relatively rapid restructuring of executive strategies. The assumption is that the child's capacity for such learning is present from birth but that it must await a certain size working memory (which in turn results from another, slower type of learning) before it may be observed. For misleading tasks, the critical size of working memory may be from 2 to 4 or 5 units; for facilitating tasks, it is only 2 units.

Relationship of the Present Theory to Piaget's and Pascual—Leone's Theories

As the reader may have noticed, the present theory deviates only moderately from Piaget's original account. With regard to the *content* of development, the following four Piagetian postulates have been preserved:

1. Development proceeds through a series of four major stages: the sensorimotor stage, the preoperational stage, the concrete operational stage, and the formal operations stage.

2. Within each stage, a series of at least four qualitatively distinct substages is identified.

3. The structures of each stage build on and transform the structures of earlier stages.

4. The sequence of substages at one level often exhibit formal parallels to the sequence of substages at other levels. (In Piagetian terminology, this is referred to as *vertical décalage*.)

With regard to the *process* of development, four other Piagetian postulates have been preserved:

1. Experience is only a partial explanation of the series of stages and substages.

2. What a child learns from any given experience is a function of his general developmental level.

3. The child's attempt to introduce consistency or "equilibrium" into his cognitive system plays a major role in motivating his progress through the various stages and substages.

4. To the extent that instruction simplifies or eliminates the child's equilibrative activity, it limits the applications of the structures.

At the same time, the theory introduces a number of changes that make the thrust of the theory more compatible with the current zeitgeist in cognitive psychology and that also permit a finer-grained analysis of cognitive tasks. The two most important changes are:

1. Developmental structures are conceptualized as groups of executive strategies that can be modeled by computer simulation rather than as logico-mathematical systems modeled by symbolic logic.

2. The general developmental factor (i.e., the factor transcending the presence or absence of any specific structure) is conceptualized as a quantifiable level of working memory rather than as a general level of "operativity."

Neither of these two changes is incompatible with Piagetian theory, particularly since the subject's level of working memory is ascribed to the automaticity of his basic operations. Rather, the two changes might better be regarded as explications of Piagetian concepts that would otherwise be difficult to operationalize. Whether the aforementioned two changes are considered to be theoretical modifications or explications, they clearly introduce at least one important change in emphasis, which might be listed as a third point of difference. Instruction is seen as being able to reduce the age at which a given executive structure is acquired by reducing the demand that acquisition of the strategy places on the subject's working memory. Although structures acquired by this sort of process may be more limited in application, I do not believe that they necessarily reflect a lower level of understanding. Finally, although the change is perhaps more one of emphasis than substance, the theory describes the structures of the preoperational stage as being distinct entities rather than as mere precursors of the structures of the concrete operational stage.

If my theory shares a good deal with Piaget's, it shares even more with Pascual–Leone's. This is not surprising, because my theory resulted from an attempt to apply Pascual–Leone's theory to a wider age range. In spite of the obvious similarities between the two theories, however, there are a number of points on which they differ. These differences came about as a result of my attempt to explain the cyclic pattern of growth which my sensorimotor and representational analyses revealed.

1. In my theory, the underlying reserve of attentional energy (Pascual–Leone's M) is seen as being fixed from a very young age. In Pascual–Leone's theory, it is seen as growing.

2. In my theory, differences in attentional span are ascribed to differences in operational automaticity. In Pascual–Leone's theory, this possibility is explicitly rejected (although the mechanism for it exists by means of overleaning and C-weighting).

3. In my theory, I distinguish between qualitative change within a Piagetian stage (change in the executive) and qualitative change across stages (change in the underlying operation). In Pascual–Leone's theory, no such distinction is made although the mechanism once again exists using hierarchical LM learning.

4. In my theory, it is assumed that rapid structural learning occurs only when items whose relations are appreciated are actively attended to (i.e., placed in working memory). In Pascual–Leone's theory, it is presumed that equally rapid learning can occur between unattended items, as long as the sensory or affective conditions are appropriate.

ACKNOWLEDGMENTS

In developing the ideas presented in this paper, I profited greatly from my weekly interaction with Paul Ammon, Veronica Fabian, Midian Kurland, Wendy Portnuff, Steven Pulos, and Irene Subelman. I also profited from less regular, but equally important, interactions with Michael Cole, Micki Chi, Frank Dempster, and Juan Pascual-Leone. Finally, I am indebted for comments on a previous version of the manuscript to Carl Bereiter, Frank Dempster, and Marlene Scardamalia. The empirical work reported in this paper was supported by grants from the Spencer Foundation, the United States National Institute of Mental Health and Child Development, the United States National Institute of Education, the Canada Council, the Campus Research Committee of the University of California, Berkeley, and the Small Scale Research and Development Fund of the Ontario Institute for Studies in Education.

REFERENCES

Arlin, P. K. Cognitive development in adulthood: A fifth stage? *Developmental Psychology,* 1975, *11,* 602–606.

Bates, E. *Language and context: The acquisition of pragmatics.* New York: Academic Press, 1976.

Bever, T. G. The cognitive basis for linguistic structures. In J. R. Hayes (Ed.), *Cognition and the development of language.* New York: Wiley, 1970.

Bever, T. G., & Langendoen, D. T. A dynamic model of the evolution of language. *Linguistic Inquiry,* 1971, *2,* 433–463.

Biemiller, A., Boychuk, L., & Rochford, M. *A new measure of M-space.* Unpublished manuscript, University of Toronto, Institute of Child Study, 1977.

Bower, T. G. H. *Development in infancy.* San Francisco: W. H. Freeman, 1974.

Bronner, A. F., Heart, W., Lowe, G. M., & Shimberg, H. E. *A manual of individual mental tests and testing.* Boston: Little Brown, 1927.

Bruner, J. On the conservation of liquids. In J. Bruner, R. R. Oliver & P. M. Greenfield (Eds.), *Studies in cognitive growth.* New York: Wiley, 1966, 183–208.

Bryant, P. E. The understanding of invariance by very young children. *Canadian Journal of Psychology,* 1972, *26*(1), 78–96.

Bucher, B., & Schneider, R. E. Acquisition and generalization of conservation by preschoolers, using operant training. *Journal of Experimental Child Psychology,* 1973, *16,* 187–204.

Case, R. *Difficulties encountered by disadvantaged children in solving a visually represented problem.* Unpublished masters thesis, University of Toronto, 1968.

Case, R. Validation of a neo-Piagetian capacity construct. *Journal of Experimental Child Psychology,* 1972, *14,* 287–302.

Case, R. Mental strategies, mental capacity, and instruction: A neo-Piagetian investigation. *Journal of Experimental Child Psychology,* 1974, *18,* 372–397. (a)

Case, R. Structures and strictures: Some functional limitations on the course of cognitive growth. *Cognitive Psychology,* 1974, *6,* 544–573. (b)

Case, R. Gearing the demands of instruction to the development capacities of the learner. *Review of Educational Research,* 1975, *45,* 59–87.

Case, R. *A constant capacity model for the growth of figurative and operative space.* Working paper, University of California, Berkeley, 1976.

Case, R. *Intellectual and linguistic development in the preschool years.* Final report submitted to the Spencer Foundation, December, 1977. (a)

Case, R. Responsiveness to conservation training as a function of induced subjective uncertainty, M-space, and cognitive style. *Canadian Journal of Behavioral Sciences,* 1977, *9,* 12–25. (b)

Case, R. *The process of stage transition in cognitive development.* (Final Report, Project #R01 HD09148-01 NIMHCD), Ontario Institute for Studies in Education, 1977. (c)

Case, R., & Globerson, T. Field independence and central computing space. *Child Development,* 1974, *45,* 772–778.

Case, R., & Kurland, M. *Operational efficiency and the growth of M-space: A test of the constant capacity hypothesis.* Unpublished manuscript, OISE, 1978.

Case, R., Portnuff, W., & Fabian, V. *The development of short-term memory in the preschool period.* Unpublished manuscript, Ontario Institute for Studies in Education, 1976.

Case, R., & Serlin, R. A new model for simulating performance on Pascual-Leone's Test of M-space. *Cognitive Psychology,* in press.

Chi, M. *The development of short-term memory capacity.* Unpublished doctoral dissertation, Carnegie–Mellon University, 1975.

Chomsky, C. *The acquisition of syntax from 5 to 10.* Cambridge, Mass.: MIT Press, 1969.

Dale, L. *A neo-Piagetian investigation of some factors affecting performance on Piaget's flexibility of rods problem.* Unpublished doctoral dissertation, LaTrobe University, Australia, 1976.

Daneman, M. *An experimental paradigm to explore the cognitive prerequisites, both semantic and formal, for the development of language.* Unpublished masters thesis, The Ontario Institute for Studies in Education, 1977.

DeAvila, E., & Havassy, B. *Intelligence of Mexican American children.* Austin, Texas: Dissemination Center for Bilingual and Bicultural Education, 1974.

Dempster, F. *A developmental investigation of memory span: Storage capacity or organizational strategies?* Unpublished doctoral dissertation, University of California, Berkeley, 1976.

Diaz, S. *Cucui scale: Technical manual.* Multilingual Assessment Program, Stockton Unified School District, Stockton, California, 1974.

Fabian, V. *When are children hard to understand? A neo-Piagetian glimpse at language acquisition.* Unpublished manuscript, University of California, Berkeley, 1977.

Gagné, R. M. Contributions of learning to human development. *Psychological Review,* 1968, *75,* 177–191.

Gelman, R. Conservation acquisition: A problem of learning to attend to relevant attributes. *Journal of Experimental Child Psychology,* 1969, *7,* 167–187.

Gibson, F. J. *Principles of perceptual learning and development.* New York: Appleton-Century-Crofts, 1969.

Goodson, B. D., & Greenfield, P. M. The search for structural principles in children's manipulative play: A parallel with linguistic development. *Child Development,* 1975, *46,* 734–746.

Halford, G. S. A theory of the acquisition of conservation. *Psychological Review,* 1970, *77,* 302–332.

Halford, G., & MacDonald, C. Children's pattern construction as a function of age and complexity. *Child Development,* 1977, *48,* 1096–1100.

Inhelder, B., Bovet, M., Sinclair, H., & Smock, C. D. On cognitive development. *American Psychologist,* 1966, *21,* 160–164.

Inhelder, B., Sinclair, H., & Bovet, M. *Learning and the development of cognition.* Cambridge, Mass.: Harvard University Press, 1974.

Jackson, E., Campos, J. J., & Fischer, W. *The question of décalage between object permanence and person permanence.* Unpublished manuscript, University of Denver, 1977.

Klahr, D., & Wallace, J. G. The role of quantification operators in the development of conservation of quantity. *Cognitive Psychology,* 1973, *4,* 301–327.

Knobloch, H., & Pasamanick, B. *Gesell & Amotruda's developmental diagnosis* (3rd ed.). New York: Harper & Row, 1974.

Kurland, M. *A new measurement technique for assessing the subjective organization of children's speech perception.* Unpublished masters thesis, Ontario Institute for Studies in Education, University of Toronto, 1977.

Lefebvre, M., & Pinard, A. Apprentisage de la conservation des quantites par une methode de conflict cognitif. *Canadian Journal of the Behavioral Sciences,* 1972, *4*(1), 1–12. (Translation available from R. Case, Ontario Institute for Studies in Education, University of Toronto, Toronto.)

Lefebvre, M., & Pinard, A. Influence du niveau initial de sensibilité au conflit sur l'apprentissage de la conservation des quantités par une methode de conflit cognitif. *Canadian Journal of Behavioural Science,* 1974, *6,* 398–413.

McLaughlin, G. H. Psychologic: A possible alternative to Piaget's formulation. *British Journal of Educational Psychology,* 1963, *33,* 61–67.

McNemar, Q. *The revision of the Stanford–Binet scale, analysis of the standardized data.* Boston: Houghton Mifflin, 1942.

Miller, G. A. The magical number seven, plus or minus two: Some limits on our capacity for processing information. *Psychological Review,* 1956, *63,* 81–97.

Noelting, G. *Stages and mechanisms in the development of the concept of proportion in the child and adolescent.* Paper presented at the 5th Interdisciplinary Seminar on Piagetian Theory and Its Implications for the Helping Professions, University of Southern California, Los Angeles, January 1975.

Parkinson, G. M. *The limits on learning.* Unpublished doctoral dissertation, York University, 1976.

Pascual–Leone, J. *Cognitive development and cognitive style.* Unpublished doctoral dissertation, University of Geneva, 1969.

Pascual–Leone, J. A mathematical model for the transition rule in Piaget's developmental stages. *Acta Psychologica,* 1970, *32,* 301–345.

Pascual–Leone, J. *A theory of constructive operators, a neo-Piagetian model of conservation, and the problem of horizontal décalages.* Unpublished manuscript, York University, 1972.

Pascual–Leone, J. Personal communication, Berkeley, 1975.

Pascual–Leone, J., & Bovet, M. L'apprentissage de la quantification de l'inclusion et la theorie operatoire. *Acta Psychologica,* 1966, *25,* 334–356.

Pascual–Leone, J., Parkinson, G. M., & Pulos, S. *Constructive abstractions (structural learning) and concept development.* Paper presented at the Canadian Psychological Association, Windsor, 1974.

Pascual–Leone, J., & Smith, J. The encoding and decoding of symbols by children: A new experimental paradigm and a neo-Piagetian model. *Journal of Experimental Child Psychology,* 1969, *8,* 328–355.

Piaget, J. Une forme verbale de la comparaison chez l'enfant. *Archives de Psychologie,* 1920, *18,* 141–172.

Piaget, J. Logique et equilibre dans les comportements du sujet. In L. Apostel, B. Mandelbrot, & J. Piaget (Eds.), *Etudes D'epistemologie genetique, II: logique et equilibre.* Paris: Presses Universitaires de France, 1957.

Piaget, J. Development and learning. In R. E. Ripple & V. N. Rockcastle (Eds.) *Piaget rediscovered.* Ithaca, N.Y.: Cornell School of Education Press, 1964.

Piaget, J. Piaget's theory. In P. N. Mussen (Ed.), *Carmichael's manual of child psychology,* Vol. I. New York: Wiley, 1970, 709–733.

Piaget, J. Problems of equilibration. In C. F. Nodine, J. M. Gallagher, & R. D. Humphreys (Eds.), *Piaget and Inhelder on equilibration.* Philadelphia: The Jean Piaget Society, 1971.

Posner, M. I. Short term memory systems in human information processing. *Acta Psychologia,* 1967, *27,* 267–284.

Scardamalia, M. Information processing capacity and the problem of horizontal décalage: A demonstration using combinatorial reasoning tasks. *Child Development,* 1977, *48,* 128–137. (a)

Scardamalia, M. *The interaction of perceptual and quantitative load factors in the control of variables.* Unpublished manuscript, York University, 1977. (b)

Siegler, R. S. Three aspects of cognitive development. *Cognitive Psychology,* 1976, *8,* 481–520.

Simon, H. A. An information processing theory of intellectual development. In W. Kessen & C. Kohlman (Eds.), *Thought in the young child. Society for Research in Child Development Monographs,* 1962, *27*(2), 150–155.

Simon, H. A. On the development of the processor. In S. Farnham–Diggory (Ed.), *Information procesisng in children.* New York: Academic Press, 1972.

Simon, H. A. How big is a chunk? *Science,* 1974, *183,* 482–488.

Slobin, D. I. Cognitive prerequisites for the development of grammar. In C. A. Ferguson & D. I. Slobin (Eds.), *Studies of child language development.* New York: Holt, Rinehart and Winston, 1973.

Spelke, E., Hirst, W., & Neisser, U. Skills of divided attention. *Cognitive Psychology,* 1976, *4,* 215–230.

Strauss, S., & Langer, J. Operational thought inducement. *Child Development,* 1970, *41,* 163–175.

Suci, G. J., Ammon, P., & Gamlin, P. The validity of the probe latency technique for assessing structure in language. *Language and Speech,* 1967, *10,* 69–80.

Sullivan, E. V. Acquisition of conservation of substance through film modelling techniques. In D. W. Brison & E. V. Sullivan (Eds.), *Recent research on the acquisition of conservation of substance.* (Educational Research Series No. 2.) Toronto: Ontario Institute for Studies in Education, University of Toronto, 1967, 53–72.

Uzgiris, I. C., & Hunt, J. McV. *Assessment in infancy: Ordinal sclaes of psychological development.* Urbana, Ill.: University of Illinois Press, 1975.

Watson, J. S. Memory and contingency analysis in infant learning. *Merrill Palmer Quarterly,* 1967, *13,* 55–76.

Watson, M. W., & Fischer, K. W. A developmental sequence of agent use in late infancy. *Child Development,* 1977, *48,* 828–837.

Wechsler, D. *The measurement and appraisal of adult intelligence* (4th ed.). Baltimore: Williams & Wilkins, 1958.

White, B. L. The initial coordination of sensorimotor schemas in human infants – Piaget's ideas and the role of experience. In D. Elkind & J. H. Flavell (Eds.), *Studies in cognitive development.* New York: Oxford University Press, 1969.

White, S. H. Some general outlines of the matrix of developmental changes between five and seven years. *Bulletin of the Orton Society,* 1970, *20,* 41–57.

Winograd, T. *Understanding natural language.* New York: Academic Press, 1972.
Zimmerman, B. J., & Rosenthal, T. L. Observational learning of rule-governed behavior by children. *Psychological Bulletin,* 1974, *81*(1), 29–42.

3 Knowledge Structures and Memory Development

Michelene T. H. Chi
University of Pittsburgh

My research has recently centered on the general question of what determines memory development. Roughly 99.9% of developmental data indicate improvement with age: The question is "why"? My research attempts to answer this question in the domain of memory and also the domains of metamemory and reasoning.

The issues addressed in this chapter are very general ones. In the memory domain, the question is: Why do older children and adults remember more than younger children? In the metamemory domain, the question is: Why are older children and adults more aware of their own memory performance than younger children?

FACTORS IN MEMORY DEVELOPMENT

Three factors influence memory development: strategies, knowledge, and capacity. The influence of each are briefly elaborated.

Strategy

The strategy component is an important factor in memory development because older children are adept at acquiring and using strategies to cope with memory tasks. In metamemory tasks, the strategy component may arise from older children's ability to perceive the useful outcomes of strategic intervention. That is, adults are better predictors of their own memory performance because they can judge the strategic requirements and the usefulness of certain strategies for a task (Brown, in press).

What is a strategy? Broadly, a strategy is a set of decision processes that determines what sequences of actions to perform. Some strategies that have been extensively studied are rehearsal, recoding, and grouping. As we will see, there are also many subsidiary strategies that a person can adopt for a given situation.

The findings on strategy development have consistently shown that the use of strategies increases with age. It is clear that part of memory and the improvement of metamemory performance must reflect this factor.

Why do we need to go beyond this? Why not simply adopt the view that strategy changes are responsible for all memory (and metamemory) development? There are three reasons: (1) If an adult strategy is taught to children, recall is still generally better in adults (Butterfield, Wambold, & Belmont, 1973); (2) if a strategy is taught to both children and adults, the initial difference in performance is generally maintained (Huttenlocher & Burke, 1976); and (3) if adults are prevented from using certain strategies, their performance remains superior to that of children (Chi, 1977).[1] In general, it is becoming more and more apparent that strategies (at least our traditional notion of strategies) do not account for all the developmental trends or individual differences in memory performance. Hence, it is necessary that we turn to other factors to account for the remaining differences.[2]

Knowledge

Knowledge affects development through the growth of the knowledge base. By growth I mean simply that there are more concepts, more relations among concepts, and so on in the semantic memory of an adult as compared to a child. Associated with the growth of knowledge is a better structure for that knowledge. A better structure may be one that has, in some sense, a more appropriate or valid set of relations among the concepts as well as a greater number of relations.

No one disputes the assumption that adults have a richer knowledge base than children. However, if one looks at the developmental literature on memory, few researchers emphasize this difference or test directly its effect on memory performance. Researchers often regard knowledge as a catchall for any age

---

[1]The results obtained by Huttenlocher and Burke are also true in adults' individual differences data (Lyon, 1977). That is, the initial individual differences in digit span was not reduced when all the subjects were required to use a certain strategy.

[2]It is conceivable that for each of the reasons listed above strategy usage could still be an underlying factor in the performance differences. For example, one alternative interpretation for all three points is that adults are using unidentified strategies. Such was precisely the case in Chi's (1977) memory span for faces study. However, I would like to propose that frequently an alternative factor (namely, amount and structure of knowledge) can override the effect of incidental strategy usage.

differences not explained by the experimental variables. No one is certain of the extent to which knowledge influences performance.

This chapter highlights the contribution of amount and structure of knowledge to memory and metamemory performance. The contributions of other components, particularly strategies, have been amply stressed elsewhere. This chapter attempts to place the knowledge factor in a proper perspective.

Capacity

The capacity hypothesis states that the improvement of performance with age can be partially explained by an increase in the capacity of working memory (Baron, in press; Carroll, 1976; Case, 1974). If one examines the developmental data in the area, the hypothesis of capacity increases seems obvious. However, the data may obscure an important issue, namely, that age and knowledge are often confounded.

To define what I mean by *capacity*, one needs to distinguish *performance* capacity from *actual* capacity. Memory capacity can be estimated empirically only by measuring the performance of an individual on a given task. For

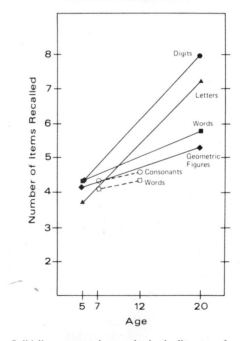

FIG. 3.1   Solid lines summarize results in the literature for memory-span performance for different stimulus materials as a function of age. Dotted lines are Dempster's (1976) results for consonants (open circles) and words (open squares).

example, in a memory-span task, the digit span for college students is about 7.98 units (Brener, 1940), whereas for 5-year-olds it is about 4 units (Starr, 1923; see Table 3.1). Hence, the performance capacity of an adult is superior to that of a child.

Since the introduction of the concept of the chunk (Miller, 1956), researchers have concluded that the actual capacity of working memory for adults is around seven chunks. For any given domain of stimuli, then, adults' performances can vary, as demonstrated in the memory-span estimates, but the theoretical interpretation is that the underlying chunk capacity of working memory is invariant (Simon, 1974). The solid lines in Fig. 3.1 summarize the literature on performance estimates for various stimulus materials.

For any given domain of stimuli, children consistently exhibit a smaller memory span. The obvious dilemma is whether the results depicted in Figure 3.1 reflect a smaller actual capacity in children or a smaller chunk size. In other words, it could be argued from Figure 3.1 that children are simply unfamiliar with these stimulus materials and that the variability in the adults' data is due to different amounts of experience with (or knowledge about) the stimuli.

Both Chi (1976) and Dempster (1976) used the latter notion to argue that memory capacity is constant, at least beyond the age of 5 years or so. That is, they assumed that children show a smaller memory span in all the materials shown in Figure 3.1 because these materials are less familiar to them. It follows from this argument that if a class of stimulus materials can be found that is equally familiar (or unfamiliar) to both age groups, then children and adults should exhibit the same memory span. Indeed, Dempster found that with consonants and words, span estimates for first graders (4.3 and 4.07) were not significantly different from those for sixth graders (4.6 and 4.3). These data suggest that knowledge of stimuli may be the critical variable in producing differences in memory-span performance among age groups. However, these data are not sufficient to conclude that capacity is invariant with age. Further data are needed to (1) pinpoint knowledge of the stimuli as the critical variable producing age differences in memory-span performances and (2) show better recall in children than in adults when the stimulus materials are more familiar to children. The studies discussed in the following paragraphs attempt to meet these objectives.

MEMORY SPAN FOR FACES

Throughout this paper, the role of strategies has been minimized and the role of knowledge has been emphasized. This orientation was derived from my first research effort, which assessed the extent to which strategies account for developmental differences in memory span and the extent to which remaining age differences are not explained by differential strategy usage (Chi, 1977). A

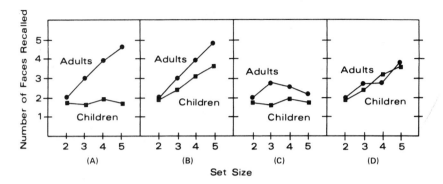

FIG. 3.2   Number of known faces recalled by adults as a function of set size. Panels A and B are 600 msec presentations per face for both adults and children. Panel A used ordered scoring, and Panel B used free scoring. Panels C and D used 300 msec presentation time for adults, replotted with children's data, using ordered (C) or free (D) scoring. In addition, the results of Panel D further prohibited the adults from using a constrained retrieval strategy.

question raised was: If there are age differences not explained by differential strategy usage, can these differences be attributed to differential knowledge of the stimuli?

The study used a reversal of training procedure to identify the specific factors within the knowledge and strategy domains that produce adults' superior memory performance. The usual assumption underlying a training approach is that a specific deficit in the child has already been identified. It is also assumed that the component to be trained is crucial to successful adult performance. These assumptions tend to overemphasize certain components and to overlook other not-so-trainable ones, as well as ignoring how the components interact.

In contrast to the training approach, Chi (1977) attempted systematically to reduce the availability of certain components that are crucial to successful adult performance in order to see whether adults' performance capacity could be brought down to the level of children's. If we can equalize performance capacity (memory span) by manipulating certain variables, then we can ask if these variables are related to actual capacity.

The first goal was to prevent adults from using the major mnemonic strategies that have been well documented in the literature — rehearsal, grouping, and chunking. Both the rehearsal and grouping strategies presumably take time to execute (Lyon, 1977), so we reduced their utility to adults by presenting the stimuli for short durations (600 msec each). Because the set size (number of stimuli in a given presentation array) varied from two to five, the total presentation time varied from 1200 msec to 3000 msec. To reduce the possibility of adults' using a chunking strategy, the stimulus material needed to be equally unchunkable by either age group. At the same time, the stimulus material had to be equally familiar to all, in order to limit the adults' advantage of greater knowledge. The stimuli chosen were faces of classmates. Faces of peers do not seem to be chunkable unless two or three consecutive faces form a familiar unit. Care was taken not to use twins, siblings, or stable couplets. Faces of peers were also an attractive choice because there was some control over how long (3 years of schooling) the subjects (kindergarteners and graduate students) had been acquainted with them. However, we did not ascertain whether the faces were equally familiar to each age group. Each subject could identify by name all the eight faces used in the experiment.

Summarizing the outcome of this serial recall task, we learned that adults remembered more faces in the correct order than did 5-year-olds, even though the use of major strategies was reduced (see Fig. 3.2A). For supporters of a constant capacity hypothesis, this initial outcome was very alarming. It suggested that adults had a larger performance capacity even when (1) mnemonic usage was minimized and (2) children seemed to know the stimuli (could name them) as well as adults. To remain skeptical, we had to probe further to see what produced the age differences. There were three potential factors: ordered recall, naming deficiency, and subsidiary strategy usage.

Ordered Recall

As shown by the data on face recall, children had greater difficulty remembering the faces in their correct order. What processes were responsible for the differences in encoding order information? It seemed that where order was defined in terms of a serial array, adults had multiple and redundant ways of encoding it, such as temporal, spatial, and numerical ordering. Children may not have the abilities to encode serial order in such multiple fashions or to realize that they were all redundant. To eliminate this dimension of developmental differences, we simply scored the data without regard to position errors (free as opposed to ordered scoring). We found that adults were still superior to children, although the differences were reduced (see Fig. 3.2B).

Naming Deficiency

The children's second limitation was their retarded speed of accessing the names of the faces, as measured by vocalization latencies. It took children more than twice as long to retrieve the name of a face (about 1½ sec) as it took adults (about 2/3 sec). This naming-time limitation cannot be ascribed entirely to a perceptual or encoding deficiency, in the sense that the children did not have enough time to scan the stimulus or to extract a sufficient number of relevant features to identify the face. We found this out by presenting the faces in a tachistoscope and measuring the identification thresholds for children and adults. This technique avoids measuring the naming component. The results showed that although adults were faster at encoding (25 msec versus 138 msec for encoding one face), the magnitude of the difference was not large enough to account for the differences in the vocalization latencies (Chi, 1977).

What is the implication of children's naming deficit for memory performance? The most important implication is that naming can be a very powerful mneumonic device because it provides an "external" memory aid. For adults, the recall task was memory for a serial list of names, because the presentation time (600 msec/face) was sufficiently long to allow them to name each face. For the children, on the other hand, the task was memory for faces only, because the presentation time was only half as long as the time they needed for name retrieval.[3]

To illustrate this point, we simulated the children's task environment by limiting adults' viewing time so that the task demand for adults also became memory for faces only. Reducing adults' presentation time to half of their naming time (i.e., 300 msec/face) did reduce their recall scores, but their scores remained superior to those of children (using ordered scoring) (see Fig. 3.2C).

Additional Strategy Usage

The adults' third advantage was their spontaneous adoption of various subsidiary strategies that were often not of initial interest to the experimenter. In particular, adults changed their strategies as the task demands changed. When their viewing time was reduced, they altered the task from one of serial recall to one of constrained recall. That is, they reproduced the response in the order that they could retrieve, rather than in the actual order of presentation — for example, first recalling the last two faces, then the first two, then indicating that the first two preceded the last two. The use of such a retrieval strategy can be confirmed by examining the serial position curves. Having identified this strategy, we were able to eliminate it by simply telling the adults not to use it. As shown in Fig. 3.2D, this manipulation, together with the reduced exposure time and use of the free recall measure, yielded equivalent performance in children and adults.

The foregoing discussion centers on three factors — better ordered recall, faster name retrieval, and modified retrieval strategy — that can facilitate adults' recall of serial arrays. We have shown that eliminating any single advantage did not substantially reduce adults' superior recall performance. However, when all possible strategy usage was eliminated and adults' exposure duration limited, we then obtained equivalent recall performance for children and adults. The foregoing findings raise a fundamental issue: How did adults retrieve the names of

---

[3]Notice that we cannot equate the task demands simply by increasing children's viewing time, because adults would still have had the additional strategic advantages (such as rehearsal).

the faces so quickly? This is the issue that led to the present research. My hypothesis was that the amount and structure of knowledge children had stored in semantic memory about their peers may not have been sufficient to permit fast access to that information. It is as though the information was so poorly structured that children require a longer period of activation (or search) in order to retrieve it.[4] One could speculate further that the inaccessibility of the names prevents the children from actively using any mnemonic strategies that required name manipulations.

Although this research could not conclusively implicate knowledge and structure of the stimuli as the sources of developmental differences in memory span performance, it did seem to suggest that *above and beyond the usage of strategies*, children do have a more limited knowledge of the stimuli, as indexed here by the naming time.[5] Because this difference in knowledge could be of sufficient magnitude to produce an age effect resembling ones supposedly produced by increased capacity, it seemed as valid to speculate that the remaining age differences showed increased knowledge as well as increased capacity.[6]

MEMORY FOR CHESS POSITIONS

As mentioned previously, in order to converge on the notion of constant capacity, we need to attribute developmental differences in recall performance to alternative factors. Throughout this paper, I have argued that in addition to the role played by strategies, recall performance is further influenced by the amount and structure of knowledge children and adults have about the stimuli. The intention of the following study is to assess the extent to which knowledge can affect memory performance independent of age.

Because knowledge generally increases with age and because there appears to be a relation between developmental differences in recall and knowledge of the stimuli (Dempster, 1976), it seems at least plausible to assume that recall improves with age primarily because adults know more, rather than because adults have a bigger capacity. We already know, for example, that recall varies directly

---

[4]Similar arguments may also be applied to adults with large and small memory spans. Baddeley, Thompson, & Buchanan (1975) found a substantial correlation between adults' memory span and reading speed.

[5]A majority of developmental studies assess children's familiarity with the stimuli by whether they can label (or name) them. In cases where children cannot provide the appropriate labels, the experimenter simply provides them. The differential name-retrieval speed of children and adults in this study clearly highlights the danger of making that assumption.

[6]Remaining age differences will henceforth refer to those not explained by differential strategy usage.

with knowledge for adults. Chase and Simon (1973) found that chess knowledge influenced performance on both a perception and a memory task, and similar results have been found with games such as "Go" (Eisenstadt & Kareev, 1975; Reitman, 1976) and baseball (Chiesi, Spilich, & Voss, 1977). However, such a direct relation between knowledge and recall cannot be inferred from existing developmental studies, even though we normally assume that adults know more than children. This is because, first, the amount of knowledge an age group has about a set of stimuli has seldom been directly measured, and second, too many other variables exist to permit such a simple deduction. On the other hand, a more direct relation between knowledge and developmental changes in recall can be shown if we demonstrate better recall in children who have greater knowledge in a content area than adults. The purpose of the next study is to provide such a demonstration.

The subjects for this study were six children (third through eighth grade) solicited from a local chess tournament. Their mean age was around 10.5 years. The adult subjects were research assistants and graduate students from an educational research center. All could play chess to some degree.

Two tasks were used to test memory for chess positions: immediate recall and repeated recall. In each condition, a chess position was presented for 10 sec, followed by recall. In the immediate recall task, the subject immediately placed the appropriate chess pieces on a blank board. Pieces, colors, and location all had to be reproduced perfectly for an answer to be counted as correct. On the repeated recall task, if the subject did not reproduce the entire board correctly the first time, the trials continued until perfect performance was achieved. The sequence and timing of each reproduction trial were recorded on audiotape. The stimuli were eight middle-game positions (averaging 22 pieces) selected from a chess quiz book (Reinfeld, 1945). Four positions were used for each memory task. At the end of the repeated recall trials, each subject was asked to draw partitions around those pieces that s/he thought formed a chunk.

Because only one of the 12 subjects had an official chess rating, some way of assessing the chess knowledge of each age group was needed. This was done in two ways: (1) by how well the subject could predict good moves in a position, and (2) by how quickly subjects could perform the knight's tour task. Following the memory trials and the chunk-partitioning task, subjects were asked to predict the next few moves from the same position. The subject made a move, and if it was correct, the experimenter replied; the subject then predicted the next move, and so on, for two or three moves, depending on the position. When the subject made a wrong move, the experimenter corrected him/her, and the moves were continued from there.[7] The knight's tour task was a modified

---

[7]The correctness of the move was determined by the solution to the chess puzzle in Reinfeld's (1945) book.

version of the one used by Chase and Simon (1973), in which subjects had to move a knight across two rows of the board, with certain constraints, using legal knight moves.[8] The time it takes to complete the moves has been shown to be a gross index of chess knowledge.

As a control, four lists of 10 digits were presented for immediate and repeated recall. The procedure was identical to the chess conditions, except that recall consisted of a written response, and no partitionings were requested from the subjects at the end of the repeated recall task.

Results

The mean knight's tour time for children was around 2.5 min for the two rows, versus 5.5 min for the adults. Hence, the children appeared to have greater knowledge of chess than the adults. On the other indication of chess knowledge, the moves prediction, children's predictions were accurate on about 59% of the moves, whereas adults predicted 44% of the moves correctly. This prediction task did not seem as sensitive as the knight's tour in assessing chess skill, perhaps because the experimenter corrected the wrong moves, which considerably constrained potential subsequent moves.

The most important result of the experiment, though, was that children's immediate recall for chess positions was far superior to adults' (9.3 versus 5.9 pieces), $F(1, 10) = p < 0.05$) (see Fig. 3.3A). In contrast, the children's digit span was lower than that of the adults' (6.1 versus 7.8 digits). Although the digit span differences was not statistically significant, it did replicate the findings in the literature (cf. Table 3.1). The same pattern of results was obtained in the repeated recall task (Fig. 3.3B). It took children an average of 5.6 trials to learn the entire chess position, whereas adults required 8.4 trials, $F(1, 10) = 6.2, p < 0.05$. For the digits, on the other hand, the typical developmental trend was again found — children required 3.2 trials to learn a list of 10 digits, whereas adults required only 2.2 trials — although the difference was not significant.

These results are consistent with Chase and Simon's (1973) findings that subjects with high knowledge recognize many more patterns than do subjects with low knowledge. In conjunction with the previous results on naming time, they suggest that memory performance in developmental studies reflects, to a large extent, the influence of knowledge in a specific content area rather than strategies per se. That is, with the exception of knowledge-specific strategies, the availability of general strategies useful for memory performance should have been comparable in both the digit and chess situations. Hence, general strategies such as rehearsal could not have played a major role in determining developmental differences in recall in this study.

---

[8]This modified version was used to save time and simplify the instruction for the children. Basically, the difference was that the knight was permitted to land on the four squares controlled by the two pawns.

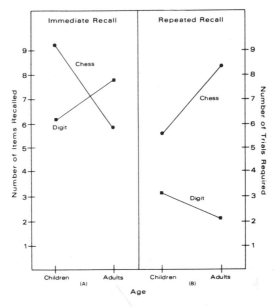

FIG. 3.3   The amount of recall in immediate and repeated recall tasks, for digits and chess stimuli.

Can we similarly rule out the role of capacity in these results? The difference in digit span replicates the standard developmental pattern. Such findings would normally be attributed to a deficient strategy or to a smaller capacity. One way to address the capacity issue is to compare the present results with Chase and Simon's results, in which only adult subjects were tested and in which the adults were assumed to be similar in capacity and strategies. If the results of this study replicate those of Chase and Simon's results in every respect, despite the manipulation of age, then we add support to the hypothesis that capacity is not a very important component.

So far, my results have replicated Chase and Simon's findings in terms of the number of pieces recalled in immediate recall, as well as the number of trials needed to learn the entire board position. It is also important to know how large the memory span is for chess chunks for children and adults. Chase and Simon found that better players recalled more chunks and more pieces per chunk on the first recall trial when chunks were partitioned by an interresponse latency

TABLE 3.1
Digit Span as a Function of Age

Age	4–5	6–8	9–12	College Students
Span	4	5	6	7.98

(IRT) of greater than 2 sec. Using a similar technique, the first trial data of the repeated recall task were partitioned into chunks using a 2-sec IRT as boundary. Then the incorrect pieces were eliminated, and the remaining pieces with their existing chunk boundaries were tabulated. From this analysis, we found that children, on the average, retrieved about 4.33 chunks whereas adults retrieved about 2.63 chunks for the first trial, $F(1, 10) = 6.98, p < 0.05$. Hence, children have a larger memory span for chunks, which confirms Chase and Simon's (1973) results. Second, the size of the first and second chunks also tended to be larger for children, although the differences were not statistically significant (see Table 3.2, rows *A*, *B*, and *C*).

In general, these results replicate those of Chase and Simon in showing that better players (here, the children) tend to (1) retrieve more chess pieces from memory in a single recall trial, (2) require fewer trials to memorize the entire chess position, (3) retrieve a larger number of chunks on the first trial, and (4) have larger chunk sizes for the first and second chunks, irrespective of age.

One of the dilemmas these results present is that if the concept of a constant memory capacity is being proposed for children and adults, we should feel as uneasy about obtaining data when children recalled more chunks as when children recalled fewer. Two likely hypotheses have been suggested by Chase and Simon (1973). One is that the better player's chunk structures may have more overlap, so that pieces from one chunk can serve as retrieval cues for pieces from another chunk. The existence of overlapping chunks has since been documented by Reitman (1976) for the game of "Go." By using a pause technique, we can capture what appear to be separate chunks, but these chunks may actually be overlapping and related. A second hypothesis was that a "chunk" is of different sizes and structures for differently skilled players. Suppose we assume that a chunk, such as a rook-queen-rook configuration, is hierarchically organized and that the better player needs only store the "name" of the chunk in a location in working memory. For the poorer player, however, a rook-queen-rook configuration may be composed of two or more chunks, such as rook-queen and queen-rook. (This is the standard explanation used throughout this kind of research to account for greater recall in the better player.) One interpretation of the chunk recall results is that it may take the skilled player more than 2 sec to "unpack" his chunk, so that it looks as if he has many more chunks, even though the number of chunks was limited by the capacity of his working memory.

Both of these hypotheses, although reasonable, are speculative because the technique of partitioning chunks by a 2-sec interval cannot capture the complete structure of the chunk. What we hoped to do, therefore, was justify the notion of constant capacity, even between 10-year-olds and adults of different skills, by obtaining comparable recall of chunks using a different technique to access the chunk structure. We requested the subjects to partition the board position into chunks at the last (the correct) trial of the repeated recall task. This technique

TABLE 3.2
Chunk Structures

	Children	Adults
A. Number of chunks on the first trial	4.33	2.63
B. First chunk size of first trial	2.50	2.25
C. Second chunk size of first trial	1.75	1.21
D. Number of chunks on last trial	6.83	7.33
E. IRT between chunks on last trial	3.03 ±1.00	2.71 ±1.03
F. IRT within chunks on last trial	1.40 ±0.51	1.37 ±0.50
G. Number of overlapping chunks on last trial	1.29	1.29

was first used by Reitman (1976) for "Go" positions. Using subjects' own partitionings, we can redefine a chunk as a cluster of pieces that the subject has grouped within one boundary. By this definition, children and adults organized the positions into the same number of chunks, about 6.8 and 7.3, respectively, and the average chunk size was about three pieces.

How do we resolve the apparent discrepancy between the final trial, in which children and adults both represented the chess position in terms of the same number of chunks, and the first trial, in which children seemed to recall more and bigger chunks? The answer may lie in the technique of accessing the chunk structure. Both hypotheses proposed by Chase and Simon (1973) seem reasonable, mainly because partitioning by a 2-sec retrieval interval does not take into consideration either the overlapping nature of the chunk structure or the fact that it may take longer than 2 sec to unpack a chunk. A third possibility is that a better player may not exhaustively retrieve all the pieces from a given chunk and may reenter the same chunk later after seeing it on the board. A fourth interpretation is that first trial performance may be limited mainly by the size and quantity of chunks already stored in memory. As subjects learn a position, they do so in the most economical way: by representing the position with as few chunks as possible and as many pieces as possible per chunk. What took the adults so long to memorize the position (around 8.5 trials) was their slower rate of assembling the pieces into chunks, because they have fewer of these components in memory. That is, if we assume that the adults' memory structure for chess contained smaller patterns, with fewer pieces per pattern, then their slower learning rate can be explained by the longer time required to recode smaller chunks to form larger ones. One simple interpretation, first proposed by Broadbent (1975), is that chunk size is limited by how much capacity of working memory is available for this recoding, because all the elements must be held in working memory while the chunk is being constructed. If adults and children have the same capacity of working memory, then eventually they will both represent the position with the same number of chunks.

Granted that partitioning by a 2-sec interval may not completely capture the chunk structure, can we, on the other hand, rely on the subject's introspections

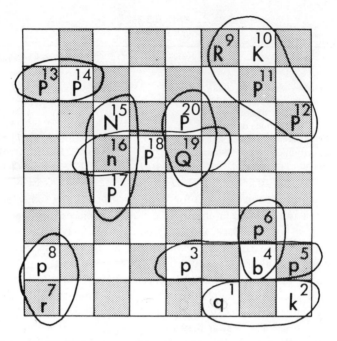

FIG. 3.4   Example of one subject's partitionings. Lower case letters are white pieces and upper case black pieces.

of the chunk structures? It seems necessary to compare subjects' partitionings directly with their recall latencies. If there is any reality to the 2-sec chunk boundary, then we hope to find that the IRTs within a chunk are less than 2 sec and that the IRTs between chunks are greater than 2 sec. To test this, the IRTs between pieces for the last trial of each subject were divided into two categories: between- and within-chunk IRTs, where chunks were defined by the subjects' partitionings. For example, Fig. 3.4 illustrates the partitioning of one subject. The letters represent pieces on the board, the encircled areas are the subjects' partitioning, and the numbers by each piece indicate the order of recall on the last trial. This recall sequence started at the lower right corner, with two pieces, the king and queen, constituting the first chunk; the IRT between these two pieces was considered to be a within-chunk time. Likewise, the IRTs for the next three pieces, pawn, bishop, and pawn, were also considered to be within-chunk times. However, the IRTs between the king and the pawn (the second and third pieces), or between the next two pawns (the fifth and sixth pieces) were considered to be between-chunk times because neither pair was enclosed within the same boundary.

If there is any reality to partitionings, between-chunk times should be longer than within-chunk times. Averaging across subjects and positions, the amount of time it took subjects to cross a chunk boundary was longer (around 3 sec) than the amount of time it took to place pieces within a chunk (around 1.5 sec) for both adults and children, even though sometimes there were overlapping chunks.[9] (See Table 3.2, rows E and F.) This analysis supports Chase and Simon's assumption that retrieval time between chunks is greater than 2 sec, whereas retrieval time within chunks is less than 2 sec.

To summarize the results: Children and adults exhibit typical developmental trends for digits in two memory tasks, immediate recall and repeated recall. However, when chess materials are used and children have greater knowledge of chess, children exhibit better recall on both tasks. Furthermore, children also have a larger span for chess chunks in immediate recall (and the first trial of the repeated recall task) but represented the board position in terms of the same number of chunks as adults on the last trial, suggesting that the capacity of working memory limits the number of chunks into which a board position can be organized.

KNOWLEDGE AND METAMEMORY

Metamemory refers to the knowledge people have about memory storage and retrieval rather than to memory performance itself. We can summarize Flavell's (1977) review of metamemory research by saying that memory-relevant knowledge is acquired throughout development. Certain types of knowledge about memory tasks (task variables) and memory strategies (strategy variables) are acquired at an earlier age than others. For example, even kindergarteners know that a memory task is harder if it has a large number of items, whereas only older children know that a recall task is harder if one has to learn two sets of words that are easily confusable (Kreutzer, Leonard, & Flavell, 1975).

Another important variable in metamemory, according to Flavell (1977), is a person's knowledge about intrinsic and stable characteristics of self and others as a memorizer (person variable). The data have consistently showed that younger children are less aware (or have less knowledge) of their recall potential than are older children. To be more specific, metamemory about person variables has been investigated in a span estimation paradigm in which the subjects are asked to predict their own recall potential. The findings have consistently showed that (1) young children are not realistic in predicting their own span performance, and (2) this inaccuracy seems to disappear beyond the third grade (Brown, Campione, & Murphy, 1977; Flavell, Friedrichs, & Hoyt, 1970; Markman, 1973; Yussen & Levy, 1975).

The intention of this research is to suggest another factor influencing metamemory: subjects' knowledge of stimuli. There are two ways to test whether

---

[9]Table 2, row G shows the number of overlapping chunks represented by subject's partitioning of the last trial. There were no significant differences between the two age groups.

knowledge of stimuli is an important variable in metamemory performance. One way is to vary the amount of knowledge subjects have about the stimuli. For example, we could vary the chess skill of the subjects. A second way is to use two different kinds of stimuli on the same task and compare a subject's metamemory performance on them. Both of these strategies are discussed in the following paragraphs.

Span and Trials Predictions by Children and Adults

The 12 subjects in the previous study, six children and six adults, were asked to predict their performance on both immediate and repeated recall tasks for both digit and chess stimuli. The immediate recall (memory span) prediction task consisted of showing a subject a chess position (or 10 digits) for 10 sec, followed by a request for a prediction of how many of the chess pieces or digits he thought he could recall. The repeated recall (trials) prediction also consisted of a 10-sec presentation, followed by a prediction of how many such 10-sec looks would be needed to memorize the entire chess position or all 10 digits. These predictions were all made prior to the actual recall phase of the study.

According to the literature (cf. Brown, in press), there should be no significant differences between children and adults in predictions of memory span because the children were fifth graders, on the average. If no differences in accuracy of memory span prediction occurred for either type of stimuli, it would suggest that a metamemory task such as prediction of memory span is not very sensitive to the knowledge factor. On the other hand, it could also be the case that a memory span prediction task does not usually project a developmen-

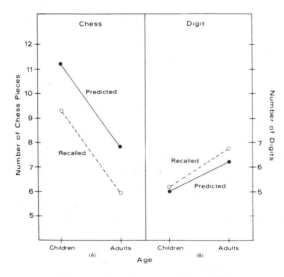

FIG. 3.5   Predictions for immediate recall by children and adults for digits and chess.

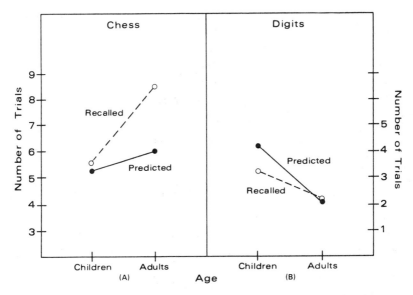

FIG. 3.6   Predictions for repeated recall by children and adults for digits and chess.

tal trend — not because the task is insensitive to the knowledge factor but because the task is too simple. That is, the task may be very conducive to an immediate simulation, so that any child (beyond the third grade) who is aware of a simulation strategy can be an accurate predictor. For a more complex task, in which simulation is not as easily accomplished, however, recall prediction may indeed be sensitive to the knowledge component. Hence, we anticipate that children might be more accurate in the trials prediction.

The immediate recall predictions are shown in Fig. 3.5. Panel *B* shows no developmental differences in either the predictions or the accuracy of the predictions between children and adults for digits. This result replicates the usual findings in the literature, namely, that no developmental differences in prediction accuracy can be observed for children beyond the third grade. For the chess stimuli (panel *A*) there were also no significant differences either in the predictions or the accuracy of the predictions between children and adults.

However, the more important result seems to be that, even though both children and adults were equally accurate in the chess and digit predictions for immediate recall, they both underpredicted their recall for digits and overpredicted their recall for chess pieces. One way to interpret this is to assume that the prediction task itself required identical processes for both types of stimuli, so that the observed performance differences were a function of the type of stimuli. Supposing that this prediction task required a simulation strategy, the results would then suggest that simulating recall in a spatial array (chess) is different from simulating recall in a linear array (digits), if there is any reality to the simulation strategy. Alternatively, one could interpret this result as suggesting that the demands of the immediate recall prediction task were quite different for the two types of stimuli, with one requiring knowledge of recalling nonverbal location information and the other requiring knowledge of recalling verbal serial lists. In either case, it suggests that a prediction task per se, which is supposed to tap knowledge of person variables, can interact with both the stimuli and the demands of the recall task.

The results on the trials prediction are shown in Fig. 3.6. Again, children did not predict significantly differently from adults for either type of stimuli, although the expected trend occurred. That is, children's accuracy was greater than adults' for chess (because the children had more knowledge of chess), whereas adults' accuracy was greater for digits. It seems to suggest that a more complex task (trials prediction) is more sensitive to the knowledge variable than a simpler task (span prediction).

The results of this study suggest that knowledge of stimuli is an important variable in determining metamemory (prediction) performance, in that different patterns of results were obtained for the chess and digit stimuli. On the other hand, no reliable differences were obtained between children and adults, suggesting that either a prediction task is not very sensitive to the knowledge variable, or else the knowledge differences (about the stimuli) were not large enough to produce an age effect. The next study addressed this latter possibility by using adults with a wider range of knowledge about the stimuli.

Memory Predictions by Adults

The study of memory predictions by adults tested the hypothesis that adults' metamemory predictions may depend on their amount of knowledge about the stimuli. Eighteen adults were divided into three groups according to their knight's tour times. In this case, the knight's tour was identical to the one used by Chase and Simon (1973). The six fastest subjects (two rows in an average of 2.5 min) were classified as the high-knowledge group. Three of the six players in this group also had official chess ratings that averaged around 1600. The medium-knowledge group averaged about 6 min, and the low-knowledge group about 9.5 min. Hence, in this study the high-knowledge group would be classified as Class B players and the low-knowledge group as novices. Thus, the skill range probably spanned about four levels.

Each subject was presented with two coherent and two random chess positions; both the coherent and the random positions contained a middle game (23 pieces) and an end game (15 pieces). The subject viewed each position for 5 sec and then gave two predictions: the number of pieces he thought he could recall immediately and the number of trials he thought he would need for complete recall. Following the predictions, the subjects were given a repeated

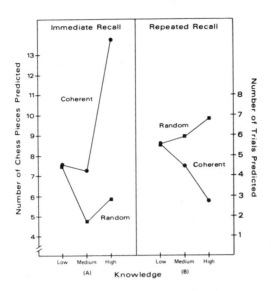

FIG. 3.7   Predictions by adults of high, medium, and low knowledge for coherent and random positions. Panel A is immediate recall predictions, and Panel B is repeated recall predictions.

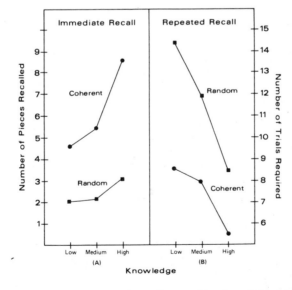

FIG. 3.8   Actual recall for high, medium, and low-knowledge subjects in immediate and repeated recall tasks.

recall task, using a different set of four positions — two coherent and two random — each containing a middle and an end game.

The results are straightforward and for the most part provide good support for the hypothesis. Figure 3.7A illustrates the prediction data for immediate recall (number of pieces) and Fig. 3.7B shows the predictions for repeated recall (number of trials to learn the position). In both cases, as the skill level increases, there is a systematic increase in the ability of subjects to discriminate the coherent from the random positions ($p < 0.01$). In other words, better chess players predicted that they would remember coherent positions much better than random ones whereas the differentiation for less good players was less dramatic.[10]

How do the metamemory predictions compare with actual performance? Figure 3.8 shows the recall performance on the repeated recall task. In this case, the first trial data are used as an indication of immediate recall performance (panel A). Panel B shows the number of trials needed to recall the entire position. The data are consistent with those in the literature.

Figure 3.9 shows the accuracy data (i.e., the differences between predicted and actual performance). There are two things to notice about these data. First, subjects consistently overestimate their memory abilities: They tend to predict more pieces than they will actually recall, and they tend to predict fewer trials than they will actually need. Second, with one exception, the prediction accuracy tends to improve with skill level (Fig. 3.9). The one reversal is due to three high-knowledge subjects who insisted that they could remember all the pieces of the coherent positions.

To summarize, these data taken together provide good support for the hypothesis that people with more knowledge about chess assess their ability to remember chess material more accurately. This is mainly shown by the better players' ability to predict the relative difficulty of coherent versus random positions. There is also a tendency for the better players to make more accurate absolute predictions.

Discussion of Metamemory Research

The metamemory studies discussed here have shown that metamemory performance can vary as a function of knowledge about the stimuli, in addition to knowledge about the task, strategies, and person variables. The lack of significant differences between children's and adults' metamemory performances, coupled with significant differences in memory performance, suggest that memory performance is more sensitive to knowledge (stimuli-relevant) than is metamemory

---

[10]Subjects were not told in advance that they would see random versus coherent positions.

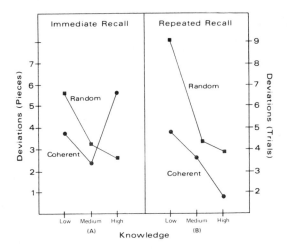

FIG. 3.9   Accuracy of subjects' predictions, as determined by absolute difference between number predicted and number recalled for each position.

performance. Metamemory performance, however, can also be sensitive to the knowledge factor if subjects vary widely in what they know.

What does this tell us about the metamemory process? Since the present studies were designed to demonstrate the importance of knowledge about the stimuli, the data are not specific enough to support any detailed theory. However, one can speculate that the underlying processes responsible for recall prediction performance can be separated into at least two general components. The first component is the amount of stimuli-relevant knowledge activated; the second is a decision process that evaluates the activated knowledge. In the case of chess positions, we assume that coherent positions will activate many more chess patterns in the memory of high-knowledge persons because they have many more patterns stored. The decision process, then, could be as simple as counting the number of activated patterns. Such a simple mechanism is sufficient to account for the immediate recall predictions. The theory would have to be expanded to account for the complexities of the number-of-trials predictions.

It should also be apparent that there are complexities in the decision processes. Suppose the decision does involve some quantification processes. For the high-knowledge persons, a 5-sec look will activate a large quantity of information, which may necessitate reliance on estimation rather than on counting. Because estimation processes are less accurate, the prediction accuracy of high-knowledge subjects using estimation may also be less accurate. Recall that three of the six high-knowledge subjects insisted that they could remember all the pieces in the coherent positions (23 and 15 pieces). Such an erroneous decision could have been based on some gross quantification process such as estimation.

Other subjects, by contrast, counted on their fingers before making an immediate recall prediction. The experimenter recollected that one of these "counting" subjects was a low-knowledge player. Clearly, the exact nature of metamemory mechanisms must await further research.

GENERAL DISCUSSION

This paper has attempted to show that the amount of knowledge a person possesses about a specific content area can determine to a large extent how well he or she can perform in both memory and metamemory tasks. The implication is that the sources of some of the age differences we often observe in developmental studies must be attributable to knowledge about the stimuli rather than to capacity and strategic factors alone. Notice that this knowledge is about the stimuli only, not about the task (i.e., we tested memory and metamemory performances, not chess playing).

In the introduction of this paper, both the knowledge and strategy factors were discussed in very gross terms, and they were treated as separated entities. Clearly, there is a need to remark on the distinction or lack of distinction between the two components, because strategies are obviously part of our knowledge system. Perhaps a better distinction would be to classify them as procedural versus declarative types of knowledge. However, without reiterating the distinction between data and process, let me stress the distinction that needs to be made concerning strategies.

Most of the developmental research has centered on what can be called "general strategies," such as rehearsal and grouping. These strategies can be applied to a wide variety of tasks. It may be misleading, however, to think of adults' superiority in terms of these few, limited mnemonics. As we saw in the first set of studies on memory span for faces, adults usually perform better than children, even without the use of these general strategies. This may be due, in part, to the fact that adults have a general scheme for adopting or inventing new mnemonics to cope with a task. (This scheme, I believe, is what Flavell referred to as knowledge about the strategy variables.) Hence, it may be necessary to introduce a subclass of general strategies, which we shall call task-specific strategies. For example, we may want to classify the following behavior as a task-specific strategy: One adult subject in the chess study always looked at the remaining chess pieces during recall to see whether any of the pieces could cue her in further recall. In fact, this particular adult subject did as well as the children, even though her chess knowledge was inferior to theirs. She seemed to have sophisticated task-specific strategies. However, overall, the adults' task-specific strategies did not overcome the children's greater advantage from years of accumulated knowledge in chess.

Another obvious subclass of strategies is knowledge-specific strategies, which can be defined as strategies applicable only to a specific body of knowledge.

The following behavior might be classified as a knowledge-specific strategy: Two of the subjects in the chess study continually memorized the chess board in mirror images. For example, if they found a rook in the left-hand corner, they would then check to see if there were also rooks in the other three corners, so that they could code all the rooks together. This is nothing more than a chunking strategy, but it is knowledge-specific. It requires some minimum knowledge of chess to predict that given a rook in one corner, there is a high probability that a rook will also be in the other corners.

Adults seemed capable of using all these strategies — general, task-specific, and knowledge-specific. There is no evidence at this time about children's proficiency with them. It appears as if the children performed better in the memory task by virture of their sheer volume of knowledge. Clearly, more research is needed to identify whether or not children's inefficient use of strategies is intimately related to their lack of knowledge.

ACKNOWLEDGMENTS

The preparation of this manuscript was supported by funds provided by the Learning Research and Development Center, University of Pittsburgh, which is funded in part by the National Institute of Education, United States Department of Health, Education and Welfare. I am grateful to William Chase and Robert Siegler for critical comments on the manuscript, as well as to John Flavell for his insightful discussion of an earlier draft. The paper also benefitted from discussions with my colleagues at LRDC — Bob Glaser, Jim Greeno, Alan Lesgold, Don Lyon, and Jim Pellegrino. Technical editing from Connie Faddis and laboratory assistance from Rita Sallis are greatly appreciated. Above all, I thank the children, their parents, and Mrs. Richey, the librarian who sponsored the chess tournaments, for their participation in the chess experiments.

REFERENCES

Baddeley, A. D., Thompson, N., & Buchanan, M. The word length and the structure of short-term memory. *Journal of Verbal Learning and Verbal Behavior,* 1975, *14,* 575–589.

Baron, J. Intelligence and general strategies. In G. Underwood (Ed.), *Strategies in information processing.* New York: Academic Press, in press.

Brener, R. An experimental investigation of memory span. *Journal of Experimental Psychology,* 1940, *26,* 467–482.

Broadbent, D. E. The magic number seven after fifteen years. In A. Kennedy & A. Wilkes (Eds.), *Studies in long term memory.* New York: Wiley, 1975.

Brown, A. L. Knowing when, where, and how to remember: A problem of metacognition. In R. Glaser (Ed.), *Advances in instructional psychology.* Hillsdale, N.J.: Lawrence Erlbaum Associates, in press.

Brown, A. L., Campione, J. C., & Murphy, M. D. Maintenance and generalization of trained metamnemonic awareness in educable retarded children. *Journal of Experimental Child Psychology,* 1977, *24,* 191–211.

Butterfield, E. C., Wambold, C., & Belmont, J. On the theory and practice of improving short-term memory. *American Journal of Mental Deficiency,* 1973, *77,* 654–669.

Carroll, J. B. Psychometric tests as cognitive tasks: A new "structure of intellect." In L. B. Resnick (Ed.), *The nature of intelligence.* Hillsdale, N.J.: Lawrence Erlbaum Associstes, 1976.

Case, R. Structure and strictures: Some functional limitations on the course of cognitive growth. *Cognitive Psychology,* 1974, *6,* 544–573.

Chase, W. G., & Simon, H. A. The mind's eye in chess. In W. G. Chase (Ed.), *Visual information processing.* New York: Academic Press, 1973.

Chi, M. T. H. Short-term memory limitations in children: Capacity or processing deficits? *Memory and Cognition,* 1976, *4,* 559–572.

Chi, M. T. H. Age differences in memory span. *Journal of Experimental Child Psychology,* 1977, *23,* 266–281.

Chiesi, H. L., Spilich, G., & Voss, J. F. *Cognitive processes and structure in individuals with high and low baseball knowledge: The first inning.* Unpublished manuscript, University of Pittsburgh, 1977.

Dempster, F. N. *Short-term storage capacity and chunking: A developmental study.* Unpublished doctoral dissertation, University of California, 1977.

Eisenstadt, M., & Kareev, Y. Aspects of human problem solving: The use of internal representation. In D. A. Norman & D. E. Rumelhardt (Eds.), *Exploration in cognition.* San Francisco: Freeman, 1975.

Flavell, J. H. *Metacognitive development.* Paper presented at the NATO Advanced Study Institute on Structural/Process Theories of Complex Human Behavior, Banff, Alberta, Canada, June, 1977.

Flavell, J. H., Friedrichs, A. G., & Hoyt, J. D. Developmental changes in memorization processes. *Cognitive Psychology,* 1970, *1,* 324–340.

Huttenlocher, J., & Burke, D. Why does memory span increase with age? *Cognitive Psychology,* 1976, *8,* 1–31.

Kreutzer, M. A., Leonard, S., & Flavell, J. H. An interview study of children's knowledge about memory. *Monographs of the Society for Research in Child Development,* 1975, *40* (1, Serial No. 159).

Lyon, D. Individual differences in immediate serial recall: A matter of mnemonics? *Cognitive Psychology,* 1977, *9,* 403–411.

Markman, E. M. *Factors affecting the young child's ability to monitor his memory.* Unpublished doctoral dissertation, University of Pennsylvania, 1973.

Miller, G. A. The magical number seven, plus or minus two: Some limits on our capacity for processing information. *Psychological Review,* 1956, *63,* 81–97.

Reitman, J. S. Skilled perception in Go: Deducing memory structures from inter-response times. *Cognitive Psychology,* 1976, *8,* 336–356.

Reinfeld, F. *Win at chess.* New York: Dover, 1945.

Simon, H. A. How big is a chunk? *Science,* 1974, *183,* 482–488.

Starr, A. S. The diagnostic value of the audio-vocal digit memory span. *Psychological Clinic,* 1923, *15,* 61–84.

Yussen, S. R., & Levy, V. M. Jr. Developmental changes in predicting one's own span of short-term memory. *Jouranl of Experimental Child Psychology,* 1975, *19,* 502–508.

4 Comments

John H. Flavell
Stanford University

The three papers in this part are very different from one another in most respects, but they do share one important attribute: All three are at the leading edge of the contemporary field of cognitive development. They say new things; they reflect novel trends. Brown and DeLoache discuss metacognitive development plus other new research topics. Case presents a new theory of cognitive growth. Chi's studies are radically and refreshingly different from most memory-development studies of the past decade. Therefore, one answer to the question, "What develops?" is well illustrated by these three papers: new theoretical and research approaches to the study of children's thinking develop.

COMMENTS ON BROWN AND DELOACHE'S PAPER

I found reading Brown and DeLoache's paper an infuriating experience. There I was, discussant knife ready, only to encounter page after page of much the sort of paper I would have tried to write if I had been a presenter rather than a discussant. In the words of Gilbert and Sullivan, I felt I had nothing whatever to grumble at, and that was terribly frustrating. I occasionally think that Ann Brown and I must be reincarnations of one another, so similar are our ideas about how and where to find Truth in cognitive development. So what I will mostly have to do with the Brown and DeLoache paper is underscore and elaborate on some of its more important points. I will also strive to grumble a bit, whenever possible.

Brown and DeLoache's critique of the modal memory strategy experiment and related matters is very well taken. There certainly has been an undue concentration on tasks rather than processes — and a severely limited range of tasks at that. We do indeed lack, and badly need, detailed and explicit models of how memory strategies develop. It is also true that we know virtually nothing about what nonproducers do. Another way to talk about this problem is to say that the modal memory strategy experiment can unearth only one half of what I have called (Flavell, 1972) an addition sequence. For example, it might show that the growing child will eventually add rehearsal, (the final half of the addition sequence) to his memory-strategy repertoire, but it usually does not show what was in that repertoire previously (the initial, missing half). Furthermore, such experiments almost never tell us anything about possible substitution, modification, inclusion, or mediation sequences (Flavell, 1972) that may also occur in strategy development. One would search the memory development literature in vain for anything formally similar to Case's modal sequence, for example.

Brown and DeLoache correctly argue that the field of memory development should import some developmental tractability from the field of problem solving. They might or might not agree with the argument that the Genevan Genevans (as contrasted with the non-Genevan ones) also have a lot to teach us about developmental tractability. I am thinking here of their wide age ranges, their countless stages and substages, their no-genesis-without-structure credo, and their recent accentuation of the preoperational child's competencies. A minor point: Although Brown and DeLoache are right in saying that we know practically nothing about memory development during adolescence, a few studies have been done recently (Flavell, in press).

And how could I possibly grumble at statements such as "What develops is metacognition" (p. 26) and "We select the metacognitive skills of self-interrogation and self-regulation as prime candidates for what develops" (p. 17)? Brown and DeLoache offer two reasons why young children may not engage in metacognitive activity. First, they contend that novices at anything do not metacognize much when performing a new task and that children are "universal novices" (p. 14). (Contrariwise, I would think that novices would metacognize a lot, although perhaps not well. Simon and Simon's paper (this volume) seems to suggest this.) Second, young children may not realize that there are certain metacognitive skills that are almost universally applicable, useful in nearly all situations. Both reasons appeal to insufficient experience, which young children obviously have in abundance. Maturational factors almost certainly comprise a third reason, one would think. If, as I believe, such factors constrain the rate of development of cognition about things, they undoubtedly do the same with respect to cognition about cognition.

Brown and DeLoache subsequently outline several excellent criteria for selecting tasks and strategies for developmental study. I completely agree that anything meeting all those criteria is eminently worth researching, but I would not try to defend the thesis that anything that doesn't isn't. For instance, the development of the ability to produce and comprehend pointing gestures is a beautiful research problem (e.g., Lempers, Flavell, & Flavell, 1977; Leung & Rheingold, 1977), but it does not meet the Brown and DeLoache criteria of having a very lengthy development or being of clear instructional relevance.

Brown and DeLoache go on to describe three candidates for developmental study that do come close to meeting their criteria, namely, extracting the main idea, scanning, and retrieval processes. I found this section of their paper particularly imaginative and insightful. Who would ever have expected to see extracting the main idea and scanning in a list of important cognitive developables and, moreover, be convinced that they belonged there? Who would ever have expected to see Piagetian object-permanence behavior convincingly categorized as an early retrieval strategy? Brown and DeLoache say they know of no study of children's conscious knowledge of their own visual scanning behavior, and they add the fervent hope that this topic will not be labeled *metascanning* if it does get researched. The development of children's knowledge of attention has, in fact, been studied recently by Miller and Bigi (1976); Brown and DeLoache will be pleased to learn that the term *meta-attention* does not appear in the written report of this research.

The final section contains well-reasoned pleas for supplementing controlled laboratory experimentation with naturalistic observation and for making our experimental tasks more meaningful and motivating for the child subject. It is hard to grumble at pleas for the adaptation of tasks to children rather than vice versa, for naturalistic approaches, for ecological validity, and other such God-and-country type of virtues, but it is not quite impossible. Coming to cognitive maturity in cultures such as ours may also involve learning how to think effectively even when motivation and meaningfulness are low. People learn how to learn things they would not have chosen to learn. They learn how to follow senseless-sounding directions and rules, fill out meaningless forms, comprehend and reason about uninteresting information or subject matter, and compose symposium discussions when tired. School, job, social relations, and other aspects of everyday life often demand cognitive activities of this dreary ilk, and many young children develop into older children, adolescents, and adults who can meet these demands. That is not much of a grumble to end on, but it is the best I can muster.

COMMENTS ON CASE'S PAPER

Of the three papers presented in this session, Case's is by far the most ambitious and venturesome. The reason is that he actually attempts to sketch out a serious theory of cognitive development. There have been precious few such attempts in the literature, although their number is growing (e.g., Fischer, 1976; Klahr & Wallace, 1976; Schaeffer, 1975). It is an embarrassing fact that the field of cognitive development continues to be much shorter on explicit, testable theories than is the field of adult cognitive psychology, and therefore papers like Case's are particularly welcome. In a sense,what he is trying to do makes it the most "important" paper in this part of the book. At the same time, any such effort is bound to provide an awfully big critical target for a discussant. I have two major criticisms to make of Case's paper. One has to do with the working-memory notion, the other with the four-step developmental sequence proposed for each Piagetian stage.

The first criticism must by now be a familiar one to Case, Pascual—Leone, and their coworkers: How are we to decide, in a consistent, principled fashion, exactly what constitutes an "item" in working memory for any given problem-solving strategy, and hence, how are we to decide exactly how much memory load the use of that strategy imposes? To put it another way, how are we to guarantee good interpsychologist reliability in assigning memory-demand numbers to executive strategies or other cognitive episodes? I can best illustrate this problem by pointing to a few instances in which Case and I did not show high interpsychologist reliability.

Consider first the Noelting task described at the beginning of Case's paper. In that task, children were asked to decide which of two sets of water tumblers and orange juice tumblers would, if mixed together in a large pitcher, taste most strongly of orange juice. The second of Noelting's four proposed strategies for solving this problem involves counting the number of juice tumblers in each set and picking the set that has the greater number. Case says that a child must hold two items in working memory to use this strategy: (1) the number of juice tumblers in one set, and (2) the number of juice tumblers in the other set. The fourth strategy involves picking the set that has the greater excess of juice tumblers over water tumblers, and Case says it has a memory demand of four items. Children of 4 to 5 years of age can use the second strategy, and children of 9 to 10 years of age the fourth. But what if there were five sets of tumblers instead of two? Wouldn't Case have to say that the memory demand for the second strategy is now 5 rather than 2 and thus larger than that of the fourth strategy? And wouldn't that imply, contrary to intuition, that the second strategy ought now to be unusable by some children who can use the fourth strategy, for example, 9-year-olds?

Later in the paper, Case makes similar memory-demand computations on Piaget's stages of development of means-ends schemes during the sensori-motor period. He defines a Stage 4 in which two strategies are acquired. These are referred to as "birelational centration with particularization" and "trirelational centration." Both are assigned a maximum memory demand of four items, but a justification for this assignment is provided only in the case of trirelational centration (Table 2.7). Birelational centration with particularization refers to trying a number of new actions to see if any of them are effective means to a desired end (e.g., trying different ways of removing an obstacle that blocks access to a desired object). I simply cannot figure out why that behavior was assigned a 4-item memory demand. Moreover, I doubt if Case could persuade any randomly chosen group of 10 cognitive psychologists that the number should be 4, or 3, or 5, or any other number.

As must now be apparent, I am very troubled about the working-memory notion. I have the feeling that The Theory of Cognitive Development we are all waiting for will incorporate something akin to this notion. That is, I believe Pascual–Leone, Case, and company are right in emphasizing its importance. But the questions remain. How should working memory and its limits or capacity be conceptualized? Would children really progress from less to more memory-demanding strategies all that much faster if we did their remembering for them, that is, if we dramatically reduced each strategy's memory demands in some fashion? What about all those tests of working memory that Case describes (p. 54)? They obviously ought to correlate very highly with one another, but Case doesn't say whether they do or not. Won't it be even harder to decide that a mental operation is "sufficiently automatized" (p. 62) than to decide how many such operations have to be held in working memory during the execution of a strategy?

The second criticism bears on Case's ideas about developmental sequences. He suggests that all strategy development exhibits a common form. Different developments within the same Piagetian period exhibit this form, and so do developments occurring in different periods. The form is a four-step developmental sequence in which each step has characteristic properties. For example, the first step is always called "isolated centration." In the case of Noelting's task, this first step is the strategy of evaluating each set of tumblers separately. If a set is seen to contain juice, the child says it will taste of juice; if it is not, he says it will not. Notice that I have merely illustrated the meaning of Case's first step; I have not formally defined it or carefully explained what all instances of it have in common. One part of my criticism is that Case has not done this either, for any of his four steps. The other part of the criticism is a fear that he mght have trouble doing so. The various illustrations of each step given in Tables 2.2 through 2.8 do not look as similar in form to me as they apparently do to Case. Compare, for example, the fourth step in the beaker problem of Table 2.3, the sentence repetition problem of Table 2.6, and the vanished object problem of Table 2.8. Furthermore, the developments Case cites may be divisible into steps additional to or even different from those he mentions, and it is also uncertain how well his four-step model would fit developments he does not cite.

Finally, there are several parts of Case's paper that seem particularly interesting and noteworthy. For example, he argues (p. 47) that different types of experience (for instance, simple practice versus modeling) may be differentially effective in promoting strategy acquisition, depending on the child's general developmental level. I was also intrigued with his suggestion (p. 58) that we should try to develop measures of sensorimotor capacity. His proposed explanation (p. 59) of how cognitive operations might become more automatic and hence require less space in working memory is likewise very interesting (cf. Schaeffer, 1975). The same is true of his suggestion (pp. 61–62) that many, if not most, of the tasks the child encounters in everyday life are both familiar and facilitating. They may, therefore, require less working-memory capacity than the typical Piagetian task, which often misleads the child and causes him to use a simpler strategy than the one needed.

COMMENTS ON CHI'S PAPER

Chi's paper presents a refreshingly different slant on memory development than is to be found in the writings of the strategy and metamemory buffs. Early in the paper she offers three reasons why strategy development cannot wholly explain age differences in memory performance. Although I believe that her conclusion is basically correct, I have some problems with the reasoning leading to it. For example, I wonder if there may not be subtle, strategy-like differences in what children and adults actually do when we think both are using the same strategy. As Brown and DeLoache's paper implies, there are many possible variations in the exact nature and manner of execution of the "same" strategy. Conversely, adults may manage to slip bits of strategic activity through the cracks even when you think your task conditions absolutely rule out strategy use. There is, in short, a danger of underestimating, as well as of overestimating, the influence of age differences in strategic activity.

Chi also makes the point that researchers seldom actually test the hypothesis that older subjects' richer knowledge base partly explains their better memory performance. However, I think there are two bodies of developmental research that she does not cite that are relevant to this issue. One is the Piagetian research on the effects of concrete-operational development on memory (Liben, 1977). The other is the work on age changes in constructive memory by Scott Paris and his associates (Paris & Lindauer, 1977). Both lines of research show how developmental changes in knowledge influence what is stored in and retrieved from memory.

It is both impressive and important to demonstrate that children can recall better than adults when the stimulus materials are more familiar to them than to adults. Chi's clever study comparing good child chess players with adult chess novices is such a demonstration. At the same time, such demonstrations cannot rule out the possibility of a capacity increase with increasing age. We could come closer to doing that if we could find stimulus materials that are equally familiar, codable, and so on for both children and adults. Would that really be so difficult? In her research on face recall, Chi could perhaps reduce the mean group difference in speed of naming faces by using subjects older than 5 years as her child group. She might then be able to match child and adult groups on face-naming speed by using only the slower-naming adults and the faster-naming children. It might be illuminating to see if these two groups then differed in memory performance. I also wonder if a correlational approach would help to answer the question. For instance, wouldn't we expect speed of naming to correlate quite highly with span within each age group? Similarly, what if Chi had equated the child and adult groups on chess proficiency instead of deliberately constituting groups in which the children would be more proficient than the adults? Once again, it seems to me that equating child and adult groups on variables of interest is the design of choice.

Chi's metamemory study, using adult subjects of high, medium, and low chess ability, is also thought-provoking. It is possible that the results are partly due to the better chess players' greater ability to recognize the coherent arrays of chess pieces *as* coherent and hence more likely to re recallable, and also to recognize the random arrays *as* random (non-chesslike?) and hence probably harder to recall? It looks that way from Figure 3.7, where the best players predict that they will have *more* difficulty with the random arrays than the poorest players do. Chi's paper raises the interesting question of what makes a person better or worse at predicting retrieval of a particular body of information. I suspect a person will be better at it to the extent that he or she (1) detects whatever structure the information affords (e.g., the possibility of meaningfully linking this item with that), (2) has had experience in retrieving that or similar types of information, and hence is aware of its retrieval demands, (3) actually samples the retrieval test (simulates, tries to recall a few) before venturing a prediction. Apropos of (3), it is interesting that some of Chi's subjects counted on their fingers before making their immediate recall predictions (p. 94).

Chi thinks Brown and I believe that whether a child is accurate at predicting his or her memory performance may depend on how well he or she can predict the usefulness of certain strategic intervention, such as rehearsal. I don't know about Brown, but I personally do not believe that. Although predicting the usefulness of particular strategies is undoubtedly an important part of metamemory, I doubt if it plays a major role in predicting memory performance, at least in the prediction tasks Chi used. For example, it doesn't seem very likely that her child subjects first decided the best way to study and memorize the chessboard arrays and then somehow made their recall predictions as a function of their strategy choice. I also doubt her conclusion that there do not seem to be any substantial developmental differences in children's ability either to identify which strategies would lead to the best memory performance or to generate potential strategies for facilitating retrieval. On the other hand, I like her idea that older subjects may realize better than younger ones how to use such strategies as simulation and quantification to sharpen their evaluation and prediction process. As indicated earlier, some of her subjects apparently tried to do some actual recalling before making their recall predictions. Similarly, Flavell, Friedrichs, and Hoyt (1970) found that second- and fourth-graders, when asked to study items until they were sure they could recall them all without error, quite sensibly practiced the act of recall until they could, in fact, perform perfectly on the recall test. A developing strategy to handle this sort of evaluation and prediction problem may be to browse through the material one needs to learn and remember in order to get an estimate of how much material there is, how much of what there is seems new, unfamiliar, hard to comprehend and remember, and so forth. Moreover, one is likely to assist this estimation by actually trying a little comprehending and remembering, that is, by sampling the retrieval test in advance.

Chi concludes her paper with a highly interesting distinction between general strategies, task-specific strategies, and knowledge-specific strategies. I have two minor disagreements with her classification of particular strategies in terms of these three categories. First, she makes the important suggestion that adults have "a general scheme for adopting or inventing new mnemonics to cope with a task" (p. 94), but she does not classify that scheme as a general strategy; a strategy could hardly be more general, it seems to me. Second, a subject of hers who looked at the remaining chess pieces to see if any of them would cue further recall was said to be using a task-specific strategy. I would rather think of it as a task-specific manifestation of a very general retrieval strategy that the growing child gradually acquires, namely, to make a deliberate search for retrieval cues that may trigger recall of one's retrieval target, if the target will not come to mind spontaneously (Flavell, in press).

Finally, some very brief conjectures about what develops and how. There may be more heterogeneity and diversity in both the "what" and the "how" than current theories can readily handle. The "what", of course, includes things like Case's executive strategies plus all the Piagetian and other knowledge they may generate. I agree with Brown and DeLoache that the "what" also prominently includes metacognition. In addition, however, there are all manner of attitudes, beliefs, aspirations, fantasies, and feelings regarding the social and nonsocial world that also evolve, and I don't see our theories trying to deal with them. The problem is similar for the "how" of development. We all know that the processes producing cognitive-developmental change operate when the child is dealing with some external situation, some input from the outside world. The tables in Case's paper illustrate such situations. However, a great deal of cognitive development may also occur independent of any immediate perceptual input (cf. Klahr & Wallace, 1976, pp. 186–187). It may occur when the child is free to ruminate about remembered or imagined objects and events — when walking to school alone, when lying awake in bed, and so on. Those "out-of-the-blue" questions about the world that children so often surprise us with attest to this sort of underground, non-task-related processing. So how do children develop all those "whats?" Partly by experiences that begin in the inner world, perhaps.

REFERENCES

Fischer, K. W. *A theory of cognitive development: Seven levels of behavior and understanding.* Unpublished paper, University of Denver, 1976.

Flavell, J. H. An analysis of cognitive-developmental sequences. *Genetic Psychology Monographs,* 1972, *86,* 279–350.

Flavell, J. H. Metacognitive development. In J. M. Scandura & C. J. Brainerd (Eds.), *Structural-process theories of complex human behavior.* Leyden, The Netherlands: Sijthoff, in press.

Flavell, J. H., Friedrichs, A. G., & Hoyt, J. D. Developmental changes in memorization processes. *Cognitive Psychology,* 1970, *1,* 324–340.

Klahr, D., & Wallace, J. G. *Cognitive development: An information-processing view.* Hillsdale, N.J.: Lawrence Erlbaum Associates, 1976.

Lempers, J. D., Flavell, E. R., & Flavell, J. H. The development in very young children of tacit knowledge concerning visual perception. *Genetic Psychology Monographs,* 1977, *95,* 3–53.

Leung, E. H. L., & Rheingold, H. L. *The development of pointing as social communication.* Paper presented at the meeting of the Society for Research in Child Development, New Orleans, March, 1977.

Liben, L. S. Piagetian investigations of the development of memory. In R. V. Kail & J. W. Hagen (Eds.), *Perspectives on the development of memory and cognition.* Hillsdale, N.J.: Lawrence Erlbaum Associates, 1977.

Miller, P. H., & Bigi, L. *Children's understanding of attention; or you know I can't hear you when the water's running.* Unpublished paper, University of Michigan, 1976.

Paris, S. G., & Lindauer, B. K. Constructive aspects of children's comprehension and memory. In R. V. Kail & J. W. Hagen (Eds.), *Perspectives on the development of memory and cognition.* Hillsdale, N.J.: Lawrence Erlbaum Associates, 1977.

Schaeffer, B. Skill integration during cognitive development. In A. Kennedy & A. Wilkes (Eds.), *Studies in long-term memory.* New York: Wiley, 1975.

II PROBLEM SOLVING

5

The Origins of Scientific Reasoning

Robert S. Siegler
Carnegie-Mellon University

Children and scientists have many traits in common. Both strive to know as much as possible. Both are eager to acquire new strategies for learning. Both are perennially fascinated by how things work. The comparison can be drawn even more closely. To learn about their worlds, both children and scientists formulate hypotheses, perform experiments, analyze data, and draw conclusions. This "child-as-scientist" metaphor has been advanced previously by Inhelder and Piaget (1958) to describe the reasoning of adolescents. The purpose of the present paper is to describe some of the developments occurring between the ages of 3 and 5 years that make scientific reasoning possible.

The chapter is divided into three sections. The first section reviews the considerable body of knowledge that we have accumulated about 5- to 17-year-olds' scientific reasoning. The second describes a new program of research concerning the origins of such reasoning in early childhood. The third attempts to integrate the new findings with other aspects of our knowledge of 3-, 4-, and 5-year-olds and to address directly the issue of what develops in this age period.

SCIENTIFIC REASONING IN CHILDHOOD AND ADOLESCENCE

To understand any type of development, it is helpful to know where the development is leading. In the case of scientific reasoning, the pioneering work of Inhelder and Piaget (1958) and a rapidly growing empirical literature on the development of formal operational thought provide considerable information about the typical progression in preadolescence and adolescence. This information may be divided into three parts: children's existing knowledge, their ability to acquire new knowledge, and the more basic processes that presumably underlie development in the first two domains.

Children's Existing Knowledge

Much of what we know about children's scientific reasoning derives from Inhelder and Piaget's (1958) description of the formal operations stage. This stage is not limited to scientific reasoning but is closely linked to it. The relationship is reflected both in the tasks that Inhelder and Piaget chose to illustrate formal operations thinking and in the characteristics they ascribed to formal operational thinkers. The tasks are the classics of elementary physics: balance scales, pendulums, projections of shadows, falling bodies, and so on. The intellectual attributes are those of the ideal scientist: the abilities to engage in purely abstract thought, to reason both inductively and deductively, to consider all possible outcomes, and to recognize and admit when the evidence is insufficient to reach any conclusion. There is also an interesting similarity between Piaget's description of the events leading to formal operational thought and Thomas Kuhn's (1962) description of the events leading to new scientific paradigms. In each case, two conditions are thought to be crucial. One is thorough familiarity with the old way of doing things, either concrete operations or the established paradigm. The other is frequent encounters with problems in which the existing framework is clearly inadequate, problems in which the usual approach either yields no answers or incorrect ones. At this point the child (scientist) is thrown into a state of disequilibrium (paradigm clash). Both Kuhn and Piaget indicate that cognitive growth is especially likely in such periods.

In Inhelder and Piaget's account, the development of formal operations begins in the preoperational period, roughly at age 5, continues through the concrete operational period, between ages 7 and 11, and ends in the formal operational period, between ages 12 and 15. On virtually all the 15 formal operations tasks that Inhelder and Piaget present, 5-year-olds are described as having little or no systematic understanding, 10-year-olds are described as understanding the qualitative but not the quantitative relationships, and 15-year-olds are described as understanding both qualitative and quantitative relationships and as having some notion of the relevant theoretical constructs. These levels of performance are ascribed to children's general cognitive developmental stages, which are said to limit the types of relationships that they can understand.

Considerable empirical work has been undertaken since 1958 to replicate Inhelder and Piaget's findings using more carefully standardized techniques, conventional statistical procedures, larger and more representative samples, and children of a variety of nationalities. The results have been quite uniform. As Inhelder and Piaget reported, there is steady improvement in scientific reasoning throughout childhood and adolescence (Dale, 1970; Dulit, 1972; Jackson, 1965; Lovell, 1961). Also as they suggested, there is a fairly high degree of consistency in the level of performance across different tasks (Jackson, 1965; Lee, 1971; Lovell, 1961). Unlike Inhelder and Piaget's reports, however, subsequent investigators have found that only a minority of adolescents, even 16- and 17-year-olds perform at the highest levels on the formal operations tasks (Dale, 1970; Lee, 1971; Lovell, 1961; Martorano, 1977; Tomlinson–Keasey, 1972). In response to these findings, Piaget (1972) has suggested that formal operations competence may be manifested only in the area of an adolescent's greatest interest, not necessarily scientific reasoning, and has also conceded that the protocols cited in the Inhelder and Piaget (1958) book were chosen for being illustrative of certain aspects of formal operations structures, rather than for being representative of adolescents' reasoning.

There is an additional problem common to both Inhelder and Piaget's original studies and to the subsequent ones. In virtually all cases, investigators have relied on clinically derived ratings of children's stage of reasoning as the primary index of knowledge. This practice has several shortcomings, both conceptual and methodological. Conceptually, it is difficult to infer from a stage classification just what a child knows; we lack detailed knowledge of what aspects of the child's performance caused him to be assigned to the particular stage. Methodologically, the stage classifications raise serious questions of intra- and interexperiment reliability. The intraexperiment reliability issue arises because in many studies only one rater is used to decide what stage a child is in. The problem could be dealt with relatively easily by using several raters and correlating their judgments, but often even this minimal step is not taken. More complex is the issue of interexperiment reliability. Even if interrater reliability within a given experiment is obtained, there is still the problem that different laboratories may develop different standards for judging when a child is in a particular stage. Thus, within each research team there may be high reliability of stage ratings, but the standards for placing a child in Stage I or II or III may be different among different research teams (cf. Neimark, 1975). In an effort to overcome these conceptual and methodological problems, some investigators have argued in favor of using the number of correct answers as the sole dependent measure, totally bypassing the stage classifications (Brainerd, 1971, 1977). This approach has the advantage of objectivity and easily attainable reliability, but it is even less helpful than the stage classifications in revealing exactly what children know.

What seems needed to assess children's knowledge, then, is a methodology that is both reliable and revealing. In several recent papers, I have proposed a methodological approach aimed at meeting these objectives (Siegler, 1976, 1978; Klahr & Siegler, 1978; Siegler & Vago, in press). The approach is based on two assumptions. One is that children's problem-solving strategies are rule-governed, with the rules progressing from less sophisticated to more sophisticated with age. The second is that a powerful means of validating hypothesized rule progressions is to create problem sets that yield sharply differing patterns of correct answers and errors depending on what rule is being used. The way in which this system works is best illustrated by an example. In an earlier paper (Siegler, 1976), I applied the methodology to a variant of Inhelder and Piaget's balance scale problem. The apparatus that was used is shown in Fig. 5.1A. On each side of the fulcrum were four equally spaced pegs on which metal weights could be placed; the arm of the balance could rotate left or right or remain level depending on how the weights were arranged. The child's task was to predict

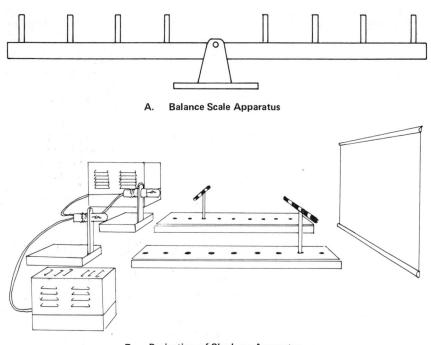

A.   Balance Scale Apparatus

B.   Projection of Shadows Apparatus

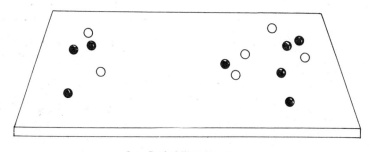

C.   Probability Apparatus

FIG. 5.1   Problems used in Experiment 1.

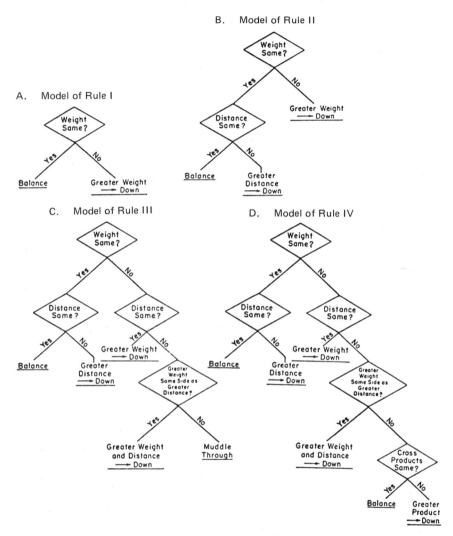

FIG. 5.2   Decision tree model of rules for performing balance scale task.

which (if either) side would go down if a lever, which held the scale motionless, were released.

A rational task analysis of the problem, Inhelder and Piaget's (1958) empirical work, and my own pilot studies suggested that the different types of knowledge that children might have about the balance scale could be represented in terms of four rule models (Fig. 5.2). A child using Rule I considers only the numbers of weights on each side of the fulcrum: If they are the same, the child predicts that the scale will balance, otherwise he predicts that the side with the greater number will go down. For a child using Rule II, a difference in weight still is conclusive, but if weight is equal on the two sides, then the distance dimension is also considered. A child using Rule III considers both weight and distance in all cases. If both dimensions are equal, the child predicts that the scale will balance; if only one dimension is equal, then the other one determines the outcome; if both are unequal and one side has the greater value on each of them, then that side will go down. However, in a situation in which one side has the greater weight and the other has the weights farther from the fulcrum, a Rule III child does not have a consistent way to resolve the conflict. Therefore, he "muddles through" or guesses. Finally, Rule IV represents mature knowledge of the task: The child computes the torques on each side by multiplying the amounts of weight on each peg by the peg's ordinal distance from the fulcrum (the pegs are equidistant from one another, so that the third peg from the fulcrum is three times as far away as the first one), and then compares the sums of the products on the two sides. Thus, if there were five weights on the third peg to the left of the fulcrum and four weights on the fourth peg to the right, $5 \times 3 = 15; 4 \times 4 = 16; 15 < 16;$ so the right side would go down.

But how could we determine whether children actually used these rules? This is where the rule assessment methodology came in. It was possible to establish which — if any — of the four rules accurately described a child's knowledge by examining his pattern of predictions for the following six types of problems (see Table 5.1 for an example of each type):

1. Balance problems, with the same configuration of weights on pegs on each side of the fulcrum.

2. Weight problems, with unequal amounts of weight equidistant from the fulcrum.

3. Distance problems, with equal amounts of weight different distances from the fulcrum.

4. Conflict—weight problems, with more weight on one side and more "distance" (i.e., occupied pegs farther from the fulcrum) on the other, and the configuration arranged so that the side with more weight goes down.

5. Conflict—distance problems, similar to conflict—weight except that the side with greater distance goes down.

6. Conflict—balance problems, like other conflict problems, except that the scale remains balanced.

Children whose knowledge corresponded to the different rules would display dramatically different patterns of predictions on the six types of problems (Table 5.1). Those using Rule I would consistently make correct predictions on balance, weight, and conflict—weight problems, and they would never be correct on the three other problem-types. Children using Rule II would behave similarly, except that they would solve distance problems. Those following Rule III would consistently make accurate predictions on weight, balance, and distance problems

TABLE 5.1
Predictions for Percentage of Correct Answers and Error
Patterns for Children Using Different Rules

Problem–Type	Rule			
	I	II	III	IV
Balance	100	100	100	100
Weight	100	100	100	100
Distance	0 (Should say "Balance")	100	100	100
Conflict–Weight	100	100	33 (Chance Responding)	100
Conflict–Distance	0 (Should say "Right Down")	0 (Should say "Right Down")	33 (Chance Responding)	100
Conflict–Balance	0 (Should say "Right Down")	0 (Should say "Right Down")	33 (Chance Responding)	100

and would perform at a chance level on all conflict items. Those using Rule IV
would solve all problems of all types.

To the extent that there was a correlation between children's ages and the
rules that best represented their knowledge, a clear developmental pattern on
each problem-type was anticipated (Table 5.1). Most interesting was the predicted developmental decrement in performance on conflict–weight problems.
Younger children, using Rules I and II, were expected to get these problems
right consistently, whereas older children, using Rule III, were expected to
"muddle through" on them and to be correct only one third of the time.
Another prediction of the rule models was that performance on distance
problems would show the most dramatic improvement with age, from 0%

correct for those who used Rule I to 100% correct for those using all subsequent rules. Finally, for balance and for weight problems, the rule models predicted consistently correct responding among children of all ages, since all four rules would solve such problems.

These predictions were made at the group level. The rule models also allowed unambiguous prediction of individual performance. That is, the statement that a child was using Rule I or Rule II or Rule IV indicated which one of the three possible predictions he would make on each problem — right side down, left side down, or balance. Given the 24-item posttest (four items from each of the six problem-types) that I have usually used, this meant that there were 3^{24} distinct possible patterns of responses; of these, less than one-millionth fit the criterion for rule usage that was adopted (20 of 24 responses conforming to a rule). Thus, the likelihood that a random responder would be misclassified as using a rule was almost nonexistent.

As mentioned earlier, this methodology was applied to Inhelder and Piaget's balance scale problem; 5-, 9-, 13-, and 17-year-olds who attended a girls' upper-middle-class private school in Pittsburgh were presented the various problems. It was found that the rule models accurately characterized the predictions of 107 of the 120 children — 89%. This percentage ranged from 80% of the 5-year-olds to 100% of the 17-year-olds. The rule models were successful in characterizing both the children's spontaneous performance and their performance following instruction. The children's explanations of how they made their choices closely followed their predictions; more than 90% of the children were classified as using the same rule on the two measures by "blind" raters. The expectations at the group level were also supported. Performance on conflict—weight problems declined from 89% correct among the 5-year-olds to 51% correct among the 17-year-olds. Correct answers improved most dramatically on the distance problems, from 9% correct among 5-year-olds to 88% correct among 9-year-olds and 100% correct among 13- and 17-year-olds. Finally, performance was consistently high on weight and balance problems, ranging from 88% to 100% correct among the various age groups. Thus, the results provided considerable support both for the particular rule models as characterizations of children's knowledge about the balance scale and for the general rule assessment methodology as a psychometric technique for indicating what children know.

Ability to Acquire New Knowledge

As noted above, two children with similar initial knowledge may be differentially able to acquire new knowledge. Inhelder and Piaget deemphasized this distinction, strongly implying that the same stage considerations that governed existing knowledge determined ability to learn. Subsequent research, however, suggests that the two domains are pragmatically as well as logically distinct. In contrast to the finding that even 16- and 17-year-olds often do not know how to solve

formal scientific problems spontaneously, much younger
found able to *learn* to solve them. Children ranging in age
have learned to solve the flexibility of rods problem (Case,
problem (Kuhn & Angelev, 1976; Siegler, Liebert, & Lieb
cals problem (Barratt, 1975; Kuhn & Angelev, 1976; Siegler & Liebert,
and the law of floating bodies problem (Brainerd & Allen, 1971). These studies
suggest that there is a substantial difference between what children typically
know and what they are capable of learning.

The studies do not mean, however, that ability to learn is independent of
chronological age. On the contrary, it has been found that older children learn
from some treatments that do not benefit younger ones at all (Siegler & Liebert,
1975), that some treatments benefit older children more than younger ones
(Brainerd & Allen, 1971), and that virtually all older children benefit from
some treatments that benefit only younger children with special personality
characteristics (Case, 1974).

A basic question suggested by these findings is whether older children's
superior learning reflects more advanced initial knowledge about the various
tasks or whether it reflects a more general learning ability. The rule assessment
methodology described above seemed to provide a tool for investigating this
issue. In Siegler (1976; Experiment 2), 5-year-olds and 8-year-olds were equated
on a pretest as being at the Rule I level; their pretest performance was comparable on all problem-types. Then the children were exposed to one of three
conditions: a control condition, in which they were presented problems solvable
by Rule I; a distance-training condition, in which problems one rule beyond
their existing levels were presented; and a conflict-training condition, in which
conflict problems two or more rules beyond their level were presented. Finally,
they were given the same type of posttest as previously.

The most interesting results of the experiment concerned reactions to experience with conflict problems: Given such problems, the older children most
often advanced to Rule III, whereas not one younger child advanced beyond
Rule I. Thus, at least in this condition, older and younger children with similar
initial knowledge about the task derived very different lessons from the same
experience.

Explaining Developmental Differences: Basic Psychological Processes

There can be little doubt that both children's existing knowledge and their
ability to acquire new knowledge improve substantially with age. The question
is how to explain these developmental changes. A number of different strategies
have been used. Inhelder and Piaget (1958) analyzed the protocols of their
preadolescent and adolescent subjects and argued that the protocols indicated
that a lack of appropriate logical structures was what prevented young children
from reasoning in a formal scientific manner. Unfortunately, the data they used

to infer the existence and importance of these logical structures were the same data that the logical structures were said to explain. Case (1974) took the approach that there were three prerequisites for solving formal operations problems: sufficient memorial capacity (M-space), exposure to situations that would provoke cognitive conflict, and the personality trait of field independence. He demonstrated that children lacking any one of these prerequisites often failed to master a formal operations problem (the flexibility of rods problem), whereas those possessing all three almost always succeeded. Yet a third approach was taken by Brainerd (1976), who assessed a variety of proposed explanations for conservation (reversibility, addition–subtraction, compensation, and identity), and found that prior knowledge of only one — reversibility — was predictive of the ability to learn from a conservation-training technique.

The approach emphasized in this chapter is similar to those described earlier in that it involves a search for limits and prerequisites: What do younger children not have (or what do they not know) that older children do have (or know) and that is necessary to learn? Younger children might know less and be less able to learn because their short-term memory capacity is not as great, because their encoding of stimuli is incomplete or inaccurate, because they lack helpful memorial strategies, because they lack the verbal skills to understand the instructions, and so on. Illustrating this approach, in the Siegler (1976) paper, I suggested that the reason 8-year-olds were able to benefit from the conflict-problem training that did not help 5-year-olds was that they encoded the balance-scale configuration more accurately. That is, older children were thought able to benefit because they encoded both weight and distance dimensions, whereas younger children were thought unable to benefit because they encoded only weight. Evidence was found that (1) as measured by performance on an independent assessment instrument, older children indeed did encode both weight and distance, whereas younger children encoded only weight; (2) through instruction, it was possible to change the younger children's encoding so that they, like the older children, encoded both dimensions; and (3) when both age groups encoded distance as well as weight, both were able to benefit from the experience with conflict problems that had previously benefited only the older children. Thus, it was concluded that differential encoding explained much of the differential ability of older and younger children to learn.

THE ORIGINS OF SCIENTIFIC REASONING

As described in the foregoing section, the scientific reasoning of children 5 years old and older has been studied fairly extensively. By contrast, virtually nothing is known about the scientific reasoning of 3- and 4-year-olds. Thus, one purpose of the present investigation was simply to extend our knowledge to a younger age group than had been previously studied.

There was also a more theoretical reason to expect that studying 3- and 4-year-olds would be valuable. This arose from previous studies of rule-governedness among 5- to 17-year-olds. Children as young as 5 years have been found to perform in a rule-governed fashion on balance scale, projection of shadows, fullness of a water jar, and probability concept tasks (Klahr & Siegler, 1978; Siegler, 1976; in press; Siegler & Vago, in press). The particular rules that children use change substantially with age, but in terms of percentage of children classified as using a rule, degree of adherence to (absence of exceptions from) the rules, and agreement between explanations and predictive performance, there is little change from age 5 years to adulthood. The theoretically interesting question is whether performance on scientific reasoning problems is rule-governed from very early in life, or whether rule-governedness as such develops, with the development being virtually complete by age 5 years.

This question raises the more basic issue of what it means to say that someone is using a rule. In one sense, rules can be thought of as a means of summarizing data, as when a set of responses is symbolized by a single verbal sentence, a mathematical equation, a production system, or some other formalism. Within this usage it makes little sense to inquire if rule-governedness develops, because the rules are merely representations (they are merely in the experimenter's head); any failure of the rules to fit the particular responses tells us only that the representation is inadequate. An alternative approach, however, is that the rule statements not only summarize data but also have some correspondence to the way in which the data were generated (they are in the subject's head as well as the experimenter's). Consider Carpenter and Just's (1975) description of their model of sentence verification:

> The proposed model postulates that sentences and pictures are represented in abstract propositional forms. To verify the sentence, the constituents in the two representations are compared — tested for identity at an abstract level. The number of operations in the comparison process is the primary determinant of the verification latency [p. 47].

Such models (rule systems) clearly act as both summarizations of data and theories of how the data came to be. They can be stated at the level of flow diagrams, as in Carpenter and Just's model; computer simulations, as in Newell and Simon's (1972) and Klahr and Wallace's (1976) models; verbal statements, as in Inhelder and Piaget's (1958) models; or decision trees, as in the present models. In all cases, the rule systems function as theories of how responses were generated as well as descriptions of what happened.

Closely related to the question of what it means to say that someone uses a rule is the question of what it means to say that someone is not using a rule. This statement can never be made with absolute certainty, for even if no pattern is apparent in a series of responses, there is always the possibility that one exists.

For example, a child might always predict which side of the balance scale would go down on the basis of which side had an even number of weights; unless one knew what to look for, the responses would not show any obvious pattern, but they would be conforming to a rule. Nonetheless, at least in fairly structured situations, it is possible to check whether any straightforward rule is being used. On the balance scale task, we can check whether a child is consistently predicting that the side with greater weight will go down, the side with less weight will go down, the side with the weights farther from the fulcrum will go down, the side with the weights nearer to the fulcrum will go down, one or the other side will always go down, the sides will alternate in going down, the side with a particular number of weights will always go down, and so on.

Of course, it could be argued that the rules being used may be more complex than these simple formulas. There are two replies to this argument, one specific to the present investigation, the other more general. The specific argument derives from our observation that 5-year-olds almost always rely on very simple rules, such as that the side with more weights will always go down. Given the simplicity of the formulas used by 5-year-olds, it seems unlikely that 3- and 4-year-olds would use much more complex rules. The general argument is that if a given age group, or even a sizable minority within an age group, adopted a particular task-related formula, however complex or nonintuitive, they would answer consistently correctly (consistently quickly) on some problems and consistently incorrectly (consistently slowly) on others. This would show up in any summary of the data that was organized by the individual item. Such unanticipated rules have in fact been discovered in past uses of the rule assessment methodology (cf. Siegler & Vago, in press).

It might still be argued that some children may use rules that are unrelated to the experimenter's organization and also unrelated to the rules used by other children, or that some children may shift from rule to rule from one problem to the next. In an epistemological sense, this may well be reasonable; all responses and all response patterns must be generated somehow, after all. However, it is difficult to see the utility of speaking of rule usage in such situations when we cannot even distinguish the patterns of responses from those likely to be produced by a random process.

In sum, it seemed at least potentially profitable to investigate very young children's scientific reasoning. The work that I have done can be organized into three domains, paralleling the work done previously with older children: existing knowledge, ability to acquire new knowledge, and more basic processes that might underlie developmental differences in the first two domains.

Experiment 1: Young Children's Existing Knowledge

The first study involving 3- and 4-year-olds was part of a larger effort to investigate the stability of rule usage over time and over tasks. In this study, children of six ages — 3, 4, 5, 9, 13, and 17 years — were presented three problems each —

the balance scale, projection of shadows, and probability tasks – on each of two occasions separated in time by one month. The particular three tasks were chosen because all had been used previously by Inhelder and Piaget (1958) as indexes of formal operations reasoning, because all were based on the concept of proportionality, and because all seemed likely to have parallel rule systems. The present focus is on the performance of 3-, 4-, and 5-year-olds on these tasks.

Method

Participants.   The children were 10 3-year-olds ($\overline{CA}$ = 41 months, σ = 2.91), 10 4-year-olds ($\overline{CA}$ = 52 months, σ = 3.63) and 10 5-year-olds ($\overline{CA}$ = 63 months; σ = 3.62). Half of the children of each age were girls and half were boys. Like all of the participants in this series of experiments, they were selected randomly from a middle-class preschool. The experimenter, a 23-year-old white female research assistant, also was constant throughout the series of experiments.[1]

Tasks.   The balance scale task was the same one described in Siegler (1976) and depicted in Fig. 5.1A. It involved putting a particular number of metal disks on one of the pegs on each side of the balance scale's fulcrum, and asking the child, "What would happen if I lifted this lever? Would this side go down, or would this side go down, would it stay the same as it is now [balance] "?

The projection of shadows task (Fig. 5.1B) involved two 25-watt point light sources, two wooden bases each having eight holes spaced at 2-in. intervals, a projection screen, and a number of T-shaped bars. These bars had identical vertical components (4 in. high), but their horizontal portions varied in length from 1 in. to 8 in. The horizontal span was denoted by alternating 1-in. segments of red and blue tape wrapped around the metal bar; thus, a 4-unit bar would have a blue segment, a red segment, another blue segment, and another red segment (or the reverse). On each problem, children saw a T bar in a hole in each of the two bases and were asked the question, "If I turned on these lights, which side would cast a longer shadow [motioning to indicate that the question referred to the horizontal span] – this side, this side, or would the shadows be just as long?"

Finally, the probability task, modeled after that of Piaget and Inhelder (1951), involved two piles of marbles, some red ones and some blue ones in each pile (Fig. 5.1C). The total number of marbles in each pile never exceeded 10. On each problem, children were asked, "Which pile would you want to choose

---

[1]Due to the large number of 3- and 4-year-olds participating in this series of experiments and the small size of nursery school populations, it was necessary to include children from four different schools in the study. The children in Experiment 1 were from one school, the children in Experiment 2A were from a second, those in Experiments 2B and 3A were from a third, and those in Experiments 3B and 3C were from a fourth. There were no appreciable differences among the schools in terms of social class or racial and sexual composition.

from if you wanted a red (blue) marble and had to choose with your eyes closed – would you rather choose from this pile, from this pile, or wouldn't it matter?"

Rule Models and Problem Types. The rule models for children's performance on the balance scale task and the problem-types used to assess them have been described. The rule of greatest importance for the present study was Rule I, involving sole reliance on a single dimension. In the case of the balance scale, a child using Rule I bases all predictions on the weight dimension. If one side has more weight, that side will go down. If the two sides have equal weight, then the scale will balance. In terms of the various problem-types, this model implies perfect performance on balance, weight, and conflict—weight problems and consistently incorrect performance on distance, conflict—distance, and conflict—balance problems (Table 5.1).

The problem-types and rules for performing the projection of shadows task were exactly analogous to the balance scale rules and problem types; the only difference was that span of the bar and distance from the light source were the relevant dimensions, rather than weight on a side and distance from the fulcrum. Rule I involved total reliance on the relative spans of the bars. If one bar had a longer span, then it would cast the longer shadow; if the spans were equal, then the shadows would be equal. This rule would always solve the three types of problems analogous to balance, weight, and conflict—weight problems, and it would always err on the three types analogous to distance, conflict—distance, and conflict—balance problems.

The relationship of the probability concept task to the other two problems was superficially more complex but actually quite similar. Like the balance scale and shadows tasks, the probability task was conceptualized as having two important dimensions – the number of marbles of the desired color and the number of marbles of the undesired color. Also, as in the other tasks, Rule I involved basing judgments entirely on the states of one dimension – in this case, the number of marbles of the desired color – so that the collection with the greater number of marbles of the desired color would be preferred, unless the numbers were equal, in which case the child would say that the two piles were equivalent. However, for reasons somewhat outside the scope of the present investigation (cf. Siegler, in press), the problem types used were somewhat different from those in the other tasks. The importance for the present investigation is that on the probability task, children using Rule I always would be expected to solve two types of problems (for the sake of brevity call them types *A* and *C*) in which judgments based solely on the number of desired-colored marbles would always be correct, and always to err on four problem-types (*B*, *D*, *E*, and *F*) where this strategy would always lead to the wrong answer.

Assessment Instruments. Children were presented parallel assessment instruments for the balance scale, shadows, and probability tasks. On each instrument there were 24 items, four each of the six problem-types. The items were ordered within each test by means of stratified random sampling, so that one item of each type was included in the first six items, one in the next six items, and so on. The tests were also parallel in the sense that all items on them could be answered in one of three ways: Side A was the right answer, Side B was the right answer, or Sides A and B were equivalent. In this regard, it should be noted that Rule I predicted not only whether answers would be correct or incorrect on the given posttest items but which one of the three possible answers would be chosen. Thus, the probability that a random responder would meet the criterion for using Rule I remained constant across the three tasks (5×10^{-7}).

Procedure.   Children were taken individually by the experimenter from their classrooms to a vacant room in their school on each of three successive days. Each time, they were told they would be playing a game and given instructions such as the following (for the projection of shadows task).

> Today we're going to be playing a game with these pieces of wood, these colored bars, this screen, and these lights. I'm going to be putting the colored bars in these holes in different ways, and I'm going to ask you whether you think the bar on this side would have a longer shadow if the light were on (indicating horizontal length) or whether the bar on this side would have a longer shadow, or whether the two shadows would be just as long as each other. Now the light is not really going to be on, but I want you to tell me what would happen if we turned the light on.

At this point, the experimenter turned on one of the point light sources so that the child could see that they indeed worked. Then the 24-item test was presented. On each item, the experimenter would set up the problem, ask the child what he thought would happen, and the child would make his prediction. At no time was feedback provided; if children ever asked how they were doing, they were simply told "fine." The next day the child was presented one of the two remaining tasks; the third day he was presented the final one. The order of presentation was randomized within age groups so that three children of each age did each task first, three did it second, and three did it third. The tenth child of each age was arbitrarily assigned to orders so that for the sample as a whole, task order was balanced.

A month later the experimenter returned to the school and repeated the procedure, again testing each child on the three tasks on three successive days.

Results

In this section, I will put the cart before the horse, describing the conclusions before the results. The purpose of this ordering should soon become clear.

The data appeared to indicate that rule usage as such undergoes substantial development between ages 3 and 5 years, or at least that use of Rule I on these

TABLE 5.2
Derivations of Predictions for Balance Scale Task

1. The Rule I and random response models make the following predictions for the percentage of correct answers on the six problem types:

				Problem type			
	B	W	D	CW	CD	CB	Overall
Rule I Model	100	100	0	100	0	0	50
Random Model	33	33	33	33	33	33	33

2. If we assume that all 5-year-olds always use Rule I, half of 4-year-olds use Rule I and half respond randomly, and all 3-year-olds respond randomly, then:

A. Since all 5-year-olds use Rule I; and
Since Rule I solves 50% of problems;
∴ Five-year-olds will solve 50% of problems.

B. Since half of 4-year-olds use Rule I, which solves 50% of problems; and
Since half of 4-year-olds use the random model, which solves 33%;
∴ Four-year-olds will solve (50 + 33)/2 = 42% of problems.

C. Since all 3-year-olds use the random model; and
Since the random model solves 33% of problems;
∴ Three-year-olds will solve 33% of problems.

D. Since half of 3-, 4-, and 5-year-olds use Rule I, which solves balance, weight, and
conflict−weight problems 100% of the time; and
Since the other half use the random model, which solves them 33% of the time;
∴ Balance, weight, and conflict−weight problems should each be solved 67% of the time.

E. Since half of the children use Rule I, which solves distance, conflict−distance, and
conflict−balance problems 0% of the time; and
Since the other half use the random model, which solves them 33% of the time;
∴ Distance, conflict−distance, and conflict−balance problems should each be solved
(0 + 33)/2 = 17% of the time.

F. Since 5-year-olds always use Rule I, which solves some types of problems 0% of the
time and others 100% of the time; and
Since 3-year-olds always use the random model, which solves all types of problems
33% of the time:
∴ Five-year-olds' performance on the different problem types should show a much
greater range (0% to 100%) than that of 3-year-olds (33% to 33%).

G. Since 5-year-olds always use Rule I, which correctly answers all balance, weight, and
conflict−weight items 100% of the time; and
Since 3-year-olds always use the random model, which correctly answers all balance,
weight, and conflict−weight items 33% of the time;
∴ Performance on each of the 12 balance, weight, and conflict−weight problems
should show developmental improvements.

H. Since 5-year-olds always use Rule I, which correctly answers all distance, conflict−
distance, and conflict−balance items 0% of the time; and
Since 3-year-olds always use the random model, which correctly answers all distance,
conflict−distance, and conflict−balance items 33% of the time;
∴ Performance on each of the 12 distance, conflict−distance, and conflict−balance
items should show developmental decrements.

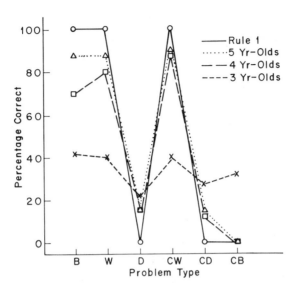

FIG. 5.3   Spontaneous performance – balance scale task.

three tasks undergoes substantial development in this period. Virtually all 5-year-olds seemed to use Rule I, approximately half of the 4-year-olds did, and virtually none of the 3-year-olds did. Both the statement that some children used a particular rule to perform a task and the statement that other children did not use any rule are probably controversial. Therefore, to provide evidence for the utility of such statements, I will take them to their logical extremes. Assume that any child who is said to follow Rule I will conform to it on all 24 predictions. Assume further that any child who is said to be using no rule performs entirely randomly, solving each of the 24 three-choice items at exactly the chance level, 33%. From these two assumptions, we can derive a wide range of predictions not only of the relative success of different age groups, relative difficulty of problem-types, and so on but of the *absolute* levels of performance as well. To the extent that these absolute predictions fit the data, they should provide convincing evidence for the claims about rule-governedness. This should be especially true given the scarcity of predictions about the absolute level of almost anything in the area of cognitive development.

Balance Scale Task.   The general model described earlier makes a number of specific predictions concerning performance on the balance scale task; the derivations of these predictions are shown in Table 5.2. First, consider the overall level of performance for each age group. Rule I solves 50% of the problems, and the random level is 33% correct. If all the 5-year-olds use Rule I, they should be correct on 50% of the problems; if half of the 4-year-olds use Rule I and half perform randomly, they should be correct on 42% of the problems; if all the 3-year-olds answer at random, they should be correct 33% of the time.

Next, consider the level of performance on the different problem-types. If balance, weight, and conflict—weight problems are (1) always answered correctly by all 5-year-olds and by half of the 4-year-olds, as implied by the Rule I model, and (2) answered correctly 33% of the time by the other half of the 4-year-olds and by all of the 3-year-olds, as implied by the random model, the overall percentage correct on such problems should be 67%. Analogously, if distance, conflict—distance, and conflict—balance problems are (1) always answered incorrectly by all 5-year-olds and half of the 4-year-olds, and (2) answered correctly 33% of the time by the remaining 4-year-olds and all of the 3-year-olds, then the overall percentage correct for these problem-types should be 17%.

Now consider the range of performance on the different problem-types: It should be considerably more discrepant for 5-year-olds, varying from 0% to 100% correct, than for 3-year-olds, clustering around 33% correct.

Finally, consider the developmental patterns for individual test items. There should be developmental improvements (from chance to above chance) on all 12 balance, weight, and conflict—weight items and developmental decrements (from chance to below chance) on all 12 distance, conflict—distance, and conflict—balance problems.

How well did the data fit this model? A 3 (age: 3, 4, or 5 years) x 6 (problem-type: balance, weight, distance, conflict—weight, conflict—distance, or conflict—balance) analysis of variance of performance on the first occasion (Fig. 5.3) revealed significant main effects for age, $F(2,27) = 8.48$, and for problem-type, $F(5,135) = 31.81$, and a significant interaction between the two variables, $F(10,135) = 4.92$. (Unless otherwise stated, all effects are significant beyond the .01 level.) As shown in Fig. 5.3, the percentage of correct answers improved from 34% for 3-year-olds to 44% for 4-year-olds, to 49% for 5-year-olds (predicted = 33%, 42%, and 50%). Performance on balance, weight, and conflict—weight problems ranged from 67% to 73% correct (predicted = 67%), whereas performance on distance, conflict—distance, and conflict—balance problems ranged from 11% to 18% correct (predicted = 17%). Five-year-olds' predictions ranged from 0% to 90% correct on the different problem-types (predicted = 0% to 100%); 3-year-olds' performance ranged from 23% to 40% (predicted = 33%). Performance on all 12 problems on which developmental increments were expected showed the predicted increments, and performance on 10 of the 12 problems on which developmental decrements were expected showed the expected decrements.

Individual performance also closely followed the model. Among the 10 children of each age, eight 5-year-olds, six 4-year-olds, and no 3-year-olds adhered to Rule I on at least 20 of 24 responses.

Similar analyses were undertaken of performance on the second occasion, one month after the first. The age-by-problem-type analysis of variance revealed significant main effects for age, $F(2,27) = 13.57$, and for problem-type $F(5,135) = 24.27$, and a significant interaction between age and problem-type $F(10,135)$

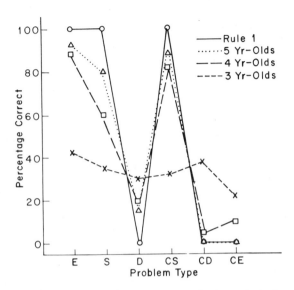

FIG. 5.4   Spontaneous performance — projection of shadows task.

= 4.81. The details of the fit of the data to the predictions will not be described at length, but in general they were very similar to the fit for the first occasion. In terms of individual children, nine of the 10 5-year-olds, seven of the 10 4-year-olds, and none of the 10 3-year-olds used Rule I.

Projection of Shadows Task.   The model made predictions for the shadows task that were exactly analogous to those for the balance scale, except for the names of the problem-types. An age-by-problem-type analysis of variance on the number of correct answers on the first occasion revealed significant main effects for age, $F(2,27) = 9.39$, and for problem-type, $F(5,135) = 29.07$, and a significant age-by-problem-type interaction, $F(10,135) = 5.79$. As shown in Fig. 5.4, the percentage of correct answers improved from 33% for 3-year-olds to 44% for 4-year-olds, to 48% for 5-year-olds (expected = 33%, 42%, and 50%). On the three problem-types for which 67% correct answers were expected, performance ranged from 63% to 74% correct, whereas on the three types on which 17% correct answers were expected, performance ranged from 11% to 22% correct. As on the balance scale, performance was far more diverse for the 5-year-olds, ranging from 0% to 92%, than for the 3-year-olds, ranging from 23% to 40%. Finally, developmental increments were again present on all 12 items for which they were anticipated, whereas the expected decrements were present on 10 of 12 items for which decrements were anticipated, with no changes on the other two items. In terms of individual children, nine of the 10 5-year-olds used Rule I on the first occasion compared to four of the 10 4-year-olds and none of the 10 3-year-olds.

The age-by-problem-type analysis of variance for the second occasion revealed significant main effects for age, $F(2,27) = 7.68$, and for problem-type, $F(5,135) = 37.29$, and a significant interaction between age and problem-type, $F(10,135) = 4.29$. Each age group differed reliably from the other two, and all three of the problem-types solvable by Rule I were solved more often than any of the other three. The interaction once more was due to the pattern on the different problem-types diverging far more for the 5-year-olds (0% to 90%) than for 3-year-olds (23% to 51%). On the individual level, nine of the 10 5-year-olds, seven of the 10 4-year-olds, and two of the 10 3-year-olds conformed to Rule I.

Probability Concept Task.   The predictions of the model were somewhat different for the probability concept task because Rule I would solve two rather than three of the six problem-types. Thus, no differences in percentage of correct answers among the different age groups were expected because the chance and Rule I levels of correct performance were both 33%. As previously, however, 67% correct performance was expected on the two types of problems that Rule I would solve (*A* and *C* of Fig. 5.5), and 17% correct performance was expected on the other types, where Rule I would err. Also as previously, an interactive pattern was expected, with 5-year-olds showing much more diverse performance on different types of problems than did 3-year-olds.

The usual analysis of variance revealed a significant main effect for problem-type, $F(5,135) = 9.25$, and a significant age-by-problem-type interaction, $F(10,135) = 1.91$, $p < 0.05$. As expected the effect for age did not approach significance ($F < 2$). On the two problem types where 67% correct answers were expected, performance was at 75% and 70%; on the four where 17% correct performance was expected, the percentage correct ranged from 21% to 38%. The 5-year-olds' performance on the different problem-types ranged from 0% to 88% correct, and the 3-year-olds' ranged from 38% to 60% correct.[2] Performance improved developmentally on all eight of the items on which increments were expected (the problems that Rule I would solve), and it decreased on 14 of the 16 items on which developmental decrements were expected (the problems

---

[2]The model's predictions concerning percentage of correct answers by 3-year-olds and percentage correct on the different problem types were clearly inaccurate on the probability task. There was a simple explanation for this inaccuracy, having to do with children's reluctance to say "It doesn't matter" and the particular problem types that were used. It turned out that "Doesn't matter" was never the correct answer on the problems that were presented and that the majority of 3-year-olds virtually never said "It doesn't matter"; four of the 10 3-year-olds never used the response, two others used it only once, and one other only twice, among their 48 responses (two occasions by 24 items each). The effect of this coincidence between the children's response bias and the makeup of the problem set was to shift the items from three-choice problems, with a 33% correct chance level, to two-choice problems, with a 50% correct chance level.

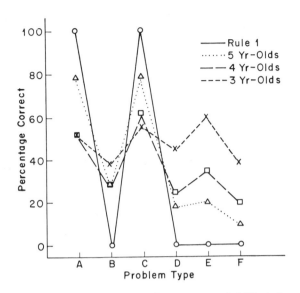

FIG. 5.5   Sponstaneous performance – probability task.

where Rule I would err). At the level of individuals, six of the 10 5-year-olds, two of the 10 4-year-olds, and none of the 10 3-year-olds conformed to Rule I.

The analysis of variance of correct answers on the second occasion again revealed a significant main effect for problem-type, $(F(5,135) = 13.77$, a significant problem-type-by-age interaction, $F(10,135) = 6.49$, and no significant main effect for age $(F < 2)$. The pattern was similar to that observed on the first occasion. Among the 10 children of each age, five 5-year-olds, three 4-year-olds, and no 3-year-olds used Rule I.

Stability Over Time.   A major purpose of the investigation was to inquire into the stability of rule usage over time. Would children who used a particular rule on one occasion use the same rule a month later? Would children who did not initially conform to any particular rule continue to do so later? Would children who did change move in the direction of more sophisticated rules, or would rule usage vary randomly?

As shown in Table 5.3, performance was quite stable over time on all three tasks. On the balance scale problem, 26 of the 30 children were classified as performing in the same way on the two occasions; on the shadows task, 21 of 30; and on the probability task, 27 of 30. Not surprisingly, the degree of stability varied with the children's age. Three-year-olds were the most stable, virtually never using a rule on either occasion. Five-year-olds were the next most stable, generally adhering to Rule I on both occasions. Four-year-olds were the least stable, with six of the 10 children progressing on at least one task from no rule to Rule I, whereas only one child moved in the opposite direction.

TABLE 5.3
Consistency of Rule Classifications Over Time

| | | Balance Scale First Experience | | |
		NR	I	II or III
Second Experience	NR	12		
	I	2	14	1
	II or III	1		

| | | Probability Task First Experience | | |
		NR	I	II or III
Second Experience	NR	21	1	
	I	1	6	1
	II or III			

| | | Shadows Task First Experience | | |
		NR	I	II or III
Second Experience	NR	10	2	
	I	7	10	
	II or III			1

Relationships Among Tasks.   Although the tasks were designed to be as comparable as possible, there was good reason to believe that even perfectly isomorphic problems might well differ in difficulty (Greeno, 1974; Reed, Ernst, & Banerji, 1974; Siegler, 1977). Table 5.4 represents a comparison of the children's performance on each pair of problems. If children performed identically on them, all scores would be on the diagonal from top left to bottom right, and differing numbers of scores above and below the diagonal would reflect differences among the tasks. Within this analysis, performance on the balance scale and shadows tasks is seen to be quite comparable, while performance on the probability task is at a somewhat lower level. Note, however, that for each pair of tasks, more than 60% of the children performed at the same level.

TABLE 5.4
Consistency of Rule Classifications Over Tasks

		Probability		
		NR	I	II or III
Balance Scale	NR	26		
	I	17	13	1
	II or III	1	1	

		Shadows		
		NR	I	II or III
Balance Scale	NR	22	4	1
	I	7	24	
	II or III		1	1

		Probability		
		NR	I	II or III
Shadows	NR	26	3	
	I	18	10	1
	II or III		2	

Discussion

The results suggested that in solving balance scale, shadows, and probability tasks, 5-year-olds generally rely on Rule I, 4-year-olds sometimes rely on Rule I and sometimes do not use any rule, and 3-year-olds almost never conform to any easily describable formula. This generalization was supported by the classifications of individual performance, the absolute percentages of correct answers for the different age groups and problem-types, and the pattern of developmental increments and decrements on the individual test items. Rule usage was found to be quite stable over time, and there was a consistent ordering in the difficulty of the three tasks, with the probability task being the most difficult and the balance scale and shadows tasks being consistently less difficult and roughly equivalent to each other.

The most interesting question raised by these findings concerned the performance of 3-year-olds. Why were they not using Rule I or any other easily describable formula? Examination of the individual protocols ruled out the possibility that the seemingly random performance on the different problem-types was due to side preferences, stimulus preferences, or alternation strategies. There were only two clear instances of these stereotyped approaches (both side preferences) among the 60 protocols. Nor could the finding be attributed to difficulty in working with large numbers; performance on items with few weights on each side was no more orderly than performance on items with many. Nor did the children's protocols reveal long runs of Rule I performance, which might indicate that children knew the rule but applied it only sporadically.[3] The 3-year-olds' explanations of how they generated their responses also were less than revealing. To quote three of them: "I chose the one that was tight," "I chose the one that was special," "I chose the one I wanted to." Not surprisingly, it was difficult to identify the behavioral referents of these explanations. The question of why 3-year-olds were not using any apparent rule thus remained.

Experiment 2A: Responsiveness to Experience

At least as important as what children know is what they can learn. Especially with 3- and 4-year-olds, it seems likely that children are often capable of more than their current knowledge but are simply awaiting exposure to the proper stimulation. The notion is closely akin to the classic theoretical construct of "readiness."

Perhaps the most basic instructional experience is direct physical interaction with objects. Part of the charm of Piaget's formal operations problems is that they provide children the opportunity to formulate and test hypotheses based on their observations of real objects — pendulums swinging, chemicals changing colors, pieces of metal, wood, and glass sinking or floating. Intuitively, we suspect that such situations, involving physical feedback and minimal reliance on language, are among the truest tests of children's cognitive capacities.

In the present context, the focus was on 3- and 4-year-olds' ability to induce Rule I on the balance scale task from simple feedback experience. First, children were pretested to ensure that they did not already know the rule. Then they were presented a set of 16 weight and balance problems, all solvable by Rule I. On each item, the weights were arranged on the pegs, the child was asked what

---

[3]Another possibility was that 3-year-olds might be consistently able to solve balance scale problems that had weights either on only one side of the fulcrum or on neither side. To test this possibility, an additional group of 10 children were presented 12 items with weights on only one side, mingled among the usual 24 posttest items. Only one of the 10 children correctly answered as many as 10 of 12 of the new items (paralleling the 20 of 24 criterion usually used for rule usage). It should be noted, however, that on the new problems the mean percentage of correct answers for the group was 57%, substantially better than the 33% chance level. Thus, it seems likely that 3-year-olds knew something about these problems but not enough to solve them consistently.

he thought would happen, and the lever was released so that the child could see if the prediction was correct. Finally, the 24-item posttest, used previously to assess existing knowledge about the balance scale, was presented.

This design was intended to focus on two issues. One concerned whether there were differences between older and younger children's ability to learn independent of differences in their existing knowledge. Three- and 4-year-olds were matched closely for pretest performance so that there was no reason to believe that one group initially knew more about the balance scale task than the other. Then they were exposed to feedback problems intended to promote acquisition of Rule I. The question was whether the 3- and 4-year-olds would emerge with similar or different knowledge.

The second issue had less to do with developmental differences in ability to learn than with a potential explanation for the previously described differences in existing knowledge. This potential explanation might be labeled the "misunderstanding of instructions" hypothesis (Vago & Siegler, 1977). Briefly, the hypothesis suggests that young children may fail to reveal their cognitive competence because they do not understand what the experimenter wants or what the instructions mean or, alternatively, because they have not had any experience with the task. The classic remedy for such misunderstanding is the provision of nonverbal feedback (cf. Braine, 1964; Braine & Shanks, 1965). Such feedback provides a direct index of what the experimenter wants; it also provides experience with the task and with the experimental situation. Thus, if the misunderstanding of instructions explanation applied to the present situation, we would expect substantial numbers of both older and young children to rely on Rule I following the feedback experience.

Method

The experiment included three parts: pretest, experience, and posttest.

Pretest. The pretest consisted of eight items: two weight, two distance, two conflict–weight, and two conflict–distance. The task and apparatus were the same as those used in the test of existing knowledge in Experiment 1. At no time during the pretest was any type of feedback provided.

Experience. Children were presented the 16-item feedback set used in Experiment 2 of Siegler (1976) in the weight experience condition. On each item, they were asked to predict what would happen if the lever was released. After their prediction, the lever was lifted and they observed the outcome. If the child's prediction was correct, the experimenter would say "Very good. You were right." If the prediction was wrong, the experimenter would say, "No, that's not right. Look carefully at the balance scale to see if you can figure out what would have told you the right answer." After a 10-sec interval, the weights were removed and placed on the scale in a different arrangement and the process started anew.

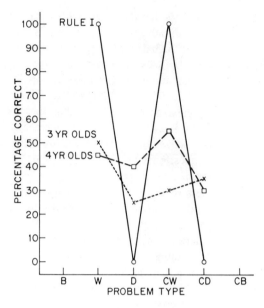

FIG. 5.6   Pretest performance (before feedback).

Posttest. The posttest was the same 24-item balance scale assessment instrument described in the previous experiment; its administration was also identical to that described previously. Pretest, training, and posttest sessions were consecutive and together lasted about 35 min.

Participants. In order to participate in the experiment, children needed to show a pattern of pretest performance that did not conform to Rule I or any other apparent formula. Pretests were given to 3- and 4-year-old boys and girls until groups of 10 children of each age, half of each sex, could be formed. The first 10 3-year-olds and 10 of the first 15 4-year-olds who were pretested were eligible under the criterion of not having more than five of eight responses conform to Rule I. The mean CA of the 3-year-olds was 43 months ($\sigma = 2.72$); that of the 4-year-olds was 55 months ($\sigma = 2.46$).

Results

Pretest. A 2 (age) x 4 (problem-type) analysis of variance on the number of correct pretest answers revealed no significant main effects or interactions (Fig. 5.6).

Experience. Correlated *t*-tests comparing the number of correct answers on the first eight and last eight feedback items revealed that the 4-year-olds progressed from 45% to 66% correct answers (t(9) = 2.35, $p < 0.05$), whereas 3-year-olds' performance remained quite constant (30% vs. 31%) (t(9) < 1).

Posttest. Analysis of the individual posttest protocols revealed that six of the 4-year-olds learned Rule I from the feedback experience, but none of the 10 3-year-olds did. This statement allows the same types of comparisons between predicted and observed results as were made in Experiment 1. The assumptions in the present case are that six of the 10 4-year-olds always used Rule I and that the other four 4-year-olds and all the 10 3-year-olds performed at a chance level on all items.

An age-by-problem-type analysis of variance on the number of correct answers (Fig. 5.7) revealed a significant main effect for problem-type, F(5,90) = 6.34, and a significant interaction between age and problem-type, F(5,90) = 3.58. Performance improved from 32% correct for 3-year-olds to 40% for 4-year-olds (predicted = 33% and 43%). Problem-types answerable by Rule I were correctly solved 51% of the time versus 20% for the other three problem types (predicted = 52% and 23%). The 4-year-olds diverged to a much greater extent on problems solvable and not solvable by Rule I (observed = 67% and 13%; predicted = 73% and 13%) than did the 3-year-olds (observed = 35% and 28%; predicted = 33% and 33%). Finally, developmental increments were observed on all 12 of the items for which they were expected; developmental decrements were observed on 11 of the 12 items for which they were expected, with no difference on the 12th item.

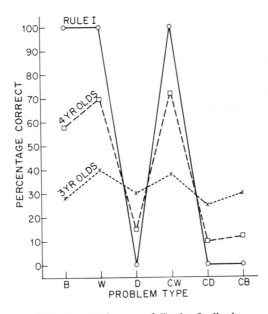

FIG. 5.7   Performance following feedback.

Discussion

The experimental findings gave clear answers to both questions posed by this experiment. There were substantial differences in 3- and 4-year-olds' ability to acquire Rule I from exposure to feedback problems. Not one of the younger children adopted Rule I, but six of the 10 older children did. As in Experiment 1, the 3-year-olds' performance did not differ in any substantial way from that which would be expected from a random model. With regard to the second issue, the findings offered no support for the view that the previously observed developmental differences in existing knowledge were caused by 3-year-olds' lacking experience with the task or not understanding the instructions. Instead, it seemed most likely that there were developmental differences in both existing knowledge and ability to learn.

A plausible counterargument to the view that these results were caused by differential learning ability, however, would be that the pretest assessment instrument was inaccurate and that the 4-year-olds who were chosen already knew more than the 3-year-olds; in this view, the selection procedure incorporated a certain amount of test unreliability and thus produced a group of 4-year-olds who actually knew more than their pretests indicated. To test this possibility, another experiment was run in which children were chosen according to the same pretest criteria and given the same experience and posttest problems as those used previously; the only difference was that no feedback was given on the experience problems. In addition to controlling for regression toward the mean, this procedure also tested the possibility that sheer exposure to the problems, rather than feedback experience with them as such, was what helped the 4-year-olds.

Experiment 2B: Exposure Control

Method

The procedure used in Experiment 2B was almost identical to that described in Experiment 2A. The 3- and 4-year-olds were pretested until comparable groups of 20 children, none meeting the criterion for using Rule I, were established. This involved testing 10 3-year-olds and 16 4-year-olds. Then the 10 3-year-olds and the 10 4-year-olds who were chosen were presented the same weight experience problems as used previously but without feedback. Finally, the usual 24-item posttest was administered.

Results

Pretest.   An age-by-problem-type analysis of variance revealed no significant main effects or interactions.

Experience.   Without feedback, 3- and 4-year-olds performed quite similarly on the problem set. T-tests revealed that neither group changed substantially between the first and second halves of the problems (t's <1.5); the direction of change in each case was toward fewer, rather than more, correct answers (for 4-year-olds, 46% to 35%; for 3-year-olds, 31% to 29%).

Posttest.   Assessment of the individual protocols revealed that two of the 10 4-year-olds appeared to adopt Rule I versus none of the 10 3-year-olds. These insubstantial differences were reflected in the age-by-problem-type analysis of variance, which revealed no significant main effects or interactions. Older children solved 38% of the problems, younger children 35%. Among problems solvable by Rule I the 4-year-olds responded correctly on 43%, compared to 34% for those not solvable by the Rule; 3-year-olds were correct on 37% and 34% respectively. Thus, neither pretest unreliability nor simple exposure to the problems appeared to explain the previously observed developmental differences in ability to benefit from feedback experience.

Experiment 3: Explaining Developmental Differences

How could we explain the differences between 3- and 4-year-olds' ability to learn? The encoding hypothesis advanced by Siegler (1976) in a similar situation provided a clue. Initially, it had been found that 8-year-olds benefited from experiences with conflict problems that did not in any way help 5-year-olds. To account for the differential learning, the encoding hypothesis was proposed; it stated (Siegler, 1976) that "5-year-olds are less able to acquire new knowledge than 8-year-olds because their encoding of stimuli is less adequate [pp. 504–505]." Several sources of evidence were collected to support the hypothesis. First, it was shown on an independent assessment instrument that 8-year-olds effectively encoded both weight and distance dimensions, whereas 5-year-olds encoded only weight. Then it was shown that 5-year-olds could be taught to encode both dimensions accurately. Finally, it was shown that 5-year-olds who had learned to encode both weight and distance were able to benefit from the same conflict problem experience that had previously helped only 8-year-olds.

It was possible to analogize from this previous situation to the present one. If 8-year-olds accurately encoded both weight and distance dimensions and 5-year-olds encoded only weight, it seemed at least plausible that 3-year-olds might encode neither weight nor distance and that this might account for their inability to benefit from feedback experience. Four-year-olds, by contrast, might be hypothesized to encode the weight dimension accurately and thus to be ready to benefit from experience with simple feedback problems even if they did not yet know Rule I. If these statements were true, we would expect the following. First, independent assessment of 3- and 4-year-olds' encoding would reveal that the 4-year-olds encoded weight much more effectively than did the 3-

year-olds; second, it might be possible to improve 3-year-olds' encoding of weight through instruction; and third, if 3-year-olds could be taught to encode weight accurately, then they, like the 4-year-olds, should be able to benefit from feedback experience.

Experiment 3A: Assessment of Encoding

The first step was to determine whether the weight encoding of 3- and 4-year-olds did indeed differ. In order to make this test, the assessment procedure used by Siegler (1976) was adapted to the present situation. Children were presented a balance scale with weights on each side of the fulcrum and were allowed to view it for 15 sec. Then it was hidden from their sight, and a second identical balance scale without any weights on the pegs was presented. The child's task was to place weights on the "new" scale so as to reproduce the configuration that he had seen on the "old" one. It should be noted that this procedure allowed fully independent assessment of encoding on the weight and distance dimensions. A child could reproduce the correct number of weights on each side of the fulcrum, could reproduce the correct distance of the weights from the fulcrum, could do both, or could do neither. The details of the scoring system are described in Siegler (1976).

Several adjustments were made in this encoding assessment procedure to accommodate the very young children we were working with. Rather than having three, four, or five weights on each side of the fulcrum, one, two, or three weights were used; it was ascertained that all children in the experiment could correctly count and identify at least three weights. In addition, the instructions were simplified and made extremely explicit and redundant as follows:

> The idea of the game is for you to look at how the weights are set on the pegs on my balance scale; then I want you to make the same problem by putting the weights on the pegs on your scale. You want the same number of weights on each side of your scale as I had on mine. You want the same number of weights on this side of your scale as you saw on this side of my scale, and you want the same number of weights on this side of your scale as you saw on this side of mine. Do you understand?
>
> First I'll put the weights on the pegs on my balance scale, but the board will be up so you won't be able to see. Then I'll take the board away. You should watch closely to see how the weights are set on the pegs and how many weights there are on this side and how many there are on this side. Then I'll put the board back up so you can't see my scale. You will then need to put the weights on the pegs on your scale in the same way that you saw them on my scale.

After receiving these instructions, children were given the 16-encoding items. Before being given each item, they were reminded of the importance of putting the same number of weights on their balance scale as they had seen on the experimenter's.

Examination of the data revealed that 4-year-olds correctly encoded the weight dimension on 73% of items versus 35% for the 3-year-olds ($t(18) = 4.39$). By contrast, the older and younger children's encoding of distance were at similar low levels, both being below 10% correct. These results were clearly consistent with the encoding hypothesis, although the 3-year-olds' superiority on the weight dimension over the distance dimension (35% vs. 4% correct) might suggest that they had also begun to learn to encode weight (another interpretation might be that their superiority on the weight dimension simply reflected the instructions' constant emphasis on reproducing weight). In any case, the predicted large discrepancy between 3- and 4-year-olds' encoding of weight was apparent. The next question was whether 3-year-olds could learn to encode weight effectively and if so, whether this knowledge would automatically engender use of Rule I.

Experiment 3B: Teaching of Encoding

Children were given the same instructions describing the task as in the previous experiment. Then they were provided the following additional advice about how best to do it:

> You do it like this: first you count the number of weights on this side, one—two; then you count the number of weights on this side, one—two—three; two weights on this side and three weights on this side. Then, when I put the board back up, you put the same number of weights on this side as you saw on this side (pointing) and the same number of weights on this side as you saw on this side (pointing). Let's see if I did it right. Is there the same number of weights on this side as this side, and is there the same number of weights on this side as this side? Good, let's practice some more.

The experimenter and child did four more problems, with the child taking increasing responsibility for their execution, until on the last two trials, the child took full responsibility. Following the last practice problem, children were told:

> Now you're going to be doing everything by yourself. Remember, first count the number of weights on this side, then count the number of weights on this side. Put the same number of weights on this side as you saw on this side and put the same number of weights on this side as you saw on this side.

Children then performed the 16 encoding items, being told before each item to count the number of weights on both sides. They were taken back to the experimental room roughly one hour after finishing and were given the standard 24-item predictions posttest.

Following the detailed instruction in how to encode, the 3- and 4-year-olds' encoding performance was quite comparable. The 3-year-olds encoded the weight dimension correctly on 82% of items, compared to 83% for the 4-year-olds. Again, neither group exceeded 10% correct encodings on the distance dimension. Thus, it was clearly possible to teach the young children how to encode weight effectively.

Knowledge of encoding might have led directly to use of Rule I on the predictions task. This did not happen. Only two 4-year-olds and no 3-year-olds met the criterion for Rule I usage on the predictions test. The reasons that 4-year-olds did less well than previously were unclear, but it was certainly apparent that engendering correct encoding did not automatically lead to improved predictive knowledge. The finding was similar to that of Experiment 3D of Siegler (1976) and again affirmed the distinctiveness of encoding from the predictions task.

This set the stage for the crucial test. If lack of accurate weight encoding was what previously prevented the 3-year-olds from learning from the feedback experience and they now knew how to encode weight accurately, then they should now be able to learn. This prediction was tested in Experiment 3C.

Experiment 3C: Responsiveness to Experience Following Encoding Training

The procedure was divided into four parts: encoding training, encoding test, predictions training (feedback), and predictions test. On Day 1, children were given the encoding training described in the previous experiment and then the usual 16-item encoding test. On Day 2, they were presented the feedback problems described in Experiment 2 and then the standard 24-item predictions test. Along with the feedback problems on Day 2, children were provided two supplementary parts of the encoding training that were intended to make encoding more directly salient in their reaction to feedback. First, when they arrived, the children were told, "Remember yesterday we found that it was very important to count the number of weights on each side? Well, it's also important to do that today." Second, on each feedback problem, the experimenter would precede the usual question by asking, "How many weights are on this side? How many weights are on this side? Is this side bigger or is this side bigger, or are they the same?" The intent was to encourage children to encode the quantity of weights on each problem. After the 16 feedback trials, children were given the standard posttest in the standard way.

As in Experiment 3B, both older and younger children were able to learn to encode weight. The 3-year-olds correctly encoded the weight dimension on 69% of items versus 82% correct encoding for the 4-year-olds ($t(18) = 2.10, p = 0.05$). Also, as previously, children of both ages were correct in encoding distance less than 10% of the time.

The most important finding of the experiment, though, concerned the children's posttest performance. For the first time, a large percentage of 3-year-

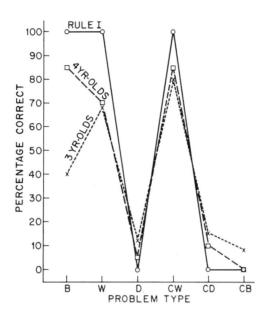

FIG. 5.8   Performance following encoding instruction and feedback.

olds responded in a rule-governed fashion. Having been given both encoding training and feedback experience, five of the 10 3-year-olds (and seven of the 10 4-year-olds) adopted either Rule I or a close cousin, Rule I'. Like the usual Rule I, Rule I' asks whether the numbers of weights on each side of the fulcrum are equal, and whenever the numbers of weights are unequal, it predicts that the side with more weights will go down. Unlike Rule I, however, when there is the same amount of weight on the two sides of the fulcrum, Rule I' does not predict "balance"; instead, it guesses randomly that one side or the other will go down. In terms of the different problem types, Rules I and I' make the same predictions on weight, conflict–weight, conflict–distance, and conflict–balance problems, but on balance and distance problems, where Rule I predicts that the child will say "balance," Rule I' predicts that he will guess one side or the other but specifically *not* say "balance." Among the five 3-year-olds who seemed to use rules, two adopted Rule I', conforming to it on 22 of 24 and 24 of 24 posttest items respectively; the other three adopted the more typical Rule I.

On examining Fig. 5.8, the influence of encoding training and feedback experience on the 3-year-olds' posttest predictions should be quickly apparent. For the first time, they, like the 4-year-olds, showed the characteristic spiked pattern of well-above-chance performance on some problem types and well-below-chance performance on others. The main deviation from the Rule I model – percentage correct on balance problems – is precisely where such a deviation would be expected, because although children using Rule I would always be correct on such problems, children using Rule I' would always be wrong.

The same types of absolute predictions as described previously can be made for this experiment by assuming that seven of the 10 4-year-olds always used Rule I, that the remaining three performed randomly, that three of the 10 3-year-olds always used Rule I, that two always used Rule I', and that five performed randomly. The age-by-problem-type analysis of variance revealed a significant main effect for problem-type ($F(5,90) = 35.03$) and a significant age-by-problem-type interaction ($F(5,80) = 2.92$, $p < 0.025$). Performance improved slightly with age from 38% to 45% correct (predicted = 40% to 45%). On the three problem-types solvable by Rule I, performance ranged from 64% to 81% (predicted = 64% to 71%), whereas on the other three, performance ranged from 5% to 14% (predicted = 14% to 17%). Finally, for the first time, performance showed a similar range for 3-year-olds, 8% to 80% correct (predicted = 17% to 68%) as for 4-year-olds, 2% to 88% (predicted = 10% to 80%).

The results of the experiment provided additional support for the encoding hypothesis. We now know that (1) 3- and 4-year-olds differed substantially in their encoding of the weight dimension; (2) that it was possible to teach 3-year-olds to encode weight accurately; and (3) that 3-year-olds who had been taught to encode weight could benefit from the feedback experience that previously had not been helpful. Thus, differential encoding seemed to explain at least a part of the differential responsiveness to instruction of 3- and 4-year-olds.

WHAT DEVELOPS IN SCIENTIFIC REASONING?

The present series of experiments, together with previous ones, allows us to tell a long and complex story about the origins and subsequent development of scientific reasoning. At present, the story can be told most confidently and in greatest detail for the balance scale problem, although we have collected considerable converging evidence on other tasks and are currently collecting more. In any case, the story's basic plot is outlined in Table 5.5. It includes four subplots — the development of existing knowledge, the development of encoding, the development of ability to acquire new knowledge, and the development of ability to benefit from a variety of supplements to feedback — and it can be divided into six chapters. At the age of three years, children do not possess any rule for solving the balance scale problem, do not encode either weight or distance very accurately, and do not benefit from feedback aimed at inducing Rule I. If given prior instructions in how to encode weight, however, the feedback often is effective in helping them attain Rule I. By the age of 4 years, there is progress in several domains: Some children use Rule I spontaneously, most children accurately encode weight, and those children who do not already use Rule I often are able to learn it from feedback. By age 5, almost all children use

TABLE 5.5
Modal Course of Development on Balance Scale Task

	Aspect of Development			
Age	Existing Knowledge	Encoding	Response to Feedback	Supplements That Aid Response to Feedback
3 years	No rule	Neither weight nor distance	Does not learn Rule I from weight and balance problems	50% learn Rule I if given weight-encoding training before feedback
4 years	50% Rule I 50% No Rule	Weight	Learns Rule I from weight and balance problems	–
5 years	Rule I	Weight	Does not learn Rule III or IV from conflict problems	Learns Rule III if given weight and distance encoding training before feedback
8 years	50% Rule II 50% Rule I	Weight and distance	Learns Rule III from conflict problems	–
13 years	Rule III	Weight and distance	Does not learn Rule IV from conflict problems	50% learn Rule IV if given both quantitative encoding instructions and external memory aids along with feedback
17 years	Rule III	Weight and distance	Does not learn Rule IV from conflict problems	Learns Rule IV if given either quantitative encoding instructions or external memory aids along with feedback

Rule I and encode the weight dimension. Feedback intended to induce Rule III or IV is by itself ineffective. Again, however, if the feedback is preceded by instruction in how best to encode, it is often helpful, this time in the attainment of Rule III. By age 8, children typically use either Rule I or Rule II, encode both weight and distance dimensions, and can learn Rule III directly from feedback. Thereafter, there is an increasing trend toward use of Rule III, and children generally encode both weight and distance dimensions. Development occurs primarily in the conditions under which they can learn Rule IV. Thirteen-year-olds require two supplements to feedback — external memory aids and instructions intended to encourage quantitative encoding — to benefit from the experience, whereas either the memory aids or instructions alone are sufficient for college students (cf. Siegler, in press).

There is a certain cyclical flavor to these data. First, children's knowledge, ability to learn, and encoding are at the same level. Then, encoding and ability to learn change. Finally, the level of existing knowledge follows. We see this happening between ages 3 and 5 with regard to acquisition of Rule I and weight encoding, and again between ages 5 and 8 with regard to higher rules and encoding of weight and distance. The theoretical implication, backed by both correlational and experimental evidence, is that improved encoding contributes to improved ability to learn, which in turn contributes in time to an improved level of existing knowledge. The model of development is similar to Piaget's model of assimilation/accommodation but differs in two important ways. First, there is a strong distinction in the present model between what children know and what they can learn. For example, improved encoding is thought to contribute directly to children's ability to learn but only indirectly to their existing knowledge. Second, within the present model all components are independently measurable. Being able to measure the explanatory construct — encoding — in particular offers a number of advantages. At a theoretical level, it helps us escape the circularity that is inevitable when we explain behavior in terms of constructs that have no observable basis except the behavior they are said to explain. At a psychometric level, it can help us predict exactly who is ready to benefit from new experience and who is not. At an applied level, it suggests an indirect approach to instruction that might be successful when more direct approaches fail.

Pursuing the model one step further, however, we might ask, "Where does encoding come from? Why is it limited in the ways that it is, and why does it improve when it does?" At present, there are no direct answers to these questions, but it is possible to analogize and to speculate. Consider the correspondence between the present notion of encoding and Gibson's (1969) account of perceptual learning:

> Perceptual learning is defined as an increase in the ability of an organism to get information from its environment as a result of practice with the array of stimulation provided by the environment. This definition implies that there are potential variables of stimuli which are not differentiated within the mass of impinging stimulation but which may be, given the proper conditions of exposure and practice. There is a change in what the organism can respond to. The change is not acquisition or substitution of a new response to stimulation previously responded to in some other way, but is rather responding in any discriminating way to a variable of stimulation not responded to previously [p. 77].

Gibson's account suggests that sheer exposure to and experience with the relevant stimuli may be important. In the present case, though, it seems unlikely that children of any age would have encountered the balance scale apparatus in previous situations; any perceptual learning of the type Gibson discusses would have to come about through some process of analogy. How this would work and the exact types of experiences that would be analogized from (teeter-totters? simple levers?) thus remain speculative.

Another possible explanation for the development of encoding would be in terms of memory development. Either the development of mnemonic strategies or the development of short-term memory capacity might account for why 3-year-olds do not spontaneously encode either the weight or the distance dimension, why 5-year-olds encode only weight, and why 8-year-olds encode both. At present we are starting an experiment aimed at testing this interpretation. Young children are presented the encoding task, either in the usual way where the board hides the initial arrangement of weights on pegs or in an alternative way, with the board absent. If memorial difficulties are crucial, then even very young children should be able to reproduce correctly the arrangement of weights on pegs when the board is absent.

The Development of Rule-Governedness

How do the present findings with the balance scale, projection of shadows, and probability tasks relate to previous observations of development in the preschool period? Consider the following, admittedly nonrandom but hopefully representative, sampling of what we know about young children's thinking:

1. Between ages 3 and 5, there is a shift from the use of "complexive" classes whose members are linked idiosyncratically, if at all, toward the adoption of "true" classes in which membership is exhaustive and exclusive (Ricciuti & Johnson, 1965).

2. Three-year-olds are virtually as adept as 4-year-olds at solving oddity problems at the level of "basic" categories ("Which is different: a Persian cat, a green Chevrolet, or a calico cat?") but the 3-year-olds' performance falls off sharply when the problems involve "superordinate" categories ("Which is different: a Persian cat, a green Chevrolet, or a cocker-spaniel?") (Rosch, Mervis, Gray, Johnson, & Boyes-Braem, 1976).

3. On the middle-sized problem, where 3- and 4-year-olds perform comparably in the absence of a verbal statement of the desired rule, provision of such a statement improves the performance of the older but not the younger children (Reese, 1966).

4. Three-year-olds rely on intuitive coordinations of length and density to estimate the relative numerousness of rows of dots, whereas 4- and 5-year-olds more often base their estimates exclusively on the relative lengths of the rows (Pufall & Shaw, 1972).

5. In probability-learning tasks where no determinate solution exists, 3-year-olds, who apparently are content to settle for a 70% hit rate, choose the correct alternative more often than 5-year-olds, older children, or adults, who search indefinitely for the "correct" solution rule (Weir, 1964).

There seems to be a common core to these observations. Three-year-olds are seen as proceeding in an intuitive manner, whereas 5-year-olds are described as proceeding systematically. Three-year-olds are seen as being content with approaches that identify the correct answer most but not all of the time, but 5-year-olds search for the single "correct" strategy. Experiential manipulations that help 4- and 5-year-olds adopt more systematic approaches do not necessarily help 3-year-olds to do so.

It appears, then, that something important happens between ages 3 and 5. We might call it the development of systematic strategies or perhaps the development of rule-governedness. Of course, this is not to say that children age 3 years and younger never use rules or that they are never systematic. Roger Brown's work on the acquisition of past tense forms (e.g., Brown, Cazden, & Bellugi, 1969) and the literature on perceptual illusions (cf. Pick & Pick, 1970), for example, demonstrate that very young children seem to perform in a rule-governed fashion in some situations. Nonetheless, there seems to be impressive growth in the range and variety of situations in which rules are used. Impressionistically, the growth appears to be most dramatic in children's approaches to new "problem-solving" situations. It is unlikely that before entering the experimental room, either 3- or 5-year-olds would ever have been asked which side of a balance scale would go down, whether a cat was more like a dog or a Chevrolet, or which object was the middle-sized one. These constitute novel problems. By contrast, the perceptual and linguistic contexts described by Brown and by the students of perceptual illusions seem much more akin to the child's everyday experience. There are obviously different ways of conceptualizing the differences between situations in which 3-year-olds perform systematically and situations in which they do not, and only rigorous empirical work can hope to distinguish among them, but in any case, it seems likely that one thing that develops between ages 3 and 5 is the ability and inclination to generate systematic rule-governed approaches.

Several explanations for this development have been proposed. One suggestion is that very young children suffer from a "mediation deficiency" in which verbal statements do not have the usual semantic influence (Luria, 1957; Reese, 1962). Others contend that the problem is a failure to understand the experimental situation (Braine, 1964; Braine & Shanks, 1965). Yet a third approach, the present one, is to explain young children's behavior in terms of inaccurate or incomplete encoding. As yet, we do not have very good means for comparing the value of these explanations or even of knowing whether they differ in important ways. What seems necessary is to develop independent means of measuring the constructs so that their predictive power and the effects of manipulating them can be directly assessed. In this regard, the encoding explanation has an early leg up, but with the development of methods for measuring the other explanatory constructs, this lead could well disappear or be reversed.

EPILOGUE

Typically in the study of cognitive development, 5-year-olds are portrayed in a peculiarly negative light. They are said to be egocentric, to lack reversibility and compensation, to attend to states rather than transformations, and to be perceptually rather than conceptually oriented. Much emphasis is given to their errors on conservation, class inclusion, seriation, and other tasks. As Flavell (1976) pointed out, even their label, "preoperational" or "preconceptual," indicates their lowly status.

In the present series of investigations, the tables are turned. Five-year-olds appear as the heroes, for they are systematic. What is in one context a lack of decentration, an attention to states rather than transformations, or a perceptual orientation is in another context the culmination of a profound developmental change. It is no accident that we so often choose 5-year-olds as the group to contrast with 7- and 8-year-olds, for the 5-year-olds are comparable to the older children in a way that 2- and 3-year-olds are not. To put it another way, it seems possible to divide the development of scientific reasoning into two phases: one lasting from birth until age 5, in which children progress from nonrule-governed to rule-governed approaches, and the other lasting from age 5 to adulthood, in which children adopt increasingly sophisticated rules. It is difficult to say which development represents the more profound change.

ACKNOWLEDGMENTS

The preparation of this manuscript was supported in part by Grant MH−07722 from the National Institute of Mental Health and by a grant from the Sloan Foundation. Thanks are due to Ms. Sandra Schneider of the YIKC chidren's school, to Dr. Ann Taylor of the Carnegie−Mellon children's school, to Mrs. Natalie Kaplan of the Carriage House preschool, and to Mrs. Kathy Downing of the Morewood Day Care Center, without whose help and cooperation this study could not have been run. Thanks are also due to Renee Dennis, who served as experimenter throughout the study, and to Jola Jakimik, Dave Klahr, Elaine Shelton, and Herb Simon, who read and commented on earlier versions of the manuscript.

REFERENCES

Barratt, B. B. Training and transfer in combinatorial problem solving: The development of formal reasoning during early adolescence. *Developmental Psychology*, 1975, *11*, 700−704.

Braine, M. The development of a grasp of transitivity of length: A reply to Smedslund. *Child Development*, 1964, *35*, 799−810.

Braine, M., & Shanks, B. The development of conservation of size. *Journal of Verbal Learning and Verbal Behavior,* 1965, *4,* 227–242.

Brainerd, C. J. The development of the proportionality scheme in children and adolescents. *Developmental Psychology,* 1971, *5,* 469–474.

Brainerd, C. J. Does prior knowledge of the compensation rule increase susceptibility to conservation training? *Developmental Psychology,* 1976, *12,* 1–5.

Brainerd, C. J. Cognitive development and concept learning: An interpretive review. *Psychological Bulletin,* 1977, *84,* 919–939.

Brainerd, C. J., & Allen, T. W. Experimental induction of the conservation of "first order" quantitative invariants. *Psychological Bulletin,* 1971, *75,* 128–144.

Brown, R., Cazden, C., & Bellugi, U. The child's grammar from I to III. In J. P. Hill (Ed.), *Minnesota Symposia on Child Psychology* (Vol. II). Minneapolis: University of Minnesota Press, 1969.

Carpenter, P. A., & Just, M. A. Sentence comprehension: A psycholinguistic processing model of verification. *Psychological Review,* 1975, *82,* 45–73.

Case, R. Structures and strictures: Some functional limitations on the course of cognitive growth. *Cognitive Psychology,* 1974, *6,* 544–574.

Dale, L. G. The growth of systematic thinking: Replication and analysis of Piaget's first chemical experiment. *Australian Journal of Psychology,* 1970, *22,* 277–286.

Dulit, E. Adolescent thinking à la Piaget. *Journal of Youth and Adolescence,* 1972, *1,* 281–301.

Flavell, J. H. *Cognitive development.* Englewood Cliffs, N.J.: Prentice-Hall, 1976.

Gibson, E. J. *Principles of perceptual learning and development.* Englewood Cliffs, N.J.: Prentice-Hall, 1969.

Greeno, J. C. Hobbits and orcs: Acquisition of a sequential concept. *Cognitive Psychology,* 1974, *6,* 270–292.

Inhelder, B., & Piaget, J. *The growth of logical thinking from childhood to adolescence.* New York: Basic Books, 1958.

Jackson, S. The growth of logical thinking in normal and subnormal children. *British Journal of Educational Psychology,* 1965, *35,* 255–258.

Klahr, D., & Siegler, R. S. The representation of children's knowledge. In H. Reese & L. P. Lipsitt (Eds.), *Advances in child development* (Vol. 12). New York: Academic Press, 1978.

Klahr, D., & Wallace, J. G. *Cognitive development: An information processing view.* Hillsdale, N.J.: Lawrence Erlbaum Associates, 1976.

Kuhn, T. *The structure of scientific revolutions.* Chicago: University of Chicago Press, 1962.

Kuhn, D., & Angelev, J. An experimental study of the development of formal operational thought. *Child Development,* 1976, *47,* 697–706.

Lee, L. C. The concomitant development of cognitive and moral modes of thought. A test of selected deductions from Piaget's theory. *Genetic Psychology Monographs,* 1971, *85,* 93–146.

Lovell, K. A follow-up study of Inhelder and Piaget's "The growth of logical thinking." *British Journal of Psychology,* 1961, *52,* 143–153.

Luria, A. R. The role of language in the formation of temporary connections. In B. Simon (Ed.), *Psychology in the Soviet Union.* Stanford: Stanford University Press, 1957, 115–129.

Martorano, S. C. A developmental analysis of performance on Piaget's formal operations tasks. *Developmental Psychology,* 1977, *13,* 666–672.

Neimark, E. D. Intellectual development in adolescence. In F. D. Horowitz (Ed.), *Review of child development research* (Vol. 4). Chicago: University of Chicago Press, 1975.

Newell, A., & Simon, H. A. *Human problem solving.* Englewood Cliffs, N.J.: Prentice-Hall, 1972.

Piaget, J. Intellectual evolution from adolescence to adulthood. *Human Development,* 1972, *15,* 1–12.

Piaget, J., & Inhelder, B. *La Genesee de l'idee de hazard chez l'enfant.* Paris: Presses Universitaires de France, 1951.

Pick, H. L., Jr., & Pick, A. D. Sensory and perceptual development. In P. H. Mussen (Ed.), *Carmichael's manual of child psychology* (3rd ed.), (Vol. 1). New York: Wiley, 1970.

Pufall, P. B., & Shaw, R. E. Precocious thoughts on number: The long and short of it. *Developmental Psychology,* 1972, *7,* 62–69.

Reed, S. K., Ernst, G. W., & Banerji, R. The role of analogy in transfer between similar problem states. *Cognitive Psychology,* 1974, *6,* 436–450.

Reese, H. W. Verbal mediation as a function of age level. *Psychological Bulletin,* 1962, *59,* 502–509.

Reese, H. W. Verbal effects in the intermediate-size transposition problem. *Journal of Experimental Child Psychology,* 1966, *3,* 123–130.

Ricciuti, H. N., & Johnson, L. J. *Developmental changes in categorizing behavior from infancy to the early pre-school years.* Paper presented at the meeting of the Society for Research in Child Development, Minneapolis, March, 1965.

Rosch, E., Mervis, C. B., Gray, W. D., Johnson, D. M., & Boyes–Braem, P. Basic objects in natural categories. *Cognitive Psychology,* 1976, *8,* 282–339.

Siegler, R. S. Three aspects of cognitive development. *Cognitive Psychology,* 1976, *4,* 481–520.

Siegler, R. S. The 20-question game as a form of problem solving. *Child Development,* 1977, *48,* 395–403.

Siegler, R. S. Cognition, instruction, development, and individual differences. In A. M. Lesgold, J. W. Pellegrino, S. D. Fokkema, & R. Glaser (Eds.), *Cognitive psychology and instruction.* New York: Plenum, 1978.

Siegler, R. S., & Liebert, R. M. Acquisition of formal scientific reasoning by 10- and 13-year-olds: Designing a factorial experiment. *Developmental Psychology,* 1975, *10,* 401–402.

Siegler, R. S., Liebert, D. E., & Liebert, R. M. Inhelder and Piaget's pendulum problem: Teaching preadolescents to act as scientists. *Developmental Psychology,* 1973, *9,* 97–101.

Siegler, R. S., & Vago, S. The development of a proportionality concept: Judging relative fullness. *Journal of Experimental Child Psychology,* 1978, *25,* 371–396.

Tomlinson–Keasey, C. Formal operations in females from eleven to fifty-four years of age. *Developmental Psychology,* 1972, *6,* 364.

Vago, S., & Siegler, R. S. *The misunderstanding of instructions explanation in developmental psychology.* Paper presented at the meeting of the Society for Research in Child Development, New Orleans, March, 1977.

Weir, M. W. Developmental changes in problem-solving strategies. *Psychological Review,* 1964, *71,* 473–490.

6 How Do Children Solve Class-Inclusion Problems?

Tom Trabasso
University of Minnesota

Alice M. Isen
University of
Maryland Baltimore County

Phyllis Dolecki
Princeton University

Alexander G. McLanahan
Stanford University

Christine A. Riley
University of Iowa

Teressa Tucker
University of
Maryland Baltimore County

INTRODUCTION

The main method by which we assess children's logical competence is to ask them questions. We cannot assume that they understand these questions in the same way we do. Nor should we assume that only logical operations are required to answer the questions. At the outset, the child does not know our intentions; he must consider the form in which the question is posed and use whatever contextual information is available to make a correct inference. Relevant information may be contained in the question, the external context, or both, and variation in either can lead to a correct or incorrect answer, independent of the logical abilities theoretically being assessed.

The purpose of this chapter is to examine how perceptual, semantic, referential, quantification, comparison, and decision processes are affected by contextual variation in a cognitive development task. The central thesis is that logical ability cannot be assessed independently of these processes and that what develops cognitively is a broader competence than just competence in logical operations. The particular case that we will examine is a problem of critical importance within Piaget's theory, namely, class inclusion. The ability to compare a superordinate with a subordinate class and to perform reversible operations on quantified classes is supposed to mark the transition from preoperational to concrete operational thought. We will analyze the class-inclusion problem from the point of view of the demands it places on the child and the way the child might try to meet these demands. Variation in the task necessarily changes its requirements and may also change the child's performance, thereby calling into question the assumption of all-or-none logical competence.

The traditional class-inclusion problem involves a number of objects belonging to a superordinate class (e.g., 8 animals), which can be divided into two subordinate classes (e.g., 5 dogs and 3 cats). After the child is asked to name the superordinate and subordinate classes, he is asked: "Are there more dogs or more animals?" The surprising result is that a majority of children under 8 or 9 years of age respond, "Dogs." (See Klahr & Wallace, 1972, for a summary of earlier findings.)

In studying this problem, Piaget (1952) was initially concerned with the development of number and class concepts. For him, classes and numbers had

> ... an important common basis, namely the *additive operation,* which brings together the scattered elements into a whole, or *divides these wholes into parts.* ... The difference between number and class, on the other hand, lies in the fact that in number, the parts are homogeneous units, while the parts of a class are still only qualified classes, and are united only by virtue of their common qualities [p. 162, italics added].

Later, Inhelder and Piaget (1964) indicated that young children fail to solve class-inclusion problems because they are unable to differentiate the intension of a class (its shared properties) from its extension (the properties of its individual members or parts). Let A stand for the superordinate class, A_1 for the majority subordinate class, and A_2 for the minority subordinate class. Then, when the preoperational child is asked the class-inclusion question, "Are there more A or more A_1?" he is assumed to be *unable* to compare the superordinate class (A) with the subordinate class (A_1). More specifically, Piaget (1952) wrote:

> ... when he thinks of the whole, he can envisage the parts which have not yet been dissociated, but when he tries to dissociate one of the parts he forgets the whole, or disregards it, and merely compares the part in question with the remaining part [p. 171].

In 1964, Inhelder and Piaget translated this explanation into a logical form and analyzed the class-inclusion problem within the context of the transition from the preoperational to the operational stage. The preoperational child's thinking is characterized by *intuition,* that is, according to Piaget (1967) the

> ... simple internalization of percepts and movements in the form of representational images and "mental experiences" — which prolongs the sensorimotor schemata without true rational coordination [p. 30].

In contrast, the concrete operational child can use logic, and the class-inclusion problem represents a test of the child's operational level. As Piaget (1967) says:

> Intuitions become transformed into operations as soon as they constitute groupings which are both composable and reversible. . . . Thus the action of combining (logical or arithmetic addition) is an operation. . . . No operation exists in an isolated state; it is always formed as a function of the totality of operations of the same kind. For example, a logical concept of class (combination of individuals) is not constructed in an isolated state but necessarily within a classification of the grouping of which it forms a part [p. 49].

Thus, the development of classification is an outcome of the development of operations in the concrete operational child. The preoperational or intuitive child can add two subordinate classes $(A_1 + A_2)$ to equal the superordinate class (A), but he fails the class-inclusion problem because he lacks three components: (1) reversibility of the transformations, or the logical operations of addition and subtraction; (2) awareness of the inclusion relation or "mobility of parts"; and (3) conservation of the whole.

Inhelder and Piaget (1964) describe the mental processes involved in the class-inclusion task as follows:

> Only when all three are present can we legitimately speak of operational addition. The only decisive test is to ask the subject to compare the extension of A with that of A_1. If he recognizes that there are more primulas (A) than yellow primulas (A_1) in a bunch, he must be aware of A as the sum of $A_1 + A_2$. Such simultaneous awareness, which is characteristic of operational thinking, implies the conservation of the whole A. . . . When the problem of inclusion cannot be solved, the most frequent error is to compare A_1 and A_2, instead of A_1 and A [p. 106].

Formally, this model of class-inclusion performance is represented as $(A_1 + A_2 = A) \leftrightarrow (A - A_2 = A_1)$. Thus, the hypothesized mental operations are:

1. $A_1 + A_2 = A$
2. $A - A_2 = A_1$

Preoperational children's difficulty in solving class-inclusion problems is said to reside in the fact that when they perform Equation 2, A is "mentally destroyed" (Piaget, 1967, p. 53), and only A_1 remains. Hence the response "A_1" to the question, "Are there more A or A_1?"

A number of questions can be raised about the validity and generality of this model. Wilkinson (1976) comments:

Taken literally, this model implies that inclusion problems having the same logical structure should all elicit the same pattern of errors from young children. Empirically, however, there is wide variation in performance on problems having this basic structure (Klahr & Wallace, 1972). Admittedly, even Inhelder and Piaget (1964) do not interpret the model so strictly, but neither do they offer a qualifying amendment to their logical equation. Furthermore, no detailed description has yet been given of the psychological processes that accomplish the logical reversal. These deficiencies suggest the need for an alternative model [p. 65].

Thus, with respect to the Piagetian tradition, two questions emerge: (1) Can young children compare a superordinate class with a subordinate one? and (2) Do they have to use logically reversible operations to do so? We address both of these questions. The more basic question, however, is how children go about solving the class-inclusion problem.

A TASK ANALYSIS

Our main purpose is to do what Wilkinson (1976) suggests, namely, to provide an alternative model of class-inclusion reasoning. We use task anslysis and an information-processing approach (cf. Klahr & Wallace, 1972, 1976) to formulate this model. Both new experimental findings and previous ones will be considered in our effort to determine how children solve or fail to solve class-inclusion problems. Our analysis will reveal that a variety of complex skills, including perceptual, semantic, linguistic, and quantitative operations, are crucial to performance on class-inclusion problems.

The analysis follows from a simple question: "What processes are required by class-inclusion problems?" Given a physical display of objects that are identifiable, countable, and partitionable into a superordinate class (A) with two subordinate classes $(A_1$ and $A_2)$, and given the question, "Are there more A_1 or A?," we can identify at least eight required components.

1. Representing the physical display.
2. Interpreting the question as a request to compare two quantities.
3. Finding a referent for A_1.
4. Quantifying A_1 as $Q(A_1)$.
5. Finding a referent for A.
6. Quantifying A as $Q(A)$.
7. Comparing the resulting quantities.
8. Responding with a set of decision rules:
   If $Q(A) > Q(A_1)$, respond "A."
   If $Q(A_1) > Q(A)$, respond "A_1."
   If $Q(A_1) = Q(A)$, respond "Same" or guess "A_1" or "A."

The remainder of this paper is organized around these eight hypothesized components. We examine how they are affected by task variables and provide tests, evidence, and discussion on each of them in turn.

Component 1: Representing or Encoding the Display

The physical display of objects may be internally represented in several ways. The main options are to encode the objects (1) as a single, superordinate class, A, (2) as two subordinate classes, A_1 and A_2, or (3) hierarchically, as both a superordinate class, A, and two subordinate classes, A_1 and A_2. Other encodings are possible and probably occur; however, these are the effects of interpreting the question rather than perceptual encoding of the displays.

A standard class-inclusion problem procedure is to ask the child for the names of the superordinate and subordinate classes. For example, the experimenter points to the dogs and asks, "What are these?" The child typically responds, "Dogs." Then the experimenter points to the cats and asks, "What are these?" The child answers, "Cats." Finally, the experimenter points to the whole array and asks, "What do you call all of these?" The child may answer, "Pets." The experimenter than uses the child's terms in his question, "Are there more pets or more dogs?" If the child does not reply with a label, the experimenter proceeds with his own terms.

This approach may not guarantee that the child has represented, in memory, both the superordinate and subordinate classes. We tested this idea with a group of 50 first- and second-grade children, ranging in age from 6–7 to 9–4 years (median = 7–6), on standard class-inclusion problems with or without the experimenter explicitly identifying the superordinate and subordinate classes. The subordinate classes were in a 5:3 ratio. Two problems under each condition (labels versus none) were given to each child in a counterbalanced order. There were no reliable differences or interactions ($p > 0.05$). Children who received labeled problems gave 60% superordinate answers; those who received problems without labels averaged 70%.

Labeling.   Having the child name the objects does not guarantee that he will encode the display in these terms nor that he will represent the display hierarchically. Whether a superordinate class name applies to the objects depends on whether or not the objects are frequent or typical exemplars of the category (Rosch, 1973). For example, the child may accept the label "Animal" for horses but not for robins.

Carson and Abrahamson (1976) systematically investigated the effects of typicality of subordinate classes. Children were asked to sort a group of objects hierarchically. They placed the objects in small boxes, labeled them, then placed them in a larger box, and labeled them again. If the child's label differed from the adult's, the child was asked whether or not he would accept the adult's label.

Four different kinds of class-inclusion questions were then asked, varying the four combinations of predetermined typical/atypical exemplars. Children who succeeded on problems where both subordinates were typical and who accepted the adult labels for atypical subordinates maintained a high level of success (80% correct) with atypical subordinate exemplars. However, children who succeeded on problems with typical exemplars and who rejected the adult labels for atypical ones dropped to a 28% success rate on problems with one or two atypical subordinate exemplars.

How might encoding affect subsequent performance in terms of our component processes? Carson and Abrahamson (1976) reported some observations relevant to this question. If the labels are typical and accepted by the child, he is assumed to encode the display with Option 3, namely, as A_1 and A_2 with A applying to both A_1 and A_2. In this case, subsequent identification of A_1 and A poses no problem. If, on the other hand, atypical exemplars are used, the child's initial encoding may be different. If there are five flies and three horses, the child may represent the display as A_1 and A_2 with A also applying to A_2. That is, there are flies and horses, and only the horses are also animals. In this case, the child is likely at Component Process 5 to identify A as A_2 and quantify A as three and to respond, "Flies." If both subordinates are atypical, as in five bees and three flies, the encoding may simply be A_1 and A_2, because A does not apply to either subordinate class. Here the child may choose A_1 as more because it is more than nothing. In this case, A is not identified, remains an empty set, and is *not* misidentified as A_2. Suppose, furthermore, that the exemplars are typical/atypical as when there are five dogs and three bees. Carson and Abrahamson (1976) pointed out a dilemma. One strategy (used by most of the children) is to identify A as A_1 and respond "Same." Another is to adopt the subclass encoding, A_1 and A_2. A third possibility is to reevaluate the atypical exemplars and apply the superordinate term. Carson and Abrahamson reported that all of these strategies were used.

Thus, *the labels used may determine how the display is encoded* and how the terms in the question are subsequently identified, quantified, and compared. Whether the child encodes the display as a hierarchical representation A with A_1 and A_2 as subordinates depends on his knowledge about the objects in A_1 and A_2 as exemplars of A, as well as his willingness to accept such exemplars as members of the class. A robin may be a more typical bird than a chicken; in time, though, most children do accept chickens as birds.

Perceptual Grouping.   Another factor that may influence the way children encode the display is suggested by Wohlwill's (1968) "perceptual set" hypothesis. According to Wohlwill, young children rely heavily on the perceptually salient cues common to subordinate class members, and therefore they tend to encode the displays by Option 2, namely, as A_1 and A_2. If a child adopts this representation, he is likely to respond "A_1" to the class-inclusion question; he will properly identify and quantify A_1 but he will *misidentify A* as A_2 in Component Process 5.

Wohlwill (1968) manipulated the perceptual features of the display by providing contrasting objects. For example, after starting with a display of jackets and hats, he added pots and musical instruments. The addition of such contrasting objects facilitated class-inclusion performance by about 15%. Presumably, the contrasting objects aided the child in seeing the objects of clothing as clothing rather than as being only jackets and hats.

Influencing Encoding of the Display: An Experiment.   We asked ourselves if we could affect the child's initial representation of the display and thereby influence his class-inclusion performance. We adopted Wohlwill's (1968) procedure of adding contrasting elements. However, we wished to promote encoding of objects as superordinate classes, so we added an additional, contrasting *superordinate class* to the display, rather than unrelated elements. In a standard class-inclusion problem, there is only one superordinate class (e.g., animals) and only two subordinate classes (e.g., 6 dogs and 2 cats). We added another superordinate class (e.g., fruits) with two subordinate classes (e.g., 4 apples and 4 oranges).

Let A stand for the superordinate class (animals) and let A_1 and A_2 stand for the corresponding subordinate classes (dogs and cats, respectively). Likewise, let B stand for the superordinate class of fruits, B_1 for apples, and B_2 for oranges. Our reasoning was that if the child compared perceptual features of the objects (or considered their functional or semantic properties), he would be more likely to consider the dogs (A_1) and cats (A_2) as members of the class of animals (A) and, likewise, the apples (B_1) and oranges (B_2) as members of the class of fruits. This representation of the display in terms of both the superordinate and the subordinate classes was intended to promote proper identification of the referents for A_1 and A and, hence, facilitate class-inclusion performance.

We also tried a second procedure to promote hierarchical encoding. Here, children answered questions about *all possible pairwise partitionings* of the two classes. Questions such as, "Are there more dogs or more apples?" (A_1B_1), "Are there more dogs or more fruits?" (A_1B), and "Are there more animals or more fruits?" (AB) were asked in an irregularly ordered series along with the standard class-inclusion question for each class, A and B.

In one experiment, Isen, Riley, Tucker, and Trabasso (1975) contrasted three conditions. Each condition was given to 24 children in each of three age groups, averaging 4, 7, and 9 years respectively. Toy objects were used in the displays and formed eight classes (animals, fruits, letters, numbers, people, silverware, vegetables, and vehicles). The subordinate class ratios were either unequal (6:2) or equal (4:4).

The one-class condition used the standard, one-class, class-inclusion problem throughout testing and served as a control. The two-class condition also had only

TABLE 6.1
Proportion of Superordinate Class (A) Answers[a]

| | Conditions | | |
Age	One-class	Two-class	Multiple Partitioning
5	0.10	0.27	0.33
7	0.27	0.42	0.52
9	0.44	0.52	0.66

[a]Data from Isen, Riley, Tucker, and Trabasso, 1975, Experiment I, 6:2 ratio problems.

class-inclusion problems, but a second class was present in the display. The third condition, called the multiple-partitioning condition, had two classes in the display, and all possible pairwise partitionings were presented in the "Are there more ____ or more ____?" format. There were a total of 15 questions. Although the other 14 are of interest (see the later discussion), we focus on the class-inclusion problems with unequal ratios (6:2). All the children in each condition were initially tested on two (6:2) ratio problems. The problems were counterbalanced across the subjects, and all eight classes were used; likewise, the order of mention of the A_1 and A classes was counterbalanced over subjects.

Both procedures facilitated performance. The proportion of correct answers (A) to the class-inclusion question, "Are there more A or more A_1," is given in Table 6.1 for each age group under each condition. Age and condition exercised significant effects $(p < 0.01)$, and the three conditions were judged to be reliably different by means of individual comparisons $(p < 0.05)$. There were no effects of order of mention of the A or A_1 classes in the question and no reliable age-by-condition interaction.

As can be seen in Table 6.1, the multiple-partitioning condition led to the most improvement, averaging 23%. Adding a contrasting class in the two-class condition produced a facilitation of 13%. Thus, both attempts to improve encoding were effective, with the greater effect attributable to the addition of a contrasting class and to having the child compare superordinate and/or subordinate classes within and between the two classes. Children were likely to compare a subordinate class to its whole if they first encoded the superordinate class and its subordinates.

McLanahan (1976) replicated the Isen et al. one- and two-class conditions in a senior honors thesis at Princeton University. In his study, 48 children ranging in age from 6–0 to 8–9 years (median = 7–0) were given 12 different class-inclusion problems with 4:2 ratios. The two-class group's performance was superior to the one-class group's on 10 of 12 problems $(p < 0.01)$; the overall improvement was 10% (42% versus 32% superordinate answers). Thus, in our two experiments, the contrasting class effects were not large, averaging 13% and 10%. Wohlwill (1968) obtained 10% to 15% increases by simply adding unrelated objects to the display. Apparently, *any* set of contrasting objects promotes contrastive comparisons and superordinate identification. The more effective procedure, however, was to force the child to identify, quantify, and compare all the classes over a series of problems.

A Critical Test of Alternative Models. The multiple-partitioning procedure allowed us to perform a critical experiment. In the standard class-inclusion problem, there is a within-class, superordinate versus subordinate comparison (hereafter called an $A_1 A$ problem). In the multiple-partitioning condition, there is another superordinate versus subordinate comparison but the comparison is between classes: A_1 (dogs) versus B (fruits) (an $A_1 B$ problem). Notice that the $A_1 A$ problem has the inclusion relation; the $A_1 B$ problem does not. These two problems allowed us to test the predictions of several major theories of class inclusion.

First, from the Piagetian perspective, $A_1 A$ problems should be more difficult than $A_1 B$ problems. The $A_1 A$ problems demand both addition and subtraction of classes as follows: (1) to quantify A, count A_1 and add the sum to the count of A_2; and (2) to quantify A_1, subtract the count of A_2 from the count of A. For the $A_1 B$ problem, there is only the addition of classes: (1) to quantify B, count B_1 and add the count of B_2; and (2) to count A_1. The $A_1 A$ problem involves both addition and subtraction of classes and thus *reversible* operations; the $A_1 B$ problem does not. The $A_1 A$ problem involves a comparison of a subordinate class with its superordinate; the $A_1 B$ problem does not. The $A_1 A$ problem requires "conservation of the whole"; the $A_1 B$ problem does not. According to our previous quotations from Inhelder and Piaget (1964), the preoperational child can do logical addition and therefore should be able to solve the $A_1 B$ problem but not the $A_1 A$ problem. Thus, for the range of ages studied (5 through 9 years), one would expect children to give more superordinate class answers to the $A_1 B$ than to the $A_1 A$ problem.

Two other models yield similar predictions. Wilkinson's (1976) model predicts that $A_1 A$ is more difficult than $A_1 B$ because $A_1 A$ involves double counting of the A_1 subordinate and $A_1 B$ does not. Wilkinson argues that younger children are unwilling to do such double counting and that this strategy is critical for solving class-inclusion problems.

The final model is Klahr and Wallace's (1976) computer simulation of successful and unsuccessful performance on class-inclusion problems. Their "failure" model predicts "failure" on $A_1 A$ but success on $A_1 B$. According to this model, verbal encoding is crucial; it dictates the subsequent identification and quantification of classes. For the $A_1 A$ problem (dogs versus animals), the verbal encoding for A_1 is DOG-NOT-ANIMAL, and for A it is ANIMAL-NOT-DOG. Hence, animals are misidentified as non-dogs, that is, A is misidentified as A_2 and $Q(A_2) =$

TABLE 6.2
Comparison of Within (A_1A) and Between (A_1B)
Superordinate Versus Superordinate Class Problems[a]

| | Proportion of Superordinate Answers | | | |
| | Experiment I | | Experiment II | |
Age	A_1A	A_1B	A_1A	A_1B
5	0.33	0.35	0.35	0.29
7	0.52	0.58	0.52	0.54
9	0.66	0.71	0.71	0.67

[a]Data from Isen et al., 1975.

$Q(A)$. The DOG-NOT-ANIMAL code does not apply to dogs, and, in their model, is defaulted to DOG by a negative deletion rule. The resulting comparison is $Q(A_1)$ versus $Q(A_2)$ and the model outputs: DOGS = 6, ANIMALS = 2, when there are six dogs and two cats. Thus, the model "fails." In contrast, for the A_1B problem, the "failure" model outputs the correct quantification and answer. It encodes the classes as DOGS-NOT-FRUIT and FRUIT-NOT-DOGS, respectively. Since A_1 can be identified as DOGS but NOT FRUIT and B as FRUIT but NOT DOGS, both encodings succeed in their first attempt at quantification. The model thus outputs DOGS = 6 and FRUITS = 8, and "succeeds." Thus, these models *all* predict that A_1A will be more difficult than A_1B and that developmentally, A_1A should lag behind A_1B.

In contrast, consider the hypothesis that the children fail because they initially encode the display only as subordinate classes (Option 2 in our analysis). If so, they would misidentify A as A_2 and B as B_1 or B_2. Those who succeeded would do so because they encode and identify A and B as superordinate classes. Hence, *no difference* in difficulty is predicted for the two problems. Another reason for this prediction is revealed in the following list, which demonstrates that A_1B and A_1A problems have the same number of component processes.

1. Represent the display as either A_1, A_2, or A_1, A_2, B_1, B_2.
2. Interpret the question as a request to compare two quantities, either A_1 and A, or A_1 and B.
3. Identify A_1.
4. Quantify A_1 as $Q(A_1)$.
5. Identify A as A_2, or identify B as either B_1 or B_2.
6. Quantify A as $Q(A_2)$, or quantify B as $Q(B_1)$ or $Q(B_2)$.
7. Compare $Q(A_1)$ and $Q(A_2)$, or compare $Q(A_1)$ and $Q(B_1)$ or $Q(B_2)$.
8. Respond A_1 if $Q(A_1) > Q(A_2)$, or if $Q(A_1) > Q(B_1)$ or $Q(B_2)$.

TABLE 6.3
Comparison of Within- and Between-Class Problems of Varying Ratios[a]

		Proportion Correct			
	Subordinate Class		Age		
Problem	Ratio	5	7	9	N (cell)
B_1A_1 or B_2A_1	4:6	0.82	0.96	0.96	48 x 4 = 192
B_1A	4:6	0.82	0.93	0.96	48 x 2 = 96
A_2B	2:4	0.84	0.97	0.98	96
A_2B_1 or A_2B_2	2:4	0.86	0.97	0.97	192
A_2A	2:6	0.92	0.96	0.99	96
A_2A_1	2:6	0.93	1.00	0.98	96

[a]Data from Isen et al., 1975.

The critical assumptions are that the display is initially encoded as a mutually exclusive set of subordinate classes and that the superordinate class applies to and is identified with one of these subordinate classes.

Isen et al. (1975) ran two multiple-partitioning conditions, one in Experiment I (reported earlier) and another in Experiment II. In Experiment II, the condition followed initial testing on a one-class, class-inclusion problem. The results were very similar to those in Experiment I; Table 6.2 shows the proportion of superordinate class answers for the two problems, with 24 children per age group (48 observations per cell). There were small (and statistically nonsignificant) differences between A_1A and A_1B problems within each age group for each experi-

TABLE 6.4
Comparison of Within-Class Problems of Varying Subordinate
Class Ratios[a]

		Proportion Superordinate Class (A) Answers			
			Age		
Subordinate Ratio	Problem	5	7	9	N
6:2	A_1A	0.32	0.51	0.65	48 x 2 = 96
2:6	A_2A	0.92	0.96	0.99	96

[a]Data from Isen et al., 1975.

ment. The overall proportion of subordinate answers for the A_1A problem was 0.515 and for the A_1B problem, 0.523. With $N = 288$ observations, this was a powerful test of the null hypothesis, and the data favored the subordinate-class encoding and misidentification hypotheses. Furthermore, analyses of the problems in a 2 x 2 contingency table indicated no developmental priority of the tasks. The conditional probabilities of success on an A_1A problem given a success on an A_1B problem were 0.45, 0.54, and 0.70 for the 5-, 7-, and 9-year-old children, respectively. The conditional probabilities of success on the A_1B problem given success on the A_1A problem were 0.48, 0.50, and 0.70.

Other Data on Subordinate Class Encoding and Comparison. Additional support for the subordinate class encoding hypothesis is found in the Isen et al. (1975) multiple-partitioning data. There were three problems that involved the comparison of a subordinate class with a superordinate class: B_1A (or B_2A), A_2B, and A_2A. When subordinate classes were quantified and compared, the ratios were 4:6, 2:4, and 2:6 rather than 4:8, 2:8, and 2:8 if the superordinate class was quantified and compared. There were corresponding "control" problems involving subordinate class comparisons of similar ratios: B_1A_1 or B_2A_1 (4:6), A_2B_1 or A_2B (2:4), and A_2A_1 (2:6).

If subordinate classes are encoded, misidentified, quantified, and compared, then we would expect the two sets of problems to be solved similarly. The data summarized in Table 6.3 indicate that this was the case. There were virtually no differences between the superordinate and subordinate control problems. Performance on both was virtually perfect, a fact consistent with the model, since both subordinate and superordinate comparisons yielded the same correct answer. The deviation from unity can be understood in terms of counting errors.

Another way of showing that subordinate encoding, misidentification, quantification, and comparison processes occur in class-inclusion problems is to contrast two other problems in the multiple-partitioning conditions that varied the subordinate class ratios: A_1A (6:2) and A_2A (2:6). In the A_1A problem, the comparison was between $Q(A_1) = 6$ and $Q(A) = 2$; in the A_2A problem, the comparison was between $Q(A_2) = 2$ and $Q(A) = 6$. Hence, we predicted that the A_2A problem would yield considerably more superordinate class responses than the A_1A problem. Notice that both problems involve identical logical structures and operations, so that Inhelder and Piaget's (1964) model predicts no difference.

In fact, as indicated in Table 6.4, performance on the A_2A problem was nearly perfect and far superior to performance on the A_1A problem. All comparisons were statistically reliable ($p < 0.01$).

Subordinate Identification in the A_1B Problem. A critical assumption in the foregoing analysis of the A_1B problem was that children identified B as B_1 or B_2 and quantified B as $Q(B_1)$ or $Q(B_2)$. This assumption was tested by varying the numbers of members in the B_1 and B_2 classes. There were three conditions in

TABLE 6.5
Experimental Design and Results Where the
Number of Subordinate Members Varied

| Condition | Number of Subordinate Members | | | | Percentage of B Answers |
	A_1	A_2	B_1	B_2	
1	5	3	4	4	80
2	5	3	6	2	85
3	5	3	6	6	100

this experiment, and the number of objects in each subordinate class for each condition is given in Table 6.5. Notice that $Q(A_1)$ was held constant, and $Q(B_1)$ or $Q(B_2)$ varied. In Condition 1, $Q(A_1) > Q(B_1)$ or $Q(B_2)$. If the child misidentifies B as B_1 or B_2, then he should respond "A_1." However, in Conditions 2 and 3, one or two subordinate classes of B are larger than $Q(A_1)$. Here, if the child misidentifies B as B_1 or B_2, he is increasingly likely to err. Forty children, whose ages ranged from 7–5 to 9–4 years (median = 8–3), were given the three problems in a counterbalanced series. The data, shown in Table 6.5, revealed that as $Q(B_1)$ or $Q(B_2)$ became larger than $Q(A_1)$, the percentage of "B" answers increased ($p < 0.05$).

McGarrigle, Grieve, and Hughes (in press) reported a more striking result on the same issue. Five-year-olds were shown models of farm animals in the following display:

COWS

B　　　　B　　　　W　　　　W

(WALL) XXXXXXXXXXXXXXXXXXXXXXXXXXXXXXXXXX CHILD

HORSES

B　　　　B　　　　B　　　　W

The cows and horses were black or white, and a model farmyard wall separated the two classes of objects. The experimenter pointed to the appropriate sides of the array and asked between-class A_1B questions. In one problem, the question was, "Are there more black horses (A_1) here or more cows (B) here?" Note that the A_1, A_2, B_1, and B_2 numbers were 3, 1, 2, and 2, respectively, for this problem and that $Q(A_1) > Q(B_1)$ or $Q(B_2)$. Only 14% of the children answered "Cows" (B). In another problem, the question was, "Are there more black cows (A_1) here more horses (B) here?" Note that the respective subordinate numbers were now

2, 2, 3, and 1, so that $Q(A_1) < Q(B_1)$. In this case, 58% answered, "Horses" (B), supporting the assumption that B is misidentified as B_1.

Children might make subordinate class comparisons in this situation because they interpret the adjective modifier "black" (or "white") as applying to *both* classes. "Are there more black horses or cows?" might be interpreted as, "Are there more black horses or *black* cows?" Thus, interpretation of the question may influence how children encode the display and identify the classes.

Finally, McGarrigle et al. pointed out that Piaget (1952, p. 169) himself conducted an A_1A versus A_1B experiment. He used one or two sets of wooden beads. There were five beads in each set, three of which were brown. For the A_1A problem, Piaget used only one set and asked, "Which would be longer, a necklace made of the brown beads or a necklace made of wooden beads?" This is an inclusion problem. For the between-class, non-inclusion A_1B problem, he used two sets; A_1 referred to the brown beads in the first set and B referred to the wooden beads in the second set. Piaget claims that the two problems did not differ in difficulty. He concluded, however, "It thus seems to be the relationship of inclusion that is the stumbling block for these children." This conclusion simply does not follow because the A_1B problem does not include inclusion!

Component 2: Interpretation of the Question

In our discussion here, we restrict what we mean by interpretation of the question. Obviously, the whole act of answering the question involves its interpretation. However, two aspects appear to be essential. First, the child must understand that a comparison of quantities is called for; this is signaled primarily by use of the comparative "more" (Donaldson & Wales, 1970). Second, the conjunction "or" must be interpreted. The form of the question, "Are there more A_1 or A?" may encourage comparison of subclasses because "or" is used most often in the exclusive sense (e.g., women or men) or to conjoin coordinate classes (Shipley, 1971). The exclusive interpretation of the class-inclusion question underlies Klahr and Wallace's (1972) example: "Are there more psychologists or clinicians in the APA?" One would not interpret clinicians as nonpsychologists unless one considered the classes mutually exclusive.

One way to alter this interpretation is to *explicitly state all the classes.* For example, one could ask, "Are there more pets or more dogs or more cats?" Ahr and Youniss (1970) did this and found that the percentage of correct "A" answers improved from 5% to 55%. When these same children were retested on the standard question, their performance returned to a baseline of about 10% "A" answers. Ahr and Youniss (1970) interpreted their result as showing no transfer between explicit and implicit questioning. An alternative interpretation is that the children consistently made mutually exclusive interpretations of the questions. For them, the A_1 or A form asks for a mutually exclusive comparison; the A_1 or A_2 or A form does likewise, except now it is clear that A is not

TABLE 6.6
Comparison of Binary- and Extended-Class Problems[a]

Problem	Number of Subordinate Members				Proportion of A Answers
	A_1	A_2	A_3	A_4	
Binary	4	2	0	0	0.32
Extended	4	2	2	2	0.74

[a]Data from McLanahan, 1976.

A_2 and therefore must refer to both A_1 and A_2. There is no clear basis for expecting transfer.

Another approach is to train children to make inclusive interpretations of the superordinate term A in the standard question. In the same (1970) study, Ahr and Youniss gave correctional feedback following A_1 responses to a group of 6- to 8-year-olds. Correct responding increased from 5% to 55%. Moreover, this training generalized to subsequent problems in which feedback was not given (72% correct). One could argue that the training induced a response bias, but such a bias would require the child to discriminate semantically the superordinate class, A, from the subordinate class, A_1, since the classes were not repeated.

McGarrigle, Grieve, and Hughes (in press) made the interesting observation that the child may, in some inclusion tasks, extend the adjective modifying A_1 to modify A. This interpretation holds for tasks such as theirs where black or white cows and horses are compared but does not extend to procedures using questions without adjectives. In the latter case, the child may produce an encoding similar to Klahr and Wallace's DOGS and ANIMALS-NOT-DOGS default code.

Support for this view was found in two of our studies of *extended* class-inclusion problems. In his thesis, McLanahan (1976) compared two conditions. Children in the first one received the standard class-inclusion problem with one superordinate class divisible into two subordinate classes. Children in the second received a different type of problem in which the superordinate was divisible into four subordinate classes (Table 6.6). If the child groups A_2, A_3, and A_4 and identifies these three subordinate classes as A, then class-inclusion performance should improve. This follows since the model would output $Q(A) = 6$ and $Q(A_1) = 4$ in the extended class problem. On the other hand, if only subordinate class comparisons occur, then $Q(A_1) > Q(A_2) = Q(A_3) = Q(A_4)$, and there would be no difference in performance between binary and extended class problems.

The children ranged in age from 6–0 to 8–9 years (median = 7–0); each was tested on 12 different problems. As can be seen in Table 6.6, the proportion of A answers increased 42% in the extended class problem ($p < 0.01$). These data favor the idea that the children treated the subordinate classes — A_2, A_3, and A_4 — as a class: non-A_1.

TABLE 6.7

Comparison of Binary- and Extended-Class
Problems with A_1 as the Majority (4:3)
or Minority (2:3) Subordinate Class

Condition (Ratio)	Subordinate Class Number of Members				Proportion of A Answers
	A_1	A_2	A_3	A_4	
Extended (4:3)	4	1	1	1	0.28
Binary (4:3)	4	3	0	0	0.32
Extended (2:3)	2	1	1	1	0.70
Binary (2:3)	2	3	0	0	0.92

We replicated McLanahan's (1976) finding and compared binary with extended problems in which the number of non-A_1 members was the same. In this experiment, 40 children, aged 6–7 to 9–4 years (median = 8–3), were tested on four different class-inclusion problems. The conditions (described in terms of their subordinate class members) are presented in Table 6.7, which also shows the proportion of children making A responses in each of the four conditions. When the number of members in A_1 was a minority, the number of A responses increased from 30% to 81% ($p < 0.01$).

These results seem to conflict with those on the A_1B problems, in which B was assumed to be identified with either B_1 or B_2. If there had been no difference between McLanahan's groups in Table 6.6 or between the extended and binary groups in Table 6.7, then we would have had additional evidence for A being identified with either A_2 or A_3 or A_4. The difference between the problems seems to lie in the fact that A_1B is a between-class problem with more than one superordinate present. The A_1A problems involve a partitioning between A_1 and all sets not included in A_1. The A_1B problem involves a partitioning between A_1 and B but *not* all sets not included in A_1. The A_1A problem promotes A_1 and non-A_1 encoding, but the A_1B problem does not. Hence, in the A_1A problem children may identify the unmentioned subclasses as non-A_1, since non-A_1 applies to *all remaining objects*. In the A_1B problem, by contrast, they identify B as either B_1 or B_2, since the term applies to either one or the other and not to A_2.

Components 3 and 5: Finding the Referents for A_1 and A

Children should have little difficulty identifying the majority subordinate class, A_1, assuming that the term used in the question applies only to it and that the members of the class share some common, distinctive features. Under these conditions, either of the optional encodings (2) or (3) would lead to identification of A_1. As far as we can tell, all class-inclusion studies meet these criteria.

The problem is finding the referent for A. Because the name of the superordinate class (e.g., animals) may be applied to either of the subordinates (dogs or cats), its intended referent is ambiguous, even if the child *knows* that dogs and cats are included in the set of animals. If the child encodes the display as subordinate classes and/or interprets the question as calling for a mutually exclusive comparison of A_1 and other A's, then A can properly be identified as A_2. The questions are whether this occurs and whether such an identification can be offset by semantic factors. The answer to both questions is "Yes."

Distinctive Feature Indicators of A as a Referent for A_1 and A_2. Suppose one has a display of cows, some black and some white, and one asks, "Are there more black cows or cows?" The child is being asked to compare a subordinate class having a salient feature (color) with a superordinate class whose features are undefined. The most likely outcome is that he will interpret the question as a comparison between black cows and white cows. This interpretation is consistent with an A_1 and A_2 encoding because that may be the only distinctive feature in the display. Suppose, however, that one adds a distinctive feature to the display for *all* the cows and specifies it in the question. Should this not facilitate identification of $A_1 + A_2$ as the referent of A? Consider the following two studies.

McGarrigle, Grieve, and Hughes (in press) performed two experiments, one on children 3 to 5 years old and the other on children 5 to 7 years old. They used displays with three black cows and one white cow. In one case, the cows were all standing up; in another, they were lying down. Standard class-inclusion questions were posed and contrasted with ones that had an adjective describing the superordinate class, A: for example, "Are there more black cows or *standing* cows?" With the preschool children, A responses rose from 31% to 52%; with the older age group, they rose from 26% to 43%. Thus, children can compare subordinate and superordinate classes if the referent for the superordinate class is unambiguous.

McGarrigle et al. argued that reference to the salient properties of A_1 promoted subordinate class comparison. To show this, they devised a clever series of experiments that they presented to preschool children. A teddy bear, a chair, and a table were displayed as follows. Between the teddy and the table were the chair and six colored chips called "steps." In one experiment, the alignment was as follows:

CHAIR
↓

TEDDY R R R R W W TABLE

Notice that there were four red steps to the chair and two white steps to the table. The form of the question that made A_1 salient was, "Are there more red steps to go to the chair or more steps to go to the table?" When A_1 was *not* salient, the question was, "Are there more steps to the chair or more steps to the table?"

When the A_1-salient questions were asked, the percentage of A answers was 0.38; when A_1 was not salient, the percentage of A answers was 0.64. Thus, when the question did not refer to the distinctive features of the subordinate classes, the majority of preschool children gave the superordinate class answer.

McGarrigle et al. replicated this finding using two-class displays in which the teddy had a chair to his left and a table to his right. There were four red chips between him and the chair and three red and two white chips between him and the table. The questions were, "Are there more red steps to go to the chair or more steps to go to the table?" and "Are there more steps to go to the chair or more steps to go to the table?" Notice that when the color of A_1 was mentioned, the child could interpret B as referring to the three red chips to the table so that $Q(A) = 4 > Q(B) = 3$. When the color of A_1 was mentioned, 46% of answers were correct; when the color was omitted, 71% of answers were correct. Again, naming the distinctive feature promoted subordinate class comparison. The important point of this work is that highlighting distinctive features can promote either subordinate or superordinate class comparisons, depending on which class's features are stressed.

Wilkinson's (1976) study of "percept inclusion" supports this argument. He contrasted the standard class-inclusion problem ("Are there more mothers or more grown-ups?") with one in which distinctive features of *both* A_1 and A were used ("Are there more grown-ups who have a picnic basket or more grown-ups who have a chair?"). For 48 nursery school children, the percentage of A answers rose from 23% to 60% when the contrasting distinctive features were used. Thus, a majority of 5-year-old children made accurate subordinate-superordinate comparisons when the referents for A_1 and A_2 were unambiguous.

Semantic Features of A.   One can choose a lexical item for the superordinate class so that it necessarily refers to all subordinate class members. Markman (1973) showed 6- to 8-year-olds a picture of large and small dogs. There were two large dogs and four small ones. Pointing to the picture and appropriate dogs, she said, "Here is a picture of a family of dogs. Here is the mother dog and here is the father dog and here are the baby dogs. And here is the *family* of dogs [pointing to all of the dogs]. Now who would have more pets, someone who owned the baby dogs or someone who owned the family?"

Markman compared this problem with standard class-inclusion problems. Using stringent criteria of giving the superordinate name and an adequate explanation, 60% of the children hearing the collective name succeeded on all problems; none of the control children succeeded on any of the problems.

In an extension, Markman and Seibert (1976) contrasted a number of collective and class names. Superordinate answers rose from 45% with class nouns to 70% with collective nouns. In a second experiment, Markman and Seibert contrasted three types of nouns: class nouns; unmarked plural nouns (money, food, furniture, silverware, fruit), which like class nouns refer to subordinates as well as the whole set; and collective nouns, which refer only to the totality. The respective percentages of A answers were 3%, 19%, and 62%.

Markman and Seibert argued that collective nouns develop semantically before class nouns. However, this conclusion does not necessarily follow from their results. If the same child had *equal* semantic knowledge about class and collective nouns — that is, that the class noun refers either to A or A_1 or A_2, whereas the collective noun refers only to A — he would, in our view, be led by the ambiguity to misidentify A in the first case but not in the second.

In their Experiment III, Markman and Seibert (1976) studied a problem relevant to Wohlwill's (1968) perceptual encoding hypothesis and the current model. Their experimental situation involved presenting pictures in which separable parts of a display formed an integral whole. For example, in their object condition, they said: "Here is a pig. This is the head and this is the body and this is the pig. Who would have more money, someone who filled up the body or someone who filled up the pig?" Notice that they point out A_1 and A but that the display is of an integrated figure. Here, we would not expect the child to encode the display as A_1 and A_2, that is, as body and head. Rather, the encoding is most likely to be a pig. The children — nursery, kindergarten, first, and second graders — answered correctly on 24% of class problems, 52% of collection problems, and 54% of object problems. Within each grade level, performance doubled.

In summary, then, collection names such as family, flock, pile, bunch, herd, pride, class, team, army, and the like do not semantically apply to the subordinate classes and hence cannot be misidentified with them. Neither can an object such as a pig be confused with its parts. By contrast, misidentification of A with A_2 is likely where ambiguously referenced class names are used. This ambiguity of reference seems to be responsible for a large proportion of subordinate class answers.

Misidentification of A with A_2: Direct Evidence.   We wished to find more direct evidence that children misidentify A with A_2. McLanahan (1976) developed a simple procedure to do this. After a child answered the question, "Are there more A_1 or A?" McLanahan asked him to explain his answer, and then asked, "How many As are there?" McLanahan's problems had ratios of 4:2 in the binary problem and 4:2:2:2 in the extended problem. If a child misidentified A as A_2 in the binary problem, we would expect him to say that there were two As. In the extended problem, when children may identify A with all nonmembers of A_1, we would expect them to respond "6" rather than "10." We would particularly expect these answers from children who chose A_1 in the binary problem and from children who chose A in the extended problem.

Table 6.8 shows the frequency distributions of the answers to "How many As are there?" in McLanahan's (1976) thesis study. There were 12 problems by 24 children, or 288 total answers. Evidence that the children misidentified the superordinate class, A, with the minority subordinate, A_2, was found in the binary problem answers. Here, the conditional probability of saying that $Q(A) = 2$, given an A_1 answer, was 0.38. For those who give an A answer, it was 0.01.

TABLE 6.8
Frequency of Numbers Given to the Question: "How Many As
Are There?" In Binary and Extended Problems[a]

		Are there more As or A_1s?			
			Problem		
		Binary (4:2)		Extended (4:2:2:2)	
		A_1	A	A_1	A
	2	80	1		
	6	118	71	4	90
How many As	10			61	88
are there?	other	12	6	18	27
	Total number				
	of answers	210	78	83	205
	Conditional probability of Number 2	0.38	.01		
	Conditional probability of Number 6			0.05	0.44

[a]Data from McLanahan, 1976.

In the extended problem, a similar proportion should misidentify the superordinate class, A, with the subordinate classes, A_2, A_3, and A_4, when they give an A answer. This was nearly the case. Here, given an A answer, the probability of saying that $Q(A) = 6$ was 0.44. Thus, the two conditions yielded similar estimates of the proportion of children who misidentified the superordinates with the subordinates.

In our replication of McLanahan (cf. Table 6.7), we also asked the children, "How many As are there?" but we did not ask for explanations in between. Forty children were tested on two problems in which A_1 was the majority subordinate class in a 4:3 ratio problem and in which A_1 was the minority in a 2:3 ratio problem. There were no differences between binary and extended problems within these ratio classifications, so we combined the data. Table 6.9 shows that we replicated McLanahan's results. If the children misidentify A as A_2 or as $(A_2 + A_3 + A_4)$, then when A_1 is the majority, $Q(A_1) > Q(A)$ and more A_1 answers are expected. This was found. The conditional probability of $Q(A) = 3$, given an A_1 answer, was 0.34. Given an A answer, it was lower, 0.12. When A_1 is the minority, if they misidentify A as A_2, $Q(A) > Q(A_1)$ and more A answers are expected. This too was obtained. Here the conditional probability of $Q(A) = 3$, given an A answer, was 0.37. Given an A_1 answer, it was lower, 0.13. The data

TABLE 6.9
Frequency of Numbers Given for the Question: "How Many
As Are There?" A_1 Majority and A_1 Minority Problems

		Are there more As or A_1s?					
		A_1 majority (4:3)				A_1 minority (2:3)	
		A_1	A			A_1	A
	7	29	15	5		7	37
How	3	19	3	3		2	24
Many	Other	8	6	Other		6	4
As?	Total	56	24			15	65
	Conditional probability of Number 3	0.34	0.12			0.13	0.37

are consistent with encoding Option 2 of the component process model. These data contradict Brainerd and Kaszor's (1974) claim that misidentification does not occur.

Note, however, that 51% of the children who gave A_1 responses in the 4:3 problem correctly quantified A. These data indicate that not all children misidentify A as A_2. In fact, the majority of the children knew how many members there were in the superordinate class despite the fact that they claimed that A_1 was more. Clearly, the components analysis does not capture all the data, and other alternatives are possible.

We replicated the misidentification findings in yet another study. Recall that we had 40 children answer class-inclusion questions that did or did not initially label the displays. The results showed no effect of labeling. After each question was answered, we immediately asked, "How many As are there?" The problems had 5:3 ratios; there were four questions per child. The distribution of number answers is shown in Table 6.10, along with the associated conditional probabilities. The data once again replicated the major finding which was that the conditional probability of $Q(A) = 3$, given an A_1 answer, was 0.47, whereas given an A answer, it was 0.04. One third of those children who gave an A_1 answer correctly quantified A.

In Tables 6.8, 6.9, and 6.10, the "other" answers were most frequently $Q(A)$ ±1 or $Q(A_1)$ ±1. These small numerical errors, however, can, in the case of small differences between A_1 and A_2 or A_1 and A, account for a number of cases in

TABLE 6.10
Binary Problem with A_1 Majority (5:3 Ratio)

		Are there more As or A_1s?	
		A_1	A
How	8	38	36
Many	3	53	2
As?	Other	21	10
	Total	112	48
	Conditional probability of Number 3	0.47	0.04

which the child gives an A or an A_1 answer for the wrong reasons. They also indicate that counting ability influences class-inclusion performance. Over all three tables, these inaccurate quantifications accounted for 13% of the answers.

Components 4 and 6: Quantifying A_1 and A

Suppose we had children quantify the classes prior to being asked the class-inclusion question. Then, when the question was presented, they would have already enumerated the classes, and a simple quantitative comparison would yield the correct response. We carried out a pilot study on this issue using 30 children from a summer camp (ages 5–9 to 8–2; median = 7–0). In each of three conditions, the children were asked standard class-inclusion questions with one-class displays having 5:3 ratios as follows. In the control (No Quantification) condition, children were asked *to point to but not to quantify* the superordinate and subordinate classes in response to labels provided by the experimenter. In the Quantify A condition, children were asked to count the superordinate class. In the Quantify All condition, they were asked to count A, A_1, and A_2. Each child was tested on four class-inclusion problems for a given condition.

The results suggest that quantifying all three classes aided class-inclusion performance. For the No Quantification condition, 45% of the responses were A; for the Quantify A condition, 42%; and for the Quantify All condition, 68%, an increase of 24% over the average of the other conditions.

Because the data were bimodally distributed, we compared the number of children giving no or one correct answer with the number giving three or four. For the first two conditions combined, eight children gave no or one correct answers and seven gave three or four; for the Quantify All condition, the respective frequencies were three and seven ($p = 0.097$, Fisher exact probability test).

Thus, the data are only suggestive. The number of children was small and the manipulation weak. What seems needed is a training procedure that guarantees that the children have the quantifications available at the time of questioning. Another interesting issue suggested by the experiment is whether having the child point to the classes led to implicit quantification. Wilkinson (1976, Experiment I) used an implicit quantification procedure: He asked children to "Point and show me all the A_1. Now show me all the A." This led to a significant 29% improvement over controls who did not point.

Quantification and the So-called Verbal Facilitation Effect.   As mentioned, our results suggest that Wohlwill's (1968) perceptual set hypothesis may be at least partially correct. Like Wohlwill, we were able to facilitate performance by providing a contrasting class. However, this effect was weak compared with the amount of facilitation that has been obtained by other means (Markman, 1973; Markman & Seibert, 1976; McGarrigle et al., in press; Wilkinson, 1976).

Wohlwill (1968) found stronger effects by posing a modified form of the question in the absence of the displays (for example, "If I had six roses and two violets, would I have more flowers or more roses?") and comparing performance on it with performance on the usual class inclusion task. Thus, as Winer (1974) noted, Wohlwill confounded quantification (cardinality in Wohlwill's terms) of the subclasses with absence of the display. Therefore, Winer compared Wohlwill's two conditions with a third, which involved quantification of the subordinate classes and pictorial displays. Winer found that performance increased if the subclasses were quantified, regardless of the presence or absence of a pictorial display. The proportions of A responses by 72 children in grades two, three, and four were 31% (standard class inclusion), 62% (quantified classes and no display), and 79% (quantified classes with display). Since the addition of the pictorial display did not reduce performance, Winer concluded that Wohlwill's hypothesis was wrong.

This conclusion may be unwarranted for two reasons. First, it is possible that when the classes are quantified in the statement, children simply ignore the display. Second, quantifying the subclasses may aid in answering the question. That is, given $Q(A_1)$ and $Q(A_2)$, children may find $Q(A)$ by simply adding $Q(A_1)$ and $Q(A_2)$. (Note that this *addition operation* does not involve use of the displays.) If so, then Winer's (1974) facilitation effect of 48% occurred because there was no need to encode the display.

Brainerd and Kaszor (1974) quantified the subordinate classes prior to posing the class-inclusion question and in the presence or absence of pictorial displays. Although they did not compare these conditions directly, their data are consistent with Winer's (1974) results that the pictures had no effect when they followed quantification of the subordinate classes. The overall mean proportions of A responses in their two experiments, using the appropriate questions for equal or unequal ratios, were 38% when pictures followed and 40% when they were absent. However, Brainerd and Kaszor (1974) did not replicate Winer's (1974) other findings nor did they replicate Wohlwill's (1968). Contrasting their cardinality before picture or cardinality alone conditions with their picture alone condition, the overall facilitation was, respectively, 4% and 13%, where appropriate ratio questions were used. Thus, stating the quantities of the subclasses before class-inclusion questioning appears to have a weak effect, if any. If the quantities are part of the question, it may be more effective; at least that appears to be the main difference between Winer's (1974) and Wohlwill's (1968) studies when contrasted with Brainerd and Kaszor's (1974).

A final note on the verbal facilitation effect is found in Wilkinson (1976), who provides one of the best examples of a purely verbal context in the literature. In his story context, no picture was shown:

> This is a story about two girls. These two girls went to the park one day, to have a picnic. When they arrived at the park, they saw that there were lots of grown-ups in the park. Some of the grown-ups were mothers, and some of the grown-ups were fathers. Now do you remember the two girls? Well, one of the girls said, "I have an idea. Let's go around the park and say 'Hello' to all the mothers." So this girl wanted to say "Hello" to whom, to all the ____? Then the other girl said, "I have a different idea. Let's say 'Hello' to all the grown-ups." So this girl wanted to say "Hello" to whom, to all the ____? Now which girl do you think wanted to say "Hello" more times, the one who wanted to say "Hello" to all the mothers or the one who wanted to say "Hello" to all the grown-ups, to all the mothers or to all the grown-ups [p. 79]?

In this problem, the proportion of children answering A (grownups) increased to 67% from a baseline of 29%. When Wilkinson added the pictures, he did so *after the story was told but before the inclusion question*. The A answers declined to 54%. In a 2 x 2 contingency table of success/failure on the story-only or the story plus picture condition, the story-only problem was easier $\chi^2 (1) = 3.79$, $p = 0.05$, our calculation). Thus, there was a slight but reliable decline when the pictures were presented *after* the story was read. It would be useful to know what effect the pictures would have if given before the story.

Component 7: Compare $Q(A_1)$ and $Q(A)$

The child must use his knowledge of basic quantitative comparisons to solve class-inclusion problems. Critical to this comparison are the operations carried out in the preceding steps (Components 4 and 6) that generate quantitative symbols for A_1 and A_2. These components also relate to Component 2 because the "more" in the question calls for a quantitative comparison. Little is known about these skills per se, and we are forced to assume that subroutines or rules for carrying out comparisons are acquired along with the understanding of quantitative and comparative terms.

Component 8: Decision Rules for Responding

Having compared the quantitative symbols for A and A_1, the child can now answer the original question. If A is identified as the whole class, then $Q(A)$ will be larger than $Q(A_1)$, and the correct answer, A, will be given. If A is misidentified as A_2 and if the number in A_2 is not equal to the number in A_1, then $Q(A) < Q(A_1)$ and the child will say the subordinate class name, A_1. If the number of objects in the subordinate classes is the same and if A is misidentified as A_2, then $Q(A) = Q(A_1)$ and the child will say "Same" or guess randomly between A and A_1.

These decision rules are important in interpreting "ratio" effects (Ahr & Youniss, 1970). Improvement from below chance to chance (50% correct) responding can occur if the children always choose A_1 when it is more numerous than A_2 but guess between A_1 and A_2 when their numbers are equal. In other words, there are two ways the child can arrive at the superordinate A response

TABLE 6.11
Observed (and Predicted) Ratio Effects[a]

		Proportion of Answers		
Test	Age	"A"/Unequal ratio	"Same"/Equal ratio	"A"/Equal ratio
1 (Exp. I)	5	0.10	0.06	0.42 (0.52)
	7	0.27	0.19	0.56 (0.57)
	9	0.44	0.25	0.67 (0.65)
2 (Exp. I)	5	0.17	0.04	0.35 (0.57)[b]
	7	0.43	0.16	0.64 (0.67)
	9	0.57	0.21	0.71 (0.74)
2 (Exp. II)	5	0.27	0.04	0.33 (0.62)[c]
	7	0.46	0.17	0.67 (0.68)
	9	0.54	0.21	0.75 (0.72)
3 (Exp. III)	5	0.16	0.00	0.43 (0.58)
	7	0.42	0.16	0.62 (0.66)
	9	0.56	0.21	0.70 (0.73)

[a]Data from Isen et al., 1975.
[b]$p < .05$ [c]$p < .01$

in the equal-ratio condition: He can correctly identify A as $A_1 + A_2$, or he can misidentify A as A_2, decide A and A_1 are the same, and randomly guess A. Let i be the probability that he correctly identifies A, e the probability that he decides that the quantities are the "Same," and g the probability of guessing A. Then, for an equal-ratio problem, the probability of an A response is:

$$P(A/EQUAL\ RATIO) = i + (1 - i)(1 - e)g \qquad (1)$$

To predict the performance of the equal-ratio groups, we estimate i from the observed probability of an A response in the unequal-ratio conditions and e from the observed proportion of equal responses in the equal-ratio conditions. Furthermore, we assume that $g = 1/2$, because there are two alternatives.

Isen et al. (1975) compared ratios of 4:4 with 6:2 in two experiments. Their observed and predicted data are summarized in Table 6.11. The observed proportions of A responses were predicted quite well for the 7- and 9-year-old children; however, for the 5-year-olds, Equation 1 overpredicted in all four cases. Overprediction means that the child is biased toward A_1. This could occur if the child encoded only A_1.

Although this interpretation is plausible, it is not supported in the data of others. We fitted the guessing model to the ratio data of Ahr and Youniss (1970), who tested 20 children at each age level, using two 4:4 tests and six unequal ratio tests per child. "More" and "fewer" questions were used. Although the unequal ratios varied from 5:3 to 6:2 to 7:1, the differences across them were slight, and we have averaged them for purposes of analysis. The results in Table 6.12 show that the guessing assumption was supported for all age groups. Thus, it seems that the "facilitation effect" of equal ratios is produced largely by guessing during the comparison of quantified classes.

Brainerd and Kaszor (1974) were the first to notice this possibility. They demonstrated artifactual facilitation by varying the kind of question used with different ratios. Consider an equal-ratio condition, 4:4, and a class-inclusion question that calls for a yes/no response. If the question asks for a *difference,*

TABLE 6.12
Observed (and Predicted) Ratio Effects[a]

	Proportion of Answers		
Age	*"A"/Unequal ratio*	*"Same"/Equal ratio*	*"A"/Equal ratio*
6	0.15	0.45	0.35 (0.38)
8	0.12	0.68	0.26 (0.26)
10	0.63	0.34	0.64 (0.75)

[a]Data from Ahr and Youniss, 1970, Table 3, p. 135 and Table 4, p. 137.

as in "Are there more A_1 than there are A?" the answer is "no" regardless of whether the child reaches the comparison process with $Q(A) > Q(A_1)$ or $Q(A) = Q(A_1)$. Likewise, consider the unequal-ratio condition, 6:2, with an *equivalence* question calling for a yes/no response: "Are there the same number of A_1s as there are As?" In this case, the child should respond "no" regardless of the quantified outcomes. That is, $Q(A) > Q(A_1)$ or $Q(A_1) > Q(A)$ would lead to the same "no" response. Brainerd and Kaszor (1974) found that 90% of the answers were "yes" to the difference and "no" to the equality questions. When they asked the equivalence questions with equal ratios, or difference questions with unequal ratios, performance was substantially lower, averaging 23% correct across their age groups and experiments.

These data suggest that responses depend on the classes quantified and the question asked. The decision rules of the component analysis account for this variation in performance. In line with Brainerd and Kaszor (1974), the analysis suggests that equivalence questions with equal ratios and difference questions with unequal ratios differentiate the possible interpretations. In other words, one is less likely to obtain a Type I error using these questions and problems.

DISCUSSION

With respect to the two questions raised initially, the several experiments cited, notably those of Markman (1973), Markman and Seibert (1976), McGarrigle et al. (in press), and Isen et al. (1975), show that "preoperational" children (children under 7 or 8 years of age) can make quantitative comparisons between superordinate and subordinate classes. McGarrigle et al. showed that even the majority of 3- to 5-year-olds can do so. The major factor promoting successful performance seems to be unambiguous reference to the class as a whole and avoidance of procedures stressing distinctive features of the subordinate class. The standard class-inclusion problem "loads the dice" in favor of subordinate class comparisons because it uses single-class contexts, ambiguous class reference, mutually exclusive forms of "or," and often, distinctive features of the majority subordinate task (e.g., brown beads or wooden beads).

Of theoretical importance is the success of our component analysis in helping us understand how these factors affect performance. We have presented a model that can succeed or fail in class inclusion and *not* depend on reversible operations. Furthermore, our A_1A and A_1B, within- and between-class experiments strongly suggest that reversible operations do not necessarily occur in class-inclusion reasoning. Hence, Inhelder and Piaget's (1964) claim that the only decisive way to assess reversibility, mobility of parts, and conservation of the whole is to ask the subject to compare the extension of A with that of A_1 is in doubt. Our analysis indicates that quantification of A is critical and that only addition, not subtraction, of classes is generally required.

Given the number and variety of component operations required to perform class-inclusion tasks, we also question the continued use of this task as a diagnostic tool. The reason for objecting to its use as a test of intelligence, logical ability, or semantic knowledge per se is simple: It is not a pure test of any of these abilities. Since hierarchical class concepts, language comprehension, quantification, and decision making all influence class-inclusion performance, it is not surprising that success would correlate with age and performance on intelligence and other tests. However, the number of components affecting performance on this task should make one quite careful in making inferences about individual abilities. It is also the case, we believe, the one cannot "control" for one or several components and hope to isolate and measure a component of interest. Our componential analysis suggests that these processes are highly dependent, interactive, and dynamic.

The recent attitude of researchers who have examined class inclusion (e.g., Carson & Abrahamson, 1976; Steinberg & Anderson, 1975; and Markman & Siebert, 1976) seems to be to regard it as a context in which to assess, say, linguistic variables. We have no objection to this, since what is done is to *systematically* examine a factor presumed to affect a component process. This is good science, and we hope the trend continues.

Of central concern to most people interested in class inclusion, however, is the development of the child's knowledge of class concepts. How are the concepts formed? What is their basis? How are they extended? What terms are used to refer to them? What terms are added with development? Which ones are dropped? We are, of course, talking about the development of the child's semantic memory, and class-inclusion questions probe only a small part of that knowledge. If we are interested in class concepts and their hierarchical structure, class inclusion is not a good place to start because it confounds perceptual, quantification, and decision-making skills. In addition, we have much more direct ways to study children's semantic knowledge (cf. Carson & Abrahamson, 1976).

Although we are considering the question of what develops, we recognize, as did Piaget, that quantification skills are also essential to class inclusion. Again, however, if that is what we are interested in, then why not study these skills directly (cf. Gelman, 1972; Schaeffer, Eggleston, & Scott, 1974)?

Thus, to the question of what develops in class inclusion, we offer the unsatisfactory answer: "Everything." A host of component skills and knowledge seems to develop together. Particularly important are children's assumptions about what the superordinate and the queried subordinate classes are, and what their relationship to one another is.

Another part of what develops is Piaget's notion of inclusion — knowledge that A_1 and A_2 are subordinate members of A. Another possibility is that, lacking this hierarchical knowledge, the child assumes that the superordinate class (animals) is prompted by different syntactic cues than is the queried subordinate class. The development of a fuller understanding of the inclusion relationship or semantic hierarchies may override the misleading syntactic cues. Given this more advanced semantic knowledge, the child still needs to quantify and compare the classes. Of the two, class concepts seem to begin earlier and to take longer to develop. Given the fact that we develop so many kinds of class concepts, it seems unlikely that this knowledge follows a simple age progression or is structurally linked to quantification. Although the most critical skills and knowledge on this task center on language and quantification, contextual variation either elicits or does not elicit this knowledge. We hope that our report has helped to raise the consciousness of the reader as to what some of these variations are and as to what component processes may operate or be affected when we ask a child a question.

ACKNOWLEDGMENTS

This research was supported by National Institute of Mental Health grants, Nos. 19223 and 29365 to T. Trabasso and by a National Institute of Child Health and Human Development program project grant (5 P01 HD05027) to the University of Minnesota's Institute of Child Development. We wish to thank Lucie Johnson, Dan Keating, and especially Marion Perlmutter for their comments on an earlier draft of this paper. We are also indebted to Robert Grieve and Ellen Markman for helpful suggestions on our research.

REFERENCES

Ahr, P. R., & Youniss, J. Reasons for failure on the class inclusion problem. *Child Development,* 1970, *41,* 131–143.

Brainerd, C. J., & Kaszor, P. An analysis of two proposed sources of children's class inclusion errors. *Developmental Psychology,* 1974, *10,* 633–643.

Carson, M. T., & Abrahamson, A. Some members are more equal than others: The effect of semantic typicality on class inclusion performance. *Child Development,* 1976, *47,* 1186–1190.

Donaldson, M., & Wales, R. J. On the acquisition of some relational terms. In J. R. Hayes (Ed.), *Cognition and the development of language.* New York: Wiley, 1970.

Gelman, R. The nature and development of early number concepts. In H. Reese (Ed.), *Advances in child development* (Vol. 7). New York: Academic Press, 1972.

Inhelder, B., & Piaget, J. *The early growth of logic in the child: Classification and seriation.* New York: Humanities Press, 1964.

Isen, A. M., Riley, C. A., Tucker, T., & Trabasso, T. *The facilitation of class inclusion by use of multiple comparisons and two-class perceptual displays.* Paper presented at the meeting of the Society for Research in Child Development, Denver, Colorado, April 1975.

Klahr, D., & Wallace, J. G. Class-inclusion processes. In S. Farnham–Diggory (Ed.), *Information processing in children.* New York: Academic Press, 1972.

Klahr, D., & Wallace, J. G. *Cognitive development: An information-processing view.* Hillsdale, N.J.: Lawrence Erlbaum Associates, 1976.

Markman, E. The facilitation of part–whole comparisons by use of the collective noun "family." *Child Development,* 1973, *44,* 837–840.

Markman, E., & Seibert, J. Classes and collections: Internal organization and resulting holistic properties. *Cognitive Psychology*, 1976, *8*, 561–577.

McLanahan, A. G. *The class-inclusion problem: An information processing interpretation.* Senior Honors Thesis, Princeton University, 1976.

McGarrigle, J., Grieve, R., & Hughes, M. Interpreting inclusion: A contribution to the study of the child's cognitive and linguistic development. *Journal of Experimental Child Psychology,* in press.

Piaget, J. *The child's conception of number.* New York: Humanities Press, 1952.

Piaget, J. *Six psychological studies.* New York: Random House, 1967.

Rosch, E.   On the internal structure of perceptual and semantic categories. In T. E. Moore (Ed.), *Cognitive development and the acquisition of language.* New York: Academic Press, 1973.

Schaeffer, B., Eggleston, V. H., & Scott, J. L. Number development in young children. *Cognitive Psychology*, 1974, *6*, 357–379.

Shipley, E. *An experimental exploration of the Piagetian class-inclusion task.* (Technical Report 18. The acquisition of linguistic structure.) Unpublished manuscript, University of Pennsylvania, 1971.

Steinberg, E. R., & Anderson, R. C. Hierarchical semantic organization in six year olds. *Journal of Experimental Child Psychology*, 1975, *19*, 544–553.

Wilkinson, A. Counting strategies and semantic analysis as applied to class inclusion. *Cognitive Psychology*, 1976, *8*, 64–85.

Winer, G. A. An analysis of verbal facilitation of class inclusion reasoning. *Child Development*, 1974, *45*, 224–227.

Wohlwill, J. F. Responses to class inclusion questions for verbally and pictorially presented items. *Child Development*, 1968, *39*, 449–465.

7

Goal Formation, Planning, and Learning by Pre-School Problem Solvers or: "My Socks are in the Dryer"

David Klahr

Carnegie–Mellon University

INTRODUCTION

This is a report on a project aimed at understanding and ultimately improving the problem-solving abilities of young children. There are both practical and theoretical grounds for such an effort. The practical justification comes from the observation that problem-solving abilities are implicitly assumed in early school activities: for example, in the puzzles and games used to teach and test fundamentals of reading and arithmetic. Not only are rudimentary problem-solving skills assumed in the early curricula, but also advanced and general problem-solving skills are an explicit goal of subsequent instruction. We have all heard the claim that training in mathematics or reading (or your favorite subject) enhances the ability of students to think logically. It is somewhat curious, then, that for all the implicit and explicit emphasis on problem-solving skills, they are rarely taught directly to young children. One long-range goal of this project, then, is to instruct preschool children on general problem-solving methods.

The theoretical interest in such a study derives from a look at the other side of the coin: Children learn about problem solving, even without direct instruction. Both intuition and casual observation indicate that, as children approach school age, they acquire a range of problem-solving abilities that are typically characterized simply as "common sense."

Let me give an example of what I mean by common sense reasoning in a young child. Consider the following scenario:

Scene: Child and father in yard. Child's playmate appears on bike.
Child: Daddy, would you unlock the basement door?
Daddy: Why?
Child: 'Cause I want to ride my bike.

Daddy: Your bike is in the garage.
Child: But my socks are in the dryer.

What kind of weird child is this? What could possibly explain such an exchange? Let me propose a hypothetical sequence of the child's mental activity:

Top goal: ride bike.
    Constraint: shoes or sneakers on.
    Fact: feet are bare.
      Subgoal 1: get shod.
      Fact: sneakers in yard.
      Fact: sneakers hurt on bare feet.
        Subgoal 2: protect feet (get socks).
        Fact: sock drawer was empty this morning.
        Inference: socks still in dryer.
          Subgoal 3: get to dryer.
          Fact: dryer in basement.
            Subgoal 4: enter basement.
            Fact: long route through house, short route through yard entrance.
            Fact: yard entrance always locked.
              Subgoal 5: unlock yard entrance.
              Fact: Daddies have all the keys to everything.
              Subgoal 6: ask daddy.

The *example* is real (in fact it is from my own experience) and should be plausible to everyone who has spent time around young children. On the other hand, the *analysis* of the example is less convincing, based as it is on a host of assumptions. Some of these assumptions are easily testable. We could determine whether the child knows *constraints*, such as the one about riding bikes only when shod. Similarly, we could assess the child's knowledge of *facts* about dryer location, shortest route to the basement, and so on. Somewhat more difficult, but still reasonable, would be the job of finding out what sorts of *inferences* the child was capable of making about her day-to-day environment, such as the one about where the socks might be, given that they were not in the drawer. However, the dominant feature of the hypothesized thought sequence is not any one of these features in isolation. Rather, it is their organization into a systematic means—ends chain. Thus, I am suggesting that by the time the child is old enough to exhibit the sort of behavior just described, she has already acquired some *general problem-solving* processes. These enable her to function effectively — that is, to achieve desired goals — by noticing relevant features of the environment and organizing a wide range of facts, constraints, and simple inferences in some systematic manner.

As it stands, such a suggestion is unremarkable. The interesting questions concern the detailed nature of such processes, their generality, and their developmental course. Paraphrasing Newell & Simon (1972, p. 663), the question is whether we can view the child in some task environments as an information-processing system, and if so, whether we can identify problem spaces, search strategies, heuristics, goal structures, and so on in a relatively precise fashion. Furthermore, can we determine which aspects of problem solving derive from the task environment and which from characteristics of the subject?

There are two rather distinct approaches one could take in studying children's problem solving. One approach, suggested by Charlesworth (1976), would study the child from an ethological perspective and observe the occurrences of everyday problem solving in the child's normal environment. This is clearly a laborious and time-consuming way to go about the task, although the naturalistic approach has certainly enriched our knowledge about early language development, and it may be the only way to observe interesting problem-solving episodes in children less than 2 years old. The other approach, which we have taken, is to study in the laboratory formal problems whose structure we can thoroughly analyze and over whose systematic variants we can maintain reasonable control. Although Neisser (1976) inveighs against such "artificial" and "academic" environments, it seems unlikely that young children acquire and hold in reserve a special set of cognitive processes for laboratory experiments that bear little relation to those they use in the "natural" environment of rooms, houses, toys, cars, and playgrounds.

Thus, the initial phase of this project has focused on the performance of children between the ages of 3 to 5 years on a variety of well-defined tasks. The first task in the series, and the only one I will report on here, is the Tower of Hanoi.

THE TOWER OF HANOI

The standard version of this task consists of a series of three pegs and a set of n disks of decreasing size.[1] The disks sit initially on one of the pegs, and the goal is to move the entire n-disk configuration to another peg, subject to two constraints: Only one disk can be moved at a time, and at no point can a larger disk be above a smaller disk on any given peg. A standard three-disk problem is shown in Fig. 7.1.

To solve this problem you might reason as follows:

I have to build the stack up from the bottom, which means that I must get disk 3 from A to C, but 2 is in the way, so I'll have to move 2 to B. But

---

[1] The many uses of this task reveal some of the changing goals and methods of experimental psychology over the last 50 years (cf. Byrnes & Spitz, 1977; Cook, 1937; Egan & Greeno, 1974; Gagné & Smith, 1962; Hormann, 1965; Klix, 1971; Neves, 1977; Peterson, 1929; Piaget, 1976; Simon, 1975; Sydow, 1970).

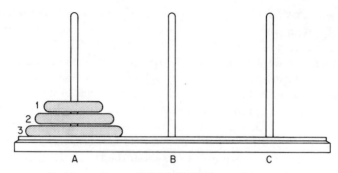

Problem: Move all the disks from peg A to peg C.

FIG. 7.1   Three-disk Tower of Hanoi problem.

if I want to move 2 to *B*, I must first get 1 out of the way, so my first move will be 1 to *C*. Now let me reconsider the new configuration. To get 3 to *C*, I still have to move 2 to *B*, which I can now do. Now to get 3 to *C* I must remove 1 from *C*, so I will put it on *B*, and at last I can move 3 to *C*. And so on.

Although, as will become evident, there are other ways to solve the problem, the example shows that even this simple version of the puzzle can tax one's ability to coordinate sequential reasoning, perceptual discrimination, quantitative ordering, and short-term memory processes. The task involves a well-defined initial state, an unambiguous desired state, and a very limited set of rules about how to change states. The difficulty lies in organizing a sequence of rule applications (legal moves) that ultimately transform the initial physical configuration into the desired one.

Children's Version of the Puzzle: Monkey Cans

For use with young children, we modified the task in three ways that changed its superficial appearance while maintaining its basic structure.

Materials.   We use a set of nested inverted cans as shown in Fig. 7.2. The cans are modified so that they fit very loosely on the pegs; when they are stacked up, it is impossible to put a smaller can on top of a larger can. Even if the child forgets the relative size constraint, the materials provide an obvious physical consequence of attempted violations: Little cans simply fall off of bigger cans. Furthermore, the materials are intuitively more "reasonable" in two regards. First, unlike the standard problem in which small disks may obstruct larger ones, with these materials, bigger cans obstruct smaller cans, either by sitting atop them or by being on a goal peg. Second, larger cans not only sit on top of but also partially contain the smaller cans. Each can is a different color and makes a satisfying clunk with each move.

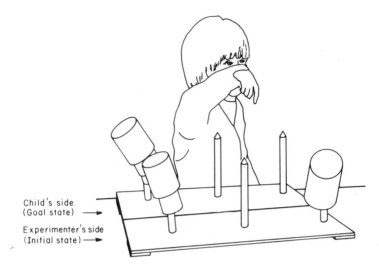

FIG. 7.2   "Monkey cans" arranged for a one-move problem. Initial configuration = state 2; goal configuration = state 1 (see Fig. 7.3).

Externalization of Final Goal.   In addition to the current configuration, the goal — or target — configuration is always physically present. We set up the child's cans in a target configuration and the experimenter's cans in the initial configuration. Then the child is asked to tell the experimenter what he (the experimenter) should do in order to get his cans (*E*s) to look just like the child's. This procedure can be used to elicit multiple-move plans: A child is asked to describe a *sequence* of moves, which the experimenter then executes.

Cover Story.   The problem is presented in the context of a story in which the cans are monkeys (large daddy, medium size mommy, small baby), who jump from tree to tree (peg to peg). The child's monkeys are in some good configuration, the experimenter's monkeys are "copycat" monkeys who want to look just like the child's monkeys (more details on the cover story are given later). The cans are redundantly classified by size, color, and family membership to make it easy for the child to refer to them. The subjects find the cover story easy to comprehend and remember, and they readily agree to consider the cans as monkeys.

Formal State Properties

Figure 7.3 shows all possible legal states and all legal moves for these materials. It is called the "state space." No configuration is repeated in the 27 states. The states are indicated by circled numbers, and the can that is moved is indicated by the number on the line connecting adjacent states. The solution to a problem can be represented as a path (a series of states) through the state space. For

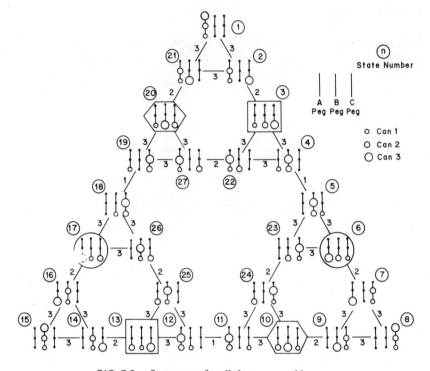

FIG. 7.3   State space for all three-can problems.

example, the minimum solution path for the problem that starts with all three cans on peg A and ends with them on peg C is shown along the right-hand side of the large triangle in Fig. 7.3, moving from state 1 to state 8. The first move involves shifting the largest can (can 3) from peg A to peg C, producing state 2. The next move places can 2 on peg B (state 3), followed by a move of can 3 to peg B (state 4), and so on.

There are no dead ends in this task — any state can be reached from any other state — so that it is possible to consider very many distinct problems (702 to be exact) simply by picking an arbitrary initial and final state. However, there are no two states for which the *minimum* path requires more than seven moves.

Three pairs of special states are indicated by the large squares, circles, and hexagons: these are seven-move problems that begin and end with all pegs occupied. We call these problems "flat-ending" problems, and the "standard" seven-move problems "tower-ending" problems.[2] As we will see, they have somewhat different properties.

_____

[2]Tower of Hanoi buffs should note that the "monster problems" of Simon and Hayes (1976) are all five-move flat-ending problems (e.g., (17 to 3, or 13 to 6). An initial state having all the objects on the wrong pegs leads to a shorter solution path then when one of them is already (prematurely) in the right location (e.g., 13 to 3 or 17 to 6).

General Procedure

The general procedure is designed to assess the upper limit (measured by the length of the minimum solution path) of children's ability to solve this problem. The child is introduced to the materials, the rules, and the cover story and presented with a one-move problem (see Fig. 7.2), then a two-move problem, and so on.

SOLUTION STRATEGIES

We can expect children to vary widely in their ability to solve these problems. Indeed, if we look ahead to the most global description of the children's performance, we can see from Table 7.4 that the best subject could reliably solve seven-move problems, whereas the poorest subjects could do no better than two-move problems. To interpret such results, we need to propose hypotheses about the cognitive processes that enable a child to solve problems reliably up to, but not beyond, length n. In this section, we start with a model for perfect performance, then consider — and reject — alternative models for such performance, and finally present a series of "partial" models to account for different degrees of less-than-perfect performance.

Consider the best performers: the 5-year-olds who could reliably solve six- and 7-move problems. When they began to do the task, they knew nothing about the Tower of Hanoi; after 15 or 20 minutes, they were solving our hardest problems with a high degree of confidence. What had they learned? What could they ultimately have acquired as experts on this task?

An Idealized Model

The model to be described is essentially the one first proposed by Simon (1975). He called it the "sophisticated perceptual strategy." The general procedure is:

1. Compare the current state to the goal state and note all items that are not in their final location.
2. Find the most constrained item (in our case, the smallest can; in the standard form of the problem, the largest disk) that is not yet on its goal peg.
3. Establish the goal of moving that item to its goal peg.
4. Determine the smallest can (if any) that is preventing you from making the desired move.
5. If there is no such can (no culprit), then make the desired move and start all over again (go to step 1).
6. If you can't make the move, then *replace* the current goal with a goal of moving the culprit from its current location to a peg other than the two involved in your current goal.
7. Then return to step 4.

```
SOLVE(C,G)          C = Current state, G = goal state
 S1:  Find differences between C and G.  If none, then done.
 S2:  n <- (Select smallest can).
 S3:  New.goal <- (Move can n from X to Y)
                  <X = current peg of n, Y = goal peg of n>.
 S4:  culprit <- TEST (new.goal)
 S5:  If culprit = nil, then MOVE (nXY); go to S1.
 S6:  else new.goal <- (Move culprit from X' to Y'); go to S4.
      <X' = current peg of culprit, Y' = other of (X,Y)>


TEST(nXY)
 T1:  f.list <- See.from(X) <all cans above n on X>
 T2:  t.list <- See.to(Y) <all cans on Y larger than n>
 T3:  if f.list = nil & t.list = nil, then culprit <- nil
 T4:  else culprit <- min(f.list,t.list); exit
```

FIG. 7.4   SOLVE: A set of rules and tests for the "sophisticated perceptual strategy."

Figure 7.4 shows a concise semiformal description of this strategy.[3] In addition to the six numbered steps just described, there are four "test" steps that describe the details of the "determine" in step 4. These correspond to a series of perceptual tests used to determine whether there is a culprit blocking the current goal and, if there is more than one, which one should be dealt with first. T1 notes any cans currently above the item whose move is being considered (i.e., on the "from" peg). T2 notes any cans on the current "to" peg that are larger than n. T3 tests for whether both of these lists are empty (nil): If they are, then there is no culprit. T4 chooses as culprit the smallest of the obstructors on the combined f. ("from") and t. ("to") lists.

Figure 7.5 shows the first several steps that SOLVE would take when presented with the seven-move flat-ending problem starting with state 13 (2/1/3) and ending with state 3 (1/2/3).[4] All the steps listed *precede* the first move. The full seven moves are shown in Fig. 7.6 (in abbreviated form). The figure shows the series of goals and tests that precede each move. For example, lines 9 to 15 in Fig. 7.6 show that the first goal (line 9) is to get from can 1 from peg B to peg A (G1:1BA). The test detects that can 2 is blocking that goal. Therefore, in line 11 a new goal (G2:2AC) is generated, and so on. Notice that the full listing

---

[3]The models in Figs. 7.4 and 7.8 are written as a sequence of FORTRAN- or ALGOL-like steps in which there are several subroutines that are undefined but whose functions are clear from the context. These models are not written as production systems simply because the increased complexity required by such a representation is unwarranted by the level of analysis we are using here (cf. Klahr & Siegler, 1978; Simon, 1975).

[4]The notation (2/1/3) is used to indicate that peg A is occupied by can 2, peg B by 1, and peg C by 3. As another example, state 27 in Fig. 7.3 would be described as $31/-/2$.

Change C into G
> C: initial state: 2/1/3   (State 13)
> G: final state: 1/2/3   (State 3)

S1: What's wrong? 1 not on A, 2 not on B.
S2: What's the smallest misplaced can? 1.
S3: Get 1 from B to A.

S4: Can 1BA be done?
T1: nothing on top of 1
T2: something in the way of 1 on A: 2
T4: 2 is the culprit.
S6: Get 2 out of way of 1BA: Get 2 from A to C.

S4: Can 2AC be done?
T1: nothing on top of 2
T2: something in the way of 2 on C: 3
T4: 3 is culprit.
S6: Get 3 out of the way of 2AC: Get 3 from C to B.

S4: Can 3CB be done?
T1: nothing on top of 3
T2: nothing in the way of 3 on B
T3: No culprit.
S5: Make move: 3 from C to B.

FIG. 7.5   Trace of first few steps of SOLVE on flat-ending problem from state 13 (2/1/3) to state 3 (1/2/3).

of Fig. 7.5 is condensed into lines 9 to 15 in Fig. 7.6. The actual move that is made is shown under "Move" column, and the resulting configuration is shown under "Config." (The last column shows the type of move that this new configuration will require. Move types will be described in the next section.) Figure 7.7 shows SOLVE operating on a standard tower-ending problem (state 15 to state 1).

Simon's (1975) labeling of this strategy as "sophisticated" is apt. The sophistication lies in the strategy's use of the principle that hard problems should be solved before easy ones. More specifically, the most important thing to attend to is the most constrained object.[5] If it can get to where it is going, the rest will be easier. This principle is utilized in two places: S2 and T4. In S2, the smallest

---

[5]In Piaget's (1976) study of this puzzle, children were asked about which of the disks traveled the most and whether they traveled more on one problem or another. Although the rationale for this line of inquiry was never described, it may have been related to this same issue. If children are aware of the very different numbers of moves that the disks make during the solution, they may begin to get a rudimentary appreciation of the notion of the relative degree of constraint that the task imposed on the different items.

		Move	Config.	Type
03	13 →3 SOLVE strategy on flat-ending problem			
04				
05	initial: 2/1/3 Final: 1/2/3			
06				
07				
08			2/1/3	T2
09	G1: 1BA			
10	Test: from (nil), to (2); culprit:2.			
11	G2: 2AC			
12	Test: from (nil), to (3); culprit:3.			
13	G3: 3CB			
14	Test: from (nil), to (nil); culprit:nil.			
15		3CB	2/31/−	T1
16				
17	G1: 1BA			
18	Test: from (3), to (2); smallest:2, culprit:2.			
19	G2: 2AC			
20	Test: from (nil), to (nil), culprit:nil.			
21		2AC	−/31/2	F2
22	G1: 1BA			
23	Test: from (3), to (nil), culprit:3			
24	G4: 3BC			
25	Test: from (nil), to (nil); culprit:nil.			
26		3BC	−/1/32	D3
27				
28	G1: 1BA			
29	Test: from (nil), to (nil), culprit:nil.			
30		1BA	1/−/32	F1
31	G5: 2CB			
32	Test: from (3), to (nil), culprit:3			
33	G6: 3CA			
34	Test: from (nil), to (nil); culprit:nil.			
35		3CA	31/−/2	D2
36				
37	G5: 2CB			
38	Test: from (nil), to (nil), culprit:nil.			
39		2CB	31/2/−	D1
40	G7: 3AC			
41	Test: from (nil), to (nil), culprit:nil.	3AC	1/2/3	goal

FIG. 7.6   Full trace of SOLVE on 13–3 flat-ending problem.

can not yet on its goal peg is selected as the one to attend to. In T4 the smallest (most constrained) of the obstructors of the current goal is chosen as the culprit.

Move Type.   Thus far, problems have been characterized by their minimum solution length. It is also instructive to consider the *type* of moves that need to be made. There are three move types, distinguished by the immediate reason for the move.

D moves: Move a can *directly* to its final goal configuration on the target peg.
F moves: Move a can *from* a peg in order to get to one beneath it.

T moves: Move a can from a peg in order to facilitate moving a different can *to* that peg.

Table 7.1 shows the sequence in which these moves occur along increasingly longer tower-ending solution paths.[6] The two shortest problems consist entirely of moves *directly* to the goal configuration. Problems of length 3 start with the removal of the largest can *from* on top of the middle-sized can in order to move it (the middle can) on the next move. Four-move problems start with the *direct* move of the smallest can to the goal peg, and so on. Notice that this classification of moves according to why they are taken implies some sort of goal structure on the part of the problem solver.

The basis for this classification is revealed by close examination of Fig. 7.7. If we ask for the proximate reason for any move, the answer is obtained by looking for the immediate supergoal that the accomplishment of the current subgoal will allow. Working from the bottom to the top of Fig. 7.7, we see that D1 and D2 have no supergoals other than the implicit "solve" goal. F1 moves an object that was discovered to be on a *from* peg for the preceding goal (2CA). D3 is another direct move. T moves can 3 again, but this time because it was on the *to* peg of the supergoal. F2 and F3 both involve moving cans from the *from* pegs of the respective supergoals. A similar classification for flat-ending problems is shown in the rightmost column in Fig. 7.7. Notice that for a path length beyond four moves, the flat-ending problems have a different sequence of move types from those of the tower-ending problems.

Alternative Models

The SOLVE model in Fig. 7.4 is very powerful: It will generate the minimum path solution for any three-disk, flat-ending problem and for any n-disk, tower-ending problem. Thus, it can be viewed as a possible "cognitive objective" (Greeno, 1976), that is, as the ultimate goal of training someone to perform expertly on this task. What about other functionally equivalent strategies for expert performance? In this section we summarize three quite different strategies, described in detail by Simon (1975), for perfect performance on the Tower of Hanoi. We argue that none of them are as likely to be acquired by our subjects as the sophisticated perceptual strategy represented by SOLVE. Then, in the next section, we describe a series of increasingly powerful partial models that culminate in the SOLVE model.

Goal Recursion. The goal recursion strategy solves the n-disk problem by recursively decomposing it into three parts: (1) removal of the $n-1$ disk pyramid from the initial peg to the other peg, (2) moving disk n from the initial to the

---

[6]The numbers following the move type indicate the order of occurrence for that type of move as longer and longer problems are presented. Thus D2 is the second D-move, F3 is the third F-move, and so forth.

TABLE 7.1
Move Types Along Tower-Ending Path

	States	Minimum	Move Type Sequence						
	Initial , Final	Path Length	1st	2nd	3rd	4th	5th	6th	7th
	2 , 1	1	D_1						
	3 , 1	2	D_2	D_1					
	4 , 1	3	F_1	D_2	D_1				
Tower-ending	5 , 1	4	D_3	F_1	D_2	D_1			
	6 , 1	5	T	D_3	F_1	D_2	D_1		
	7 , 1	6	F_2	T	D_3	F_1	D_2	D_1	
	8 , 1	7	F_3	F_2	T	D_3	F_1	D_2	D_1

	15 →1 SOLVE strategy on Tower-ending problem	Move	Config.	Type
03				
04				
05	Initial: −/321/− Final: 321/−/−			
06				
07			−/321/−	F3
08				
09	G1: 1BA			
10	Test: from (33.2), to (nil); smallest:2, culprit:2.			
11	G2: 2BC			
12	Test: from (3), to (nil), culprit:3.			
13	G3: 3BA			
14	Test: from (nil), to (nil), culprit:nil.	3BA	3/21/−	F2
15				
16	G1: 1BA			
17	Test: from (2), to (3); smallest:2, culprit:2.			
18	G2: 2BC			
19	Test: from (nil), to (nil), culprit:nil.	2BC	3/1/2	T
20				
21	G1: 1BA			
22	Test: from (nil), to (3); culprit:3.			
23	G4: 3AC			
24	Test: from (nil), to (nil); culprit:nil.			
25		3AC	−/1/32	D3
26				
27	G1: 1BA			
28	Test: from (nil), to (nil), culprit:nil.	1BA	1/−/32	F1
29				
30	G5: 2CA			
31	Test: from (3), to (nil), culprit:3.			
32	G6: 3CB			
33	Test: from (nil), to (nil), culprit:nil.	3CB	1/3/2	D2
34				
35	G5: 2CA			
36	Test: from (nil), to (nil); culprit:nil.			
37		2CA	21/3/−	D1
38				
39	G7: 3BA			
40	Test: from (nil), to (nil); culprit:nil.			
41		3BA	321/−/−	goal

FIG. 7.7   Full trace of SOLVE on 15−1 tower-ending problem.

final position, and (3) moving the $n-1$ disk pyramid from the other peg to the goal peg. Steps 1 and 3 are accomplished by recursively applying the same strategy. Two considerations make it unlikely that our subjects acquired this strategy. First, they were given only limited exposure to "pyramids" that seem necessary to induce the approach. The only example of recursion they encounter is the seven-move, tower-ending problems. Second, as Simon (1975) notes, to execute this strategy, the full goal stack must be retained in memory. It is both necessary and sufficient for solution: "At each stage, the problem solver can decide what to do next without any reference to the current distribution of the

```
SOLVE.2(C, G)
   S1:  Find differences (C-G).  If none,  then done.
   S2:  n <- (Select smallest).
   S3:  New.goal <- [nXY]
   S4:  Move; go to S1.
```

```
SOLVE.4(C, G)
   S1:  Find differences (C-G).  If none,  then done.
   S2:  n <- (Select smallest)
   S3:  New.goal <- [nXY]
   S4:  culprit <- TEST.4(new.goal)
   S5:  If culprit = nil,  then MOVE[nXY]; go to S1.
   S6:  else MOVE[culprit, current.of(culprit), empty]; go to S1.

TEST.4(nXY)
   T1:  f.list <- See.from(X)
   T3:  culprit <- top(f.list)/nil
```

```
SOLVE.5(C, G)
   S1:  Find differences (C-G).  If none,  then done.
   S2:  n <- (Select smallest)
   S3:  New.goal <- [nXY]
   S4:  culprit <- TEST.5(nXY)
   S5:  If culprit = nil,  then MOVE[nXY]; go to S1.
   S6:  else MOVE[culprit, current.of(culprit), other.of(X, Y)]; go to S1.

TEST.5(nXY)
   T1:  f.list <- See.from(X)
   T2:  t.list <- See.to(Y)
   T3:  if t.list = nil,  then culprit <- top(f.list)/nil,
   T4:  else culprit <- top.(t.list), exit.
```

FIG. 7.8   Partial strategies: SOLVE.2, SOLVE.4, SOLVE.5

disks among the pegs. If only he can retain the unaccomplished part of the goal hierarchy in memory, he can calculate what needs to be done without sight of the puzzle and without holding a visual image of it [p. 270]." Given the highly salient display of both initial *and* final configurations, as well as the severe memory demands of this strategy, it seems unlikely to be acquired by young children.

Notice that the memory demands of the sophisticated perceptual strategy are far smaller. Each new goal needs to be retained only long enough either to make the move directly associated with it or to generate its immediate subgoal. The subgoal *replaces* the immediately prior goal. After a move is made (or imagined), the entire procedure is restarted and the differences between the actual (or imagined) new configuration and the goal (which is physically present) are again determined.

Rote.   The move—pattern strategy involves three simple rules that allow one "mindlessly" to solve any tower-ending problem.[7] (If you really want to impress your friends, you should learn this and then apply it to a seven-disk problem... 127 moves without a hitch!) This strategy, like Model IV for the balance scale (Siegler, 1976), is easy to remember and execute, but it is very hard to induce, even for adults. It is quite implausible that our children acquired it in this study.

Another form of rote strategy is based on a memorized list of moves. To solve any specific tower-ending problem, the subject simply cycles through the move sequence he has memorized for that problem. Such a rote strategy could include some degree of generality by being couched in terms of initial, final, and other pegs, which are then instantiated for any particular n-disk problem. Another form of rote strategy would consist of a large collection of $S-R$ pairs in which S is a description of a specific current-final pair of configurations, and R is the appropriate move in that situation (e.g., "state 5 to state 8: move 3 to C"). Given the huge number of such specific associations and the limited exposure the subjects get to most of them, this seems to be an unlikely acquisition. Furthermore, it could not explain how subjects who have seen, for example, problems 20—1 and 3—1 immediately solve 6—8 or 13—15.

Partial Strategies

We have rejected as unlikely the major alternative strategies that subjects might acquire as they become expert in this task. Now let us attempt to characterize the different levels of performance in terms of weakened versions of the sophisticated perceptual strategy (SOLVE) just described. Figure 7.8 shows three such partial strategies. In each of the models, steps have been numbered to correspond to the steps in SOLVE (Fig. 7.4). Each model is named according to the length of the problem that precedes the first error the model would make.

SOLVE.2 will solve up to two-move problems, but it will fail on all longer ones except D3. In step 2 it determines which of the differences involves the smallest can, and it establishes (in S3) the goal of moving that can directly to its goal peg. Having set the goal, it then makes the move (S4) without any further perceptual testing or comparisons. When presented with anything other than a D problem, SOLVE.2 makes the wrong move because it immediately attempts to move the smallest can not yet on the goal peg. For anything other

---

[7]Simon (1975) describes it as follows:

  1. On odd-numbered moves, move the smallest disk; 2. On even-numbered moves, move the next-smallest disk that is exposed; 3. Let Peg S be the initial source peg, T the target peg, and O the other peg. Then if the total number of [disks] is odd, the smallest disk is always moved from S to T to O to S, and so on; while if the total number of [disks] is even, the smallest disk is always moved in the opposite cycle: from S to O to T to S, and so on [p. 273].

TABLE 7.2
Move Selected by Partial Strategies for Each Problem Type
Along Tower-Ending Path
goal: 321/ — / —

		Config.	Partial Strategies			
λ	Type	A/B/C	SOLVE.2	SOLVE.4	SOLVE.5	SOLVE
1	D_1	21/3/—	3BA	3BA	3BA	3BA
2	D_2	1/3/2	2CA	2CA	2CA	2CA
3	F_1	1/—/32	2CA—	3CB	3CB	3CB
4	D_3	—/1/32	1BA	1BA	1BA	1BA
5	T	3/1/2	1BA—	1BA—	3AC	3AC
6	F_2	3/21/—	1BA—	2BC	3AC*	2BC
7	F_3	—/321/—	1BA—	3BA, or 3BC*	3BC*	3BA

— illegal
*Off minimum path

than D problems such moves are illegal. SOLVE.2 differs from SOLVE (the model in Fig. 7.4) in three respects: (1) It does not test the feasibility of the move it wants to make, (2) the only goal it sets always includes the ultimate goal peg rather than any temporary, internally generated, subgoal peg, and (3) it never determines the smaller of two obstructors.

SOLVE.4 will solve all problems up to five-move problems. The steps are similar to those in the SOLVE model, with two important exceptions, both contained in S6. When a culprit is detected, S6 does not establish a new goal and then return to S4. Instead, it immediately moves the culprit. Furthermore, S6 does not have the concept of "other": The target peg for the culprit is simply an *empty* peg. Further differences between SOLVE.4 and SOLVE lie in the very weak tests that are used to determine whether a move can be made. These tests determine only whether there is anything on top of the can to be moved. If there is nothing there, the move will be attempted (i.e., there is no culprit, if the f.list is empty).

SOLVE.5 will solve problems up to length 5 correctly and then will begin to makes moves that are not on the minimum path. Unlike SOLVE.4, SOLVE.5 now uses the concept of "other" when determining where to move the culprit, but — like SOLVE.4 — it makes the move directly, instead of generating a new goal. SOLVE.5 also lacks the full testing capacity of SOLVE. In particular, TEST.5 does not determine the smallest of the potential obstructors on both the t.list and the f.list. Rather, if the t.list is empty, then the culprit is whatever is sitting at the top of the f.list, if anything. If the t.list is not empty — that is, if there is something larger than the can to be moved on the target peg — then it is assumed to be the obstructor (steps T3 and T4).

Table 7.2 shows the move selected by each of the partial strategies for each of the seven problem types along the tower-ending path from state 15 to state 1.

Consider the F2 configuration in the sixth line of the table. The goal (shown at the top of the table) is to get the three-can stack on peg A. SOLVE.2 would notice that cans 2 and 1 are not on the goal peg. Then it would select can 1 as the can to be moved and would attempt to move can 1 directly to the goal peg, which is, of course, an illegal move. SOLVE.4 would establish, in steps S1, S2, and S3, the goal of moving can 1 from B to A, and then test it. TEST.4 would determine that can 2 on the f.list was the culprit, and steps S5 and S6 would move the culprit, can 2, from where it is, peg B, to an empty peg, in this case peg C. This turns out to be — serendipitously — the correct move. SOLVE.5 would also enter the test phase with the goal of moving can 1 to A. However, T3 would fail, since the t.list — the list of cans on the "to" peg that are larger than the can to be moved — would contain can 3. Steps 5 and 6 in SOLVE.5 would then move can 3 to the "other" peg, that is, move 3 from A to C, which, although legal, is not on the minimum path. Of course, SOLVE would correctly decide to move 2 from B to C. (The details are shown in lines 16 to 19 of Fig. 7.7.)

The pass/fail patterns in Table 7.2 are predicted not only for the particular configurations shown but also for any configurations of the specified type. Thus, they suggest an empirical approach similar to that used by Siegler (this volume) for determining which, if any, of the strategies a child is using. However, such a procedure assumes that the strategy being used remains stable during the assessment. Although the stability assumption is reasonable in cases where the assessment yields no feedback for the subject (as in a typical pretest condition), it is untenable in the situation that our subjects faced. For each item, they were required to produce a solution, and they were well aware of how successful they had been. Furthermore, in this initial study, the problem sequence was designed to assess only their first point of failure. Thus, although the partial models appear to have a potential for precise diagnosis, in this chapter we utilize only the predictions they make about the longest problem reliably solved.

A STUDY OF CHILDREN'S PERFORMANCE

The study was run in two phases, with the second to some extent being contingent on the outcome of the first. The two procedures are described separately, and then their results are combined in the analysis. The main difference between the phases lies in the age groups used and the amount of intervention by the experimenter.

Subjects

Thirty children attending the Carnegie–Mellon University Children's School participated. There were 10 children in each of three age groups "3s" (mean 3:10, range 3:8 to 4:4), "4s" (mean 4:5, range 4:1 to 4:9), and "5s" (mean

5:9, range 5:2 to 6:3). The sex ratio was approximately 50/50 in each age range. The children came from predominantly — but not exclusively — upper-middle-class professional families.

Phase I: Purpose and Procedure

There were three goals for the first part of the study, which used the 4-year-old group: (1) Explore the basic ability of uninstructed 4-year-old children to solve problems of various lengths; (2) explore the extent to which they could describe a multiple move sequence; and (3) explore the effectiveness of some rudimentary instruction, including a graduated sequence of problems and a few simple hints about goals and subgoals.

The child was familiarized with the materials shown in Fig. 7.2. Then the rules and objectives were described in the context of a cover story. The cover story went something like this:

> Once upon a time there was a blue river [point to space between rows of pegs]. On your side of the river there were three brown trees. Can you count your trees? On my side there were also three brown trees. On your side there lived three monkeys: a big yellow daddy [put yellow can on a peg], a medium-sized blue mommy, and a little red baby. The monkeys like to jump from tree to tree [according to the rules]; they live on your side of the river. On my side there are also three: a daddy, [etc.] Mine are copycat monkeys. They want to look just like yours, right across the river from yours. Yours are all stacked up like so [state 1], mine are like so [state 2 or 21]. Mine are very unhappy; can you tell me what to do so mine can look like yours?" [The actual script is, of course, more elaborate.]

The problem sequence was generated by choosing increasingly longer problems from alternating sides of the two tower-ending paths terminating in state 1 (Fig. 7.3), for example, 21–1, 3–1, 19–1, 5–1, and so on. If the child suggested an illegal move, the experimenter would point out the illegality. If the child had no suggestion for a move, the experimenter would make the correct first move and then ask the child to continue. If the child was successful at completing the problem in the minimum number of moves, the experimenter would give him either another problem of the same length from the other side of the state space triangle or one that was one move longer. The idea behind all of this was to get an estimate of the upper performance level of the child without either having the child give up because of too many failures or generating lucky solutions.

As the child appeared to reach his upper limit, the experimenter would begin to give a systematic series of hints, attempting to move the child through the steps of the SOLVE strategy described earlier.

For the first few problems, the children were asked to state not just the next move but the next *several* moves. Children varied widely in their ability to do

TABLE 7.3

Pairs of Initial →Final States for Problems of Different
Path Length

Path Length	Problem Order	Tower-ending	Flat-ending
3	a	19 → 1	19 → 3
	b	4 → 1	23 → 3
	c	18 → 15	22 → 6
	d	5 → 8	11 → 6
4	a	5 → 1	18 → 3
	b	18 → 1	24 → 3
	c	19 → 15	27 → 6
	d	4 → 8	12 → 6
5	a	17 → 1	26 → 3
	b	6 → 1	11 → 3
	c	20 → 15	19 → 6
	d	3 → 8	25 → 6
6	a	7 → 1	25 → 3
	b	16 → 1	12 → 3
	c	21 → 15	18 → 6
	d	2 → 8	26 → 6
7	a	15 → 1	14 → 3
	b	8 → 1	16 → 6
	c	1 → 15	13 → 3
	d	1 → 8	17 → 6

this, and the experimenter tried to adapt to these variations. For many children, the attempt to elicit multiple-move plans was given up after the first few problems.

Phase II: Purpose and Procedure

The three objectives of Phase II were as follows:

1. Further investigation of the effects of types of moves. This required varying the goal configuration so that the possibility of specific stimulus configurations being associated with specific moves could be ruled out. This was accomplished in two ways. First, both tower-ending and flat-ending problems were presented. Second, within a problem type, the goal configuration was systematically changed.

2. Elimination of the confounding of the two types of instruction. In this phase, no guidance was given when children reached their peak performance.

TABLE 7.4

Number of children in Each Age Group Who Could Reliably Solve Tower-ending Problems Up to But Not Beyond Given Length

Age				Problem Length (λ)								
Nominal	Mean	Range	n	1	2	3	4	5	6	7	λ	
3	3:10	3:8 – 4:4	10	0	5	1	4	0	0	0	2.9	(0.99)
4	4:5	4:1 – 4:9	10	0	1	1	5	1	2	0	4.2	(1.2)
5	5:9	5:2 – 6:3	10	0	0	0	0	5	4	1	5.6	(0.7)
			30	0	6	2	9	6	6	1		
		Cumulative[a]		30	30	24	22	13	7	1		
		Nontransition probability		0.00	0.20	0.08	0.40	0.46	0.86			

[a]Total number (all groups) solving problems up to and including given problem length.

The only "instruction" consisted of presenting the increasingly longer problem sequence and making the correct first move when subjects did not know what to do.

3. Beginning to measure age-related differences on this task. The 3- and 5-year-old children described at the beginning of this section served as subjects in Phase II. The apparatus, cover story, instructions, and so on were identical except, as just mentioned, no hints were given when subjects began to falter.

Table 7.4 lists the initial and final states for the problems used in this study. (Reference to a problem as having "n-moves" means that the minimum path has n moves). Of course, one could solve an n-move problem in *more* than n moves. All the T–T problems end with states 1, 8, or 15 and start somewhere on the outer contours of the exterior triangle in Fig. 7.3. All minimum paths for T–T problems are also along these contours. All the flat-ending problems end in states 3 or 6 and start in some state on the interior irregular hexagon in Fig. 7.3 (except for the seven-move, flat-ending problems). Notice that along the minimum path for all flat-ending problems there are no flat configurations other than the final one (again, except for the seven-move, flat-ending problems).

The problem sequence was generated by selecting initial-final pairs as follows. The first two problems were 21–1 (one-move) and 3–1 (two-move). (These were always solved correctly.) Then a series of tower-ending problems was selected from the list in Table 7.4. For a given problem length, n, problem a was presented first. If it was correctly and confidently solved, then n was incremented by 1, and problem a of the next length was presented. If there was hesitation or apparent uncertainty, problem b of the same length was presented. If there were any errors, the problem was reinitialized and the first move was made by the experimenter (this would convert the a problem of length n into the b problem of length $n - 1$). If two of the three remaining problems were correctly solved, then n was increased again. Otherwise, the T–T sequence was terminated, and a shift to flat-ending problems was made, starting with length $n–2$, where n was the current level for the tower-ending series. This procedure was designed to present a series of longer and longer problems ending in state 1 until the subject reached his upper limit. Then problems ending in states 15 and 8 were presented to assess one level of generality of what had been learned. Following this, the flat-ending series was presented to test generalization still further.

Results

Path Length.   At any point in the solution of a problem, the child can suggest either the correct move or several kinds of "incorrect" moves. These include legal moves not on the minimum path, illegal moves, and "don't knows."

TABLE 7.5
Number of Children Reliably Solving Tower-ending and Flat-ending
Problems of Each Length[a]

		Length of Tower-ending						
		2	3	4	5	6	7	
	1	1	–	–	–	–	–	1
	2	2	–	2	–	–	–	4
	3	–	1	1	1	–	–	3
Length of	4	–	–	–	4	3	–	7
Flat-ending	5	–	–	–	–	1	–	1
	6	–	–	–	–	–	1	1
		3	1	3	5	4	1	

[a]Three-year-olds ($n = 7$), 5-year-olds ($n = 10$).

A global measure of the child's ability is the length of the longest problem (or subproblem) for which he reliably stays on the minimum path.

The distribution of subjects reliably solving problems of a given length is shown in Table 7.5. The age differences are clear and striking. The regularity of the age effect indicates that the semiclinical procedures used in Phase 1 did not seriously distort the assessment of maximum performance levels, although it may have increased the spread of the 4-year-old group somewhat.

Consider first the 4-year-olds from Phase I. None of them could solve the seven-move, tower-ending problem reliably. However, two of them could do the six-move problem, that is, they could solve the seven-move problem if the first move had already been made. One child could do no better than the two-move problem, and most of the children could reliably do up to four-move problems before they began to err.

Five-year-olds were just about evenly divided between five- and six-move problems, and one of them could solve seven-move problems. The 3-year-olds fell into two major groups: those who could not get beyond two moves and those who could do four-move problems.

Recall that in the tower-ending series, subjects received problems ending in different goal states to ensure that they had not simply learned moves from specific stimulus configurations. Thus, we are fairly confident that a subject classified as an n-move child could solve problems starting n moves away from any tower. Flat-ending problem performance further assesses the generality of what subjects know about the problem. Table 7.5 is a cross classification of three- and five-year-old children according to their maximum performance on tower-ending and flat-ending problems. (Only seven of the three-year-olds are included here. The others were never run on flat-ending problems). The data suggest that flat-ending problems are uniformly harder. For example, of the four children who could solve up to six-move, tower-ending problems, only one could solve the five-move, flat-ending problem, and three could solve only four-move, flat-ending problems. No child could solve a flat-ending problem beyond his tower-ending level, and most of them dropped down two levels. Table 7.5 is also very regular in that the 10 entries in the lower right-hand quadrant are all 5-year-olds, the others are all 3 years of age. These results are consistent with the partial models in a weak sense. It can be demonstrated that for problems beyond length 2, the partial models make nonoptimal or illegal moves on flat problems before they make any errors on tower problems of the same length.

The decline in performance as path length increases is very irregular, as shown in the last line in Table 7.5, indicating the conditional probability that a subject who can solve an n-move problem will fail an $n + 1$-move problem. Of the 30 children who could solve two-move problems, six (20%) could go no further; of the 24 who solved three-move problems, only two (8%) could not solve four-move problems; and so on. For the total group of subjects, it is clear that very few "peak" at three-move problems: They can either do no better than two-move problems or they go on to the longer ones.

These results motivated the set of partial models described earlier. There is no SOLVE.1 because every subject could solve at least two-move problems. The other SOLVE models were proposed because of the substantial frequency with which subjects at levels 4 and 5 could go no further. Although not shown, a SOLVE.6 model can be derived from SOLVE by removing the capacity to generate a new goal, that is, by replacing S6 in SOLVE with S6 from SOLVE.5.

One measure of the relative difficulty of different move types is the relative frequency with which the correct move is made for problems *starting* with that type of move.[8]

Figure 7.9 shows the mean relative frequency with which 4-year-olds make the correct first move on problems starting with different types of moves. Performance on D1 and D2 is perfect on first encounter: For D1, there is little that the child could do wrong, and for D2, the major problem is to determine the correct order in which to move the two cans to the goal peg.

F1 requires the removal of the largest can from the medium one. The most frequent error here is an attempt to move the medium can directly, without first removing its obstructor. Another frequent error is to attempt to move the medium one while the large one is held aloft or while the large one is temporarily placed in the "river." The incorrect moves here are almost always such illegal

---

[8]In a *sequence* of moves, the heuristic of never moving the same can twice in a row gives a 0.5 probability that the correct move will be made. However, for initial moves, the chance level is only 0.33 (except for the first move in the seven-move problems, where it is 0.5). Even this overestimates the chance probability of a correct move, since subjects may suggest illegal moves as well.

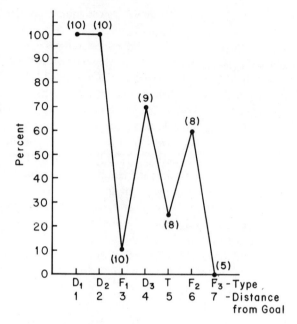

FIG. 7.9   Mean relative frequency of correct first move for problems starting with a given move type (number of subjects).

suggestions; rarely are they either of the two legal moves off the minimum path. In our procedure, the F1 items represent the child's first "real" problem; as Figure 7.9 shows, few of the children know what to do at this point.

Although D3 is four steps from the goal, it is a move that would *a priori* seem obvious, but 30% of the children err on their first encounter with it. Since all the models predict a correct move here, this result poses another challenge to the proposed partial models.

Move T is unique. It is the only one requiring that a can be moved *away* from its ultimate goal peg, and it has a low initial score. SOLVE.5 is the first model with sufficient power to solve T problems.

This analysis reemphasizes what the models are intended to convey: The relationship between initial and final states is not simply one of distance in the state space. Instead, the *type* of move — implicitly characterized by the mental operations that generate it — appears to be of central importance.

Learning.   The distinctiveness of the move types is further revealed by an analysis of the rate at which they are learned. One rough measure of the rate of learning is a plot of frequency of correct moves as a function of the occurrence of that type of move. The 4-year-olds' "learning curves" are shown in Fig. 7.10 for four move types. Figure 7.10 shows, for example, that the first time move type F1 is encountered, it is never made correctly. For 50% of the second occurrences of F1, the correct move is made, and by the third time any particular subject has encountered an F1 move, the probability is about 0.9 that the correct move will be made.

The quotation marks around "learning curves" are a reminder of the rather complex data base that underlies them. Recall that the first occurrence of a move type is also a problem that *starts* with that move. Subsequent occurrences are almost always reached *en passant* from longer problems. However, this is not invariably the case, because the experimenter would, for example, occasionally drop back to a 3 or 4-move problem if the subject had erred on a longer problem when only three or four moves from the goal. Furthermore, as subjects reached their peak performance, they dropped out of the data base completely, so that the later occurrences of any move type include only the higher performing subjects. For example the 9 points for the F1 curve are based on the following ratios of correct moves to number of instances: 0/10, 5/10, 8/9, 8/8, 7/7, 5/6, 3/3, 2/2, 2/2. For F2 the ratios are 5/8, 3/5, 2/3. As a result of these complications, the curves in Fig. 7.10 overstate the rate at which the moves are learned and understate the differences in the types of moves.

What could subjects be learning? First, let us consider what they are *not* learning. The data lend no support to the notion that what subjects learn is a list of moves. That is, having learned that from state 2 they can get to the goal (state 1), and from state 3 to state 2, subjects do not, upon first encountering state 4 (requiring an F1 move), search for a move that produces a familiar state (3) that is known to lead to a solution. If this were the case, then the data for first-move accuracy (Fig. 7.9) and acquisition (Fig. 7.10) would be much more

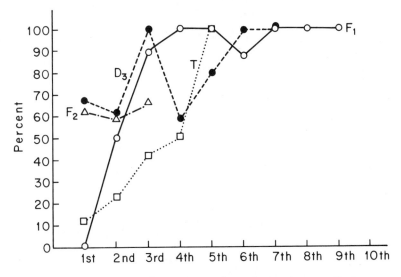

FIG. 7.10   Frequency of correct moves for each move type on *n*th occurrence (4-year-olds).

systematic than is actually the case. For example, even though D2, when it is physically present, always produces the correct move, when it is one of several *possible* states that could be reached from F1, it is not immediately recognized as being a desirable subgoal along the solution path. Figure 7.10 suggests that the F1 and D3 moves are acquired quickly relative to the T, F2, and F3 moves. Success on these first two move types corresponds directly to the transition between SOLVE.2 and SOLVE.4. The additions to the SOLVE.2 strategy are a simple test before attempting a move (S4, and TEST.4 in SOLVE.4) and a direct action contingent on the outcome of that test (S5 and S6 in SOLVE.4). The transition from SOLVE.4 to more advanced strategies requires an elaboration of the test for legal moves, the introduction of the concept of the "other" peg, and for SOLVE (i.e., for F3 problems), the generation of a new goal rather than a direct move. As suggested by Fig. 7.10, these acquisitions and their organization posed a formidable challenge to our subjects.

Mixed Strategies. Subjects who manage to get beyond the three-move, tower-ending problems almost invariably run off the last three moves very rapidly and smoothly. Even with the experimenter moving the cans, this sequence, which always involves moving a two-can stack to the goal peg, takes no more than a few seconds to execute. Recall that this is the sequence starting with F1, the move that is never correctly made on first occurrence. From first occurrence to last, there is a reduction by a factor of at least five in the time it takes to run off the three moves.

What seems to be happening is a shift from a simple, direct strategy (SOLVE.2), to one that has additional steps and tests (SOLVE.3), to the further development of a specialized local procedure. As SOLVE.3 first develops, the child appears to consider the differences between initial and final states and to proceed in a means–ends fashion to reduce those differences. After several such experiences, he acquires not just the single correct move but the entire sequence. For example, in the case of F1, what appears to be acquired is the three-move sequence for moving a two-can stack to the goal peg. A possible form for the "subroutine" is

Goal: [32 → Goal.peg]
   Move [3 → empty.peg]
   Move [2 → Goal.peg]
   Move [3 → Goal.peg]

This representation is "rote" in that it generates a move sequence without any further reference to the stimulus configuration, once it is evoked by the need to move the 32 stack. It is "general" to the extent that the peg containing the stack and the goal.peg are variables to be instantiated by the particular evoking circumstance. However, the goal.peg must be the peg in the *final* goal and not

19300	P5 E 3/1/2
19400	S 321/—/—

19500	5:44	S: Like that, like that.
		E: Like that, and they all want to be over here (A).
19800	5:49	S: Well, that is pretty hard, but I can do it.
19900		E: O.K.
20000	5:57	S: Oh. Take... I'm thinking.
20200	6:10	E: What are you thinking about?
20300	6:12	S: How we should do this.
20400		E: Tell me what you're thinking?
20500	6:15	S: About how to do this.
20600		E: O.K. What do you think? How should we do it?
20800	6:19	S: I don't know yet.
20900	6:38	Take the yellow (3) off and put the yellow one on here (C),
21000		and then take the red (1) and put it on there (A), and take the...
21100		and then put the yellow one and put it on here (B), and then
21200		put the blue one (2) on the red, and then put the yellow one on
21300		the blue one.
21400	6:54	E: Let's try that.
21500		What's the first thing I should do?
21600		You said...
21700	7:01	S: Take this one (3) and put it on there (C)...etc.

––

23400	P6 E 3/—/21
23500	S 321/—/—
23600	

23700	7:26	S: Oh, that.
23800	7:31	O.K. That's easy.
23900		Just take the yellow one and put it on there (B).
24000	7:37	Take the (pointing to 2(C)...and take...and take, take the b...
24100	7:41	No, take the blue one, put it on there (B), and then, then,
24200		take the yellow and put it on the blue (points toward C, then
24300		to B), and then take the red one and put it on here (A)).
24400	7:51	And then take the blue one and...No, and then...and then put
24500		the yellow one here (C), and then put the blue one on the
24600		red one, and then put the yellow one on the blue one.
24700	8:04	E: O.K. What's first?
24800	8:07	S: First, take this (3) and put it on there (B).
25900		E: (3 →B)
25000	8:13	S: No, I was wrong. Forget it.
25100		(E puts 3 back on A).
25200	8:15	First take the blue one and put it on there (B).
25300		E: (2 →B)
25400		S: Now take the yellow one and put it on there (B)...etc.

FIG. 7.11   Protocol from subject aged 4:11, showing five-move (a) and six-move (b) plans.

some intermediate goal. This limited generally keeps this routine from being evoked at the start of a seven-move problem. Even if the goal of moving the two top cans off the smallest was generated at this point, the routine just described would not be evoked because the target for this first placement of the two-can stack is not the goal.peg. A further limitation of this routine is its ineffectiveness on flat-ending problems.

All the partial strategies described earlier (except for SOLVE.2) are likely to have something like this routine in addition to the steps shown in Fig. 7.5. When it is evoked, it takes over, running off the last few moves. However, since it is of no use on flat-ending problems, the strategies listed would maintain control to the very end.

Planning. At times, the experimenter asked the child for not only the next move but the next several moves. Few children verbalized multiple-move sequences beyond a few moves. Repeated requests to do so appeared to confuse them and had to be terminated. However, those who could and would verbalize showed a remarkable ability to describe a series of imagined future states and actions on those states.

Perhaps the most impressive plans are shown in Fig. 7.11. They came from a boy, aged 4:11. At the top of Fig. 7.11, the complete five-move plan is verbalized after about 60 sec of study (lines 209–214). The next problem for the same child has a six-move minimum path. The child starts verbalizing a move sequence after just a few seconds, (239–240), corrects himself, and then smoothly rattles off a six-move plan (241–246). Notice that when he starts to make actual moves, he makes the same initial error and recovery (248–252) that was in his verbalizations.

This protocol (as well as several others not included here) is in striking contrast to Piaget's results and interpretations of his investigations of the same task (Piaget, 1976). He reports that before the age of 7 or 8 years children did not plan, even with the two-disk problem. He concludes that they cannot "combine inversion of the order" (in our context, putting the baby under the mommy, while the mommy is moved first) with a "sort of transitivity" (using an intermediate peg to hold a can temporarily). There is, Piaget says, "a systematic primacy of the trial-and-error procedure over any attempt at deduction, and no cognizance of any correct solution arrived at by chance [p. 291]." I find it hard to reconcile this interpretation with these protocols.

Summary of Results

The following picture is emerging: (1) Path length is a factor in problem difficulty, but it is confounded with move type, which seems to be much more important. (2) Path type is important, but we cannot conclude that flat-ending problems are intrinsically more difficult than tower-ending problems because they are always given after tower-ending problems. Rather, we can conclude that whatever is acquired on tower-ending problems is less effective on flat-ending problems. (I will hazard a guess, though, that even with a different training sequence, flat-ending problems will turn out to be harder. The reason for this prediction is given later.) (3) Age effects are clear, significant, and monotonic. There are no U-shaped performance curves. (4) Planning, or at least verbalization of move sequences, is difficult to elicit. The rare occurrences are, however, quite impressive. Notable in all the protocols is the *absence* of a seriously incorrect plan. Subjects either can say what they are going to do correctly or they say nothing at all. (5) Learning rates are very sensitive to move type.

Goal Ordering

Recall the earlier comments about the locus of "sophistication" in the SOLVE model. Built into every model, as the second step, is the knowledge that the smallest cans must be attended to first. No child, even the 3-year-olds, ever attempted to invert the order of moves on two-move problems. This ordering takes place every time a new situation is assessed (Step 2) and, for the six- and seven-move problems, when the smallest obstructor is sought.

One explanation for the flat-ending performance being poorer than tower-ending performance may be that the latter provides a highly salient external representation for the ordering of the goals, whereas the former does not. A target display such as (321/-/-) provides very strong clues that the last can to be placed is 3, the second from last 2, and the first 1. However, a target such as (1/2/3) provides no such compelling reminders that small things must be taken care of before large things. In fact, for all the seven-move, flat-ending problems, there are *two* minimum paths. One of them achieves its goals in the "proper" order, and the other one does not. (See, for example, 13 to 3 via 24 in the state diagram, Fig. 7.3.) The more likely that the correct goal ordering is not maintained, the longer the solution path will be, because incorrect goals are generated during solution. This is exactly what happened: The average solution path length is longer for all flat-ending problems than for corresponding tower-ending problems. There appears to be much more meandering around the state space with flat-ending problems. For tower-ending problems, the goal display may serve as a physical manifestation of the notion of a "goal stack."

CONCLUDING COMMENTS

What develops? That is the theme of this text, and I suppose I should take a stab at an answer. I must remind you that at this point in the research program only the roughest outlines of a picture are emerging, and much remains to be done even on this one task, not to mention others. In proposing an answer I go beyond the limits of the study described here and try to characterize the ways in which the question might be answered. There seem to be three kinds of answers. I call them the *empirical*, the *characteristic,* and the *procedural.*

Empirical descriptions consist of performance measures and their changes over time. Typically, we see monotonic improvements with age, but often a careful observational paradigm reveals dips and peaks on specific tasks. It seems to me that improvements in both the analysis and the measurement procedures used in cognitive development research have substantially enhanced the precision and interest of answers to what develops simply by pointing to the data. For example, in Siegler's (1976) balance scale task we see dramatically different paths in the pass/fail patterns for different problem types. For the task studied here, Table 7.4 is an example of an empirical description of what develops.

A second way to talk about what develops is to propose *global characteristics of the child.* The child is wholistic or analytic, he is rule-governed or not, he is familiar with specific stimulus materials, he is systematic, he is egocentric or metamemoric. For the Tower of Hanoi problem, the characteristic description of what develops includes terms like orderliness, planfulness, undistractability, and focus. Sequential ordering is crucial to problem solutions; furthermore, the child must focus on the newly generated subgoal and not be misled by the still unsatisfied supergoal. (In the model proposed, such supergoals are supposed to be obliterated by new goals, but it is difficult to forget on command.) The child must be able to decompose the desired end state into a series of attainable, temporally ordered, intermediate states, and he must then reintegrate the parts into a whole.

Finally, we can formulate *procedural descriptions* of what develops. The Tower of Hanoi models provide examples. At the present stage of this project, the proposed models are but the roughest approximations to what children know when they exhibit a particular performance level on this task. Younger children's strategies contain no tests: They are very direct in their attempt to get to the goal. Older children make tests before they move, but they still move directly, rather than by generating new goals that are further tested. Only the most advanced children have the ability both to generate subgoals and to utilize the concept of the "other" peg.

But remember, there is more to the developmental story — even to the procedural account — than just performance models. The full story of what develops must account for the psychological processes that enable a child to listen to the task instructions, assimilate them to his existing general problem-solving processes, and produce something approximating the performance models we have previously described. There are several components to that sequence, and a child who can do only two-move problems may differ from one who does seven-move problems with respect to any of them. His general problem-solving abilities may be less, his assimilation capacity may be inadequate, or his information-processing system may lack the capacity to run the task-specific model (cf. Klahr, 1976; Klahr & Wallace, 1976).

There seem to be ways of isolating these components. For example, in a study with adult subjects Neves (1977) is teaching different Tower of Hanoi strategies with direct instruction to get precise measures of the demands they make on the information-processing system. This procedure eliminates the effects of the general problem-solving capacity and the assimilation procedure. In fact, subjects are not even told what the problem is, they are told only how to go about making a move. We can shed some light on the child's general capacity by extending the sort of analysis described in this chapter to a range of other problems, and such studies are in progress in my own lab. Finally, we can study the assimilation problem by adding to the precision of the measures. A cleaner procedure for getting at latencies and eye movements (see also Neves, 1977) would enable us to trace the information of the kind of subroutines — or procedural chunks — described earlier.

It is probably clear that, of the three forms of answer to the question of what develops, my preference lies with the procedural. It seems to me that, no matter what the domain we are studying, we ultimately must move through characteristic and empirical accounts to procedural descriptions of what develops. Then we can all get to work on the really interesting question: *How*?

ACKNOWLEDGMENTS

This work was supported in part by grants from the Spencer and Sloan Foundations. The stimulus materials were developed in collaboration with Yaakov Kareev. Thanks to Mary Riley and Mike Zidanic for experimental and technical assistance, to Chris Glenn, Bob Neches, and David Neves for useful comments on earlier drafts, and to the parents, children, and teachers of the CMU Children's School. Finally, my grudging thanks to Bob Siegler for ruthless editorial suggestions that required a major revision of an earlier draft.

REFERENCES

Byrnes, M. A., & Spitz, H. Performance of retarded adolescents and nonretarded children on the Tower of Hanoi problem. *American Jounral of Mental Deficiency*, 1977, *81*, 561–569.

Charlesworth, W. R. Human intelligence as adaptation: An ethological approach. In L. B. Resnick (Ed.), *The nature of intelligence*. Hillsdale, N.J.: Lawrence Erlbaum Associates, 1976.

Cook, T. W. Amount of material and difficulty of problem solving: II. The disc transfer problem. *Journal of Experimental Psychology*, 1937, *20*, 288.

Egan, D. E., & Greeno, J. G. Theory of rule induction: Knowledge acquired in concept learning, serial pattern learning, and problem solving. In L. W. Gregg (Ed.), *Knowledge and cognition*. Potomac, Md.: Lawrence Erlbaum Associates, 1974.

Gagné, R. M., & Smith, E. C., Jr. A study of effects of verbalization on problem solving. *Journal of Experimental Psychology,* 1962, *63,* 12–18.

Greeno, J. G. Cognitive objectives of instruction: Theory of knowledge for solving problems and answering questions. In D. Klahr (Ed.), *Cognition and instruction.* Hillsdale, N.J.: Lawrence Erlbaum Associates, 1976.

Hormann, A. Gaku: An artificial student. *Behavioral Science,* 1965, *10,* 88–107.

Klahr, D. Steps toward the simulation of intellectual development. In L. B. Resnick (Ed.), *The nature of intelligence.* Hillsdale, N.J.: Lawrence Erlbaum Associates, 1976.

Klahr, D., & Siegler, R. S. The representation of children's knowledge. In H. W. Reese & L. P. Lipsitt (Eds.), *Advances in child development* (Vol. 12). New York: Academic Press, 1978.

Klahr, D., & Wallace, J. G. *Cognitive development: An information processing view.* Hillsdale, N.J.: Lawrence Erlbaum Associates, 1976.

Klix, F. *Information und Verhalten.* Berlin: VEB Deutscher, 1971.

Neisser, U. General, academic and artificial intelligence. In L. B. Resnick (Ed.), *The nature of intelligence.* Hillsdale, N.J.: Lawrence Erlbaum Associates, 1976.

Neves, D. *A study of strategies of the Tower of Hanoi.* Paper presented at the meeting of the Midwestern Psychological Association, May 1977.

Newell, A., & Simon, H. A. *Human problem solving.* Englewood Cliffs, N.J.: Prentice-Hall, 1972.

Peterson, J. *Studies in the comparative abilities of whites and negroes.* Mental Measurements Monograph, 1929 (No. 5), 1–156.

Piaget, J. *The grasp of consciousness.* Cambridge, Mass.: Harvard University Press, 1976.

Siegler, R. S. Three aspects of cognitive development. *Cognitive Psychology,* 1976, *8,* 481–520.

Simon, H. A. The functional equivalence of problem-solving skills. *Cognitive Psychology,* 1975, *7,* 268–288.

Simon, H. A., & Hayes, J. R. Understanding complex task instructions. In D. Klahr (Ed.), *Cognition and instruction.* Hillsdale, N.J.: Lawrence Erlbaum Associates, 1976.

Sydow, H. Zur metrischen Erfassung von subjektiven Problemzustanden und zu deren Veranderung im Denkprozess (II). *Zeitschrift fur Psychologie,* 1970, *178,* 1–50.

8 Counting in the Preschooler: What Does and Does Not Develop

Rochel Gelman
University of Pennsylvania

For some years now, I have contended that preschool children can and do count to represent the numerical value of a set of objects or pictures. I do not mean that the young child who is able to rattle off the number words is necessarily able to count. He may or may not be able to do so. It all depends on what else he can do with the list of words he rattles off. And as we shall see, the young child who is unable to rattle off the conventional words in the conventional order may nevertheless be able to count. In short, I do not rest my claim that young children can count on their ability to recite the conventional number words. If not this, then what? To what kind of evidence can I possibly be appealing? To answer this question, it is necessary to consider what is involved in counting. Thus, I begin my discussion with a summary of a counting model on which my husband and I have been working (Gelman & Gallistel, 1977). Next, I present data on the extent to which young children's "counts" are governed by the counting principles outlines in the model.[1] Finally, I address the questions of what does and what does not develop.

THE COUNTING MODEL

What does it mean to say that a young child counts to represent number? Inspection of the various count sequences that I have recorded led me to the view that the young child's ability to count is governed by several principles and

---

[1] The word *count* is in quotation marks to reflect the fact that we have yet to define the ability to count.

that adherence to some of these principles requires the coordination of several component processes. I present the counting procedure and its development by introducing the principles one by one and by examining the component processes underlying adherence to each of them. In proceeding principle by principle and component by component I make explicit the possibility that children may possess some counting principles but not others; that the individual principles could consist of several component skills, not all of which may be perfected at a given age; and that some of the principles may operate more or less in isolation in the "counting" behavior of very young children. In the end, successful counting must surely involve the coordinated application of all the principles. Indeed, as we shall see, some principles of counting require the coordinated use of other principles. Still, it is of considerable interest to determine whether any of the principles might be followed by the very young child. Should we focus solely on the appearance of completely accurate counting, we run the danger of underestimating the young child's knowledge of the counting principles. Worse yet, we might reach a conclusion of no competence, when in fact there is a partial competence. Clearly, partial competence or a limited ability to coordinate the counting principles is not the same thing as a complete lack of competence.

To account for full understanding of counting, it is necessary to appeal to five counting principles. The first three principles deal with rules of procedure or the "how to" of counting and are likely to be familiar because they are fundamental to many other counting models (e.g., Beckwith & Restle, 1966; Klahr & Wallace, 1973; Schaeffer, Eggelston, & Scott, 1974). The fourth deals with the definition of countables or the "what to" of counting. The fifth involves a composite of features of the three how-to-count and one what-to-count principles.

The Counting Principles

The One—One Principle.   It would be impossible to claim that an individual kows how to count if he were unable to follow the one—one principle. The use of this principle involves the ticking off of items in an array with *distinct* ticks in such a way that *one and only one* tick is used for each item. For a child to follow this principle he has to coordinate two basic component processes: *partitioning* and *tagging*. *Partitioning* involves the step-by-step maintenance of two categories of items — those that have not yet been counted (set U in Beckwith and Restle's notation) and those that have already been counted (set C in Beckwith and Restle's notation). Items must be transferred (either physically or mentally) *one at a time* from the U set to the C set. Tagging involves the summoning up, one at a time, of distinct tags. In the successful use of the one—one principle, tagging and partitioning must proceed in lockstep. As an item is transferred from the to-be-counted to the counted category, a distinct tag must be withdrawn from the set of tags and set aside, not to be used again. In other words, tagging and partitioning must start together, stay in phase throughout their use, and stop together.

Having outlined the component processes that contribute to the one—one principle, it becomes clear that a child who fails to adhere to the one—one principle can err in at least three ways. He can err in the partitioning process; for example, he may move two items into the "counted" category on one count. He can err in the tag withdrawal process; for example, he may use the same tag twice on different items. Finally, he can fail to keep the partitioning and tagging processes coordinated; he may keep withdrawing tags when he finishes transferring items into the already-counted category.

The Stable-Ordering Principle.   Counting obviously cannot proceed unless the one—one principle is put into practice. Still, there is more to counting than the ability to assign tags to the items in an array. To be credited with the ability to count, one must demonstrate the use of at least one additional principle — the stable-ordering principle. That is, there must be evidence that the tags used to correspond one-for-one to the items in an array are produced in a stable, that is, repeatable, order. This principle calls for the use of a stably ordered list that is as long as the number of items in an array. We might expect the young child to have some difficulty with it, for it presents a rather formidable serial-learning task. We might also expect to find that the extent to which young children adhere to the principle depends on set size.

The Cardinal Principle.   The two preceding principles involve the selection and application of tags to the items in a set. The cardinal principle deals with the fact that the final tag used in a series of tags has a special significance. This tag, unlike the preceding ones, represents a property of the set as a whole — its cardinal number.

So, not only must one be able to assign tags in a fixed order, one must be able to pull out the last item assigned and somehow indicate that it is the item that represents the number of items in the array. To the extent that the singling out of a particular item to represent cardinal numerosity requires additional processing steps, this principle should show a delayed developmental function as compared to the one—one and stable principles. Put differently, because the application of the cardinal principle presupposes the application of the first two principles, it should be more difficult to use and therefore later to appear.

The Abstraction Principle.   I have thus far focused on the "how to" of counting and have been quite evasive about the "what to" of the matter. I confess to having done this intentionally because I want to highlight the question of what constitutes countables. Those who have little intercourse with developmental theories and the assumptions they make regarding the ability of young children to count may wonder way. After all, adults behave as if they assume any collection (real or imaged) of entities can be counted. Although adults may not regard it as reasonable, they can nonetheless be induced to count sets that are made up of widely different entities, for example, a set consisting of all the great minds, all the chairs, and all the pencils in a room. This seems so obvious that one might well ask; Why elevate it to the status of a principle? There are two reasons. First, I suspect that the overgeneralization of this principle is what produces bewilderment about the claim that one cannot count all the points on a line. Second, it is an open question whether young children appreciate that the counting procedure can be applied to minds or even sets of heterogeneous objects. Indeed, many have suggested that the young child places severe restrictions on the nature of what constitutes a countable collection. For example, Ginsburg (1975) maintains that early counting — and the concept of number as well — is "tied to particular concrete contexts, geometric arrangements, activities, people, etc. [p. 60]." Gast (1957) devoted a lengthy monograph to the supposed lack of abstractness in the young child's conception of number and concluded that "Enumeration is possible for 3- and 4-year-olds only when the things to be counted are identical to one another... elements that vary in material composition or qualities (such as color) are not included in the enumeration [p. 66]."[2]

Work by Gast and others suggests that young children behave as if a collection of heterogeneous items does *not* constitute a collection of countables. Unlike adults, they seem to restrict severely the definition of stimuli to which they can apply the how-to-count rules. Whereas adults allow that *any* events may be classified together for purposes of counting, there is the suggestion that young children do not. The developmental questions, then, are: What is the permissible definition of "things" that can be included in an enumeration, and how does this definition change with age? If it is indeed true that the young child believes that he cannot apply the how-to-count principles to heterogeneous materials, then we would be loathe to say that he has a full appreciation of how a counting procedure can be used to represent number.

The Order—Invariance Principle.   Assume for the moment that a child consistently honors the how-to-count principles and can even apply them to a relatively wide range of heterogeneous collections. Can we conclude that he has a full understanding of counting as it is involved in the representation of number? I think not. Nothing I have said so far captures the fact that the order in which a particular set of objects is tagged is in fact irrelevant. Let me be more specific.

Adults know that any count word can be assigned to any item in an array — so long as no count word is used more than once in a given count. Furthermore, adults know that the order in which items are tagged and partitioned does not

---

[2]Translation by C. R Gallistel.

matter. Given a linear array of a rabbit, truck, dog, and cat arranged left to right, it is perfectly proper to count the rabbit as "one" on one trial and the cat as "one" on another trial. Likewise, it is perfectly all right to start the count with the middle object (the dog can be "one") and then skip around until all objects have been counted. We know that the result of the counting procedure will be "conserved" as objects are rearranged. Ginsburg (1975) argues that young children do not know this and cites a number of anecdotes to support his contention.

The child who appreciates the irrelevance of the order of enumeration knows a number of facts. The first is that a count item is a "thing" as opposed to a "one" or a "two." (Notice the implicit use of the abstraction principle.) Second, the verbal tags are arbitrary designates of an object and do not adhere to that object. Third, and most important, the same cardinal number results regardless of the order in which particular objects are tagged. In general, this principle captures the fact that much about counting is arbitrary.

Obviously, the doesn't-matter principle presupposes the integrated use of the other counting principles. We would expect the child who cannot apply the how-to principles in a coordinated manner to fail a test of the doesn't-matter principle. We might also expect a child who severely restricts the definition of countables to do worse on such a test than a child who is more permissive. Before examining the data that bear on these questions, though, there is one further issue we should consider.

A Caveat: You Don't Have to Use the Conventional Count Words in Order to Count

Having outlined the counting principles, I can now return to my preliminary comments. I said that a child who can rattle off the conventional count words may not be able to count. The issue is whether he uses these words in a way that honors the counting principles. At the very least, to credit him with the ability to count, we need evidence of his understanding of the one—one and stable-order principles. I also said that a child who fails to rattle off the count words may nevertheless be able to count. It is this point that I wish to dwell on.

I draw your attention to the fact that the counting model does not specify the use of conventional count words as tags. Nor does it specify that whatever words are used be conventionally ordered. This is as it should be. One does not have to use the conventional count words in a conventional order to be able to count. I suspect that the failure to recognize this contributes to the widespread belief that many African tribes cannot count. I am sure that it has led to an underestimation of the young child's ability to count. In both cases, counting ability is compared to the typical Western adult's way of counting, a way that involves the use of the traditional number—word terms and sequence. To illustrate my objection, I want to read an excerpt from Menninger's (1969) treatise *Number Words and Number Symbols.* This particular quotation appears in a passage arguing that individuals who have the number words *one* and *two* may not be able to count. Menninger demands that they have words that are equivalent to our *three, four, five*, and so on. He writes: "When a tribe of South Sea Islanders counts by twos, *urapun, okasa, okasa urapun, okasa okasa, okasa okasa urapun* (that is, 1, 2, 2′1, 2′2, 2′2′1), we distinctly feel that they have not yet taken the step from two to three. And we realize with astonishment that these people can count beyond two without being able to count to three [p. 17]." What Menninger failed to recognize is that the members of the tribe in question are using a simple concatenation rule of ones and twos for generating their tagging sequence! It is not the list that we typically employ, but is nevertheless an effective tagging sequence.

The case of a two-item concatenation rule versus a base-ten rule is but one example of why it is not necessary to use the conventional sequence when counting. In a variety of East African cultures there is a prohibition against the counting of cattle, people, and valuable possessions. Yet the same cultures are likely to place a premium on having large herds of cattle and a large number of children. It is these two factors that probably contribute to the impression that such tribes "count" with a "one-two-many" system. Consider the well-intentioned anthropologist who studies the counting abilities of such tribes. He is most likely to assume that it is best to ask individuals of the tribe to count familiar objects. And what is more familiar than children or cattle or houses in the village? Yes, they are familiar, but they also are the very items that must not be counted! The mother who is asked to count her children is confronted with two conflicting values. She must not count her children, yet she wants to tell about the fact that she has a large number of children. What to do? Answer by saying *many, a whole lot,* or something of the kind.

But how do I know that these individuals can count and that they do not treat large numbers as undifferentiated manys? Easy: They will and do count cowry shells, which are not on the taboo list of what is uncountable. Indeed, the fact that they count cowry shells allows them to get around the taboo and determine the exact number of children, cows, and so on that they have. Using one shell at a time, they touch each of the taboo items. This done, they count the cowry shells and then infer (implicity using the transitivity of one—one correspondence) the number of valuables they have.

These are but two examples of the errors one can make when assessing the ability to count. Elsewhere I take up this issue in greater detail (Gelman & Gallistel, 1977), but I trust that the point is obvious. There is no reason to require a child to use conventional count words in a conventional order. What is it that must be assumed? Intrinsic to the counting procedure is the use of unique tags to mark or tick off the items in a collection. Furthermore, the tags must be used in a fixed order. And the tags must have an arbitrary status with respect to the objects being counted; they cannot be the names of the items or properties of the items. The set of count words meets these criteria, but so do other sets of tags. One obvious candidate is the alphabet, which is, in fact, used to count in Greek or Hebrew. But the tags need not even be verbal. They can, for example, be short-term memory bins. Recognition of the fact that counting can proceed without the use of words that are count words or, for that matter, words at all, led us (Gelman & Gallistel, 1977) to introduce some terminology. We call the traditional count words of a given language *numerlogs*. Other tags (verbal or nonverbal) are called *numerons*. Notice that this distinction allows us to hold open the possibility that animals can count. It also allows for the possibility of young children using nonconventional or idiosyncratic count—word sequences.

THE DATA FOR EVIDENCE ON ABILITY TO USE HOW-TO-COUNT PRINCIPLES

Many of the data referred to in this chapter were collected in previous studies. In this section, I summarize the methodologies used in these studies so that readers can follow the arguments without having to refer to the other sources.

The Magic Experiments: Evidence for the How-To-Count Principles

Gelman and Gallistel (1977) have analyzed two major sources of evidence for the young child's ability to use the how-to-count principles. The first source constitutes a set of transcripts available from "magic" experiments I have conducted. Although children were not asked to count, many did so spontaneously. Thus, we began our assessment of the extent to which young children honor the counting principles by analyzing a subset of available protocols. The second data source is an experiment designed to elicit counting and is summarized later in this section.

Choice of Protocols. Two series of magic experiments were selected for analysis of the counting principles. One involved the use of two- and three-item displays, the other the use of three- and five-item displays. The former transcripts were included because they were available for 2-year-olds as well as for older children. The latter transcripts were included because they involved the largest set sizes that have been used so far in magic experiments.

Participants. The transcripts from the two- and three-item magic experiments involved children aged 2, 3, and 4 years. There were 16, 32, and 32 children in each of the respective age groups. The three- and five-item magic experiments involved independent groups of 3- and 4-year-old children. There were 24 subjects in each group.

Procedure and Materials.   The magic studies were initially designed to assess whether young children know that some transformations are number relevant (e.g., addition and subtraction) and that others are number irrelevant (e.g., displacement, color change, and identity change of items). The procedure involves a two-phase experiment. First, a child is shown arrays containing different numbers of objects. He is told that one is the "winner," the other the "loser." There is no mention of number. A series of trials establishes an expectancy for the numbers presented; this is revealed by the fact that answers to "why" probe trials almost always involve the child talking about the numbers. From the experimenter's viewpoint, Phase II begins with the surreptitious alteration of one or both arrays. These changes are either number relevant (addition or subtraction) or number irrelevant (e.g., displacement, color change). The data from Phase II are used to make inferences about the young child's ability to work with number-relevant and number-irrelevant transformations. The entire experimental procedure is tape recorded on an audio recorder. These tapes are then transcribed verbatim.

As indicated, we selected a set of available transcripts and analyzed all the counting sequences that appeared. In both series of magic experiments discussed here, the arrays were made up of homogeneous items (toy green mice), and these were displayed linearly.

A Videotape Experiment: Further Evidence for the How-To-Count Principles

Main Design Features.   Our second source of data on the how-to-count principles comes from an experiment designed to elicit counting. The design used heterogeneous sets of 2, 3, 4, 5, 7, 9, 11, and 19 objects. It also varied the type of display arrangement (linear versus nonlinear). The variables of set size and type of display were within subject variables; age was obviously a between-subjects variable.

Participants.   The experiment included children of four ages: 2, 3, 4, and 5 years. There were 19 2-year-olds to start. Two failed to understand our instructions; the data from one was lost due to an equipment failure. The Ns in the 2-, 3-, 4-, and 5-year-old groups were 16, 21, 19, and 15, respectively.

Procedure and Materials.   An attempt was made — not always successfully — to test each child on set sizes of 2, 3, 4, 5, 7, 9, 11, and 19 for six trials per set size. Three trials for each set size were linear displays; the remaining three trials were haphazardly arranged displays (except for set size 2). Linear trials preceded nonlinear trials. The displays were of chips of various colors. All sessions were videotapes for later transcription and analysis — thus the choice of *Videotape Experiment* as the tital of this section.

Those familiar with the vicissitudes of running young children will worry about the demands our design made on the subjects. We incorporated a variety of procedural features to enhance the likelihood of obtaining cooperation. First, we displayed two set sizes at a time, designating one set as the child's and the other as the experimenter's. A child was asked to count and/or indicate the number of items on "his plate" and then on the experimenter's plate. This was done to reduce the amount of time the experimenter took to set up trials. The set size pairs were 2 and 3, 4 and 5, 7 and 9, 11 and 19. They were shown in this order. Second, we used a puppet as a cohort to the experimenter since we have found that a three-way conversation among child, puppet, and experimenter heightens a young child's interest in almost any task.

Although we attempted to run all children on all trials, the child's proclivities were also taken into account. If a child wanted to keep working with a given set size, he was allowed to do so. This meant that in some cases we obtained 20 counts of a given set size! If it was clear that a child was frustrated or unwilling to continue, the experimental session was ended. Accordingly, I will report the number of children run on a given set size when summarizing individual tendencies to follow a particular principle or combination of principles.

Data Source for Abstraction Principle

We have not run experiments explicitly designed to assess the extent to which young children restrict the definition of what constitutes a countable collection of items. Still there are experiments that allow us to examine the effect of heterogeneity on a child's tendency to count and/or abstract the numerical value of an array. A comparison of results from the magic and the videotape experiments described above provides one source, because the former involved homogeneous and the latter heterogeneous sets of materials. The source of yet further comparisons will be described in Section III.D.

An Experiment on the Order-Invariance Principle

An example of the kind of behavior we sought to study concerning the young child's understanding of the order-invariance principle introduces the nature of the test we used. Assume for the moment that we have adults count an array of heterogeneous items, say, a toy-sized chair, dog, baby, flower, and car. To start, these are arranged left to right as listed. Likely as not, the adult will begin at the left or right end of the row and count the first item as "one," the next as "two," and so on until he counts the last one as "five." This done, we proceed to scramble the array and then once again arrange them in a row. This time the objects are arranged left to right as follows: flower, car, baby, dog, and chair. The adult counts, tagging the flower as "one," the car "two," and so on. Now we leave the objects in the same positions and point to the car and ask the adult to count all objects but start with the car. Our adult complies by tagging the car as "one," the baby "two," the dog "three," the chair "four," and then returning to tag the flower as "five." The demonstration continues as the adult meets our request to count while making the car be "three," then "four," and "five." He does this by skipping around the array to include all items present in each count. In so doing, he shows that he knows that each of the count words *one* to *five* can be assigned to any of the five items in the array. Furthermore, he shows that he knows that the order in which items are partitioned and tagged does not matter. What does matter is that the tags be assigned in a fixed order and that each item be assigned a distinct tag. Which item receives a given tag is completely arbitrary. Despite the reassignment of tags, the same count and cardinal number result.

The recognition that it does not matter which tag is assigned to which item is an explicit realization of the abstraction principle and an implicit realization of the other three counting principles. Accordingly, we should expect that the abiity to honor the doesn't-matter principle depends on the extent to which a child can coordinate his application of the other principles. By this logic, the development of this principle should be delayed compared to the developmental course of the other principles.

We have run a variety of tests of the doesn't-matter principle but will report on only one of them. In all cases, the central test was like the one we put our imaginary adult through. After a child counted a set of approximately five items, he was asked to modify his counting of the objects so as to have a particular object be tagged as "two," "three," "four," and so on. Some might be surprised that we could use the modified counting task with preschool subjects. To do so requires that the child be able to understand some rather vague instructions, skip around the array as he assigns tags, think of possible ways to move the items to facilitate assigning a particular tag to a particular object, and so forth. He also must remember which object is to be designated by which count word. For these reasons, we approached the initial experiments on this principle with considerable trepidation. As it turned out, there was little reason to worry. It quickly became apparent that most children understood what we were asking of them.

Participants.   Twelve 3-year-olds and 15 4-year-olds participated in this order-irrelevance experiment.

Materials and Procedure.   The materials used in this experiment were small trinkets that varied in color and item type (e.g., a small chair, a baby). Each child was shown a set of five objects and asked to count these five or six times. Between count trials the experimenter rearranged the trinkets, but otherwise the count trials did not differ. If it was apparent that the child could not apply the how-to-count principles consistently, the experimenter then tested the child's ability to count with a set size of four items. Children who received four-item trials were tested with the same set size during the doesn't-matter part of the experiment. Otherwise, they were tested with the five-item array.

In the doesn't-matter part of the experiment, the experimenter began by pointing to the second item in the row and asking the child to count by making that item be "one." Then he asked the child to count again, making that item be "two," or "three," and so on. This done, the experimenter pointed to the second-to-last item in the row and asked the child to make that item be "one" and then "two." Subsequent steps in the experiment will not be presented here.

THE EVIDENCE

Magic Experiments and the How-To-Count Principles

Scoring Procedure. Each count sequence was scored separately for evidence regarding the use of each of the three how-to-count principles. We identified a count sequence in the magic protocols primarily on the basis of a child having used tag items from two well-known lists — the *number words* and the *letters of the alphabet.* A child did not have to use these tags in the conventional order or, for that matter, in any order. However, he did have to use some tags. Despite our caveat regarding the use of words as evidence for counting abilities, we had no choice here. In almost all cases, a count sequence was generated spontaneously. Because the child was not asked to count, we had no other way of defining the beginning of a sequence.

A particular count sequence was scored as providing evidence for the use of the one—one principle if it had as many different verbal tags as there were items in a given array. If a child said two different number words or letters of the alphabet when shown a two-item array, he was scored as having used the one—one principle. If he said three different tags when viewing a three-item array, he was again given credit. Consistency with respect to order of tag assignment over trials did *not* serve as a criterion in this particular analysis. The one—one analysis simply addressed the question of whether children used as many different tags as there were items in the array. This done for each trial, we then considered the tendency of a child to honor the one—one principle on all his trials. If a child met the one—one criteria on at least 90% of his trials, he was judged perfect with respect to this principle. If he met the criteria on at least 60% but not more than 90% of his trials, his application of the one—one principle was judged to be shaky.

Children did have to show consistency over trials in their use of a list of tags in order to be scored positively on the stable-order criterion. The child who consistently said "two, six, ten" when he saw a three-item array on one trial and then consistently said "two, six" when he saw a two-item array was scored as being correct with respect to his ability to follow this principle. Thus, we allowed children to use idiosyncratic number lists if they used them consistently. Of course, children who chose to use the conventional sequence of number words were also given credit. And the child who used the alphabet — another stably ordered list of terms — was likewise scored as being correct. A child's use of this principle was judged to be perfect or shaky across trials in the same way as his use of the one—one principle.

We judged children's understanding of the cardinal principle by four criteria. The first involved uniquely tagging each of the display objects and repeating the last tag, for example, "one, two, three; three!", "two, six; six!" As in this examples, there were times that the repetition of the last tag was given emphasic stress. In these cases the stress on the final tag was exaggerated well beyond the bounds of the ordinary stress patterns that characterize the ends of some English sequences. Indeed, it was more like a scream or shout. We also used two indirect criteria, indirect as contrasted with the first two. A child was scored as following the cardinal principle if he shifted from assigning the correct number of tags in one sequence to stating only the last tag on a later encounter with the same set size. Again the child could do this his own way, that is, by using an idiosyncratic list. Finally, children could be scored as being correct on *this* principle if they *correctly* stated the numerical value of the set and yet seemed to not count. Why *correctly*? To do otherwise would amount to saying that any time a child says a number word, he thinks that word represents the numerical value of a given set. Maybe; but surely unlikely.

Let me anticipate a possible objection to the last cardinal criterion: that it involves a reification of my hypothesis that correct judgments of set size are almost always based on or derived from covert, if not overt, counting (Gelman & Tucker, 1975). I do not think that is a reification, and I hope to convince you with data from the varied set-size videotape experiment. But first the findings from the magic experiments.

Results.   The results are really quite straightforward. The vast majority of the children — including those in the youngest group — could and did make use of all three principles. This outcome is captured in the results regarding the children's ability to use the how-to-count principles in a coordinated fashion (see Table 8.1).

In presenting the data on the coordinated use of the three principles, I make a distinction between children who made no errors at all in their application of the how-to-count principles and children whose ability to use the three principles was shaky. If we allow that both groups of children were able to use all three count principles, then we see that even the youngest subjects were able to count rather well.

The fact that so many children can be credited with having all three count principles makes it hard to ask about their relative difficulty. The numbers in the remaining cells are small, but there is a hint. If children did not follow all

TABLE 8.1
Percentage of Subjects in Each Group in Magic Experiments
Showing a Given Composite Counting Profile

Observed Profiles of Available How-to-Count Principles	2 vs. 3 Experiments			3 vs. 5 Experiments		
	2-yr.-olds (N = 16)	3-yr.-olds (N = 32)	4-yr.-olds (N = 32)	2-yr.-olds (N = 0)[d]	3-yr.-olds (N = 24)	4-yr.-olds (N = 24)
All three perfect[a]	63	57	82	—	50	71
All three – at least one shaky[b]	25	34	0	—	50	21
One–one and stable	13	3	9	—	0	4
Stable and cardinal	0	3	0	—	0	0
Never refer to number[c]	0	3	9	—	0	4

[a]Includes Ss who used cardinal number on all trials.
[b]At least 60% of the trials involved perfect coordination of the three principles.
[c]Recall that Ss were not asked to count or use number.
[d]Not run on these set sizes.

three principles, they tended to count the number of items in the array without assigning a cardinal value to that array. That is, they behaved in accord with the one–one and stable-order principles but not the cardinal principle.

What is not reflected in the table is the typical nature of the error made by children who used all three principles but were shaky. The errors were predominantly one–one errors of two kinds: partitioning and coordination errors. The former involved the double counting or skipping of an item in the middle of an array. The latter involved a difficulty in stopping the counting procedure. A majority of the errors involved a count of one-too-few items. Tagging errors (using the same tag more than once) were almost nonexistent.

One might have the impression that since we allowed children to use idiosyncratic lists, such lists were ubiquitous. In fat, they were not. Five of the 2-year-olds used their own lists of tags (e.g., "one, thirteen, nineteen," "two, six," "A, B"). By 3 years of age, children were able to use the conventional lists in a conventional order — at least for set sizes of five or fewer objects. I do not find the latter result too surprising. After all, "Sesame Street" is watched by many a preschooler, and the program encourages children to count. What I do take as noteworthy is the fact that some 2-year-olds construct their own lists. I am particularly impressed with the occasional child who used the alphabet instead of a number word sequence. The spontaneous use of a nonnumerical sequence suggests to us that young children have available a cognitive principle in search of an appropriate list. And the alphabet is an appropriate list. Likewise, I think the tendency to construct an idiosyncratic list of number words suggests that the stable-order principle is guiding the learning. How else to explain the idiosyncratic but stable lists of number words? It is exceedingly unlikely that adults go around teaching the wrong list of count words. If I am right about this interpretation, we should find that when older children are asked to deal with larger set sizes, they too will invoke idiosyncratic lists. In particular, we should expect to see the use of lists that begin with the conventional sequence but shift over to idiosyncratic sequences, for example, 1–2–3–4–5–10–9.

This was one reason for the videotape study that involved larger set sizes. Another reason was my interest in whether use of the cardinal principle does indeed lag behind the use of the other principles. In addition, I wanted to determine whether increases in set size produce systematic increases in errors and if so what might be the nature of these errors. Finally, a study involving heterogeneous items would provide some information regarding young children's definition of the domain of countables.

More on the How-To-Count Principles: The Videotape Experiment

Because children did so well at counting the set sizes used in the magic experiments, we saw little point in presenting the results principle by principle. As expected, when children in the videotape experiment encountered larger set sizes they started to err. Accordingly, we present the results principle by principle before introducing the composite scores. Data from all these analyses are given first for the 3-, 4-, and 4-year-old children. Because our 2-year-old subjects almost resisted being tested on the larger set sizes, we think it best to treat their data separately.

Scoring the Videotape Data.   The videotapes were transcribed as described in Gelman and Gallistel (1977). The scoring was as described above for the magic protocols, with the following differences. Recall that in the magic transcripts we had no way to identify a trial independent of the child's tendency to use number words or letters of the alphabet. In the videotape experiment, we determined the start of a trial and thus were prepared to consider whatever followed as the response. Second, children invariably pointed when they counted. Thus, we could take advantage of the pointing behavior when scoring types of one–one errors. How we did this will be taken up when I discuss error types. Finally, we found it necessary to make some minor adjustments in the criteria used for judging a child's use of the cardinal principle (see Gelman & Gallistel, 1977, Chapter 8).

The One–One Principle.   The crudest index of adherence to the one–one principle is whether or not children use as many counting tags (be they unique or not) as there are items to be counted. This they generally do, as shown in Fig. 8.1.

As it turns out, the children represented in Fig. 8.1 used only number words as tags. Thus, the question becomes one of whether they tended to use as many

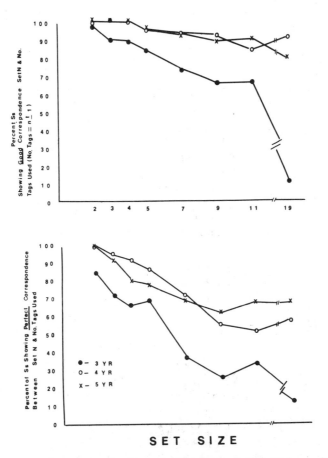

FIG. 8.1   Percentage of subjects in videotape experiment who made a good or perfect correspondence between set size and number of tags.

number words as there were tags. The bottom half of the figure summarizes the extent to which children at each of the three age levels showed perfect correspondence between set size and the number of tags they used. The top half of the figure plots the extent to which children used no more than one extra or no fewer than one less tag than the number corresponding to the set size.

The extent to which children assigned the same number of tags as there were items in the array depended on set size. Older children were better able to meet this criterion, particularly at the larger set sizes. When the 4- and 5-year-olds failed to use as many tags as items, they just missed (± 1) even for set sizes of 19. The 3-year-olds did not do quite as well as judged by the N or $N \pm 1$ criteria. But still, with the exception of set size $N = 19$, their performance in the large number range is quite creditable. For set sizes 7, 9, and 11, 73%, 65%, and 67% of their trials were tagged with either N or $N \pm 1$ tags. These figures suggest

TABLE 8.2
Tendency of Children in Videotape Count Experiment
to Make Each Type of One—One Error

Set Size	Age Group	Number Count Trials	N Error Trials/ 100 Trials	Tag-Duplication Errors/100 Trials	Rate of Each Type Error[a]		
					Partitioning Errors 100 Trials	Coordination Errors/ 100 Trials	
2–5	3 years	402	32.6	1.0	21.6	21.9
	4 years	256	10.9	0.0	5.8	5.1
	5 years	191	18.8	1.6	11.0	6.3
7–19	3 years	122	72.1	5.7	73.0	37.7
	4 years	269	42.4	3.7	30.1	22.6
	5 years	207	35.7	1.4	23.2	19.8

[a]Error trials could have more than one error; hence the rates for the different kinds of errors do not sum to the rate of error trials.

TABLE 8.3
Rate (Occurrence/100 Trials) of Each Type of Partitioning Error
in Videotape Experiment

			Type Partitioning Error			
Set Size	Age Group	Number Count Trials	Double Count	Recount	Omit	Leave Off Too Early
2–5	3 years	402	9.7	2.8	8.9	0.2
	4 years	256	3.1	0.8	1.9	0.0
	5 years	191	2.1	0.5	8.4	0.0
7–19	3 years	122	22.6	7.3	38.0	5.1
	4 years	269	13.8	0.3	14.2	1.8
	5 years	207	7.3	1.5	12.1	2.3

that young children are quite good at applying the one–one principle for relatively large set sizes. This is also evident in the kinds of errors that children made.

Table 8.2 summarizes the number of tagging, partitioning, and coordination errors made per 100 trials for set sizes 2 to 5 and 7 to 19. As shown, tagging errors seldom occur. When errors do occur, they are either partitioning errors or coordination errors. Partitioning errors are particularly notable for those trials involving the larger set sizes. Why? Or more particularly, what does it mean to make a partitioning as opposed to a coordination error? Tables 8.3 and 8.4 present the relevant data.

Table 8.3 summarizes the nature of partitioning errors, which occur mainly when the child makes a slip in going from one item to an adjacent item. Thus, the high rate in the "double count" and "omit" columns. Children seldom leave off before finishing a count. Nor do they have much of a tendency to return to

TABLE 8.4
Rate (Occurrence/100 Trials) of Each Type of Coordination Error
in Videotape Experiment

			Type Coordination Error			
Set Size	Age Group	Number of Count Trials	Beginning	End	Overrun	Dysynchrony
2–5	3 years	402	5.7	12.5	2.4	1.3
	4 years	256	1.2	2.7	0.8	0.4
	5 years	191	1.6	4.7	0.0	0.0
7–19	3 years	122	5.8	21.4	1.6	8.8
	4 years	269	0.0	19.0	2.6	0.9
	5 years	207	0.0	14.0	4.8	1.0

an item after it and subsequent ones have been tagged. All of this leads me to conclude that the children understand the partitioning process but are somewhat sloppy in their execution of it. The larger the set size, the easier it presumably is to lose track in the partitioning process and thus omit one item or double count an item. If this is the case, then errors should occur as the child moves between adjacent items; there should be little tendency to leave off with a number of items remaining to be tagged, nor should there be much skipping around. This is precisely what we observed.

The idea that errors in applying the one—one principle are owing to performance demands and not to a lack of competence is supported by a consideration of the type of coordination errors that occur (Table 8.4). Notice that errors are predominantly *beginning* and *end* errors. Beginning errors reflected a difficulty at initiating a coordinated application of the tagging and partitioning processes. A child would hesitate while his finger was poised over the array and then abruptly start tagging while pointing to the second item in the array rather than the first one. Or a child might drum two or three times on the first item before continuing. Similar failures in coordination occurred even more frequently at the end of an array. In all cases, errors that were classified as *beginning* or *end* errors involved a miss or double count of but one item. This is to be contrasted with *overrun* errors, which involved the continuation of tagging when there were no further items to tag or the repeated tagging of items that were displayed in a somewhat circular fashion. The dysnchrony category was used to capture those error trials on which the child's pointing got out of step with his recitation of number words or vice versa.

What to make of the fact that coordination errors were most frequently of the *end* error type and next most frequently of the *beginning* error type? I think this shows that the child has some difficulty starting the coordinated use of the processes involved in one—one, but once started he goes along just fine until he has to stop the coordinated effort. That the difficulty is so consistently focused on the last item suggests the presence of a faulty stop rule, a suggestion that brings to mind the Russian studies of young children's difficulties with tasks that require a verbal accompaniment to a motor response. The young children in Luria's (1961) study were reported to have found it hard to inhibit verbal accompaniment once they managed to start it up. Whether the comparison is warranted is not particularly pertinent to the point I wish to make, which is that the difficulty in stopping is not all that profound, for the child does stop and does so pretty much with the last item. If he misses, it is typically only by one.

With the results of the one—one error analyses, we can return to an earlier point, which is that the young child who, in the course of counting, fails to apply the one—one principle perfectly usually does so because he slips up in moving from item to item, thereby missing an item or tagging it twice. The categories of error that predominate lead to the conclusion that the child's failure indicates a lack of skill and not a lack of an appropriate underlying concept or rule.

TABLE 8.5
Number of Subjects in Videotape Experiment
Who Were Not Tested at Each Set Size

	Age		
Set Size	3 years (N=21)	4 years (N=19)	5 years (N=15)
2	0	1[a]	1[a]
3	0	0	0
4	1	1	0
5	1	0	0
7	4	2	0
9	9	4[b]	0
11	10	2	0
19	12	2	0

[a]E inadvertently omitted this set size for these subjects.
[b]Includes two subjects who were not run on this set size because of experimenter's error in setting up the trial.

The Stable-Ordering Principle.   Children of all three ages, when willing to count a given set, tend to honor the stable-order principle. Indeed, more than 90% of the 4- and 5-year-olds and 80% of the 3-year-olds used the same stable list on all trials, regardless of set size. Interestingly enough, many children removed themselves from the experiment when they reached a set size they could not negotiate. Thus, as shown in Table 8.5, only nine of 21 3-year-olds were willing to count set sizes of 19. We might conclude that when young children attempt to count a given set size, they apply the stable-ordering principle.

As in the previous data (from the magic protocols), we observed a tendency toward the construction of idiosyncratic lists. Unfortunately, the number of children who constructed such lists was small. There were one 5-year-old (of 15), two (of 19) 4-year-olds, and five (of 15) 3-year-olds. I say unfortunately because we had hoped to determine the relationship between set size and the tendency to construct idiosyncratic lists. For now, I simply note that when such lists appear, it is with younger children and/or larger set sizes, a result consistent with the view that the availability of the stable-order principle guides list learning. To a remarkable degree, the business of list learning is well advanced in young children, as evidenced by their facility in counting reasonably large set sizes.

The Cardinal Principle.   How did the children do with regard to the cardinal principle? It is by no means the case that the children were unable to honor the cardinal principle. Three- and 4-year-olds did rather well on the smaller set sizes, and most 5-year-olds managed to arrive at the cardinal number of set sizes as large as 9 (see Fig. 8.2). Still, as compared to the one—one and stable principles, the cardinal principle seems to be the hardest to follow. This falls out of analyses

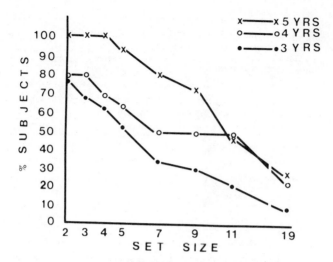

FIG. 8.2 Percentage of subjects in videotape experiment who used cardinal principle on a given set size when all criteria listed in text are applied.

on the extent to which children honor all three principles in a coordinated fashion. Before I turn to a discussion of the use of all three principles, there is an important point I want to make about the scoring criteria for the cardinal analysis.

Recall that we credit children who simply state the correct number but who do not count aloud. There was a question about the legitimacy of this criterion.

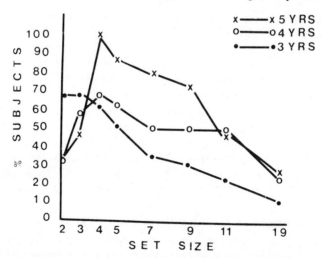

FIG. 8.3 Percentage of subjects in videotape experiment who used cardinal principle on a given set size when all criteria *except number labeling* are used.

The results of the present study allow us to address this concern. Despite the fact that the experiment involved repeated requests to count, there were children who chose not to do so — at least not aloud. As a result, we have cases where the evidence for cardinality is based on the child's having stated the correct number for that array. In Fig. 8.3 I present the results of concluding that a child who simply gave the correct answer was not using the cardinal principle — at least not in the way the counting model requires. A comparison of Fig. 8.2 and 8.3 shows no effect of shifting the scoring criteria for 3-year-olds. However, the shift in scoring criteria produces a rather odd result for the 4- and 5-year-olds; they seem to do worse than the 3-year-olds. Furthermore, they do better in applying the cardinal principle on set sizes 4, 5, 7, 9, and 11 than they do on set sizes 2 and 3. I think the only sensible way out is to conclude that some of the older children have progressed beyond the stage of having to count aloud to determine the numerical value of very small set sizes (cf. Gelman & Tucker, 1975). I also think that I am justified in assuming that a child who does not count aloud but nevertheless gives the correct answer regarding the numerousness of the set can use all three principles. This is the assumption that was followed in determining how well children coordinated the three how-to-count principles. In other words, the child who simply stated the correct numerical value of a set was assumed to have the ability to apply the one—one, stable—order, and cardinal principles for that set size. Because all children who were so scored on a small set size gave clear evidence of the coordinated use of the three principles on larger set sizes, I was satisfied that this assumption was warranted.[3] Now for the results of the analyses of the children's ability to use all three principles in concert.

The Coordinated Use of the How-To-Count Principles.   When the set size is small (and presumably the demands on the child are minimal), most children apply all three principles in conjunction. Thus, for a set size of 2, 76%, 74%, and 96% of the 3-, 4-, and 5-year-olds gave evidence of using all three principles. Similarly, for set size 3 the respective percentages were 67%, 79%, and 100%; for set size 4, 57%, 68%, and 100%. By set size 7, the respective percentages fell off to 19%, 47%, and 80%; only in the 5-year-old group do we see a majority of children able to honor all three principles for set sizes 2 through 7.

Obviously, an increase in set size made it difficult for children to continue to use all three principles in conjunction. What happened? On the basis of sequential analyses we reported elsewhere (Gelman & Gallistel, 1977), increases in set

---

[3]The reader who is unhappy about this decision will be able to make up his own mind by considering Table 8.14 in Gelman & Gallistel (1977) wherein care is taken to present the results of altering criteria for cardinality. It is of interest, however, that when this criterion of cardinality is not followed in assessing the ability to use all three principles it again turns out that 3-year-olds are better than older children because they are more inclined to count aloud.

size first led the children to stop applying the cardinal principle. When children used two of the principles rather than all three, the two they used were the one—one and stable-order principles. It was not that the latter two continued to be applied perfectly. In fact, some errors in applying the one—one principle appeared just at the point where children stopped identifying the cardinal number of the set. As set size increased still further, so did the tendency to make one—one errors. This is reflected in the fact that we eventually found ourselves crediting children with only the stable-order principle because there were too many error trials (i.e., more than 60%) on the one—one principle.

This pattern is true regardless of age, although, not surprisingly, the younger the child, the smaller the set sizes at which he began to falter. I take the pattern to mean that at a very early age children know many of the fundamentals of enumeration. The nature of development, at least from 3 years of age onward, appears to be one of skill perfection and not the apprehension of new principles. When the set size is small and the demands on the child's skill minimal, most 3-year-olds apply all three principles in conjunction. Increases in set size produce errors in the application of the one—one principle. I think the child stops using the cardinal principle when he recognizes the uncertainty of his performance on the one—one principle — successful adherence to which is presupposed when one applies the cardinal principle.

A Return to the 2-Year-Olds in the Videotape Experiment.[4]   Do 2-year-olds show any appreciation of what is involved in counting? Apparently they do. All but one of the children used lists of number words. In this regard, we identified three classes of children: One class used idiosyncratic lists, another used conventional lists, and one child used the same number word over and over again (e.g., "3—3—3"). The five (of 16) children who used idiosyncratic lists had conventional lists for the first three entries and then took up with their own lists (e.g., 1—2—3—6—5—10). One of the idiosyncratic list users recycled when he ran out of available number words and thereby produced a list of 1—2—3—1—2—3 and so on. All children who used idiosyncratic lists adhered perfectly to this order over trials. in contrast, only one of the nine children who tried to use the conventional order of numerlogs did so perfectly; the other eight met the criterion of using the same list on at least 60% of their trials and were therefore judged as being shaky in their ability to use the stable-order principle. Note that the child who follows his own list does *better* at honoring the stable-order principle than the child who follows convention.

Okay, so 2-year-olds can use a list of number words. But do they have any inkling that these words are to be assigned as tags to items in a set? I think so. First, the children pointed — to be sure, not perfectly. Still, 10 out of 16 did

---

[4]The number of 2-year-olds who were tested on set sizes 2, 3, 4, 5, 7, 9, 11, and 19 were 16, 15, 13, 11, 7, 7, and 0, respectively.

well enough for us to do error analyses vis-à-vis the one—one principle. And just as we found with older children, the main error types were coordination and partitioning errors involving one item. That such errors occurred led us to consider the possibility that the children were assigning approximately as many tags as there were items to tag. This brings us to another source of evidence on the one—one principle. We found an overall tendency for the 2-year-olds to use more tags as set size increased (Fig. 8.4) This is not to say that the number used was precise — it was not. Nevertheless, the number of words recited did tend to increase with set size.

Eight (or 50%) of the children were able to count and identify the cardinal number of a two-item array. The median age of the children who did not provide evidence of ability to indicate the cardinal number was 27 months; the median of children who did was 31 months. The four children who were scored as having followed the cardinal principle on a set size of 3 were at least 32 months old; indeed, three of them were 35 months old. It seems, then, that the younger the child, the less likely he is to give any evidence of following the cardinal principle — a result that is consistent with our position that a child must show skill on the one—one and stable-order principles before he can arrive at the cardinal representation.

To be sure, 2-year-olds are not skilled counters. Nevertheless, it is possible to identify the use of some components that make up the counting procedure. They attempt to tag items, they point (albeit less than systematically), and they appear to be guided by a stable-ordering principle. Yes, they have much to learn.

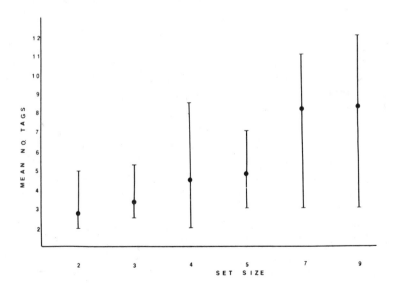

FIG. 8.4   Mean and range of mean number of tags used for each set size by 2-year-olds in videotape experiment.

But they will not be without help, for they seem to have available counting principles — principles that will guide them in their efforts to achieve performance mastery.

The Abstraction Principle

Recall that the displays in the videotape counting experiment were heterogeneous. Yet I have said nothing about the way this influenced behavior. The reason I have said nothing is that nothing seemed called for. We failed to observe any tendency for children to pick out those items that were alike (say, in color) and count only those; instead, they treated all the heterogeneous objects in our arrays as countables. We found a similar effect, or rather lack of effect, when we compared the ability of children to identify the number of heterogeneous or homogeneous items displayed on a card (Gelman & Tucker, 1975). In that study, we found that children in magic experiments take changes in identity or color of an object within an array to be irrelevant to the array's numerousness. Indeed, over and over again, I find that preschoolers are content to group together and count items of diverse composition.

Is it surprising that young children will count "things?" It is from one point of view but not from another. Developmental accounts such as Gast's (1957) are tied to a particular view of number concepts. This view holds that number concepts develop along with the child's ability to classify objects and events into organized hierarchies. It is a common (although not necessarily correct) view that children first classify together objects that share salient perceptual properties and only later develop the ability to use "abstract" criteria for the purposes of classifying. The theme that concepts are initially perceptual and then abstract (or logical) has dominated the major theoretical writings in developmental psychology. From this viewpoint it is easy to slide into the position that the ability to classify entities as "things" for the purposes of counting a heterogeneous set of objects is relatively advanced developmentally.

However, one need not assume that a complex hierarchical scheme mediates the ability to classify entities as "things." Instead, it is possible to view the ability to classify the world into things and nonthings as a derivative of the ability to separate figures from grounds. In this case, the categorization of things as opposed to nonthings may well be a very early achievement. For the child to count heterogeneous materials, he simply needs to treat them as "things." He need not know the way these things can be assigned to various levels of a classification hierarchy.

I do not mean to suggest that the young child will be willing and able to count any collection of items or nonitems I put together for a count trial. It would be amazing if there were no restrictions placed on what is countable. I know of no evidence regarding the countability of imaginary items and would not be surprised if a child said he could not count them. This is a matter for further research. Still, the young child's definition of countables seems to be relatively unrestricted.[5]

The Order-Invariance Principle

We now come to the last of the counting principles. In a sense, this principle is redundant of the other four. It captures the way the first four principles interact in contributing to a full appreciation of counting. We expect that a child who does well on the order-invariance task will use the how-to-count principles in concert. But we are getting ahead of ourselves. First, we have to consider how children performed during the doesn't-matter experiment. And to do this, we again have to consider scoring criteria.

Scoring the Data.   For purposes of the present discussion, there is no need to go over all the details of the scoring procedure. It is enough to know that performance on each trial was scored at one of four levels. Then, an overall performance score, which took into account trial-by-trial performances, was assigned each child. A child could respond in one of two ways on a given trial and be scored at Level 1 — the top grade. The child who tagged the designated object as requested and made no how-to-count errors while doing so was obviously given a Level 1 score for that trial, but so were children who adopted strategies for making a given object be X that forced them to produce errors. For example, there was the child who, when asked to make the second object in a row be four, tagged the first object *one* and then held his finger in the air while he said, "Two-three" and then dropped his finger to touch the designated item while he said "four" and continued to count the remaining objects. There were also children who rearranged the order of their lists (e.g., one, four, two, three, five) so as to be able to proceed left to right and tag each item in succession. There was a variety of such strategies (Merkin & Gelman, 1977) that enabled children to follow our instructions but then forced them to make errors. We distinguished between strategic errors and straightforward counting errors in the application of the how-to-count principles. Trials that involved simple counting errors but otherwise followed our instructions were scored as Level 2. Still poorer performances were scored as Level 3 or Level 4.

Having reliably scored the performance on each trial at Level 1, 2, 3, or 4, we assigned each child an across-trials performance rank of I, II, III, IV, or V. Distinctions in overall performance reflect the extent to which children received Level 1 or 2 scores on their individual trials. Those children who received a Level Level 1 score on *all* trials were assigned an overall performance rank of I; child-

---

[5]In Gelman and Gallistel there is a discussion of the evidence that appears to contradict this conclusion. We argue that such evidence was collected in experimental situations that set children to think that they were to count together items that were alike.

ren who scored at Level 1 on at least 60% (but not 100%) of their trials were assigned an overall rank of II; children who received Level 1 scores on no more than two trials were assigned an overall performance rank of III; children who failed to receive Level 1 scores but received Level 2 scores on at least 60% of their trials were assigned an overall performance rank of IV. All other children were ranked at level V on overall performance — reflecting the fact that they had considerable trouble with the experiment.

Results.   Recall that there were 12 3-year-olds and 15 4-year-olds who participated in the order-irrelevance experiment. Seventeen and 47% of the respective age groups received an overall performance rank of I. Another 25% and 20% in each age group received an overall rank of II. Thus, 42% and 67% of the 3- and 4-year-olds scored at least at rank II. The percentages of children scoring at each of the remaining ranks were 17%, 17%, and 25% in the 3-year-old group and 7%, 13%, and 13% in the 4-year-old group. These data reflect the fact that many children made some how-to-count errors when performing on the doesn't-matter items. Only 17% and 47% of the 3- and 4-year-olds were able to negotiate the doesn't-matter test items without making straightforward count errors. This raises the question of the relationship between the child's understanding of the how-to-count principles and his overall performance on the doesn't-matter items.

In this and all other experiments on the question at hand, it was the better counters who received the top grades for their overall performance on the doesn't-matter items. For a child to do well on the latter tests, he had to show independent evidence of being able to coordinate the how-to-count principles on at least some set sizes. However, an ability to apply the how-to-count principles in concert is not a sufficient ability for the order-irrelevance principle. In every experiment we have done, we find good counters who do very poorly on the doesn't-matter items. Thus, as expected, the ability to apply the order-irrelevance principle is dependent on the development of counting skill, yet counting skill is not enough. The question of what new knowledge develops and makes it possible for a child to honor the order-irrelevance principle is taken up in the next section.

WHAT DEVELOPS?

I address the question of "What develops?" by first considering what does not develop — at least from the age of about 2-1/2 years on. Even the youngest children in our how-to-count studies behaved in accord with the one—one and stable-order principles. They may have erred in the application of these principles; nevertheless, the errors that occurred are best characterized as performance errors rather than as errors that reflect complete lack of knowledge of the one—one and stable-order principles. How else to explain the tendency of children to assign approximately as many tags as there are items to tag? And how else to explain the appearance of idiosyncratic number lists or even the novel list of the alphabet? Surely, no one would expect to find an adult in this culture who intentionally and consistently taught their young to count with idiosyncratic lists of number words. And it is exceedingly difficult to imagine adults speaking to the beginning language learner as follows: "A, you do this; B you do that; C, you do that," and so on. It would be a violation of what speech looks like to the 2-year-olds (see Ferguson & Snow, 1977, for a review of the relevant literature). Since the use of such strings is repeatable and stable over trials, I can think of no other explanation than that the young child has a principle in search of a list.

It is perhaps a lucky thing that there is a principle to guide the acquisition of the count—word sequence. Even with its aid, the child has much to learn. The research reported in earlier sections of this chapter involved set sizes as large as 19; it did not involve set sizes of 20, 30, 100, 1000, and more. I do not know what we will find when we use such set sizes, but I venture to guess that young children will encounter considerable difficulty, for the generation of the count words involved here depends on a base—ten rule. I suspect that the child has yet to develop such knowledge. Here, then, is one candidate for development.

Another candidate for development has been highlighted in several of the preceding sections. This is the eventual perfection of skill in applying the one—one principle. For the counting procedure to work as a method for establishing the numerousness of a set, it will not do to allow partitioning or coordination errors. Over trials, a child who makes such errors will arrive at different estimates of the same set size. This will allow him to conclude that set sizes of the same number of objects represent different numbers from trial to trial. Needless to say, such a child is unlikely to conserve number. But worse yet, he is very likely to falter in making same—different judgments of those set sizes for which he still makes one—one errors. Thus, it is essential that the young child perfect his application of the one—one principle, or else his ability to compare the numerousness of sets will be exceedingly limited.

Related to the former argument as to what develops is one regarding ability to apply the cardinal principle. We have seen that the child who makes one—one errors for a given set size is disinclined to identify the cardinal number of that set. To the extent that the application of the cardinal principle depends on the coordinated use of the one—one and stable-order principles, this is as it should be. Yet it seems a bit odd to say a child can count and still not know the numerical value of the set. Until the child can state the cardinal number of a given set, it is not clear that he realizes that a given count can be used to determine cardinal number. Like others (e.g., Schaeffer et al., (1974), I conclude that the development of the cardinal principle is delayed compared to the one—one and stable-order principles.

Even when a child can apply the cardinal principle, it is not clear that he has a full appreciation of it. Recall that we observed children who could use all three how-to-count principles and still did not do well on the doesn't-matter items. A good score on the order-irrelevance tasks can be taken to reflect an understanding that once a given set has been counted it does not matter how it is recounted – the cardinal number therein will be conserved. The development of the cardinal number concept would thus seem to pass through stages. Initially, the child has to repeat the last tag of a count sequence. Then, he sees that the cardinal number is conserved across repeated counts. Presumably the next step is the ability to rely on a rule of one–one correspondence without having to count at all. If we assume that this is what Piaget's test of number conservation is about (cf. Brainerd, 1973), then we should expect a developmental lag between a child's ability to conserve number as revealed by the doesn't-matter test and the Piagetian test. In an ongoing experiment designed to test this hypothesis, this seems to be what happens.

In the end there should be yet one further development, the ability to reason about number without first having to count and thereby to achieve a specific numerical representation. It is only when the child is freed from his reliance on the counting procedure that he will be able to reason about algebraic entities, appreciate the rule of one–one correspondence, and so on. From Piaget (1952) we can conclude that these are the kinds of arithmetical knowledge that emerge during middle childhood.

ACKNOWLEDGMENTS

The preparation of this paper as well as the research reported in it were supported by NICHD Grant No. 04598 and NSF Grant BNS-77-03327 to the author. The author's address is 3813 Walnut Street, Department of Psychology, University of Pennsylvania, Philadelphia, Pa. 19104.

REFERENCES

Beckwith, M., & Restle, F. Process of enumeration. *Psychological Review,* 1966, *73,* 437–444.

Brainerd, C. J. Mathematical and behavioral foundations of number. *Journal of General Psychology Monographs,* 1973, *88,* 221–281.

Ferguson, C., & Snow, C. (Eds.), *Talking to children: Language input and acquisition.* Cambridge, England: Cambridge University Press, 1977.

Gast, H. Der Umgang mit Zahlen und Zahlgebilden in der frühen kindheit. *Zeitschrift für Psychologie,* 1957, *161,* 1–90.

Gelman, R., & Gallistel, C. R. *The young child's understanding of number: A window on early cognitive development.* Book manuscript, University of Pennsylvania, 1977. A revision will be published by Harvard University Press.

Gelman, R., & Tucker, M. F. Further investigations of the young child's conception of number. *Child Development,* 1975, *46,* 167–175.

Ginsburg, H. *Young children's informal knowledge of mathematics.* Manuscript copyrighted by author, Cornell University, 1975.

Klahr, D., & Willace, J. C. The role of quantitative operators in the development of conservation quantity. *Cognitive Psychology,* 1973, *4,* 301–327.

Luria, A. R. *The role of speech in the regulation of normal and abnormal behavior.* New York: Pergamon, 1961.

Menninger, K. *Number words and number symbols.* Cambridge, Mass.: MIT Press, 1969.

Merkin, S., & Gelman, R. *Strategic behavior among 3- and 4-year-olds in a modified counting task.* Unpublished manuscript, University of Pennsylvania, 1977.

Piaget, J. *The child's conception of number.* New York: Norton, 1952.

Schaeffer, B., Eggelston, V. H., & Scott, J. L. Number development in young children. *Cognitive Psychology,* 1974, *6,* 357–379.

A Discussion of the Chapters by Siegler, Trabasso, Klahr, and Gelman

James G. Greeno
University of Pittsburgh

AUTHOR'S NOTE

The form of this discussion is taken directly from Lakatos (1961, 1976). Although many discussions of scientific ideas have been presented as dialogues, Lakatos' book (1976) uses a quasi-historical format both to clarify and to enrich the relationships between ideas in the development of work on mathematical problems. By acknowledging my debt to Lakatos' very important book, I do not mean to pretend to anything like the degree of his achievement. Lakatos gave a thorough exploration of some fundamental issues concerning the nature of mathematical knowledge. My task is much more modest, of course. However, I do hope that this form may provide a useful context for identifying some of the interesting issues raised in the papers on which I was privileged to comment.

The discussants are based on historical figures. I do not pretend that any of the real individuals would react to the conference papers with the remarks that I attribute to them, but perhaps the remarks are reasonable within the general conceptual frameworks that these theorists have contributed to our thinking. Similarly, the responses that I attribute to characters inspired by the four authors are my responsibility, not theirs. They are merely my impressions of ways in which the positions taken in the papers might be made responsive to some of the questions that are raised, rather than ways in which I think the real authors would actually respond.

DRAMATIS PERSONAE

Discussants

Beta . . . . Binet
Delta. . . . . Dewey

Theta . . . . .Thorndike
Pi . . . . .Piaget
Omega . . . . Wertheimer

Authors

Sigma . . . . Siegler
Tau . . . . .Trabasso
Kappa . . . . .Klahr
Gamma . . . . Gelman

BETA.   We all found these chapters to be very interesting, and we thank the authors. To begin the discussion, let me offer an answer to the question in the title of this book. I believe there is a quite simple answer to the question of "What develops in children's cognitive development?" — it is intelligence. But, of course, that is merely another way of putting the question: "What is the nature of intelligence?"

I find it interesting that the main method for investigating intelligence, which we began with in 1905, is still very much in use. We made the assumption that intelligence would be indicated on tasks where older children succeeded and where younger children failed. I see that that assumption is still very much in use.

SIGMA.   By and large, that is correct. However, you probably have also noted significant changes. It is becoming more common for investigators to analyze in detail exactly what children of different ages do on various tasks rather than simply noting where they succeed and where they fail.

BETA.   Yes, I noticed that. Finding the ways in which children's performance differs, rather than merely cataloguing tasks, is a considerable advance. And I also find it quite significant that you, Sigma, have begun to examine developmental changes in children's learning of new methods for working on a problem. That strikes me as a potentially very powerful method for investigating the nature of intelligence.

PI.   I'd like to join in your enthusiasm, Beta. All these investigators have been looking very carefully at cognitive structures, which is a very encouraging development. I was particularly impressed by Tau's finding that the difficulty children have in the class-inclusion problem is a difficulty in understanding the relations between sets and subsets. I have to agree with you, Tau, regarding your very surprising result that performance is the same when judgments involve different superordinate categories as when they involve a single category. That finding makes it unlikely that children who fail in that task are ever aware of the total superordinate category. But it is still clear that the difficulty is in the children's understanding of the pattern of relations between objects and their categories; this confirms the importance of the general structure by which children represent set membership and set inclusion.

TAU. I think that's correct, Pi. I would emphasize, though, that in specifying the way in which the understanding process is affecting children's performance, we are achieving a more detailed and specific analysis of the process. And as we do that, it is no longer reasonable to consider cognitive growth simply in terms of the development of additional structures. For example, in my analysis it is clear that the source of much of the difficulty is the child's interpretation of the situation and of the questions that are asked about the situation. If we take that seriously, we surely cannot continue simply to talk about younger children lacking the logical structure of class inclusion.

PI. Oh, I think you are correct in that. However, you did not really provide a very detailed account of just what the processes of representation are. Because the difficulty for many children seems to come from incomplete representations of sets of objects, I think that a detailed analysis of the process of representing sets might show the nature of the conceptual deficiency. In any case, it would be interesting to show exactly what relations are involved in the semantic processes that lead to the representations you have hypothesized.

OMEGA. I, too, am very interested to see how the problem of representation and understanding enters into the class-inclusion situation, as well as into Sigma's findings concerning the balance scale problem. Indeed, Sigma's results suggest that the appropriate rules for solving that problem will be acquired through normal experience, as soon as the child comes to represent the relevant features of the sitatuion. I'm puzzled, though, about two things. First, I wonder whether the issue is simply one of having a more complete representation in the sense of including all the features. It seems to me that what children need to appreciate in the balance scale problem is the relationship between weight and the event of falling — and later, the way in which distance enters into that system. Do you think that the failure to encode distance — and for very young children, ro encode weight — is due to a simple lack of attention or to a more complex failure to appreciate the relation between these and the main event of the task — the falling of one end or the other of the balance scale?

SIGMA. Right now I can't tell you which of those is happening in the situations I've studied, though it's something that I have been thinking a lot about lately. When we have trained children to encode the relevant features of the situation, they have not automatically adopted the rules that use those features. However, there is something of a chicken-and-egg problem here. If children must appreciate the relevance of a feature before they encode it and if they must encode the feature before they can recognize its relevance, then the whole structure might never emerge. And yet it does. We've broken through the circle by instructing children in how to encode the information. The next step is to identify the ways in which children come to encode the relevant features in the absence of such direct instruction.

THETA.   I'd like to remark on the feature of these analyses that Sigma mentioned in his first comment — the detailed specification of the processes assumed to occur in these situations. I have generally been skeptical of the emphasis given (in some discussions) to vague notions of cognitive structure. It seems to me that what is needed is a careful analysis of the requirements of a task. We once discussed this in terms of stimulus–response bonds, but the general notion is quite compatible with the current terminology of production rules. The important idea is the benefit of identifying the component processes needed to perform a task. This is especially evident in Kappa's analysis of the young children's performance on the disk transfer problem. Many of us have felt that careful task analysis would be a boon to instruction. Gamma's emphasis on analyzing the performance of children in counting tasks seems to support this idea.

GAMMA.   There is an important difference between the idea I have in mind and the idea that knowledge can be analyzed into networks of stimulus–response bonds — or even production systems. Remember that in my analysis of counting, I proposed that there are several general principles that children must come to understand. They must also have the mechanics of the skill, and I assume the mechanics and principles must be integrated in some coherent way. But I don't necessarily think that the whole system of knowledge can be analyzed into production rules very easily.

One surprising result of our studies is that the basic principles seem to be understood by very young children — children who are not yet skilled in the mechanics of counting. This has two consequences. First, it indicates that the principles regarding number and quantity are not acquired by abstraction from well-learned skills. They do not emerge from concrete procedures, as many people have thought they might. Second, it makes it seem that the approach suggested by Theta may be exactly correct concerning the process of acquisition. If all the principles are present at a very early age, then perhaps all that needs to be added is a set of relatively simple components that can be analyzed as a set of stimulus–response bonds.

KAPPA.   This concept of a skill may be more complicated than it seems; just because we identify something as a skill, rather than as a principle, it doesn't necessarily follow that it is organized in a simple way. The organization of a system can be quite complex yet still be represented as a production system — in fact, production systems seem to provide a special clarity by showing the structural relations between different parts of a procedure. Productions function at different levels. For example, some productions set goals for the system, and the operation of other productions is contingent on them. If we can figure out how planning works, it will almost certainly involve using global features of a situation to engage in abstract analysis of the problem. Selection of subgoals will probably occur as a consequence of the planning procedures. In the evidence that I presented about goals and planning in very young children, the processes appear to be quite primitive — the factors in the situation that are driving these processes aren't yet clear. But there is definitely more involved in this skill than simple collections of stimulus—response bonds. There are hierarchies of procedures involved, and to understand intellectual skills, we must be able to represent relations between component processes, as well as the processes themselves.

DELTA.   I am very interested in this matter of goals, and I will raise a question about it later. However, perhaps Sigma could first comment about another interesting topic, that of organized skills. He reported a conclusion that 5-year-old children are more systematic in their approach to problems than are 3-year-olds. Is that another form of this phenomenon of an organized skill?

SIGMA.   Yes, I think it is, although I'm not sure how it works. It's clear that children 3 years old and younger use rules in many situations. I think that the major difference between them and older children is the tendency of the older individuals to search for and apply rules in relatively unfamiliar situations, such as these experimental tasks. It may be that the older children have more active processes for forming rules through a process of induction, or it may be that they simply have greater knowledge about the types of physical features that could plausibly be important in the types of situations we present.

DELTA.   That's very interesting, and it relates closely to the question I wanted to ask Kappa about goals in skilled performance. I've felt for a long time that the skills children develop should be useful to them. Indeed, I've argued that we should teach as much as possible in the context of problems, so that children would see the utility of the skills they are acquiring. The question that I have concerns the process of acquiring skill in setting goals. Do you think, Kappa, that this skill might involve general principles similar to those Gamma discovered when she studied counting? If so, then children's main task in learning to be more systematic or organized — as well as in learning to apply their knowledge — may be acquiring skill in applying principles rather than in acquiring the principles themselves.

KAPPA.   I agree that the issue you raise is an important one. The development of goal-setting capabilities is one of the critical issues that I hope to learn about in studying young children's problem solving. I think that what you refer to as a general principle is illustrated by the importance of sequential ordering in my procedural model. However, I think the question of whether children acquire a principle of sequential ordering, rather than a procedure for applying a principle they already have, is a poor question. What they acquire are procedures that we can interpret in relation to general principles if we choose to, but a more fruitful approach is to analyze what the procedures are.

PI.   Before we leave this topic of organized skills, there are two things about Gamma's approach that bother me. One involves the idea of modifying a procedure while maintaining constraints on its operation. The other involves the idea of applying a procedure over its total domain. I think, as a general rule, we should expect a child to be able to do both of these, if that child really understands the principles that the procedures are based on. But in two rather important cases, Gamma's results suggest that young children's counting procedures do not meet this standard.

The first of these problems came up when Gamma asked children to count objects and assign a specific number to one of them. Of course, what the children did was charming and showed considerable knowledge of the principles Gamma proposed as criteria for understanding counting. But the children also encountered some difficulties. When Gamma showed us how she solved these problems, she transformed her normal counting procedure in a way that preserved the one—one and stable-order principles. When the children tried to perform the same transformations, they were unable to preserve these constraints. I wonder whether we should conclude, with Gamma, that the children really do understand these principles fully, since they do not maintain them when the usual spatial sequence is disrupted.

The other problem is that the counting procedures are worked out only for small sets of items. The nature of counting is such that they can be applied to indefinitely large arrays. Gamma's view seems to be that if a child has mastered the counting of small sets, that is sufficient evidence to attribute understanding of the basic principles of counting, and the child merely has the technical problem of extending the skill to include a larger domain of numbers. However, given the small sizes of the sets that these very young children count, it seems to me that they may not have acquired a basic principle. We know that it takes a greater level of computing power to count indefinitely large sets than to count sets bounded in advance by some finite number. One way to achieve that additional power is to have a general principle of adding one to whatever number you had previously. Perhaps a principle of that kind is essential to counting, but is not part of the equipment of the children Gamma observed. If children lack the principle of indefinite extension, I doubt that we should conclude that they really have acquired all the principles of counting at the tender age that Gamma suggested.

GAMMA.   With regard to the first problem you raise, I think your point is too strong. I'm confident that the children understood the principles that I attributed to them. In the doesn't-matter experiment, we imposed the unusual constraint that a particular object needed to be tagged with a particular number. To meet this demand, children had to violate other constraints that they knew about. I would not want to conclude that they didn't understand those constraints — rather, they lacked the skill needed to generate a new procedure consistent with all the constraints they knew, when the added constraint of a specified number for an object was imposed.

The second problem is more complicated. I haven't really worked through the issue of counting larger arrays, as I pointed out in my chapter. Perhaps when we have done that, we will have to agree with you that an additional principle is needed. In that case, we would agree that to that extent, the understanding of our very young subjects was incomplete. Of course, when we understand what the principle is, we may be able to show it in very young children, too, which would mean that they simply hadn't gotten all their principles integrated yet. However, a judgment on that would be quite premature at this point.

One implication of your remarks is that a clear distinction between principles and skills is going to be very hard to defend. I may have presented that distinction a little more definitely than it really deserves.

THETA. I want to make a general comment about representations of skills. The idea that a skill consists of an organized set of behavioral components, complete with goals, planning, and principles, is a very important one. When I argued for the analysis of skills and knowledge into their component stimulus–response bonds, I was very interested in how the bonds were organized, but I didn't have a good way of expressing this. Modern theoretical methods seem to have gone at least part of the way toward an adequate representation of interactions between components of psychological processes.

TAU. I agree, and there may be a helpful analogy to the achievements that we study in young children. If my analysis of the class-inclusion situation is correct, when a child understands that situation, that child has available a rather complex collection of concepts and skills for representing sets of objects and their interrelations and for interpreting statements and questions about them. It seems as though we scientists are engaged in an analogous process. We observe phenomena, and the opinions we form about them often involve misconceptions at least as serious as the ones we observe children making. We shouldn't be surprised if the changes we need to incorporate in our thinking involve new ways of representing situations and new interpretive procedures for linking language to the situations, just as they do for children.

THETA. That's an interesting observation, Tau, and it relates to a question I wanted to ask you, similar to one that Pi asked you quite a bit earlier. I agree with him that your conclusions about representation and semantic interpretation seem vague. Some years ago I would have said that you need to identify the bonds involved in representing the semantic relations in the situation. Of course, a more complicated set of concepts is needed to carry out the analysis, but how do you feel about Pi's suggestion that a detailed analysis be done to specify the components involved in the representations you identified for us?

TAU.   It certainly is an appealing suggestion. It would require working out the relationships between language processing and reasoning in a way that has only begun to be achieved in some other areas. A project like that would certainly raise interesting issues about language and thinking, and an analysis of that kind may have to be done before we really understand problems such as class inclusion.

THETA.   Along that same line, when we discussed analyzing tasks, such as those in arithmetic, as a set of stimulus—response bonds, we needed to identify the stimulus condition necessary for a response to be correct. That dimension of analysis is also important now, when investigators use production rules to represent components of procedural knowledge, since the condition of each production is a test that is applied to the stimulus situation. Sigma's conclusions about the importance of encoding emphasize the importance of having relevant stimulus features in the conditions for productions.

I wonder whether an analysis of that kind isn't needed for the counting situation studied by Gamma. We have already discussed some of the puzzling issues involving relationships between principles and skills in that situation, and I'm not sure that any simple analysis will resolve them. However, some of the difficulties that children have — especially their problem with beginning and ending a count — might be clarified considerably if we had a model in which the various processing components responsible for frequent errors were made explicit. The kind of model I have in mind would be quite similar to Kappa's, where a series of processes simulate the various degrees of skill that Kappa's subjects showed. A good deal of the variance in those procedures might be accounted for by the kinds of perceptual tests applied by different children as they begin and end counting.

GAMMA.   That sounds like an interesting project. It would be even more interesting if we could see how the understanding of principles interacts with low-level components of procedural knowledge.

PI.   While we are discussing stimulus features, there is a point about Kappa's results that I want to mention. In the usual form of the Tower of Hanoi, the constraint on size ordering must be encoded and remembered. By setting up the problem with cans, Kappa made a significant change: What is ordinarily a rule to remember now becomes an obvious fact. It could be that the plans would be much harder for young children to generate in the standard situation in which they are required to remember the constraint.

KAPPA.   I suppose that's a possibility. In any case, the cognitive basis of those plans is not very clear.

OMEGA.   I'm glad that the idea of constraints in a problem space was mentioned. I have always felt that it was important for children to understand the structure of a situation they were learning about, and an important component of that may be an appreciation of the constraints that are present and the relationships between different constraints. Understanding constraints, along with strategic knowledge that involves setting goals, may provide a powerful way of characterizing the development of skill and knowledge about a class of problems.

BETA.   Well, we certainly have identified some interesting issues. Our method of comparing children of different ages on tasks where they differed did not lead to a complete understanding of intelligence. These newer techniques and approaches seem to be revealing some significant aspects of intelligence and cognitive development and thus represent real progress. On the other hand, the situation seems a little chaotic. However, I had a feeling it might turn out that way — at least for a while.

REFERENCES

Lakatos, I. *Essays in the logic of mathematical discovery.* Unpublished doctoral dissertation, Cambridge University, 1961.

Lakatos, I. *Proofs and refutations: The logic of mathematical discovery.* Cambridge: Cambridge University Press, 1976.

III REPRESENTATIONAL PROCESSES

10

How Children Represent Knowledge of Their World In and Out of Language: A Preliminary Report

Katherine Nelson
Yale University

Many people — especially those working with artificial intelligence models of language processes — have been struck by the complexity of the knowledge base necessary to understand even simple language and by the ease with which very young children appear to use this knowledge base in their everyday lives. Impressively, young children's language use appears to involve inference, prediction, and long-term memory for sequentially ordered events — cognitive skills that are usually considered underdeveloped even when the child enters school. The problem is how to characterize children's knowledge in a way that can account both for their great success in using language in their everyday lives and their great difficulty in performing many other cognitive tasks. To do this we must look to the natural language system that the child uses in his own ecology. As one means toward that end, we have been scanning baby biographies and parental diaries. Consider the routine of a 1-year-old child (from Church, 1966):

> (At 8:00 A.M.) She emits a series of whoops summoning adults, and we find her standing at the crib side grinning broadly as she greets us. . . . Once picked up, she points to or waves at all her favorite objects in the room. . . . Diapers changed, she walks quickly out to the dining room, jabbering cheerfully, and demonstrates interest in breakfast . . . by going to her table and banging. . . . She finger feeds all lumps, accepting various degrees of help. . . . She points to the cleaning tissues and, when given one, wipes her mouth and hands, very pleased with herself. . . . At [breakfast's] end she stands, grabs her piece of toast and is lifted down, and walks forthrightly off to some project or other. . . . (At about 9:30 A.M.) "Do you want a bath?" "Ess," and off she goes to the bathroom. Helps get herself

undressed, dumps bath toys into the running water. . . . She grabs wash cloth to wash face, hands, tummy, and each foot on request, drinks water from her cup with great skill [p. 50–51].

Apart from the precocity of this child, the account is unremarkable. So are the following reports of the same child 5 months later (Church, 1966): "On seeing a pair of closed pruning shears sitting idly by for the first time, she picked them up and prepared to demonstrate to me how she could clip her fingernails with them . . . [p. 70] " and, "She now occasionally usurps driver's seat in the parked car and goes through an energetic mimicry of starting and driving it, with gear-shifting and horn honking, key and wheel turning, etc. [p. 71] ."

These examples show that at the age of 1 year the child has a knowledge of daily routines that enables her to participate confidently in action sequences, to predict the sequences, and so to anticipate the next steps. She can use this knowledge to respond to questions with appropriate verbalization or action (for example, "Do you want a bath?"). Moreover, her knowledge of objects and events allows her to engage in classificatory activity, such as preparing to use the pruning shears on her fingernails — a clear demonstration of classification through use.

There is ample evidence from mothers' reports that it is not only routine events that are well remembered but novel events as well. According to one such report, "In the middle of January, M. (21 months) went to a bowling birthday party for her brother. They had a candy machine in the bowling alley and M. got money for the machine. They went back three weeks later to drop off M.'s brother. While in the car, M. asked for money to buy candy in the bowling alley." This demonstrates a type of long-term memory that is independent of language, in that it appears prior to language, and that also has much in common with our own memory for everyday events. What sort of memory is this? Does it consist of accumulated episodes, or is it formulated into some sort of structure abstracted from particular events? How does verbal knowledge map onto event knowledge?

In posing these question I am assuming that studying the type of memory relied on in everyday life is basic to understanding more advanced knowledge structures, such as those employed in more complex and structured tasks. I believe it to be basic in two ways: both to the older child's and adult's similar understanding of everyday events and to understanding the older child's competence at tasks such as story understanding, classification, and problem solving.

The framework within which we have been looking at the developing structure of event memory is that of the script (cf. Schank & Abelson, 1977). Scripts are models of familiar experiences that are called into play in the appropriate verbal or situational context. Each script (1) contains certain basic and obligatory events in sequence, (2) predicts open slots for optional objects and events and what they may contain, and (3) designates appropriate roles and actors.

That is, there is a skeletal sequential structure that is called up in context and is filled in, as needed, with context-appropriate optional slot fillers and details. As Schank and Abelson (1975) note, "The structure is an interconnected whole and what is in one slot affects what can be in another [p. 3]." The advantage of such a frame is obvious: It makes understanding a familiar event possible without constantly attending to and organizing all the subcomponents.

There are at least three possible developmental paths that scripts might follow. First, the script might develop through the accumulation of individual episodes, with each episode consisting of some common elements in a common sequence plus additional idiosyncratic details. With experience, the common elements in the sequence would be abstracted out to form a general script. This model is recognizable as one form of a general concept formation model (cf. Nelson, 1974) and has some of the same problems. For example, how does the person know that another similar episode has come along unless he already knows the basic pattern? What happens to the idiosyncratic details when the script is abstracted? Do they remain available at some lower level?

Another alternative is that a skeletal sequential structure is set up after a single experience and develops through the addition of details, slots, and roles and through the substitution of open slots for specific details. Still a third possibility is that a collection of unordered, random elements is stored at the outset, and the script develops by imposing structure on these elements.

With this last possibility we must consider the relation of general cognitive development to script development. It is possible that the young child experiences episodes more as random elements than does the older child. If so, the third possibility might be characteristic of script development in younger children, and another type of development might characterize older ones. In other words, there are two kinds of development to be concerned with: short-term development of a memory structure from the experience of similar events and long-term developmental changes in the characteristics of such structures.

If we find evidence for skeletal scripts, we are faced with additional, but somewhat more familiar, questions. Does the script direct action only; is it used also for interpreting and producing language; can the child verbalize it? The last question is crucial to the interpretation of research. Again, the case might be different at different ages. One possibility would be a three-stage progression. A young child, just building up a script, might be able to verbalize all its parts, that is, the script would be fully explicit. Then, when the script had been developed fully, it would become implicit and the child would not be able to verbalize it. Finally, when he reached a metalinguistic or metaconceptual level of development, he would again be able to verbalize the structure.

Another problem involves the relationships between nodes in the script. If there is a central, organizing element for the subcomponents of the script, is it necessary to access it in order to activate the script? In concrete terms, what calls up the breakfast or bath script for the 1-year-old child described above? In one case, a sequence of action apparently was sufficient; in the other, a word ("bath") triggered the appropriate action sequence. At this point it seems unlikely that there is an either-or answer to this question, but it in turn raises additional questions. Once accessed, is the script run off in a unidirectional manner, that is, is it nonreversible, or is it bidirectional so that the user can proceed backward and forward within it? Does this possibility change with age?

Research on young children's scripts will eventually need to tackle all these questions. At the moment, however, we are only on the threshold of the investigation, and we have just begun to study the nature of scripts, their development over time, and their accessibility to free varbalization, probes, and active reconstruction. We have looked at only one age group thus far, preschool children of 3 to 5 years of age. With children of this age, we are able to study both verbal and enactive modes of recall and reconstruction, which would be difficult with younger children. On the other hand, the children do not yet display the cognitive strategies and operations of the concrete operations stage, with its reversible, reflective abilities. They are somewhere between the infant and the 10-year-old in cognitive ability; script organization at this age might well be different from earlier and later ones.

Our first strategy was basically an interview technique. We recognized, however, that what the child was able to verbalize might be an inadequate reflection of his knowledge, so we supplemented verbal accounts with the opportunity to act out a familiar event. We felt this combination would at least give us a baseline from which we could design more sensitive experiments. We chose a routine event familiar in the life of all children — mealtime — because we were interested in mapping the common content and structure — the what and how of organized knowledge — rather than the cognitive processes of acquiring or using knowledge. We have undertaken two preliminary studies along these lines.

STUDY I

The first study was designed to discover whether there were common elements, a common structure, and a veridical sequential organization in children's understanding of familiar events. Eating in three settings was investigated: lunch at the day care center, with which all the children had common experiences; dinner at home, which would vary from family to family; and eating at McDonald's, where there was a set sequence of common events. We expected the greatest agreement in the day care reports, because the experience was common to all the children and because the interview took place at the day care center, thus allowing the children to draw on a common context in their reports. We expected that the hamburger stand situation would also elicit similar reports because of its standard event sequence. Finally, we expected the dinner-at-home situation to show the greatest variability.

Eight children (ages 48 to 61 months), attending a university-affiliated day care center, were interviewed in three sessions: each session focused on one of the three eating situations described above. In each case, the verbalization condition was presented first so that the props would not contaminate the initial report. The child was asked to tell what happened when he had lunch at the day care center (or at home or at McDonald's). The question was termed the First Pass and was followed, where necessary, by general probes such as "Anything else?" Finally, knowledge of sequence was probed directly by asking such questions as, "What happens next?", and knowledge of details was probed specifically, for example, "How do you know when it's lunch time?"

The enactive, or prop-assisted, condition always followed the verbalization condition. Children were presented with a model school, house, or McDonald's restaurant, Fisher-Price "people" toys, and other appropriate props such as chairs and tables, and were asked to show what happens when you have lunch. Again, the probes followed the general-to-specific pattern. In addition to tape-recording the children's responses, the experimenter made notes of their actions.

Analysis

The resulting protocols were analyzed in terms of a set of common elements, which we labeled *Basic Events*. These were components of the event sequences that appeared in many of the protocols, almost always in a definite sequence. Theoretically, an event component can be of any size; that is, a child might refer to an element as small as taking a bite of a hamburger or as large as eating lunch. Rather than make *a priori* decisions as to what an event component might be, we derived them from the children's protocols. Events that were mentioned by several children and that were not spontaneously broken down into further subcomponents were defined as Basic Events. There was great consistency among children in the degree to which events were specified. The Basic Events that emerged for the day care situation were verified against a teacher's account of lunchtime activity for appropriateness of sequence. Because of the common structure that emerged, we were further able to identify anchor events, central acts, and optional events as follows:

Anchor event: playing on playground, book corner
Optional events: washing hands, getting food, sitting down
Central act: eating
Optional events: dessert, throwing away plates
Anchor event: napping

Sequence

Three indications of understanding of the sequence were available. First, some children gave ordered descriptions without prompting. An example from the

McDonald's context, using props, is the following (verbalization in italics):

> The child moves the car containing the mother and father in the front seat, the child in the rear seat, up to McDonald's. Car noises are made by the child.
> *They're driving.*
> The car is parked; father, mother, and child get out. They enter through the door.
> *Now, walking through this door. I walk in there and I, I, I ask my daddy and then the daddy ask the lady and the lady gets it. One small coke, one cheeseburger. Two hamburgers. Two hamburgers and one cheeseburger and they say, they say, they say, some some fish sandwiches.*
> Moves the McDonald's men around behind the counter.
> *They want to eat here so they don't need a tray. Then we go find a table. I eat it all up. All. And throw the . . . and the paper, throw the, the cheeseburgers in the garbage can.*
> The child removes the three figures from McDonald's.
> *Goodbye. Goodbye. Jump in the car. And they jump in the car. Vroom! Vroom! Goodbye.*

A second indication of knowledge of sequence is the use of temporal order terms, including *before, after, and, then,* and *when.* A third indication is an appropriate response to a specific probe. These last two are illustrated in the following sequence, which was an addition to the above protocol:

> *Exp:* And when do you pay the waitress, when you get your food or . . .
> *Child:* No. My daddy does it. *When* we leave McDonald's.

Actually, of course, this is an incorrect response, since paying takes place when the food is ordered. This was, in fact, the only common sequence error made in any of the situations. The response may indicate a relative unawareness of other's appropriate role behavior (in this case, father's). Alternatively, it may be an interpolation from a well-developed, more general restaurant sequence where paying does take place at the end of the meal (cf. Schank & Abelson, 1975).

Combining all three types of evidence across children, contexts, and conditions revealed evidence of correct sequence in all the protocols for all situations. Table 10.1 presents the order of elements for each child in each context, derived from all sources.

If a child did not respond to the first inquiry with a sequence of events but did respond to general and specific probes such as, "What happens next?" or, "What happens after lunch?", what can we conclude? Is one type of evidence superior to another with respect to sequential organization in memory? Although spontaneous recall would appear to be the most convincing evidence, one could argue that response to probes reveals a type of organization of a higher order. Spontaneous sequential recall might be based on some inescapable

TABLE 10.1
Order of Events Mentioned by Each Child in Each Situation

	F_1	F_2	F_3	F_4	M_1[b]	M_2	M_3[b]	M_4[b]	Total No. of Mentions
Day Care									
Bring lunch			1	1	1				3
Clean up		1	2						2
Book corner			3			1			2
Wash	1		4		2				3
Sit		2	5	2	3	2			5
Eat	2	3	6	3	4	3			6
Clean up	3	4	7		5	4			5
Dessert					6	5			2
Nap	4	5	8	4	7	6			6
Mean number of elements mentioned: 5.67								$\bar{X} =$	3.78
Home									
Preactivity	1	1	1	1–2	1	1			6
Signal dinner	2	2			2				3
Wash hands	3								1
Go to place	4	3	2	3					4
Sit	5	4	3	4		2			5
Eat	6	5	4	5	3	3			6
Clean up	7	6	5		4	4			5
Afteractivity	8–12	7–9	6–10	6	5	5–6			6
Mean number of elements mentioned: 8.00								$\bar{X} =$	4.50
McDonald's									
Transportation	1	1	1	1	1	1		1	7
Arrival	2	2	2	2		2		2	6
Enter		3		3	2	3		3	5
Order	4	4	3	4	3	4			6
Receive	5	5		5	4	5			5
Pay		10	8	9	8	6		4	6
Sit	3–6	6	4	6		7			5
Eat	7	7	5	7	5	8		5	7
Garbage		8	6	8	6				4
Leave	8	9	7	10	7		9	6	7
Transportation	9	11		11			10	7	5
Mean number of elements mentioned: 9.14								$\bar{X} =$	4.90[a]

[a] Adjusted for number of subjects.

[b] These three children did not give complete data because of absence or non-cooperativeness.

pattern matching over which the child has no control. Response to probes, however, indicates (1) understanding of temporal order terms such as *next, before, after,* and *then* and (2) the ability to reorder, reverse, and reconstruct the correct sequence in response to questioning. Admittedly, our evidence for these processes is sketchy, but it is suggestive of good control over knowledge of routines.

Commonality

Table 10.1 also shows the commonality of event knowledge across children. Contrary to our expectations, the greatest number of elements and commonality of elements came from McDonald's (4.9 vs. 4.5 at home and 3.8 at the center). There are two problems with interpreting these numbers, however. First, they are combined across verbal and enactive conditions for each child, and the McDonald's prop was unquestionably the most attractive and engaged the child longest, as reflected in the number of events each child included. (Only F3 included fewer events in the McDonald's sequence than in one of the others.) Thus, although the center situation elicited equal amounts of information across both modalities (Verbal = 3.8; Active = 3.7) and the home situation elicited more in the verbal condition (7.2) than in the enactive (3.8), the McDonald's situation elicited more events in the enactive condition (7.9) than in the verbal (6.6).

A second problem with the commonality measure is that the probes more or less ensured that many elements would be mentioned by most of the children. Although some elements were never probed (e.g., dessert and garbage), others, such as paying at McDonald's, were always probed. The experimenter was not consistent in this respect, and, therefore, the commonality data should be considered only suggestive. More consistency in the probing procedure is necessary for reliable and meaningful data to result. At this point, we are unable to compare realistically across situations, but we can say with confidence that all these 4-year-old children know the routines of eating at home, at school, and at a hamburger stand and are able to verbalize them as well as act them out.

Roles, Subcomponents, and Details

In this first study we made several somewhat surprising observations. Contrary to what we expected, personal and idiosyncratic elements did not dominate the reports, although disruptions of the routine were frequently mentioned, such as "Someone spilled the milk." The enactive condition brought out more personal and fantasy material than did the verbal condition, not surprising considering that we were asking the children to engage in a play situation organized around a familiar event. *Details* of basic events were seldom mentioned except when specifically probed. For example, *playing* could mean riding bikes, playing games, playing with dolls and so on, but these were not mentioned. Similarly, *eating* was mentioned by all, but how and what was eaten was not specified, with the exception of dessert, and hamburgers at McDonald's, which were mentioned by many children. Dessert might be considered as a separate act, and hamburgers as somehow defining McDonald's. The constraint on details was not related to some arbitrary size chunk that the child could handle. For example, almost every child mentioned throwing away plates at the day care center, a minor component compared to the variety of activities included in *eating*. Why was this act mentioned? We believe it was because it was one of the ways in which eating at the day care center was differentiated from eating at home. The lack of detail in eating and playing is no doubt related to the variety of specific activities, people, and objects that could be included in these acts. Only by ignoring the specifics — that is, by defining the open slots — could the child report a general sequence that would apply to any day. These open slots are, in effect, general concepts. In the case of *playing* and *eating*, they are event concepts that subsume a number of more specific activities. One of the hypotheses that we are interested in investigating is that these general concepts, defined in terms of the conceptual superstructure of the script, may be the precursors of such well-studied hierarchical structures as categories, collections, and logical classes (cf. Trabasso, Isen, Dolecki, McLanahan, Riley, & Tucker, this volume).

Except when acting out scenes with props, the children rarely referred to the roles of teachers, parents, and other children. Their response to probes and inclusion of others in enactive sequences indicated that they knew about these roles. Their misunderstanding of paying in McDonald's indicates incomplete role knowledge, however, since paying requires understanding the relation of another person to still a third person, quite removed from the child's own activity. These facts suggest that scripts are built up from the child's point of view and from that point of view the roles of other people are of minor importance.

Implicit Structure

As shown above, there was a common skeletal structure representing the mealtime event, even where the specifics varied, as in the home situation. The children's use of linguistic forms suggested that we were tapping an implicit structure. In particular, their use of definite articles, pronouns, and deictic terms (e.g., *there*) without prior identifying reference indicates that for the child, at least, the referents were implied by the situation. For example, in the McDonald's protocol quoted earlier, we find definite articles referencing elements that have not been explicitly introduced into the situation (*the lady, the paper, the garbage can*). The child apparently assumes that these elements are implicit in the situation and do not need explicit introduction. (See Maratsos, 1976, for evidence that children of this age do understand the need for the introduction of referents for use of the definite article.) Similarly, their use of pronouns for elements that have not been specifically introduced indicates the same kind of assumption of known elements. In this case, the young child's lack of understanding of the other's perspective and assumption of shared context help to identify what she herself understands implicitly.

In summary, children's knowledge of mealtime events appeared to fit the script model. In fact, the Schank and Abelson (1975) example of a restaurant script is strikingly like the children's description of eating at McDonald's. The development of script structure was not apparent in this study, however.

STUDY II

Study II was designed to investigate the development of scripts by controlling for amount of experience with the routine. The structure of the "Eating lunch at the day care center" script that emerged from the previous study was used as a baseline. Because the children in that study were interviewed in the spring, all of them had had many months to build up their knowledge about the situation. We were interested in knowing how children new to the situation would go about structuring their experience.

In this study, 14 children were interviewed within the first week of the opening of the day care center in the fall and again 3 months later. Seven of the children were new to the center and seven were returning from the previous year. As in Study I, the interview technique was employed using the format: "What happens when you have lunch at the day care center?", followed by general probes (e.g., "Anything else?"), then specific probes for order, detail, and role. The experimenter also probed for knowledge about the entire sequence of the day's events so that the number of events was not comparable to Study I. This will complicate the analysis, but the general outcome should be clear enough. Again, the child demonstrated the activity with props after verbalizing it.

We expected the returning children to have a more complete script at the beginning of the year than did the new children because their previous year's script would be reactivated. This proved to be the case. Returning children included an average of 9.1 elements compared to the 5.4 included by the new children. There were only three elements common to all the new children (sitting, eating, and napping), whereas four were common to the returning ones. At the second interview, 3 months later, both old and new children had added elements to their descriptions, as Table 10.2 shows. The added elements were primarily after-lunch activities for the new children and prelunch activities for both groups.

More important than total number of elements is the connection between elements and the length of spontaneous sequences. Although all children showed that they were aware of sequence when specifically probed with questions such as, "What happens after lunch?," not all children produced a sequence without probing. This can be summarized in terms of the number of probes needed to

TABLE 10.2

Summary Statistics Comparing Old and New Students at Time 1 and Time 2 on Length of Event Sequences

	Script Length	Event–Probe Ratio	No. of Events Recalled to 1st Question	Total Number of Events Recalled in Sequence	Length of Longest Sequence	"Other" Role Specifications	
						Verbal	Enactive
Time 1							
New	5.4	1.24	1.86	5.86	1.85	11	16
Old	9.1	1.94	3.83	8.57	3.14	9	9
Time 2							
New	8.6^b	1.32	4.6	8.43^b	3.57	4	8
Old	11.3^b	2.34^a	5.5	11.43^c	6.57	2	3

[a]Differs from New at $0.10 > p < 0.05$.
[b]Differs from T_1 at $p < 0.025$.
[c]Differs from T_1 at $0.10 > p < 0.05$.

elicit a given number of elements — the event/probe ratio. Again, this ratio increased from Time 1 to Time 2 (1.59 and 1.83) and for returning versus new students (2.14 and 1.28). Table 10.2 shows the analogous pattern for the number of events recalled after the first general question, the length of the longest sequence of events recalled in order, and the total number of events recalled in sequence by each child (i.e., not in response to a specific probe). In every case, the returning children produced longer sequences than did the new children, and longer sequences were produced at Time 2 than at Time 1, although not all differences reached statistical significance. Thus, it appears that the children were establishing a sequence from the beginning, but they added to it and perhaps linked into a longer structure pieces that had originally been isolated.

More important for understanding the progression of knowledge over time is the analysis of individual sequences. Two sample protocols and a graphic analysis illustrate the differences between children. One of the children was new to the center, and the other was returning for the second year.

The transcripts were analyzed on the sequential analysis graphs according to the following scheme. The script's hypothesized event sequence is coded along the horizontal axis. The vertical axis represents the interview sequence. From this chart, it is possible to tell how well the child's verbalized script maps onto the hypothesized script in its event structure and sequential format. Arrows connect elements that were emitted in sequence, without being interrupted by interview probes, false starts, or departures from the script, making it possible to quantify the length of the sequence with and without probes. Inclusion of roles of other than self is indicated by triangles (as in ▲ for teacher). Inclusion of material from inappropriate scripts (e.g., having dinner at home) or additional scripts (other day care events) is indicated by ⒮. Leaving the script or bringing new material in is indicated by oblique arrows, ↗ or ↘. Probes are indicated as general, ⒢⒫, or specific, ⒮⒫.

The first script sequence (Table 10.3 and Figure 10.1) reveals a well-organized, skeletal script prompted by the general question, "What happens when you have lunch here?" Verbalization of the script begins with the central event (eat) but reverses to the preceding event (serving). The sequence is indicated by temporal markers: *after, first,* and *then.* Deleting the reversals yields a sequence of three basic events: serving, eating, and throwing away. Implicit knowledge of required roles and slots is indicated by "somebody" in the serving role and the definite "the" used to reference fork, cup, and plate. Notice that further probing elicits more event and role knowledge but leads to only one further link: that between eating and nap. (Nap is linked to dessert only through yet another probe.) Notice also the lack of specificity about the details of the central event, eating. Only *a* fork and *a* spoon are mentioned. As in Study I, young children did not break down basic events into subcomponents. Of the hypothesized seven basic events, this boy verbalized all but one (washing hands) and sequenced all correctly.

TABLE 10.3
Script No. 1

Returning Student, 4 Years, Boy	
Interviewer	*Child*
1. Can you tell me about what happens when you have lunch here?	1. I eat lunch and after lunch I throw all my stuff away. First, somebody gets me lunch. Then I eat it and . . . somebody serves it to me and then I throw the stuff, the cup and the fork and the plate. And that's all.
2. What happens afterwards? Ummum.	2. After lunch? You go outside until they play big wheels and the bikes.
3. Anything else happen?	3. We just run around. That's all. Play in the sandbox.
4. What about after that?	4. We play in those two . . . houses.
5. Let's think right before lunch. How do you know it's lunchtime?	5. Teachers tell me.
6. What are you doing when they tell you? What are you doing before lunch?	6. Uh . . . We play. No we don't play. We uh . . .
7. What do you do when the teachers tell you it's time for lunch?	7. [No response.]
8. Do you do anything special before lunch?	8. No. Just sit down.
9. And then what?	9. Then we just go back home.
10. Tell me about eating.	10. Well, we eat with a spoon and a fork. Nothing else. Then we just go to bed.
11. Oh, you just go to bed? When do you do that?	11. After we eat our, uh, dessert.

The structure in the first script may be contrasted with that of the second — produced by a new and younger student — in which naptime dominates rather than eating (Table 10.4 and Figure 10.2). General and specific probes elicited nap activities. Only one sequential link is verbalized, that between *play* and *mommies come*. This child does, however, demonstrate knowledge of three of the basic events (eating, throwing away, and napping). Because throwing away

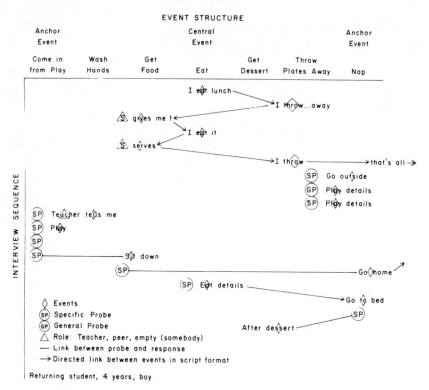

FIG. 10.1 Event Structure – First Script.

plates is specific to the day care center script, its inclusion indicates a differentiated knowledge structure. This is supported by what the script does not contain, even under probing: idiosyncratic, episodic, or irrelevant events, roles, and objects, and the material from related, well-established scripts, such as eating at home. The general question, "What happens when you have lunch here?" is interpreted in terms of a very general, skeletal sequence of events, indicating that some structure underlies the child's organization of knowledge about her world.

Admittedly, there is a difficulty in interpreting the differences between the returning and new children and between the responses at Time 1 and Time 2. In both cases, simple familiarity and ease in the day care situation may have made a difference in the complexity and length of response sequences, as would familiarity with the experimenter. Such effects are well established with children of this age and cannot be discounted. Although the experimenter was well known to all the children and skilled in establishing rapport, one cannot be certain that some effects of shyness did not remain. The strongest comparison, from this point of view, would be between the new and returning children at Time 2 when all were "old hands" at the center; this comparison remains reasonably strong.

Unfortunately, it is also the case that age (less than or more than 4 years) is confounded with returning and new status. In a center of this size, it was not possible to control for age and status simultaneously. Thus, the possibility remains that the data on development of a specific script structure may be confounded with general cognitive developmental factors, as discussed earlier.

TABLE 10.4
Script No. 2

New Student, 3 Years, Girl	
Interviewer	*Child*
1. What happens when you have lunch here at school?	1. Then you be tired.
2. When is that?	2. When you go to sleep.
3. Anything happen at lunch?	3. Lunch? You could take a nap.
4. You could take a nap?	4. Lunch. Play.
5. You play at lunch?	5. That's at the end too.
6. Lunch is at the end?	6. No, no. You play outside. That's at the end. The mommies come.
7. How do you know it's lunchtime? What do you do?	7. Take a nap.
8. How do you know it's gonna be lunchtime? Does somebody tell you? Who tells you?	8. Yup. The teacher!
9. And then what do you do?	9. Eat.
10. What do you do when you eat?	10. With a fork. [Shows mouth movements.]
11. After you eat, right right after you eat, what do you do?	11. Then you go to bed.
12. What do you do with your plate?	12. Throw it away.
13. Why do that?	13. Because! So you have a new one!
14. Do you throw your plates away at home?	14. No.

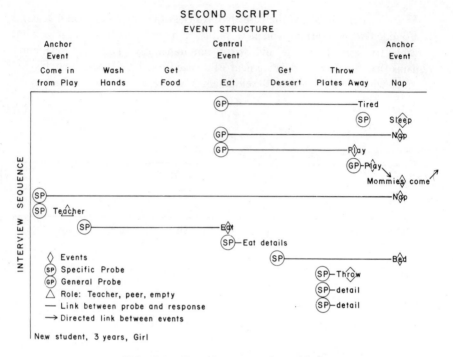

FIG. 10.2   Event Structure – Second Script.

Temporal Terms and Script Structures

The use of temporal terms such as *then, when, before,* and *after* was one type of evidence used to determine whether the child had sequential knowledge of an event. Possibly, the establishment of such sequences is in itself associated with the knowledge and use of temporal terms. Use of such terms was associated with group status, age, and time of testing. Moreover, there was a correlation between the use of temporal terms and length of the script sequence at both times for both groups of children ($r = .71$, $p < .005$ at T_1; $r = .75$, $p < .005$ at T_2). It is impossible to determine whether the temporal terms were aiding the child in establishing or recalling the sequence or whether the sequencing made the use of such terms feasible. This is a fruitful area for further investigation. *Then* was by far the most commonly used term, reflecting the typical forward nature of the recall. That *after* was next most frequent follows from the same observation and agrees with the semantic literature, which shows the order of events to be the strongest determinant of the child's understanding of temporal terms. For this reason, presumably, no child used the term *before,* which would now fit into the order-of-mention strategy.

Roles and Relations to Other Scripts

As noted with Study I, there was relatively little mention of other people's roles in the children's scripts. This was particularly true for the returning children (Table 10.2). The new children in the enactive condition mentioned the greater number of roles, whereas the number of people mentioned *decreased* over time, both within and between groups. Two factors may account for this seemingly anomolous finding. First, it may reflect the increasing skeletal nature of the script in which fewer details are specified and more slots left open. On the other hand, a striking finding is that 15 of the 27 new children's mentions of other people were of family members (vs. only three of the returning children's 18), and these appeared equally often in the verbal and enactive conditions. Family members do not belong in the children's day care lunch script, but for the new children (who were just beginning to establish this routine and who perhaps were differentiating it from the eating-at-home script), family members intrude at predictable places. For example, when the experimenter asks, "How do you know when it's lunch time?", the new child may give no response or may say, "Daddy says I have to eat," or "Mommy told me." None of the returning children gave such responses.

Interpolation from other scripts occurs with other elements as well. One frequent place is in response to requested information that the child does not have. The experimenter often (but not always) asked the child where the lunch came from. Lunch is brought to the day care center in large metal cans from one of the university dining halls by one of the teachers. However, few children were aware of this, and when asked, produced a response based on general knowledge (and inference, if you like, from other scripts) such as, "You buy it at the store," "You make it," "Mother and Daddy buy it," "They cook it," "At the baker's," and the ultimate fallback, "God makes it."

IMPLICATIONS

One of the claims about the development of scripts was that the script would become more skeletal as awareness of the variability of slot fillers led to less specification, and as awareness of necessary implications grew. Our preliminary observations of older children (age 7 to 10 years) suggest that this is the case. However, it would appear that the present data, which show increasing richness and completeness with increasing experience, argue against this kind of development. Nonetheless, the question remains open for a number of reasons. First, we are observing the building up of a script which, as the interpolations suggest, is being differentiated from an established (eating-at-home) script. It seems probable, from comparisons among the three situations in Study I, that the Basic Events of the lunch script have already been well specified in the home context and it is only the differences that need elaboration in the day care setting. This interpretation is supported by the skeletal structure already apparent in the children's protocols, where *eating*, for example, is almost never specified in any detail. When probed, the children show that they know about eating implements, who serves the food, and what kind of food they have, but these details are slot fillers and are not mentioned spontaneously.

To investigate this question more fully, we must trace the building up of knowledge of a truly novel event as well as test the effect of a novel element on the structure of an established script. Preliminary investigation suggests that script knowledge of school-age children has become so implicit that it is almost inaccessible to explicit probing. However, a novel experience produces the same kind of skeletal sequence plus slot fillers seen in the development of the younger children's scripts.

What, then, have these preliminary studies told us about children's memory, conceptual structure, or language base? First, young children know about and appear to rely on the sequential structure of familiar events. They reveal at an early age what Ann Brown describes as the ability to extract the main idea, to ignore trivia (Brown & DeLoache, this volume). All kinds of information about the world can be, and quite probably is, organized around such structures. They provide tools for interpreting the implications of speech as well as for the prediction of recurrent events. They provide a framework within which both specific and general object and event concepts may be built up. In addition, such structures may form the basis for the interpretation of recounted events and stories. The story grammars that are currently of such interest must ultimately be based on an understanding of real life events. We are not claiming that the script structure is the only representation of the child's knowledge, but for the young child it may be the most important.

The second study also suggests that the development of script structure — at least for preschool children — is very orderly, beginning with the connection of central events, which are amplified with recurrent events but which are not loaded down with irrelevant and idiosyncratic detail. Rather, a simple skeletal structure appears to build up, and slots for alternative fillers are specified. The process is neither random nor unorganized.

These studies have touched on only some of the questions raised at the outset of this paper, leaving open many possibilities for the development of script structures and their use at various ages. In particular, the script for eating lunch at the day care center is one that has presumably been differentiated from the script for eating lunch at home as evidenced in the interpolations of the new children. It might be that building up a truly novel script of a novel event will reveal different principles, and we plan to investigate that possibility in future studies.

We cannot yet give an answer to the general question posed in the title of this volume, "What develops?" However, with Rochel Gelman and a growing number of others, I believe that if you want to know what develops, you need to know where the child is starting — a point that is certainly as important as knowing where the endpoint is. There are considerable data available telling us that the conceptual and semantic knowledge of the older child becomes increasingly ordered by hierarchical categorical relationships. I think we are ready to try to answer the more interesting question of how this system develops by looking at what precedes this type of organization of knowledge and by trying to find the connections between the two. In the currently popular terminology, we are attempting to discover how semantic memory develops from episodic memory and, at the same time, how the structure and power of the latter accounts for young children's competence in dealing with everyday events.

ACKNOWLEDGMENTS

The studies reported here were carried out in collaboration with Janice Gruendel, who participated in all aspects of the planning and analysis and who acted as the experimenter in Study II. Matthew Leeds helped to design and acted as experimenter in Study I. The research was supported in part by a grant from the Carnegie Corporation of New York to William Kessen and Katherine Nelson.

REFERENCES

Church, J. *Three babies: Biographies of cognitive development.* New York: Random House, 1966.
Maratsos, M. P. *The use of definite and indefinite reference in young children: An experimental study in semantic acquisition.* Cambridge, England: Cambridge University Press, 1976.
Nelson, K. Concept, word and sentence: Interrelations in acquisition and development. *Psychological Review,* 1974, *81,* 267–285.
Schank, R. C., & Abelson, R. P. *Scripts, plans, and knowledge.* Paper presented at the 4th International Joint Conference on Artificial Intelligence, 1975.
Schank, R. C., & Abelson, R. P. *Scripts, plans, goals, and understanding.* Hillsdale, N.J.: Lawrence Erlbaum Associates, 1977.

11

Spatial Concepts, Spatial Names, and the Development of Exocentric Representations

Lee W. Gregg

Carnegie–Mellon University

Why is it that when you look into a mirror you get a left—right but not a top—bottom reversal? The mirror does not work like a lens that inverts an image. Of course, as you think about it, you come to realize that a mirror image doesn't really reverse left and right sides of objects, whereas inverting lenses do — unless you are using the lens as a magnifying glass, in which case you do not get the left—right reversal.

Just about the time you are convinced that Einstein was right — it's all relative to the perspective you take — you must then ask why the letters on the front of the ambulance you see through your rear view mirror are perfectly legible. Aha! They are legible because some genius decided to print the letters backward. But wait! Are only the individual letters reversed, or is the entire string of letter positions backward? And if the letters are reversed, doesn't that mean that the mirror, like the lens, has produced a genuine left—right reversal of the image?

If you are somewhat confused about the nature of these transformations, if you are unable to offer a completely coherent explanation of the possible perceptual phenomena involved in looking into mirrors and through lenses, you can empathize with the 5-year-old subjects who played with our computer-controlled "turtle" this past year. The "turtle" is a small, domed robot driven by two wheels and independent stepping motors (Papert, 1971a, 1971b). On a table in front of our subjects was a box with three push buttons. One of the buttons caused the turtle to move forward, the second caused it to turn left, and the third made it turn right.

We thought that the children would learn the functions of the buttons very quickly and then go on to more complex tasks. However, the children had a great deal of difficulty learning which button made the turtle turn clockwise and which made it turn counterclockwise. And so, what began as a preliminary training study became a full-blown investigation into the development of spatial concepts.

Our initial goal had been to construct process models of reading at each of several developmental stages. In another paper, Sylvia Farnham—Diggory and I developed a taxonomy of reading tasks progressing from the earliest identification of symbolic elements through skilled reading performance in a variety of complex tasks (Gregg & Farnham—Diggory, in press). The initial phases in the acquisition of reading skills involve mapping visual symbols onto real world events. However, a precursor to this cognitive mapping is the acquisition of stable perceptions of those events and the assignment of names to them. Our simple-minded hypothesis was that with a fairly minimal amount of experience with the turtle, the child would be able to make the appropriate discriminations, learn the appropriate names, and then devise complex sequences of button presses — sentences — that would cause the turtle to do more and more elaborate things. In other words, the child would learn to *write* new, higher-order ideas by a sequence of button presses.

Werner suggested a quarter century ago (Werner & Kaplan, 1950) that symbol learning is initially a differentiation process. Research in developmental semantics has indicated that this is so (Bloom, 1970; Nelson, 1973; Slobin, 1971). At first, a child may use a single word to represent many events. With growth and practice, the child learns to map his original word onto only one type of event and learns to map other words onto other events. If a similar process occurs during the early stages of learning a *visual* symbol system, some comprehension difficulties may arise because the child believes a single symbol represents more or less than it actually does. The growth of comprehension, then, is in large part the growth of the ability to parse a set of events into those elements represented by a particular symbol and to correctly assign the symbols to the elements (Gregg, 1974). Thus, the general question was, "What are the processes and stages of a child's mapping of symbols onto events?"

METHOD

To answer this question, we studied a few children longitudinally on the turtle task. Children needed to map three symbols (buttons that could be pressed) onto three events — having the turtle make a 90° left turn, a 90° right turn, or go forward. Thus, the basic turtle task was to choose the button that would make the turtle go to the desired location.

Participants

Eighteen children, twelve 5-year-olds and six 4-year-olds, served as subjects in the year-long series of studies. Three other 5-year-olds and four 4-year-olds began the study but dropped out along the way. We also tried to run a few

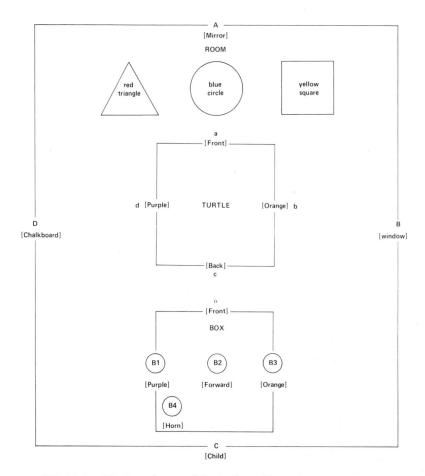

FIG. 11.1   The three frames of the turtle problem space: **ROOM, TURTLE**, and **BOX**. The **ROOM** frame as viewed by the child at C contains familiar objects A, B, and D. The names of the objects are in square brackets. The **TURTLE** frame has boundary elements [Front] and [Back]. Within the **ROOM** frame are the novel elements of the problem – the geometric figures (yellow square, blue circle, and red triangle), the turtle, and the control box. These are the elements for which the children have spatial names. Notice that in the standard condition, the control **BOX** frame does not have a front and the buttons have no names. For perspective taking, Condition IVa, the addition of the turtle head to the control box defines [front] for the **BOX** frame supplying a spatial name, a. For the color-coding condition, Condition IVb, the purple and orange earmuffs on the turtle's head and the purple and orange overlays on the pushbuttons provide common, symbolic names as indicated in the **TURTLE** and **BOX** frames.

277

3-year-olds; their data are the basis for some of the speculations on early development that we present below.

Experimental Setting

The layout of the experimental room is shown in Fig. 11.1. The child was placed at one end of the room. On his left was a chalkboard; on his right were windows; in front of him was a large one-way mirror. In the center of the room, on the floor, were three geometric shapes and the turtle. The shapes were a red circle, a blue triangle, and a yellow square. Each shape had a maximum dimension of about 20 cm. All three shapes were arranged in a row, about 2.5 m in front of the child.

The Turtle

As described earlier, the turtle was a robot that could move forward and turn left or right. When it moved forward, it went about 45 cm, roughly the distance between the shapes. When it turned, it stayed on the same spot but changed its orientation by 90°. Thus, as seen in Fig. 11.1, if a child, oriented as he was, wanted to move the turtle from the red triangle to the blue circle, he would first have to push the right turn button to get the turtle facing in the right direction, and then he would have to push the forward button so that the turtle would move from one shape to the other.

The turtle could start any problem from one of four orientations: 0°, so that it would be facing the same direction as the child; 180° rotated, so that it would be looking directly back at the child; or 90° or 270° rotated, perpendicular to the child's orientation.

The Button Box

The child controlled the turtle by means of several buttons, actually micro-switches, mounted on a square box. The box was placed directly in front of the child on a small desk. Each button on the button box operated from the turtle's rather than the child's perspective, that is, one button always made the turtle turn to its left (B1), one to its right (B3), and one made it go forward (B2), regardless of its position relative to the child. The turtle's actions followed as soon as a button was pressed. If the child pressed a button while the turtle was moving, an error was recorded and the turtle moved on.

The button box's control of the turtle was mediated by a PDP–11 computer. The turtle and computer were connected by a visible cord, although the button box was not visibly connected to either. Thus, the child would press a button, the command would be recorded by the computer, and the computer would instruct the turtle as to the desired move. A control program, "Turtle Jargon" was written to facilitate the experiments (Hester & Faddis, 1976; Gregg, 1977).

Pretesting

All the children were pretested for their knowledge of certain spatial concepts and vocabulary. The Boehm Test was given, and supplementary questions aimed at assessing the children's concepts of left and right were also presented. In addition, the children were asked to name the colors and shapes they would encounter in the experiment. On the basis of this information, we claim that the children understood the problems. All knew the names of the colors and shapes used in the experiments; furthermore, all were able to follow the instructions by walking the floor carrying a stuffed toy turtle.

Procedure

Children were taken individually by the experimenter from their classroom to the turtle laboratory. Free-play and demonstration problems were given at the beginning of each session, followed by the test problems. Children were typically able to solve about four test problems a session. Following this, they were told they had done well and returned to their classrooms.

RESULTS

The results are reported in terms of Problem Sets. Problem Set I was administered during the fall semester; Problem Sets II and III were given during the winter months; Sets IV and V were completed by late spring. Table 11.1 shows the number of correct solutions for each subject on each Problem Set.

Problem Set I

Problem Set I consisted of the 24 problems generated by the three initial locations (square, circle, or triangle), the four orientations of the turtle (0°, 90°, 180°, or 270° rotated from the child), and two remaining destinations. The problems were presented in a random order. The data for Problem Set I are broken down into two kinds of problems. The first type, shown in the first column of Table 11.1, is 0° and 180° problems. On these problems, the turtle was oriented either in the same direction as the child or facing the child, thus requiring that the first button press be a turn toward the destination. The mean of 4.72 is slightly above chance if each of the three buttons was selected randomly.

The second type of problem, shown in the second column of Table 11.1, summarizes performance on 90° and 270° problems. In these problems, the turtle was either oriented directly toward the destination, in which case the forward button had to be pressed, or was facing the opposite direction, in which

TABLE 11.1
Number of Correct Solutions by Problem Set[a]

	Subjects	I	II	III		IVa	IVb	V
				0°/180°		90°/270°		
5-year-olds	1	3	10	9	7	7	—	6
	2	7	12	9	6	—	12	8
	3	4	10	6	6	9	—	7
	4	5	8	7	11	—	—	7
	5	5	7	5	9	—	—	9
	6	4	9	7	6	8	—	8
	7	6	10	5	10	—	12	7
	8	5	11	4	4	—	6	8
	9	7	11	7	7	—	11	7
	10	5	11	9	6	9	—	10
	11	7	10	7	7	6	—	8
	12	4	10	6	6	8	—	8
4-year-olds	13	3	11	6	6	—	10	6
	14	4	10	7	4	—	6	6
	15	2	0	5	9	—	7	5
	16	5	11	10	8	8	—	11
	17	7	12	6	4	11	—	7
	18	2	9	4	3	7	—	—
	Mean	4.72	9.56	6.61	6.61	8.11	9.14	7.53
	S.D.	1.64	2.71	1.75	2.17	1.45	3.12	1.50

[a] The entries in each column are the numbers of problems correct out of a maximum of 12 problems.

case two successive pushes of either of the turn buttons would align the turtle with the goal. The children did very well on these problems, with a mean of 9.56 out of 12. When the turtle was facing toward the destination, a no-turn problem, 19 errors out of a possible 108 were committed. More striking is the result for the problems requiring two turns: Only 3 errors out of 108 were committed.

Thus, Problem Set I produced a major surprise. We had supposed that 4- and 5-year-olds, known for their egocentrism, would perform better on the 0° problems, where the turtle was aligned with them, than on the 180° problems, where it faced the opposite direction. After all, the button on the right would make the turtle turn left under these latter conditions. In fact, the mean for 0° problems was 2.00 compared to 2.72 for the 180° problems. The difference was not significant but was in the opposite direction from that predicted.

Problem Set II: The Short Way

Unfortunately, the children were already becoming bored at this early phase in the study. Our expensive toy was not as attractive as we had hoped. Worse yet, there was no evidence that the children improved during Problem Set I. Problem Set II was restricted, therefore, to only 0° and 180° problems, and the demonstration problems were dropped. A new button was added, the horn button (B4), to motivate the children to solve the problems the "short way." We wanted to make sure the children understood that they were to make the minimum number of moves. Therefore, the horn button was activated only at the end of those problems that were solved correctly.

The basic finding was that the children continued to make mistakes. Since we had eliminated the 90° and 270° problems, all problems now required selecting an initial turn button. The mean number of correct problems was 6.61 out of 12. Chance would be 6 out of 12 since most children recognized early that the forward button was not to be used first. The children had learned very little and were still bored. Their performance on the second Problem Set confirmed the original finding of no difference between 0° and 180° problems, with means of 3.50 and 3.11 respectively.

Problem Set III: Head Problems

Something had to be done to show the children what to attend to when the turtle rotated. Therefore, we added a very large smiling (of course) papier-mâché head to the turtle to create an unambiguous front—back cue and to exaggerate the swing of the turtle as it rotated about its axis. In this way, the children would be led to notice whether the turtle's head was moving left or right.

Unfortunately, once again this did not lead to any improvement. The mean level of performance in Problem Set III was identical to that in Problem Set II (6.61).

We could ascribe the difficulty of the problems to the children's egocentrism. If the child took an egocentric view of the task, the 0° problems should have been much easier than the 180° problems. In fact, as in the previous sets, there was no significant difference between performance on the two types of problems. Nor was it the case that children simply could not discriminate that the turtle was facing toward them in one instance and away from them in the other. All the children could identify the turtle's head and tail and could verbalize the direction in which the turtle was facing.

A likely place to find an explanation seemed to be the literature on left—right reversals and mirror image discrimination. However, it turns out that this literature offers many phenomena but very little in the way of process description. The following quotation (Corballis & Beale, 1976) is typical:

. . . we have argued that the confusion or equivalence of left and right is not primarily a matter of perception, at least in the most immediate sense of the term. Neither animals nor people seem to have any serious difficulty in seeing which way round an object is, for example. The problem occurs at the higher level of analysis at which patterns or objects are identified according to what they are, rather than according to where they are located or which way they are oriented. Thus there is a strong tendency to treat left—right mirror images as equivalent. They may be perceived as different simply because they are facing opposite ways, but they may be labeled and recognized as the same. These phenomena presumably have their origins in the characteristics of the natural environment [p. 191].

Thus, our analysis turned back to the original question of mapping. Clearly, the children knew what the turtle was doing; in fact, they were now becoming reluctant to do more problems. The assignment of button functions, however, remained unstable. The children made assignments, but they did not understand why the role of the button would change from session to session or even within sessions. Sometimes the right-hand button (which caused the turtle to rotate clockwise) made the turtle turn to the window, and sometimes the same button made it turn to the wall. This depended, of course, on the initial orientation of the turtle, but the children did not grasp that. At least one child was perfectly willing to accept the ambiguity as he counted the number of problems solved in one session. Since half of the problems were 0° and half were 180°, he adopted a strategy of pressing only one of the two "turn" buttons and got half of the problems correct. His comment: "Four out of eight ain't bad!"

Problem Sets IVa and IVb: Perspective Taking and Color Coding

How could the mapping function be facilitated for the children? One way would have been to place the control box in the same orientation as the turtle itself. We could pick up the box and carry it to the turtle, turn the box so that it was aligned with the turtle, and then have the child select the button on the side to which the turtle must proceed. The box was heavy and bulky, however, so we took a different tack. We built a papier-mâché head, mounted it on the control box, and asked the children to imagine that they were inside the turtle looking out. We called this condition *perspective taking*; it was administered to half of the children as Problem Set IVa.

The other half of the children received a more direct treatment, Problem Set IVb. Huge "earmuffs," colored purple and orange, were attached to the turtle's head. The right and left button on the button box were similarly color coded purple and orange. Thus, the mapping between button box and turtle was accomplished simply by selecting the same colored button. Our preliminary hypotheses were that perspective taking as such would not help appreciably and that color coding would be a foolproof (or childproof) method of turtle control. We were partially wrong on both counts. The children in the perspective-taking condition (Problem Set IVa) improved from a mean of 6.61 to 8.11, and the color-coding condition (Set IVb) improved from a mean of 6.61 to 9.14. Both improvements were significant, and the two did not differ from each other.

It should be noted that for some of the children the color coding worked well. However, it is interesting that not a single child could explain why the coding made the task easier. It was just magic as far as they were concerned.

Problem Set V: Generalization

In Problem Set V, we removed the head on the control box, the ear muffs, and the color codes. Overall performance dropped to a mean of 7.53 correct. Thus, removing the aids wiped out the gains observed in Problem Set IV. The drop was greater in the color code group (mean = 6.71) than for the perspective taking group (mean = 8.13).

So the study ended. In the next section, we try to explain what was going on.

COMPREHENDING THE SYMBOLIC FUNCTIONS OF BUTTONS

As we finally came to realize, it was not simply a matter of the children learning to associate a certain action of the turtle with a particular button. There were a number of identifiable stages that the children needed to go through in learning to solve turtle problems. Piaget would be pleased (Piaget & Inhelder, 1967). However, it turns out that most of the difficulties emerged when concepts necessary for the performance of the task had not yet been mastered by the child. Gagné would be pleased (Gagné, 1965). The following is an analysis of what children do and don't know about the turtle at different stages of development.

Developmental Stages

In our global model, we identified five stages in the acquisition of understanding of the turtle task:

Stage I is reached when the child comprehends that the buttons have some effect on the turtle.

Stage II marks the point where the child differentiates the "forward" button (B2) from the other two that make the turtle turn. However, the turn buttons are not seen as being different from each other.

Stage III involves the recognition that buttons B1 and B3, the two turn buttons, have separate functions. At this point, though, the child does not understand which button makes the turtle turn in which direction.

Stage IV marks the achievement of a different type of understanding, the knowledge that the turn buttons make the turtle rotate on its axis rather than turning in the usual sense of changing direction and going forward.

Stage V represents full understanding of the turtle task, where the turn buttons are differentiated with respect to direction of rotation.

A number of comments about the different stages may render the model more easily understandable. Stage I might seem to be a trivial achievement; surely the children would know from the outset that the buttons had *some* effect on the turtle. In fact, this was not the case. As far as the 3-year-olds we observed were concerned, pressing buttons was unrelated to the movement of the turtle, even though close temporal contiguity held. After all, although the turtle had an umbilical cord connecting it to the computer, the button box was not visibly connected to either of them. A first essential concept, then, is that the buttons make the turtles do things.

Stage II is the beginning of awareness that the orientation of the turtle can be related to button functions. The first function to be differentiated is the forward button, B2. There is ample evidence in our data to show that the forward button is learned first.

In Stage III, the child learns that buttons B1 and B3 perform different functions. However, the idea of turning is not a unitary concept, and so the difference in function is not clear. The children give a deictic description of the effects of buttons, saying, B1 makes the turtle go this way and B3 makes the turtle go that way, pointing to spatial locations in the room. The children confuse the end point — where they wish the turtle to look — with direction of rotation. Our evidence for this stage is based principally on the verbal responses of the children when they were asked what the buttons do.

At the beginning of Stage IV the child realizes that the simple, egocentric assignment of spatial location is not sufficient. Characteristic of this stage is the shifting of button function assignments. There is an increased awareness of the different properties of the $0°$ and $180°$ problems. The outcome for a few of the children was a more appropriate representation of the concept of a turn. The turtle rotates on its axis. The button function is identified with an action of the turtle, not a spatial location. However, the mapping of the button functions for B1 and B3 — counterclockwise and clockwise rotation — has yet to be learned.

Finally, there is the question of what it means to understand fully the turtle task, that is, to reach Stage V. Close analysis reveals this to be a much more substantial achievement than we had at first anticipated. Even if we limit consideration to $0°$ and $180°$ problems, we find that the child must possess a biconditional "truth table" similar to the following rules:

Rule I.   If the turtle is facing $0°$ and the goal direction is toward the window, then press button B3.

Rule II.   If the turtle is facing $0°$ and the goal direction is toward the chalkboard, then press B1.

Rule III. If the turtle is facing 180° and the goal direction is toward the window, then press B1.

Rule IV. If the turtle is facing 180° and the goal direction is toward the chalkboard, then press B3.

None of the children discovered this "truth table" representation. To learn these rules by induction and to apply them would seem to require formal operational reasoning (Siegler, 1976) and the ability to deal with multidimensional tasks. In this sense, the turtle task imposes demands similar to the Piagetian conservation-of-volume problem — a problem much too difficult for our preoperational subjects.

ARE THERE ALTERNATIVE STAGES?

The sequence of developmental stages, by definition, should be invariant. Do the stages described above come from the particular ways in which we introduced the problem-solving task to the children? Are there other ways to set up the experiments, to design the layout of the button box, or to engineer the switches so that children can learn button functions? Obviously we do not know, but there have been some suggestions. One possibility is to make switches that twist in clockwise or counterclockwise directions, thus providing immediate tactual feedback when the child attempts to throw the wrong switch. Another possibility is to use a large wheel that rotates from a spring-loaded neutral position. Here, the movement of the wheel more closely matches the rotational movement of the turtle. Or we could have used symbols on the switches themselves — arrows arcing to left or right, above and below the pushbutton switches.

Each of these experimental manipulations poses a new task. We chose two operations that made sense to us in the context of the general developmental literature and in light of our long-range goals. Since we wished to assign arbitrary symbols to the buttons, each button should have equal status as an abstract concept. Building semantic features into the manipulation of a button would defeat the purpose. We wanted to study the way abstract symbols *acquired* semantic properties. On the other hand, we did not want to deal with the long-range problem of right/left discrimination learning and the mirror range image reversals that were confusing the children. An information-processing approach to these issues is described in the next section.

AN INFORMATION-PROCESSING ANALYSIS

A process description of a child solving a turtle problem prescribes a sequence of steps, each one a cognitive act of a simple sort. Only a few are required for the task; all are within the basic repertoire of the child. A list of these processes is as follows:

1. Notice the present location of the turtle.
2. Find out where the turtle should go (its goal).
3. Test if the current location of the turtle is different from the goal.
4. Test whether the turtle is facing the goal.
5. Find the button with value X, i.e., $f(B1) = X$, where X is the name of the direction the turtle must turn in to face the goal.
6. Assign a spatial name to an object (e.g., to a button or the goal location).

Such a set of processes forms a program very much like GPS (Ernst & Newell, 1969; Newell & Simon, 1972). The turtle task is a clear example of a problem in which means—ends analysis is appropriate. The children visually detect the difference between the current state and the desired goal state. The differences are of two kinds. Either the turtle is facing the correct way and the forward button must be pressed, or the turtle is not facing the correct way and one of the turn buttons must be pressed. The children must then try to reduce these differences, test if the problem is solved, and, if it is not, reduce the differences further until it is.

The important part of this process description is not the program: GPS will work for children or adults at any stage of practice or development. What is crucial to performance on the task is the representation of the visual space, the semantics of the visual objects, and their spatial relations. Fig. 11.1 is an attempt to organize the information in the child's problem space. This is the data base on which the processes operate.

We believe that the spatial names are organized as frames. Here, quite literally, a frame outlines a scene just as a picture frame defines the boundaries of a picture. Frames are not visual snapshots but are more likely composites of many viewing occasions. There are three frames indicated in Fig. 11.1. For the ROOM frame, the *boundary* objects are [mirror], [window], [child], and [chalkboard]. These are familiar objects that have names known to the child and establish a more or less veridical pseudometric. There are also objects within the ROOM frame that may themselves be frames. For example, the objects G1, G2, and G3, the colored geometric shapes, are part of the ROOM frame. The other two main frames are the TURTLE and the BOX. For the children, the TURTLE had boundaries [front] and [back], but not boundaries [left] and [right], since the children had not mastered the left/right concept. At the start of the experiment, the BOX frame had no distinctive boundaries that could be related to the task. The result was that the children were unable to map the appropriate buttons onto the appropriate turtle parts and therefore were unable to select the appropriate turn button. I imagine that we could have run the children for hundreds of additional problems under these conditions.

Perspective Taking

In the perspective-taking condition, we added a large turtle head to the button box. The effect was to create the spatial name [front] for the **BOX** frame. No distinctive features were added to the turtle; hence, the **TURTLE** frame remained as before. The question was how this small manipulation created the rather large observed effect.

To address this issue, we first need to define formally the construct of mapping. The important thing about the **TURTLE** frame is that its boundary elements change with respect to the elements of the other frames. The turtle rotates in 90° increments so that it can "look at me [child]" or "look at the [mirror]", and so on. For any orientation of the turtle, there exists a mapping of its boundary elements to any other frame of reference. A mapping, then, is a set of corresponding spatial names. Thus, as illustrated in Fig. 11.1,

$$M_{TW} \; :: \; = a \rightarrow B$$

describes the turtle looking to the window. A complete theory of the semantics of visual space would require several constructs — turning angles, distance measures, a basis for determining centroids and generating origins, superposition operators, and more. For our purposes here, we need only deal with the pairwise relationships and postulate a mechanism for orienting the button box, a plausible superposition operator.

In a similar fashion, we can map the button box onto the room or onto the turtle. For example, the map of **BOX** on **TURTLE** as shown in Fig. 11.1 is

$$M_{BT} \; :: \; = a \rightarrow a.$$

With the turtle rotated 180° the map would be,

$$M_{BT} \; :: \; = a \rightarrow c.$$

With the turtle head on the button box, and the addition of just one symbolic element, there is now a basis for detecting a difference between the 0° and 180° problems. Just as important, the distinctive features provide a basis for learning. What is learned appears simple enough to say, but it is exceedingly complex to lay out in the form of a program. Simply said, the child learns to orient the button box to the turtle, that is, to superimpose the **BOX** frame on the **TURTLE** frame.

MENTAL ROTATIONS AND EXOCENTRIC REPRESENTATIONS

Huttenlocher and Presson (1973) showed that mental rotation problems were much easier than perspective-taking problems and concluded that the mental operations in the two tasks were very different. Their experimental situation involved four response cards, each showing an array of three blocks from four different viewpoints, 90° apart. One of the four cards was the correct choice, another was the original, egocentric view of the array, and the other two were called miscellaneous. In the mental rotation condition in which the subject had to anticipate what the array would look like if *it* were rotated 90°, 180°, or 270°, the errors were distributed at just about chance level — a third of the errors were egocentric choices. In the perspective condition in which the subjects had to anticipate how the array would look (if they were related to a different location), egocentric errors comprised 80% to 90% of the total.

Although the subjects in the Huttenlocher and Presson study were considerably older than our subjects, their results suggest a possible mechanism by which our perspective-taking condition might have exercised its effect. Putting the head on the button box and creating the spatial name [Front] may have converted the task from one on which the child himself had to take the turtle's perspective to one on which he could keep his own position and think of the button box (an external object) as taking the turtle's perspective. Once the button box took the turtle's perspective, it would be a simple matter always to choose the correct button.

To implement the orienting mechanism involved in mentally rotating the BOX frame into correspondence with the TURTLE frame, we need a match routine. Therefore, we add a seventh elementary process onto the GPS-like program described above.

7. Match spatial name from frame BOX to frame TURTLE.

Since both turtle and box have a common spatial name, [Front], the mental representations of these two objects can easily be made to coincide.

Color Coding

Referring to Fig. 11.1, we can now also see how and why the color-coding manipulation (Problem Set IVb) works. The ear muffs on the turtle's head creates two new symbols, [Orange] and [Purple]. The presence of these symbols on both the TURTLE frame and on the buttons B1 and B3 of the BOX frame allows a direct reference to the correct button. The complex perspective-taking task need not be executed. Moreover, the indirect naming of buttons in terms of external references to the ROOM frame are by-passed.

As before, the child must understand the problem and determine which of the geometric objects is the goal. A direct visual act produces the symbol for the correct button, "Notice Color of Ear Muff." The mapping is immediate, and the child merely observes the spatial name correspondences. Finally, the child must attend to the button box in order to "Find Button with Value Color."

We had supposed that the simplicity of the color coding would have more pronounced effects. Why it did not, we still don't know. Encouragingly, though, we have since introduced the task to naive subjects, and it appears to work, even with 3-year-old children, provided they have the concept that the buttons cause the turtle to move.

CONCLUSION: EGOCENTRIC CHILDREN AND EXOCENTRIC REPRESENTATIONS

The present set of experiments was designed to determine the conditions under which young children could map an external symbol system onto their representation of a spatial array. We found that egocentric children typically have considerable difficulty performing this task, but with perspective taking and color code aids, their performance improves substantially. The question was how these aids exerted their effects.

An information-processing account of the task identified an exocentric representation of the relationships between the experimental objects and the larger frame of reference — the other objects in the room — as crucial. An exocentric representation is an image of objects and their spatial relations embodying the information inherent in the physical arrangement. Contrary to what might have been expected, 3- to 5-year-old children, typically thought of as egocentric, were able to form these exocentric representations. Where they seem to have encountered difficulty was in attaching spatial labels onto one of the experimental objects — the button box. Once we helped them do this, they proved quite capable of choosing the correct response. Thus, although performance was generally poor, as might be anticipated on a spatial task with egocentric children, the source of the children's difficulty was somewhat different from what the literature might have led us to believe.

Notice that we have not explained how exocentric representations are learned; our process descriptions show only how the problems were solved, given a particular representation. However, the learning process should not be a great mystery. We need only postulate a generator for spatial names, a process for controlling the child's attention to the task, and a discrimination-learning program to construct higher-order chunks — the frames — and to index them in long-term memory. After all, visual representations are neither more nor less symbolic than the associations generated in paired-associate or serial verbal-learning tasks. Names are names. Their spatiotemporal order in the environment or in long-term memory is what determines their meaning.

REFERENCES

Bloom, L. M. Language and development. *Form and function in emerging grammars*. Cambridge, Mass.: MIT Press, 1970.

Corballis, M. C., & Beale, I. L. *The psychology of left and right*. Hillsdale, N.J.: Lawrence Erlbaum Associates, 1976.

Ernst, G. W., & Newell, A. *GPS: A case study in generality and problem solving.* New York: Academic Press, 1969.

Gagné, R. M. *The conditions of learning.* New York: Holt, Rinehart, & Winston, 1965.

Gregg, L. W. Maximizing the mini-uses of on-line computers. *Behavior Research Methods & Instrumentation,* 1977, *9*(2), 67–71.

Gregg, L. W. Perceptual structures and semantic relations. In L. W. Gregg (Ed.), *Knowledge and cognition.* Potomac, Md.: Lawrence Erlbaum Associates, 1974.

Gregg, L. W., & Farnham-Diggory, S. How to study reading: An information processing analysis. In L. Resnick & P. Weaver (Eds.), *Theory and practice in early reading.* Hillsdale, N.J.: Lawrence Erlbaum Associates, in press.

Hester, M., & Faddis, C. Turtle jargon: A manual for an experimental control language. Pittsbugh, Pa.: Carnegie-Mellon University, CIP Working Paper #332, 1976.

Huttenlocher, J., & Presson, C. C. Mental rotation and the perspective problem. *Cognitive Psychology,* 1973, *4*, 277–299.

Nelson, K. Structure and strategy in learning to talk. *Monographs of the Society for Research in Child Development,* 1973, *38*(1–2, Serial No. 149).

Newell, A., & Simon, H. A. *Human problem solving.* Englewood Cliffs, N.J.: Prentice-Hall, 1972.

Papert, S. A computer laboratory for elementary schools. *Artificial Intelligence Memo No. 246,* MIT, 1971.   (a)

Papert, S. Teaching children thinking. *Artificial Intelligence Memo No. 247,* MIT, 1971. (b)

Piaget, J., & Inhelder, B. *The child's conception of space.* New York: Norton, 1967. (Originally published, 1948.)

Siegler, R. Three aspects of cognitive development. *Cognitive Psychology,* 1976, *8*, 481–520.

Slobin, D. I. Developmental psycholinguistics: Cognitive prerequisites for the development of grammar. In W. O. Dingwall (Ed.), *A survey of linguistic science.* College Park: University of Maryland Linguistics Program, 1971.

Werner, H., & Kaplan, E. The acquisition of word meanings: A developmental study. *Monographs of the Society for Research in Child Development,* 1950, *15*(1, Serial No. 51).

12 Imagery and Cognitive Development: A Teleological Approach

Stephen Michael Kosslyn
Harvard University

Many theories of development rely implicitly on a backward extrapolation strategy, in which the theorist's knowledge of the mature end state directs his conception of the developmental process (as Flavell, 1963, points out in the case of Piaget). Unfortunately, most developmentalists fail to characterize the end state in a rigorous manner, relying instead on intuitions and introspections. This has serious consequences, for if one's notions about the end products of development are awry, they can misdirect one's conception of the developmental process as well.

This chapter has two main thrusts. First, it is an initial attempt to work out a methodology for studying memory and perceptual development. This methodology is rooted in a teleological conception of development: Not only is the child father to the man, but the man is son of the child. In this view, the child's development can be seen in hindsight to have been drawn forward to the achievement of adulthood.[1] We take the backward extrapolation technique seriously and attempt first to characterize some aspects of the way adults represent information in memory. It is hoped that our characterization of adult processing will reveal junctures at which development could have taken place, and thus the characterization should help us to formulate interesting developmental

---

[1]This use of the word "teleological" does not imply that the child *knows* what he will eventually become, and is striving toward achieving that goal. Rather, the assumption is that since reproduction occurs after puberty, many of the young child's properties have been propogated because they led to adaptive properties in the adult. Further, quite aside from such tenuous arguments, the present claim is that it is *useful* to view development as being goal-directed, as being "designed" to produce the adult.

hypotheses. Second, we develop these ideas within the context of a particular issue — the representational-development hypothesis (Kosslyn, 1978a). According to this hypothesis, young children rely predominantly on imagery for representing information in memory, whereas older people tend to use more abstract linguistic representations (cf. Bruner, Olver, & Greenfield, 1966; Piaget & Inhelder, 1971). I have previously examined the literature on this issue and have found it wanting. Without an explicit conception of what imagery is and how images represent information, developmentalists have been unable to collect the data necessary to assess the hypothesis (Kosslyn, 1978a). The present chapter, then, is in part an attempt to develop a theoretical approach that will allow more precise examination of the representational-development hypothesis.

There is one fundamental problem with the teleological approach: To my knowledge, not even *one* interesting property of adults' cognition has been explained to most researchers' satisfaction (see Newell, 1973). Given this sad state of affairs, how can we hope to work backward? Patience is probably not the answer; it seems naive to expect that consensus will be reached in the near future on any interesting topic in cognitive psychology. The present approach, however, does not depend on consensus. Instead, we attempt to develop a methodology for studying adult information processing that will also serve a teleological function, that will lead us to formulate hypotheses about how this end state was reached. This approach is intended to allow us to extrapolate backward before a theory of adult processing is complete (if that ever occurs!) and also to promote the accumulation of results, the building of a big picture, about cognitive development. Unlike other theoretical frameworks (e.g., Piaget's theory), the current approach is an attempt to characterize the way real time processing develops with age, and to do so in an explicit manner.

1.0   OVERVIEW

This chapter has three major sections. The first two describe the first two phases of the enterprise: discriminating among possible classes of models of adult imagery and then using these findings to formulate a model of imagery. The final section discusses our attempt to extrapolate backward and to consider the representational-development hypothesis in this light. Since the organization of this chapter is so intimately bound with the particulars of the research strategy and basic methodology, it is helpful first to review the basic structure of the approach. A more detailed treatment is given when we consider the data.

1.1   Overview of the Methodology

Our research strategy has two distinct phases; developmental implications of very different sorts may be drawn from each.

We begin by studying the way adults use imagery to represent information in memory. In Phase I, we try to formulate key issues and generate a decision tree on which nodes represent issues and branches stand for competing hypotheses about them. Experiments are performed to eliminate one of the opposing branches (hypotheses) and to allow descent to the next issue. We begin by formulating an intuitively plausible, vague model (a proto-model), which helps us to define the basic issues and alternative stances on them. At the conclusion of this phase, we should know something about the underlying principles of imagery representation and processing, and we will have a backlog of results from the particular experiments. Each kind of information may inspire developmental work, albeit of a limited and not very interesting sort (being mostly concerned with whether children and adults are alike in regard to some principle or result).

Phase II begins when we can no longer extend our decision tree by formulating more basic issues and competing hypotheses about them. That is, there comes a time when a vague model or conception no longer helps one to formulate important questions. At this point we take the products of the Phase I research (both the derived principles and the particular findings) and attempt to account for them within a process model. This process model not only is intended to explain the findings of Phase I in an elegant (parsimonious and straightforward) way, but also should help us to formulate interesting and important research problems. As new findings emerge, the model will become more constrained. With numerous and varied results to explain, it will become increasingly difficult to provide an elegant account of all of them; it is hoped that one sort of model will clearly be the most elegant and that we eventually will be forced to closely approximate the truth.

In order for our theorizing to progress, then, it is critical that new and important results (i.e., those that help to discriminate among competing classes of models) are continually being produced. Our process model helps us to collect useful data in two ways. First, it serves a *directive function*: If we take model building seriously, we will motivate our decisions by appeal to data (not only our intuitions, as so often happens); thus, the act of constructing the model forces us to consider issues we might otherwise have overlooked. Second, it serves a *deductive function*. In attempting to account for a variety of diverse results, we will find that new predictions arise from the model as a whole.

The second phase is much more interesting than the first from a developmental point of view. Now we can consider how nature — in the form of developing processing capacity — and nurture — in the form of increasing numbers of encoded facts and rules — intereact in development. The model allows us to consider questions about the developmental process itself, about mechanisms responsible for systematic changes in structures and processes with maturation and experience.

2.0   PHASE I: DISCRIMINATING AMONG COMPETING
HYPOTHESES ABOUT KEY ISSUES

2.1   Methodology

The classic Baconian approach to science can be thought of in terms of decision trees on which branches from the same node correspond to alternative hypotheses about some issue (see Platt, 1964). Supposedly, one descends the tree, narrowing the class of acceptable explanations, by performing crucial experiments. This approach runs into trouble in psychology, however, because psychological phenomena are so complex that any given result cannot be considered crucial; a particular finding may be due to any number of obfuscating factors and/or confounded variables. The only way we can really deal with this problem is by adopting a technique of converging operations (cf. Garner, Hake, & Ericksen, 1956), that is, by performing a number of different experiments that address the issue at hand. It is hoped that one of the alternative hypotheses will provide a clearly more elegant account of our findings than do the others, which will allow us to reject them in its favor (see Kosslyn, 1978b, for an extended discussion of the rationale behind this approach).

2.1.1   The Role of a Proto-Model in Generating Alternatives.   As becomes obvious when one attempts to make these ideas concrete, it is quite difficult actually to construct trees of alternative possible structures and/or processes. Our proposal, in line with some suggestions made by Popper (1963) and others, is to allow preconceptions to guide one in initially defining issues. But more than this, we feel it is a virtue to begin with only the outline of a model, a proto-model. Proto-models are explicit only in regard to the basic skeleton, the defining principles of a class of models. They are silent regarding the actual details. Such a model seems an appropriate first step for at least three reasons. First, because a proto-model highlights the basic assumptions or claims of a class of models, it is relatively easy to see where components might be different, or missing, which aids in formulating alternative hypotheses. Second, detailed models invite research plagued by a "confirmation bias," for which data consistent with one's notions are sought. Unfortunately, only data that discriminate between *viable* alternatives are of genuine interest. That is, any piece of data is inconsistent with *some* notions, but these notions are often "psychological phlogiston," so off-base that ample disconfirming evidence already exists. Third, even if an out-and-out confirmation bias does not exist, a too-detailed guiding preconception may result in research of interest only within the context of the theory (e.g., as with estimating the value of each parameter). Since the theory is almost certainly wrong (how unlikely it would be if a "true" theory emerged at this early stage!), results relevant only to it are of dubious value.

2.1.2   A Proto-Model for Imagery Representation.   We began with the notion that visual images might be like displays produced on a cathode ray tube by a computer program (plus data). That is, we hypothesized that images are temporary spatial displays in active memory that are generated from more abstract representations in long-term memory. Interpretive mechanisms (a "mind's eye") work over ("look at") these internal displays and classify them in terms of semantic categories (as would be involved in realizing that a particular spatial configuration corresponds to a dog's ear, for example). This simple proto-model directs our attention to at least four key issues: first, it suggests that the experienced quasi-pictorial image is not epiphenomenal; second, it leads us to ask whether such images are simply retrieved or generated; third, if images are generated, we may then ask whether generation is simply a piecemeal retrieval of stored information, or whether it involves retrieving organized units; lastly, we are faced with the question of whether images are composed solely by retrieving perceptual information, or whether conceptual information is also used.

2.2   Studying the End Product: Four Key Issues

Before attempting to derive developmental implications, then, we will attempt to characterize adult processing. In Phase I we try to narrow the class of acceptable models by discovering some of the basic operating characteristics of imagery which must be accounted for by any model.

2.2.1   Issue I: Are Images Epiphenomenal?

Our cathode ray tube metaphor posits that images are produced and then processed by other mechanisms. Presumably, information implicit in long-term memory becomes explicit in an image (e.g., if asked which is higher off the ground, a horse's knees or the tip of its tail, people often claim that this information becomes apparent only when they construct an image of the beast). Alternatively, images could be nonfunctional, epiphenomenal concomitants of more abstract unconscious processing. In this view, images could simply be like the lights that flash on the outside of a computer while it is adding; although they systematically vary with the functioning of an information-processing mechanism, they take no part in the processing (see Kosslyn & Pomerantz, 1977). None of the current explicit models of imagery treat experienced images as functional representations (see Baylor, 1971; Farley, 1974; Moran, 1973; Pylyshyn, 1973; Simon, 1972). Thus, this issue must be resolved before we can even begin to understand imagery.

We performed three classes of experiments to address the image-as-epiphenomenon view. These experiments were motivated by the claim that experienced quasi-pictorial images *embody* spatial extent. If images are in fact functional, then this property should affect information processing when images are used. In contrast, if these spatial, quasi-pictorial images are not functional, then their spatial properties (which do not characterize list-like linguistically based representations) would not be expected to affect information processing.

2.2.1.1 Scanning Visual Images. If images embody spatial extent, then they should preserve relative metric distances between portions of objects. If so, then we might expect that more time should be required to scan longer distances across images. We have done a series of experiments to investigate this implication. In the first experiment, reported in Kosslyn (1973), subjects studied a set of drawings. One group later constructed visual images of the drawings, one at a time, and mentally focused on a specified point. Following this, a possible property of the drawing was presented, and the subject was to "look" for that property on his image. Upon detecting it, he was to push one button; if he "looked" and could not find it, he was to push a different one. As predicted, the farther a property was from the initial focus, the longer it took to "see" it in the image. In addition to this group, there were three control groups. In one, subjects again imaged the drawings but did not focus on any particular part before the probe. These subjects showed no effects of location of the probe per se, eliminating this factor as a possible explanation for the results of the first group. The other two groups did not image the drawings but described them in various ways; these results were sufficiently different from the imagery groups to allow us to argue that imaging and describing are not functionally equivalent processes.

But did these initial findings really indicate that distance per se was preserved in images? Unfortunately, there was a major flaw in this experiment: more items were scanned over when scanning longer distances (see Lea, 1975). Thus, one can explain the apparent effects of distance without referring to spatial images, but rather by arguing that all functional internal representations consist of networks of propositions (see Anderson & Bower, 1973; Pylyshyn, 1973). When subjects are told to focus on a location on an image, what they really do, the argument goes, is activate a particular portion of a network. When a property is presented, the relevant variable is how many links in the network must be traversed before reaching the representation of the property. Because representations of more distant properties are separated from the activated location by more intervening links, more time is required to shift activation to these representations.

We performed a number of experiments to eliminate the confounding between distance and number of items scanned. In the simplest experiment, subjects saw a series of schematic faces, one at a time. Faces consisted of eyes, a nose, and a mouth. The eyes were either 2, 3, 4, or 5 inches above the mouth and were either light or dark. A face was presented, then removed; the subject constructed a mental image of it, then "mentally stared" at the mouth of the imaged face. Finally, the word "light" or "dark" was presented, and the subject was to "glance up" at the eyes of his imaged face and decide whether the word described them. If so, he was to push one button; if not, the other. As expected, the time needed to classify the eyes increased with distance between the mouth and eyes.

One could argue that the results of this first experiment were due to a number of factors other than distance per se. Perhaps subjects simply responded to some sort of implicit demand characteristics. Or perhaps subjects intentionally regulated their responses to produce the expected results (although they denied having done so when queried after the experiment). However, because the same number of things fell between the mouth and eyes of each face, regardless of amount of separation, the same number of "links" presumably would be traversed in a propositional network representation of each face.

To rule out such explanations, we conducted a second experiment. People first learned to draw a map of a mythical island that contained seven objects (e.g., a hut, tree, rock). These objects were located so that each of the 21 interobject distances were distinct (at least ½ cm longer than the next shortest). After learning to draw the map, subjects were asked to image it and to focus mentally on a given location (each location was used as a focus point equally often). Following this, another word was presented; half the time this word named an object on the map, and half the time it did not. On hearing the word, the subject was to look for the object on his image. If it was present, he was to scan to it and push a button upon arriving at it. If it was not found on the imaged map, he was to push another button. As before, the longer the distance, the more scanning time was needed.

We included a control to rule out explanations that some sort of (unspecified) underlying representation was actually processed and that the image itself was epiphenomenal. These subjects had the same task as the experimental group just described but with one change in the instructions: After imaging the map and focusing on the initially named location, they were simply to decide — without necessarily referring to the image — whether the second word named an object on the map. Thus, if the processing of some abstract representation merely associated with the image was actually responsible for the distance effects observed before, we should find the same pattern of results here. In fact, distance had absolutely no effect on judgment time in this situation.

Finally, we can rule out one more counterexplanation: that (1) the closer two objects or parts are, the more likely they are to be encoded into the same chunk, and (2) that objects in the same chunk are accessed more quickly than those in different chunks. In this experiment, subjects again performed the imagery task with the faces. Now, however, immediately after the picture was removed, the subject was asked to image the face at one of three subjective sizes. Interestingly, time to scan increased not only with amount of separation between the eyes and mouth (as before) but also as subjective size (and overall distance) increased. The effect of subjective size cannot be ascribed to any grouping phenomenon because subjective size was not manipulated until after the picture was encoded and removed.

Taken together, these results seem to indicate that images do represent metric distance and that this property affects real time processing of images (see Kosslyn, Ball, & Reiser, 1978).

2.2.1.2   Imaging to the Point of Overflow.   The notion that images have spatial extent suggests that they also have spatial boundaries (after all, they don't extend on indefinitely). If images occur in a structure specialized for representing spatial information (e.g., within a matrix, as in our proto-model), then the maximum spatial extent of an image should be constrained by the extent of the structure. We tested this idea in the following way: Subjects were asked to image an object as if it were being seen from very far away, and then they were to imagine that they were walking toward the object. They were then asked if it appeared to loom larger; all subjects replied that it did. At some point, we suggested, the images might loom so large as to "overflow." At this point, the subject was to stop his mental walk and to estimate how far away the object seemed to be, either verbally or by moving a tripod apparatus the appropriate distance from a blank wall. Once we obtained the distance estimates and the length of the longest axis (which accounted for the most variance in distance estimates in a regression analysis) of each imaged object, it was trivial to calculate a visual angle subtended by the image at the point of overflow. (This basic experiment was performed in a variety of ways, which differed in how distance was estimated and in whether subjects mentally imaged pictures or imaged animals when given only their names and sizes.)

In all the experiments, the basic results were the same. First, subjects claimed that smaller objects seemed to overflow at nearer apparent distances than did larger objects (the correlation between object size and distance was always very high). In fact, distance estimates usually increased linearly with the size of the imaged object. Second, the calculated visual angle at the point of overflow generally remained constant for different size objects when pictures were imaged. (When named animals were simply imaged, however, the angle sometimes decreased for the larger ones.) In addition, in another experiment, we obtained a similar estimate of the "visual angle of the mind's eye" via measuring the amount of time required to scan across the longest possible non-overflowing imaged line. These results, then, support the claim that the images we experience are spatial entities and that their spatial characteristics have real consequences for some forms of information processing (see Kosslyn, in press).

2.2.1.3   Subjectively Smaller Images are More Difficult to Scrutinize.   Our proto-model suggests that images are processed by the same sorts of classificatory procedures used in classifying perceptual representations. If so, we might expect some of the same constraints that affect ease of classifying percepts also to affect ease of classifying parts of mental images. An obvious example is apparent size: Parts of subjectively smaller objects are harder to see in perception; thus, we might expect that they are also harder to see in a mental image.

Kosslyn (1975) tested this idea in a simple experiment requiring subjects to imagine animals at different subjective sizes. After a given animal was imaged at one of four relative sizes (learned by drawing squares of specified sizes prior to the experiment), a property was presented. The subject was told that we were interested in how long it took to see a property on the image or to see that it was not there. Only after the property was either clearly in view or clearly not present was the subject to respond by pushing the appropriate response button. The results indicated that more time was required to see properties on subjectively smaller images. Subjects often reported that it was necessary to zoom in on an initially small image to see a property but that such zooming in was not necessary to examine a larger image.

Do these results really demonstrate that images are quasi-pictorial entities that are examined by the mind's eye? One could argue that our subjects inferred the motivation of the experiment and simply helped us out by regulating their response times appropriately (although they denied having done so when queried after the experiment). We worried about this kind of "cooperation," and hence actually began with an indirect size manipulation. We reasoned that if images are constructed in a limited spatial display, then if we fill up most of that display with a large image, only a small portion will be available to construct a second image. Thus, we asked subjects to image target animals, such as a rabbit, next to either an appropriately scaled elephant or a fly. As expected, most people reported that the target animal seemed larger when imaged next to the fly, and they required less time to see parts of target animals in this condition.

We worried that this result was due not to size but to the nature of the context animal (elephant or fly). Perhaps people had a favorite elephant — like Dumbo — but no favorite fly and spent more time and effort constructing the image of the elephant, leaving less time and effort to detail the target animal. Thus, we conducted a second experiment in which subjects were again asked to image pairs of animals but now were told to image the elephants as tiny and the flies as giant. As expected, more time was now required to see parts of target animals when they were imaged next to the giant fly than next to the tiny elephant.

We are forced again to ask whether these results really implicate processing of a spatial image by the mind's eye. As in the initial scanning experiment, one might try to explain these findings with a model in which all information is stored in networks of abstract propositions. That is, perhaps the representation of the concept of an animal includes a list of properties of that animal, and the size manipulations merely vary how many of these properties are activated prior to the probe. According to this view, people realize that they should see more things on a larger image and move farther down (i.e., activate more entries on) the property list. Therefore, the probability that a given probed property is activated prior to query would be higher when subjects construct subjectively larger images. And verification time is faster if a sought property is already acti-

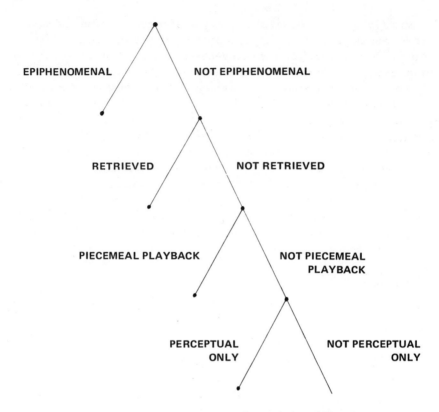

FIG. 12.1   The decision tree at the conclusion of Phase I.

vated than if it must be searched for in long-term memory, as would happen when fewer properties are initially activated when people are asked to construct a subjectively smaller image.

We did an experiment to distinguish this notion from our own, which posits that size per se is important. If the effects of subjective size are simply a consequence of probability of activation on a list, then we would expect subjects to be faster in verifying properties stored near the top of the list (because these properties are most likely to be already activated at the time of probe). People have inferred that lists are ordered by association strength, frequency of co-occurrence between a noun and property, or the like from the fact that highly associated, frequent properties are verified most quickly in standard sentence verification tasks (see Conrad, 1972; Smith, Shoben, & Rips, 1974). For example, the finding that "A lion has a mane" is affirmed more quickly than "A lion has a tail" could be taken to imply that "mane" is stored higher than "tail" on the "lion property list." If lists are so ordered, then the association strength of a property — and not its size — should dictate the time needed to see the property on an image. We tested this idea by constructing items such as "cat claws" and "cat head," where the smaller property was more associated with the noun (as determined by normative ratings). Interestingly, people were faster to see these larger properties when asked to find them on an image of the object. When no imagery instructions were given, people were faster in verifying the smaller, more associated properties. The same results were obtained using a very different technique involving a regression analysis on times to evaluate items not selected for the size-association strength tradeoff (see Kosslyn, 1976a). These results, then, allow us to distinguish between processing of images and nonimaginal representations.[2]

The total weight of these three classes of experiments — on scanning, overflow, and ease of detection — indicates that images are not epiphenomenal. The results are difficult to explain if quasi-pictorial, spatial depictions are not processed. At this point, then, we choose to descend the branch that rejects the claim that images are epiphenomenal and proceed to the next issue (Fig. 12.1.)[3]

2.2.2   Issue II: The Origin of Images: Are Images Simply Retrieved in Toto?

The second node of our decision tree is at the bottom of the branch representing the hypothesis that images are functional. This new node represents the issue of the way images arise. Two branches extend from this node: On one hand, images could be stored in toto and simply retrieved; on the other, images may not simply be replayed or projected wholistically.

We claimed earlier that larger images are more quickly examined because more information is apparent on them. If so, then subjectively larger images may require more construction time if images are in fact constructed by elaboration (adding more parts or detail). Kosslyn (1975) found this to be the case; subjectively larger images generally required more time to construct, independent of the actual size of the imaged object (within a relatively narrow range). One could

---

[2]One could argue that these results simply indicate that there is more than one list stored and that different lists are differently ordered. Given all the multiple ways in which we can order things (e.g., for parts of an animal, in terms of softness, nearness to the ground, edibility, reflectivity) — including some ways that involve hitherto unencountered dimensions such as how useful a dried part would be as writing paper — it is absurd to suggest that all possible orderings are stored. We obviously compute some orderings only when they are needed. Given this capability, why should we store more than one list ordering, which is presumably indexed by reaction times in a standard semantic memory task? And if we compute new orderings only when needed, why should we bother to reorder them in terms of size in the present imagery task? Reordering is certainly unnecessary to perform the task correctly.

[3]The initial work, which has been marshalled to deal with the issue of whether images are epiphenomenal, was not done with this systematic tree approach in mind at all but was done only to demonstrate that images are not like other forms of internal representation. The last three issues were investigated with this general approach in mind, however.

argue, however, that this reflects a criterion effect, not the effects of adding more parts. That is, since more material is packed into a smaller area, perhaps a smaller image reaches some level of brightness sooner than corresponding subjectively larger images. If an image is considered complete when it has reached a given level of vividness, then this effect could produce these findings — even if images are simply retrieved in toto, with no construction.

From this counterinterpretation, it follows that as more details are added to a picture, less time should be needed to image it. If the construction idea is correct, in contrast, more detailed pictures should take more time to image. We tested these contrasting predictions in an experiment in which subjects formed images of more or less detailed versions of pictures of animals. Subjects studied a picture, imaged it (pushing a button when the image was completed, allowing us to measure the time required to evoke the image), answered a question about the image, and then chose which picture (from a set of two) they had imaged. The results indicated that people do, in fact, require more time to image more detailed pictures.

A control group was asked not to use imagery in this task but simply to answer as quickly as possible. Instead of pushing the button when they had an image, these subjects pushed it when they had reviewed the properties of the drawing in their minds. Unlike the imagery task, this review process required the same amount of time for detailed and undetailed pictures. Thus, imagery was distinguished from nonimaginal retrieval, and the view that images are not simply played back or retrieved in toto was supported.

One could argue that more detailed pictures required more time to image not because they were constructed but because there were more things to check after the image was retrieved. That is, one may indeed simply "project" an image, requiring the same amount of time for detailed and undetailed ones. But after the image is present, one may first check over it before deciding that the image is in fact fully retrieved (even retrieval of a single unit need not be instantaneous). And because one scans to more parts on more detailed images, more time is consumed before deciding to push the button. We tested this idea by making use of two findings: First, we knew that subjectively smaller images of simple drawings require less time to scan than do larger ones. Second, other work had shown that parts of images of simple line drawings do not require more time to see than do parts of larger ones (this was also true in the analogous perceptual experiment in which people actually looked at the pictures). Interestingly, other subjects rated the properties equally discriminable on large and small versions of the pictures, suggesting that our earlier effects of size were actually due to discriminability of properties, which decreased with smaller images of actual remembered animals. We reasoned that if people are simply scanning more over the more detailed images after retrieving them, not only should larger images require more time to generate, but effects of detail should be greater with subjectively larger images (since more distance must be traversed between checking parts). New subjects were asked to image the detailed and undetailed drawings at two subjective sizes. Interestingly, detailed versions again required more time to image, and this difference was the same for both subjective sizes. In addition, there was no effect of size on generation times. Thus, our subjects were not simply scanning the images after projecting them wholistically into consciousness.

2.2.3   Issue III: Are Images Retrieved in Units or Piecemeal?

Given that images are not merely turned on like slides in a projector, are they retrieved in coherent units or simply piecemeal? People may have integral representations in memory that are sampled (perhaps at random places) and activated a portion at a time. Alternatively, coherent units could be retrieved and composed in the act of construction. We initially addressed this question by asking people to study drawings and then image them. The drawings included matrices of letters arranged to form greater or lesser numbers of units, according to Gestalt principles of organization (e.g., six columns of six letters were evenly spaced or grouped to form two wider columns three letters across). More time was, in fact, required to image drawings containing more units (even though the same number of elements was present).

One interpretation of these results would be that the image is stored integrally but that the retrieval process segregates the representation into units during construction. To rule out this possibility, we performed another experiment. First, people learned to image a set of drawings prior to the experiment proper. The drawings were divided into three groups, defined by whether (1) an animal was drawn completely on one page, (2) parts were separated and presented on two separate pages (in the correct relative locations), or (3) parts were separated and presented on five separate pages (in correct relative locations). When parts were distributed on more than one page, the subject was told to study each page as long as he liked and to "glue" the parts together in his mind to form the whole animal. This forced subjects to encode separate units and to integrate them in memory. If later images were constructed by composing these units, we would expect subjects to require more time to construct images of animals presented on more pages. This, in fact, was the case. Therefore, we have good reason to posit that the imagery system is built to retrieve and integrate "chunks" stored separately in memory. In any case, the data described in this subsection justify our concluding that images are not simply played back in a piecemeal fashion but instead are constructed in organized units. We cannot say, however, whether these units *usually* reside in memory or are formed in the act of generation. The latter alternative seems nonfunctional and superfluous, however, especially relative to the obvious uses of being able to amalgamate separate representations into a single image. We take the weight of evidence to indicate that images are composed from units and procede from here. If we have erred in this inference, it will become evident in our examination of Issue IV, because Issue IV rests on our resolution of Issue III.

2.2.4   Issue IV: Are Images Generated Only From Perceptual Information?

The fourth level in our decision tree also concerns the origins of images. Images could be generated by simply composing perceptual units, or image construction could involve an interplay between perceptual and conceptual memories. This latter view seems correct on the face of things, simply because people claim to be able to construct novel images on hearing descriptions of them. For example, most people claim to be able mentally to picture Jimmy Carter slapping Mr. Peanut on the back, although most of them have never seen this. However, knowing what Messrs. Carter and Peanut look like and the meanings of "slap" and "back" (in this context), one can construct a novel image. Since one can give oneself verbal cues and instructions, it would be surprising if people did not use verbal (or more abstract propositional) information to construct images. In fact, Weber, Kelley, and Little (1972) reported that people do use self-supplied verbal prompting in imaging words. In addition, we performed an experiment (see Kosslyn, 1978b) that demonstrates that the ease of forming a mental image is affected by how one conceptualizes it. In this experiment, people saw a 3-x-6 matrix of letters. After it was removed, they were told it would be referred to as "6 columns of 3" or "3 rows of 6." Interestingly, when it was described the first way, with more units predicated initially (and in terms of columns rather than rows), more time was required to image the matrix. Since it was the same matrix in both cases and the labels were given after the matrix was removed, these results seem to indicate that conceptual information can influence image construction.

2.3   The Conclusion of Phase I: Developmental Implications

At this point I could no longer think of issues that seemed central for discriminating between classes of theories. Many relatively minor experiments suggested themselves, but none of these touched on new, important issues. It was at this point that we ended our attempts to understand the end product of development in Phase I. Before turning to Phase II, let us consider what sorts of developmental implications arise from the approach of Phase I.

   There are two basic ways in which our enterprise thus far can speak to developmental issues. First, one can simply see whether adults and children behave similarly in regard to some derived principle or obtained result. For example, the finding that adults scan images might lead us to investigate whether chilren do also, and if so, whether they scan at the same rate and so on. Second, one can treat the results from Phase I as a *technology*, a set of tools for investigating related questions. For example, the fact that subjectively smaller images require more examination time could be used as a diagnostic test for determining whether children and/or adults use imagery in particular situations.

There are two main reasons for not adopting the first strategy, for not simply investigating whether children are like adults in regard to some variable or strategy. First, there is no clear motivation for this research. Certainly, children will differ from adults (e.g., will be worse), but is our knowledge about children or development likely to increase with a larger corpus of such descriptions? It is not enough simply to have a list of ways in which children and adults differ. As Bever (1975) said, "An encyclopedia of everything is a science of nothing." (See also Newell, 1973.) The difference between studying development in Phase I versus Phase II is the difference between child psychology and developmental psychology. In Phase I, one would examine the effects of some variables at different ages, which does not tell one much about the mechanisms of development. In Phase II, the developmental concerns are truly *developmental*: They are about the way structures and/or processes change with experience and maturation (as will be discussed shortly).

Second, we have not yet really tried to explain the findings of Phase I; we used them only to discriminate between alternative positions. For example, it was just good luck that images could be scanned, allowing us to demonstrate that metric information is preserved in them. These findings say very little about the mechanisms underlying scanning itself. There was a good reason for not trying to explain the particulars of each finding. As Newell (1973) points out so convincingly, there are simply too many ways of explaining any given finding. It is only after we try to explain a number of findings in an elegant way that we lose degrees of freedom and explanation becomes more difficult. These considerations lead us to reject trying to explain how children differ from adults on a given task. We defer explaining our results obtained thus far until Phase II, when we develop a general and explicit process model. It is quite difficult to account for a large set of diverse data with an explicit, parsimonious, and straightforward model, and the mere fact of sufficiency lends some credibility to this sort of explanation.

Therefore, from a developmental point of view, the main use of Phase I is technological. This application is limited, however, by our ability to ask good questions within the boundaries of a proto-model. The only question I could think to ask about development was an old and a simple one: whether young children tend to use imagery in retrieving information from memory. In order to investigate this question, I asked both children and adults to decide whether certain properties were appropriate for given animals. The properties were those described earlier, with the smaller ones being more strongly associated with the animal (e.g., for a cat, claws more than head). Children, like adults, were faster with larger properties when imagery instructions were given. Unlike adults, however, 6-year-olds were not faster with the smaller, more highly associated properties when no imagery instructions were given. Thus, there was some evidence (bolstered by self-report data garnered after the experiment) that young children spontaneously used imagery in memory retrieval (see Kosslyn, 1976b). However, as is evident in Kosslyn (1978a), this finding did not really lead anywhere; a number of possible variations were obvious but no novel insights or new directions.

3.0   PHASE II: CONSTRUCTING A PROCESS MODEL

After no further basic issues presented themselves, we had a backlog of information about (1) basic principles (positions on the issues) derived from converging evidence from different experiments, and (2) the particular results of experiments designed to distinguish between positions. An experiment on scanning images may have been intended to demonstrate that images preserve spatial extent, but in performing the experiment, information about scanning per se was gathered that also needed to be explained. In the second phase we wish to account for these data with a process model.

3.1   The Simulation Technique

3.1.1   Why a Computer Simulation?

There are at least four reasons for constructing a computer simulation model: First, it forces one to be explicit; hand waving maketh not a program run. Second, it allows one to be general while remaining explicit; in a way, the program serves the function of a notepad in arithmetic, saving one the effort of keeping too many things in mind at once. Third, it forces one to consider processes in a system of interacting components. Hence, explanations for individual phenomena should be self-consistent, and accumulated results form a more coherent picture than if one considers individual processes and structures in isolation. Fourth, it allows one to know whether one's ideas are sufficient to account for the data. If the program runs as expected, it is a kind of "sufficiency proof." This is an important virtue when one's ideas become complex.

The present approach is not simply to construct a detailed model and then test it; rather, we attempt to fill out the model by performing experiments to help discriminate between alternative implementations. In addition, as the model begins to take shape, predictions are derived and tested. The simulation helps us discover new, overlooked, or unfathomed issues and questions. It does so in two ways. First, it *directs* our attention to issues that must be resolved before modeling can progress further. We must base the properties of the model on actual data; making decisions arbitrarily or solely in keeping with our intuitions just will not do. Second, if parsimony and beauty are to be maintained, the simulation forces one to make certain predictions. This is its *deductive* function. Mechanisms originally posited to deal with particular sets of results do not exist independently but affect one another's operation. New predictions are generated from these interactions (as will be discussed later). Furthermore, if a mechanism *can* be easily used to explain performance in some task, it *should* be so applied, leading one to make predictions about this behavior.

3.1.2 The Simulation as Theory

I claimed that the simulation technique allows one to formulate an explicit, general, self-consistent model, and then to test whether that model is sufficient to account for some results. There is a major problem with this approach: The program will not actually run without numerous "kluges," without numerous ad hoc manipulations required by the realities of working with a digital computer and a programming language such as **ALGOL** or **LISP**. The actual simulation, then, is a mixture of structures and processes motivated by one's theory and structures and processes of no theoretical interest but of crucial practical importance. The problem is to separate the kernels from the chaff. There are two reasons we need to do this: First, there is the problem of knowing what class of models is being embodied in a simulation. That is, a given program could be taken as an instantiation of a very narrow, highly specified class (i.e., all the structures and processes are treated as defining features of the class) or as an instantiation of a very broad, underdetermined class (i.e., only a few structures and processes have theoretical import). Without knowing what is important about a simulation, we cannot know when two alternative models are functionally equivalent. The second reason for specifying the theoretically important features of the program is a practical one: Without doing so, how can we test the model? Only by claiming that certain features are sufficient to engender some consequent can we make predictions. If we can characterize the important aspects of programs, we then can compare programs that are alike in these regards but different in others. If some of these prove to be better simulations than others, this will direct our attention to study properties of the programs previously considered incidental. Thus, a description of a program's defining features could turn the simulation technique into an even more powerful tool for use in theory building. Simply by observing the workings of different instantiations of a class, we might gain information that would force us to introduce further constraints on the class of acceptable models.

It seems clear that in order for a computer program to serve as a model we must have some metadescription of the theory embodied in the program. This description should state the important principles of the theory and describe the corresponding features of the program. If this is successfully accomplished, the program can be regarded as a proof procedure that allows one to see whether certain conclusions follow from one's premises (principles). The problem, of course, is in how to specify this metadescription. Ideally, we would like a precise, explicit language in which to specify the theory and the way it maps into the program. This is beyond me; I have only the faintest of glimmerings about how this could be done. Alternatively, as a stopgap we can choose our level of discourse about the program such that only theoretically important features are described. It then becomes an empirical question (as far as I can see) whether all models that meet this description behave as claimed; if not, this would serve as a means for further defining the theory. Thus, in the following section I skirt this problem by describing only what I take to be the defining features of our theory, as embodied in the program. Although this is clearly inadequate in the final analysis, it does not seem an unreasonable way to begin.

3.2   The Model

Although the simulation is a single integral system, for expository purposes it seems best first to consider its data structures and then the processes that involve these representations. Following this, we briefly consider how the simulation operates as a "question—answerer."

3.2.1   Data Structures

3.2.1.1   The Image Proper.   The experienced spatial image is represented by a configuration of points in a matrix. A "picture" is displayed by selectively filling in cells of this matrix. This "surface" image was designed to simulate four properties of imagery discovered in the foregoing experiments. First, the image embodies information about spatial extent; it also is capable of displaying information about brightness contrast and the like. This image is not strictly pictorial because it does not share all the properties of pictures (e.g., it cannot be hung on a wall). Rather, it is quasi-pictorial in that it shares the properties of a percept of a picture. As such, parts of the surface image correspond to parts of the represented thing, and the interpoint spatial relations among the parts are preserved in the image. These properties were implied by the set of experiments described on page 295—301.

Second, activation (cells available for processing by the mind's eye interpretive procedures) decreases with distance from the center until no cells are activated (material in this region has overflowed). This property was suggested by the finding that the estimated absolute size of the mind's eye (measured in the experiments discussed on pages 297—298) was reduced when a stringent definition of overflow was provided in the instructions. This seems to indicate that images gradually fade off toward the periphery, that overflow is not all-or-none. In addition, our finding that people could scan overflowed portions of the image led us to implement nonactivated regions around the periphery of the image display (See Kosslyn, Ball, & Reiser, 1978).

Third, the surface display has limited resolution, causing contours to become obscured if an object is pictured too small (because there are not enough cells per unit area to depict details). This property is based on our finding that subjectively smaller images are more difficult to scrutinize. We have modeled this property in two alternative ways, the differences not being of theoretical importance (or, at least, so it seems at present — see Kosslyn & Schwartz, in press).

Fourth, the matrix corresponds to a "visual short-term memory" structure. Representations within this structure are transient, requiring effort to maintain. That is, as soon as an image is placed in the matrix, it begins to fade; if images are constructed by placing parts sequentially, only so much material can be placed before initially activated portions fade away. Thus, the matrix has a limited "capacity" defined by the rate at which material in it fades and the rate at which new material can be inserted (or old material "refreshed"). Inclusion of this property was motivated by results reported in Kosslyn (1975), indicating that more time is required to "see" portions of more complex images, as would be expected as it becomes increasingly less likely that all material in complex images can be maintained at once.

3.2.1.2 Long-Term Memory Representations.   There are two sorts of representations for generating images, one storing information about the "literal" appearance of an object and another storing facts about the object.

The perceptual memory of an appearance is not interpreted semantically; it is the product of "seeing that," not "seeing as." The memory of how something looked allows reproduction of the experience of "seeing" in an image. In our model, this information specifies how points should be arranged in the surface matrix to depict some object. We represent this information with pairs of *R, Theta* coordinates. We chose this representation because it allows images to be generated easily at different locations in the surface matrix and in different subjective sizes (i.e., sizes in the matrix). Available data motivated these considerations. In addition, this format implied that images could be generated at nonstandard orientations (by multiplying the *Theta* values); we now have preliminary data supporting this prediction, making this property desirable. This, incidentally, is an example of the model's deductive function.

A given object may be represented by more than a single image file in our model. One such file represents a global shape or central part (this question is open, and thus illustrates the model's directive function). Other files represent "second looks" that can be integrated into the global or central shape to form a fully fleshed-out image. Thus, our model includes hierarchical organization in long-term memory. This property was motivated by our findings that more time was required to generate images containing more units, even if the amount of material (e.g., letters in a matrix) was the same. In addition, pilot data indicated that people could construct images of pictures of different complexity in about the same amount of time if they were not required to include details.

Some subjects reported that they formed somewhat fuzzy images of more complex objects and then waited until probed before filling in the details. This sort of introspection is consistent with the notion that a global image is initially generated and then elaborated, but we have as yet no convincing evidence on this issue.

The second component of our long-term representation is a set of facts about the imaged object. These facts are represented discursively, in a propositional format, and represent (1) information about where and how a part (represented in a file of $R, Theta$ coordinates) is attached to a global or central image; (2) a description of the part's appearance (represented as an ordered set of procedures that will search an image and locate the part if executed in sequence); (3) the name of the file that contains the "perceptual memory" of the object or part; (4) the resolution necessary to see the object or part in the image; and (5) the name of the superordinate category.

The foregoing sorts of information were included to simulate some ways in which conceptual information might be used in generating images. In addition, we discovered numerous problems (e.g., if a part is not visible, should one "zoom in," or "pan back" and try again?) in the course of implementing the model, many of which necessitated including particular sorts of information (i.e., resolution level, in this case).

3.2.2   Image Processes

There are two sorts of processes used in imagery: routines for generating and classifying the image and routines for transforming it.

3.2.2.1   Image Generation and Classification.   Images are generated by printing out points in the surface display. They consist of a basic skeletal form that may be supplemented by details. These details are integrated into the image by use of two procedures: **PUT** and **FIND**. The **PUT** procedure accepts a location and relation for a part (e.g., for a chair's cushion, **SEAT** is the location, and **FLUSHON** is the relation). **PUT** then calls **FIND** to locate the relevant part of the image (the seat) by means of a set of procedures defining **SEAT** (retrieved by looking up the representation of seat and locating the procedural definition). Once **FIND** locates the foundation part (seat, in this case), it passes back the Cartesian coordinates of the part's location in the image. **PUT** then checks the location relation and, if need be, adjusts the size of the deep representation of the part (e.g., sets the size of the cushion to fit flush on the seat), and then prints the part in the correct location. Subjective size and location of the imaged object may be specified; if not, the image is centered at a medium size (as suggested by data).

If **FIND** fails to locate the foundation part (e.g., seat) during image construction, perhaps because the image is too large or too small, the part (cushion) is simply omitted from the image (explaining why subjectively smaller images are generated more quickly but the more difficult to examine). If the task is to decide whether an image has a certain property, however, **FIND** works in con junction with various impage transformations in an all-out attempt to locate the sought part. Before trying to locate a part (i.e., discover whether the definitional procedural tests may be satisfied), it looks up the resolution of the image (i.e., dot density) optimal to "see" the part. If the dot density is not within the optimal range, it expands or contracts the image (as appropriate) until the resolution is optimal. If the size of the image is correct and **FIND** still cannot locate the part, **FIND** assesses the relative location of the sought part (from information in the procedural definition) and scans until the appropriate location is in focus (as will be described shortly). If the size and location are correct but the classificatory procedures executed by **FIND** still are not satisfied (e.g., it cannot locate the configuration of points delineating the arms of a chair), the program returns a **CANNOT FIND** message. If it locates the part, it returns an affirmative response.

3.2.2.2 Image Transformation. Our program transforms images by moving the points that delineate them. All of these transformations move only a portion of the image at a time; images are transformed gradually to avoid fragmentation by moving a portion too far at any one stroke (see Kosslyn & Shwartz, 1977). Expanding an image involves moving the points outward from the center, beginning with the outermost points; contracting an image involves pulling points toward the center, beginning with the innermost points. Rotating an image involves shifting the points around a pivot. Scanning an image is treated as another kind of transformation in which points are moved across the surface matrix so that different portions of the image seem to move under the center (which is most highly activated and in sharpest focus). These implementations represent hypotheses, of course, and are but other examples of the directive function of the enterprise. More details about image transformations (and the program in general) are provided in Kosslyn and Schwartz (1977; in press).

3.2.3 Imagery in Question Answering

Our simulation also models some aspects of the way imagery is used in answering questions. Essentially, we view our model as an extension of the sort of model proposed by Smith, Shoben, and Rips (1974), although the nonimaginal claims seem compatible with any current theory of semantic memory. On being asked whether an object has some property, the program first does an overall relatedness check. If the object and property are entirely unrelated, the program exits with a negative response. (This aspect of the pro gram is totally uninteresting, however, the relatedness values being simply listed in a table instead of being computed. We leave the problem of how to compute these values to those studying the field of semantic memory per se.) If the property is not totally unrelated to the object, the program then attempts to look up the sought fact in the object's propositional file. If it is present, an affirmative response is delivered. Presumably, more associated properties will be stored directly with the representation of a concept and hence will be more quickly affirmed than properties that must be inferred. If the sought property is not located in the object's file, the program then attempts to infer this fact by looking up the name of the object's superordinate category and then searching the file associated with it. If this fails, the program looks up the procedural definition of the property's appearance, generates an image of the object, and then inspects the image for the property. For example, one might ask **ANSWERIF A CAR HAS A REARTIRE**. In this case, the program would first determine that car and rear tire are related above some criterion and — given that this is true — would then look up the propositional file associated with **CAR** and search for the entry **HASA.REARTIRE**. If this is present, the program responds affirmatively; if not, the program looks in this file for the name of the object's superordinate, **SUPERORD.VEHICLE**. On finding this in the object's file, the propositional file associated with **VEHICLE** would be checked for **HASA. REARTIRE**. If this is found, an affirmative response is made. If no superordinate name is found in the object's file or if **HASA.REARTIRE** is not found in the superordinate's file, the program looks up the procedural definition (description) of **REARTIRE** (if one is not available, the property is novel and the program stops here), generates an image of **CAR** (as described earlier), and searches the image for a rear tire. If it finds the specified pattern of points, it responds affirmatively; if it fails here, the program responds negatively. Thus, a negative response is delivered only when the program has tried to answer affirmatively but failed. This probably is not a good model of human processing because we sometimes respond "I don't know," and we often seem to reject an assertion before exhaustively searching memory. This failing is not critical, however, as the simulation is intended as a model of imagery and the interface between imagery and semantic memory. The details of a semantic memory model will be left to others.

Although the program executes these strategies in the sequence described in the foregoing paragraph, this is probably not how people perform them. Kosslyn, Murphy, Bemesderfer, and Feinstein's (1977) data suggest that images are generated and inspected at the same time that abstract propositions are being accessed. Given the inherently serial nature of a digital computer, our simulation of parallel processing would not differ much from the current implementation. To mimic the consequences of parallel processing, however, we would need to estimate how long each process took and then let only the fastest of the competing processes affect relevant aspects of subsequent processing.

4.0 EXTRAPOLATING BACKWARD: THE TELEOLOGICAL FUNCTION OF THE MODEL

The purpose of Phase II was to encourage us to consider issues fundamental to the way a real processing system would operate. We claimed that in trying to construct a simulation, we would be directed to study interesting and important phenomena and would be led to make interesting deductions and predictions. Let us first consider how the model directs our attention to interesting developmental issues and then consider the sorts of predictions that follow from the model's account of development.

4.1 Directive Functions

Virtually every component of the model leads one to ask how development proceeds. Is the extent of the image representational structure constant over age? Does image generation proceed the same way? (Perhaps children do not integrate files together, due to capacity limits or the like.) Can children (or adults) zoom in and scan in parallel, or must these operations be performed serially? Are images refreshed at the surface level, or must they be regenerated from long-term memory? (If they must be regenerated, it may be more difficult for children to hold images than it is for adults.) All of these questions are important if children really do tend to rely on imagery; if they do, then constraints on their imagery will map directly into the eccentricities of their general thought processes.

Superficially, exploration of these questions may resemble the simple investigation-over-age experiments that I disparaged at the conclusion of Phase I. But now, we are not asking isolated questions without developmental foundations. Any results we obtain from studying these sorts of questions must fit into a general framework, and our explanations must be self-consistent. Furthermore, the model suggests mechanisms that may underlie developmental change, as discussed in the next section. This sort of research feeds directly into the deductive properties of the model and thus not only extends our understanding of cognitive development but aids us in generating new predictions.

The foregoing questions hover fairly close to our model. A step back leads us to a more fundamental question: Where do the imagery files come from? That is, how are long-term memory representations of images encoded? If there are age differences here, they may have ramifications for the child's entire cognitive structure. Therefore, in thinking about how to build a "front end" to our program, a "perceptual parser," we were directed to consider rules for dividing stimuli into component parts. It seemed clear that perceptual parsing would involve both "bottom-up" processes (determined by stimulus properties per se) and "top-down" ones (determined by higher-order mental activites such as expectations and preconceptions). We began by studying bottom-up processes, looking at which sorts of changes in values along stimulus dimensions dictate part boundaries. In one set of studies, we studied the roles of contour, color, and texture changes in delineating part boundaries.[4] Enclosed nonsense shapes were used as stimuli. Different regions of the interior were colored differently, constructed on a differently patterned background (e.g., x's or o's), or defined by "pinches" (bends) in the surrounding contour. In the first experiment, first graders and adults simply indicated where a form would come apart if it were made out of slips of paper and a breeze came along. Children and adults both used changes in the stimulus properties to define parts, but young children used color and texture changes less often than did adults. This result may simply have indicated, however, that contour changes are more discriminable to young children.

Thus, in the second experiment, we systematically varied the relative saliency of the dimensions (as measured by ratings of a separate group of adults). In this experiment, there were changes in only two dimensions (e.g., color and texture) within any given stimulus. Furthermore, one of the dimensions was dominant, and changes in dimensions occurred at different places in the figure. We told these subjects that each form had only two parts and asked them to indicate where the parts met. Adults tended to choose the point of change in the dominant dimension as delineating part boundaries — even if the dominant dimension was color or texture. Young children (first grade or younger) tended to override the adult-dominant dimension and select a contour change (even a very subtle "pinch" in the outer shape) as dictating part boundaries. These findings are not surprising given the literature on dimensional preference in concept learning and attention (e.g., Brian & Goodenough, 1929; Kagan & Lemkin, 1961; Suchman & Trabasso, 1966), which shows that children of this age range tend not to utilize color if shape cues are available.

The third experiment using adults and young children attempted to show that children encoded parts into memory more in accordance with contour changes than with color changes. Children and adults saw forms that contained parts defined by changes in contour, color, or texture. As before, one dimension was more perceptually salient (as determined by prior ratings). In this case, however, the part boundaries, indicated by changes along stimulus dimensions, were not in conflict. After seeing a figure, subjects were presented pairs of parts and asked to select which one was taken from the previously shown stimulus (only one part was in fact from the figure). Parts were defined by a change in a given stimulus dimension. The results basically dovetailed with the previous findings: Children were more accurate in selecting parts defined by contour, then color, and then texture. Adults, in contrast, showed less of a difference and,

---

[4]This work was performed in collaboration with Karen Heldmeyer.

surprisingly, were better at encoding texture-defined parts than color-defined ones. Interestingly, children were much more affected by the dominance of a dimension than were adults. Children tended to encode the more salient dimension over the less salient one, but there was little difference for adults. Apparently, adults noticed the less clearly defined parts and intentionally spent more effort encoding them. We would expect this sort of top-down processing to develop with age (cf., Brown & DeLoache, this volume).

They finding that children tend to use shape information in parsing, even if this is not the most dominant dimension, led us to examine the way form is encoded in more detail. In this experiment, first-graders and adults were shown the nonsense line drawings used by Bower and Glass (1976).[5] After seeing 12 of these drawings (7 sec each for children, 5 sec for adults), subjects were shown pairs of parts, one of which was a portion of one of the drawings, and were asked to select the bona fide part. There were two sorts of parts: ones in which the line segments were organized according to Bower and Glass' system (basically a formalization of two Gestalt laws, proximity and good continuity), and ones organized more or less haphazardly.

Not surprisingly, both adults and children selected more good than bad parts, and the relative advantage was about the same over age (85% vs. 67% for adults, 67% vs. 48% for children). It appears that first-graders and adults encoded shape information by similar principles.

The second experiment is of more interest. We took the same stimuli and colored the segments corresponding to the bad parts differently from the rest of the figure. The bad parts were a very saturated blue, and the rest of the figure very light red. Thus, good color continuity now defined the previous bad part (vis-'a-vis shape) as a single unit. When a new set of adults were presented with the pairs of parts, we found that they actually selected slightly more of the bad parts (defined as before, 74% vs. 70%)! Interestingly, the first-graders' performance looked much like that in the previous experiment: They continued to select more of the good parts, even with the strong color conflict (64% vs. 55%).

Therefore, we have reasonable evidence that perceptual information in children's memory does not tend to be parsed according to color but that color becomes a more important stimulus property with age. This fact has obvious implications for children's concept development if they do in fact think primarily in terms of images, which are constructed (in part) on the basis of encoded perceptual information.

4.2   Deductive Functions

The "representational-development hypothesis" states that young children use imagery more often than do older people. In what ways does our model address

---

[5]This work was performed in collaboration with Arnold Glass.

this proposal? If a fact is not explicitly noted in an object's propositional file, it can be retrieved in two ways: It can be deduced by looking it up in the superordinate file, or it can be found implicitly represented in an image. For example, consider how you answer the following queries. "Do Volkswagen Beetles have ventwings (little triangular windows near the front of the door)?" and "Do Chevrolet Novas have wheels?" In the first case, most people report having to image the car to answer the question. It is unlikely that this information is stored directly with the concept of Beetle, and since it is not common to all cars, it cannot be deduced from information stored with the general car concept. For the second question, most people report being able to answer without consulting an image (although one may be present incidentally). Again, it seems unlikely that this information was stored directly with the Nova concept; rather, it was deducible from knowledge that the Nova is a car, and that cars have wheels (cf. Collins & Quillian, 1972).

Imagery will necessarily be used, we claim, if one is asked a question about a concrete object and one does not have the necessary information stored explicitly in the object's propositional file or in its superordinate's file. Therefore, if fewer facts are encoded explicitly, or if deduction is difficult, imagery is increasingly likely to be used. As development proceeds, then, learning (as reflected in increased propositional knowledge) and maturation (providing more processing capacity, resulting in deduction becoming easier) may result in reduced use of imagery. We examine this conjecture in some detail within the context of our model.

4.2.1   Learning With Experience.   With increasing age, the child will have increasing numbers of occasions to access facts. With increasing use of a particular fact, it becomes increasingly likely that that fact is encoded proportionally. For example, consider again whether VW Beetles have ventwings (please answer). And again. By the third time it should no longer be necessary to consult an image. Instead, the fact that the car has ventwings should now be stored explicitly (if you had the information in your image initially). This example illustrates one form of memory development in which the child may recode information into propositional form as he accesses that information repeatedly.

This recoding idea leads us to expect that frequently accessed facts will be represented in an "explicit" format and will not require imagery. Furthermore, with increasing age, we expect that frequency becomes less important, as more and more facts are recoded. We consider some data that bear on these claims after discussing additional sources of development.

In addition to internal recoding of the sort just described, people often learn by being taught. Certain facts are encountered and memorized in a linguistic format, especially facts that are important for identifying objects and/or getting around in the world. Retrieval of these sorts of facts, then, also should not require consultation of an image. In addition, people sometimes are taught rules and strategies. What is of interest here is that children sometimes are not able to learn some rule or strategy (e.g., Smedslund, 1961); sometimes rules don't "stick." Let us now consider why this may occur and why children may use imagery even when it is not absolutely necessary.

4.2.2 Effects of Maturation.   In addition to the effects of experience in using information, speed of processing may also increase as the child matures. That is, mylenization or the like may be responsible for the quicker reaction times commonly observed with increasing age (e.g., Kosslyn, 1976b; Nelson & Kosslyn, 1975). If activation starts to fade as soon as a representation is accessed, then the speed of reactivation will determine how many representations can be held in mind at once (assuming that amount of activation per unit and decay rates are relatively constant over age). It is as if one were juggling: The faster one can move one's hands, the more balls can be kept aloft. This parameter will affect how much material can be kept in an image at once. It also may affect how easily the child can make deductions. Consider what would happen in our model if it were asked **ANSWERIF A NOVA HAS WHEELS** and this fact were stored in the superordinate **CAR** propositional file but not in the **NOVA** propositional file. To deduce this fact about Novas, the program must (1) know how to infer it (i.e., which algorithm to use), (2) store the name of the sought property, (3) store the name of the superordinate, once found in the **NOVA** propositional file, and (4) store the name of the object, nova after going to the superordinate file (so it will know to which object the fact is relevant). If any one of these pieces of information is not available, the deduction will not go through. Thus, if a child has only a limited "activated memory" capacity and tends to forget some of this information, he will be unable to deduce the sought fact. Hence, although the child may seem to know any individual piece of information (including the deduction algorithm) necessary to make the inference, in practice he may often use imagery instead. That is, even when verifying something like "Dogs have four legs," children may end up consulting an image, rather than deducing the answer from their knowledge of animals, because of constraints imposed by activation/decay rates (which correspond to limits of "processing capacity").

This notion suggests many interesting experiments. First, one is tempted to devise external aids (e.g., showing a picture of an earless dog and asking about the ears), so that memory load is reduced and abstract processing can proceed without undue difficulty. In addition, it is interesting to consider a twist on Werner's old "microgenesis" techniques. If we place memory loads on adults, say, or otherwise limit their processing capacity for abstract information, we might be able to simulate childlike behavior in the adult. For example, we might ask adults to hold in mind a set of logical premises for a later problem, which might impair doing deductions in answering an interpolated question — engendering imagery use. Further, if one can increase the efficacy of each component step, the child may become able to execute the entire chain. So, for example, overlearning the fact that a dog has ears may increase the likelihood that the child uses this information in deciding whether a German shepherd has ears.

Speculation aside, these notions make a clear prediction about when imagery should be used: when retrieving relatively difficult-to-recall facts about concrete objects. Presumably, the difficulty reflects the availability of explicit encodings. Facts stored directly with an object concept should be easier to retrieve than those that must be deduced via the superordinate, and these should be easier to access than those requiring the generation and inspection of an image (given that this strategy requires more operations than do the first two). Furthermore, children should use imagery to retrieve facts about concrete objects that are easy to retrieve (for an adult) if they indeed have fewer explicit encodings and have difficulty in making deductions.

In keeping with our general tack, we began by investigating our claims about when adults use imagery before attempting to extrapolate backward. In a very simple study, we asked 20 Johns Hopkins University undergraduates to read a set of 72 sentences and to indicate whether each one was a true or false assertion; to rate, on a 7-point scale, how much they thought they had to use imagery in order to make the truth judgment; to rate, on a 7-point scale, how difficult they thought it was to make the truth judgment; and, to rate, also on a 7-point scale, how frequently they thought they had considered the asserted fact in the past.[6] There were three types of sentences, all asserting facts about the properties of concrete objects. A third had no adjectives (e.g., "Lions have fur"); a third had one adjective (e.g., "Trucks have big wheels"); and a third had two adjectives (e.g., "Donkeys have long, furry ears"). Half of each type of statement were true and half were false.

We expected that it would be unlikely that the more qualified properties would be stored explicitly, either with an object concept or its superordinate concept. Thus, we expected these statements to be more difficult to verify and to require more imagery. We also expected subjects to report less frequently that they had considered the more qualified statements in the past. And we expected that the less often one had thought of some fact, the less likely it was to be explicitly encoded and the more likely it was that imagery would be required to verify it.

The results were basically as expected. For "true" statements, for which subjects presumably found some sort of representation in memory, rated difficulty and imagery use were highly correlated, $r = .84$. Rated frequency of consideration and imagery use also were systematically related, $r = -.64$. As expected, more difficult and less frequent assertions tended to require imagery for verification. The mean imagery ratings (higher numbers indicating more use) for statements with zero, one, and two adjectives were 2.56 (Sd = .772), 3.38 (Sd =

---

[6]This work was performed in collaboration with Jim Cahill.

.909), and 3.08 (Sd = .586), respectively. Thus, although statements with one adjective engendered imagery use more than those with no adjectives, statements with two adjectives engendered less imagery than expected.

The results for "false" statements also revealed that the more difficult to assess statements required more imagery, r = .84 again, surprisingly. Interestingly, we found here that imagery use increased — not decreased as it did with "true" statements — for evaluations of more frequently considered assertions, r = .60. Perhaps the more one had encountered some association, the more plausible it seemed, and thus people used imagery as a double check when making truth judgments (cf. Collins & Quillian, 1972). The mean ratings for the zero, one, and two adjective "false" statements were 2.15 (Sd = .565), 3.29 (Sd = .807), and 3.23 (sd = .688), respectively. Again, imagery did not increase as much as expected with the two adjectives. Subjects often reported that the two adjective statements were ambiguous, which may have engendered various nonimagery inference strategies during verification. Alternatively, the increased specification may sometimes have rendered the two-adjective pair itself more or less probable (for any object), allowing easy acceptance or rejection.

The ratings task seemed not to be appropriate for use with children. Therefore, we plan to use a different task to test our developmental predictions.[7] In this task, we will examine whether the difficulty of evaluating a sentence has different effects for children and adults. We also will examine effects of rated frequency of consideration, but these ratings were taken from adults and we have little confidence that they reflect children's experience. In our experiment, 16 true and 16 false statements about properties of animals (with one adjective e.g., "A bee has a dark head") were selected from a pool of 90 statements rated by 25 Hopkins students. Subjects first decided whether each statement was true or false and then evaluated three things: how much they thought they had had to use imagery to evaluate the statement, how difficult it was to judge the truth, and how often they had thought of that fact in the past. As before, ratings were done on a standard 7-point scale. We selected our 32 items to obtain a relatively even distribution of imagery ratings, the range being from a mean of 1.3 to 5.0 (on a 7-point scale). These sentences were taperecorded in an abbreviated form (similar to that of Kosslyn, 1976b). Subjects first hear the word "large" or "small" (each word occurring on half the trials), then the name of the beast, followed 7 sec later by a possible property.

Subjects will sit in front of two square "windows" placed side by side about 36 in. in front of them. One of these frames will be 1 in. per side, and one will be 11 in. per side. Subjects will first be shown a drawing in the large frame, which is then removed. The subject will be asked if he can "pretend" to see the drawing there (even 5-year-olds seem to have no trouble with this, and in fact can point to the locations of various parts of the pretend drawings). The same

---

[7]This work is being performed in collaboration with Brian Reiser and Karen Heldmeyer.

procedure will then be repeated with the smaller frame. The subject will be told that he will soon hear the name of one of the frames, then the name of an animal, and that he should look at the appropriate frame and pretend to see the animal just filling it up. Following this, the name of a possible part of the animal will occur, and the subject will say "yes" or "no" as quickly as possible to whether the property was appropriate for the animal. A clock will be started on presentation of the property name and stopped when a voice-activated relay is triggered by the response.

Following the logic used in Kosslyn, Murphy, Bemesderfer, & Feinstein (1977), we reason that if imagery is in fact used, subjects should be faster when they begin with the relatively large image than when they begin with the very small one. In the latter case, time-consuming "zooming in" should be required before "seeing" a given property on the image. If imagery is not used, size of the initial image should be inconsequential. Thus, the primary variable of interest here is a difference score — time to verify the small image minus time to verify the large one. Since each subject receives each item at only one size (each size occurring equally often over subjects), all analyses are on item means (pooling subjects of a given age). For adults, we expect that statements rated more difficult should tend to require imagery and thus should engender effects for image size; easy statements should not require imagery, and hence initial image size should not affect verification times. In contrast, children should use imagery even with relatively easy statements.

As of this writing, only preliminary results are available. Although there appear to be trends in the predicted directions, we must wait for more data before drawing any conclusions. With our adult subjects, we have occasionally found that the items rated as most often requiring imagery actually show the reverse effect — the larger image requires more time. Subjective reports of "having to scan further" with the larger image are consistent with this finding, but they fail to account for the effects of size observed repeatedly in the past (e.g., Kosslyn, 1975, 1976a, 1976b). It will not be surprising, of course, if things turn out more complicated than we originally hoped.

5.0   CONCLUSIONS

This chapter had two foci: the role of imagery in cognitive development and a methodology for investigating questions of cognitive development. Imagery was a good topic for illustrating our methodology, if only because so many general processes and structures seem involved in it: Retrieving information from an image clearly involves memories of perceived information (which involves both perceptual and memorial processes) and also involves manipulating linguistic material (which is required to understand what to "look for" on an image). In the course of considering how to construct a model of imaginal processes we were forced to touch on these other topics, and we could have developed these offshoots into full-fledged projects.

The present approach has three major advantages over traditional piecemeal approaches. First, the problems investigated in the present context fit into a coherent framework. Thus, we have some confidence that the results will build on one another, forming a picture of the mind and the way it develops. Second, since we attempt to eliminate competing models, it doesn't matter very much whether our own conception is correct or not: We narrow down the class of acceptable models, placing constraints on future theories — of both adult cognition and its ontogenetic foundations. Finally, the backward extrapolation strategy allows one to use findings about adult cognition to guide developmental work, and it also promises to allow results of developmental work to feed back, to guide investigations of adults. This is only fitting, for not only is the man son of the child, but the child is father to the man.

ACKNOWLEDGMENTS

The present work was supported by NSF Grant BNS 76-16987. I wish to thank Steven P. Shwartz, without whom much of the actual modeling would never have progressed so quickly nor so well. This paper was written in April, 1977, and is in many respects a sequel to the paper "Investigating the Representational-Development Hypothesis," which is to appear in P. A. Ornstein (Ed.), *Memory in children,* Lawrence Erlbaum Associates: Hillsdale, New Jersey, in press. Thanks to Gordon Bower and Jerry Kagan for comments on the manuscript. For readability, I use the terms "he" and "his" to refer to both genders.

REFERENCES

Anderson, J. R., & Bower, G. H. *Human associative memory.* New York: Wiley, 1973.

Baylor, G. W. *A treatise on the mind's eye.* Unpublished doctoral dissertation, Carnegie–Mellon University, 1971.

Bever, T. G. Functional theories of linguistic structure require independently motivated theories of speech behavior. In *Chicago Linguistics Circle V: Papers on functionalism.* Chicago: Chicago Linguistics Circle, 1975.

Bower, G. H., & Glass, A. L. Structural units and the redintegrative power of picture fragments. *Journal of Experimental Psychology: Human Learning and Memory,* 1976, *2,* 456–466.

Brian, C. R., & Goodenough, F. L. The relative potentcy of color and form perception at various ages. *Journal of Experimental Psychology,* 1929, *12,* 197–213.

Bruner, J. S., Olver, R. R., & Greenfield, P. M. *Studies in cognitive growth.* New York: Wiley, 1966.

Collins, A. M., & Quillian, M. R. Experiments on semantic memory and language comprehension. In L. Gregg (Ed.), *Cognition in learning and memory.* New York: Wiley, 1972.

Conrad, C. Cognitive economy in semantic memory. *Journal of Experimental Psychology,* 1972, *92,* 149–154.

Farley, A. M. *VIPS: A visual imagery and perception system: The results of protocol analysis.* Unpublished doctoral dissertation, Carnegie–Mellon University, 1974.

Flavell, J. H. *The developmental psychology of Jean Piaget.* Princeton: Van Nostrand, 1963.

Garner, W. R., Hake, H. W., & Eriksen, C. W. Operationism and the concept of perception. *Psychological Review,* 1956, *63,* 149–159.

Kagan, J., & Lemkin, J. Form, color, and size in children's conceptual behavior. *Child Development,* 1961, *32,* 25–28.

Kosslyn, S. M. Scanning visual images: Some structural implications. *Perception and Psychophysics,* 1973, *14,* 90–94.

Kosslyn, S. M. Information representation in visual images. *Cognitive Psychology,* 1975, *7,* 341–370.

Kosslyn, S. M. Can imagery be distinguished from other forms on internal representation? Evidence from studies of information retrieval time. *Memory and Cognition,* 1976, *4,* 291–297. (a)

Kosslyn, S. M. Using imagery to retrieve semantic information: A developmental study. *Child Development,* 1976, *47,* 434–444. (b)

Kosslyn, S. M. The representational-development hypothesis. In P. A. Ornstein (Ed.), *Memory in children.* Hillsdale, N.J.: Lawrence Erlbaum Associates, in press. (a)

Kosslyn, S. M. Imagery and internal representation. In E. Rosch & B. Lloyd (Eds.), *Cognition and categorization.* Hillsdale, N.J.: Lawrence Erlbaum Associates, in press. (b)

Kosslyn, S. M. Measuring the visual angle of the mind's eye. *Cognitive Psychology,* in press.

Kosslyn, S. M., Ball, T. M., & Reiser, B. J. Visual images preserve metric spatial information: Evidence from studies of image scanning. *Journal of Experimental Psychology: Human Perception and Performance,* 1978, *4,* 47–60.

Kosslyn, S. M., Murphy, G. L., Bemesderfer, M. E., & Feinstein, K. J. Category and continuum in mental comparisons. *Journal of Experimental Psychology: General,* 1977, *106,* 341–375.

Kosslyn, S. M., & Pomerantz, J. R. Imagery, propositions, and the form of internal representations. *Cognitive Psychology,* 1977, *9,* 52–76.

Kosslyn, S. M., & Shwartz, S. P. A simulation of visual imagery. *Cognitive Science,* 1977, *1,* 265–296.

Kosslyn, S. M., & Shwartz, S. P. Visual images as spatial representations in active memory. In E. M. Riseman & A. R. Hanson (Eds.), *Computer vision systems.* New York: Academic Press, in press.

Lea, G. Chronometric analysis of the method of loci. *Journal of Experimental Psychology: Human Perception and Performance,* 1975, *104,* 95–104.

Moran, T. P. *The symbolic nature of imagery.* Paper presented at the third International Joint Conference on Artificial Intelligence, Stanford University, August, 1973.

Nelson, K. E., & Kosslyn, S. M. Semantic retrieval in children and adults. *Developmental Psychology,* 1975, *11,* 807–813.

Newell, A. You can't play 20 questions with nature and win. In W. G. Chase (Ed.), *Visual information processing.* New York: Academic Press, 1973.

Piaget, J., & Inhelder, B. *Mental imagery in the child.* New York: Basic Books, 1971.

Platt, J. R. Strong inference. *Science,* 1964, *146,* 347–352.

Popper, K. R. Science: Problems, aims, responsibilities. *Proceedings of the Federation of American Societies for Experimental Biology,* 1963, *22,* 961–972.

Pylyshyn, Z. W. What the mind's eye tells the mind's brain: A critique of mental imagery. *Psychological Bulletin,* 1973, *80,* 1–24.

Simon, H. A. What is visual imagery? An information-processing interpretation. In L. W. Gregg (Ed.), *Cognition in learning and memory*. New York: Wiley, 1972.

Smedslund, J. The acquisition of conservation of substance and weight in children: II. External reinforcement of conservation of weight and the operations of additions and subtractions. *Scandinavian Journal of Psychology*, 1961, *2*, 71–84.

Smith, E. E., Shoben, E. J., & Rips, L. J. Structure and process in semantic memory: A feature model for semantic decisions. *Psychological Review*, 1974, *81*, 214–241.

Suchman, R. G., & Trabasso, T. Color and form preference in young children. *Journal of Experimental Child Psychology*, 1966, *3*, 177–187.

Weber, R. J., Kelley, J., & Little, S. Is visual imagery sequencing under verbal control? *Journal of Experimental Psychology*, 1972, *96*, 354–362.

13

Individual Differences in Solving Physics Problems

Dorothea P. Simon
Herbert A. Simon
Carnegie—Mellon University

Children from age six onward spend a large part of their lives in elementary schools, learning school subjects whose formal structure is not very different from that of the subjects they will study in high school and college. Hence, it is perhaps not inappropriate to report some research on individual differences in adult competence in a subject, elementary physics, that is typically taught in high school and college. An understanding of the bases of adult competence may cast light on the skills the child must attain enroute to such competence, in particular prerequisite skills in arithmetic, reading, and algebra. Moreover, the method of analysis used here could also be used in studying the knowledge demands of elementary school subjects.

We follow the strategy used in other recent work in information-processing psychology (e.g., Klahr & Wallace, 1976) of trying to establish what is learned before investigating how it is learned — that is, of studying performance first and then learning. The task domain we examine is a part of elementary physics. More specifically, we are concerned with the topic of motion in a straight line, which occupies about one week of a one-year high school or first-year college physics course. Still more specifically, we use the treatment of this topic found in a widely used high school physics textbook that employs algebra but no calculus (Taffel, 1973). We are interested in what it is that students know when they have mastered the chapter and how they make use of this knowledge when they go about solving problems. Our method of study has been to gather problem-solving protocols from two subjects: (S1) a subject with a strong mathematical background and wide experience in solving problems of this kind, and (S2) a subject who had taken a single course in physics many years previously and who had an adequate, but not unduly strong, background in algebra. From the comparison of the behavior of the more experienced and the less experienced subjects, we seek to draw some conclusions about the learning process and to comment on which part of the skill is least readily learned by standard methods of studying textbooks and working examples.

A small number of analyses of school subjects appears in the literature, but not always at the level of detail proposed here (and which we think essential for our purposes). Gagné (1963) pioneered in this kind of analysis with his studies of elementary arithmetic skills. Paige and Simon (1966; see also Bobrow, 1968; Hinsley, et al., 1977) studied the processes involved in understanding and solving algebra word problems. Novak (1976) simulated the processes for solving physics problems in statics (levers). Marples (1974) has analyzed the logical structure of problems in mechanics and electricity. Bundy (1975) and Bundy, Luger, Stone, and Welham (1977) have analyzed student performance in solving pulley problems. Larkin (1976) has analyzed simple dynamics problems. Greeno (1976, 1977) has analyzed the performance of high school students solving several classes of geometry problems and has constructed a program that closely simulates their performance. Brown and Burton (1975) have constructed a computer program for tutoring students learning to solve electronics circuit problems. Bhaskar and Simon (1977) constructed a program for generating problems in chemical engineering thermodynamics, and Bhaskar (1977) has analyzed human problem-solving behavior in chemical engineering, cost accounting, and business policy cases.

THE TASK CONTENT

Motion in a straight line is taken up in the fifth chapter of Taffel (out of 32 chapters) and occupies 22 pages (out of about 550). Previous chapters of Taffel have already introduced methods and units for measuring length, time, mass, and weight (Chapters 2 and 3), and the concepts of vector, force, and motion (Chapter 4), but not acceleration. The fifth chapter introduces the notions of uniform and accelerated motion, units of acceleration, average and instantaneous speed, relative speed, motion at constant speed, and uniformly accelerated motion. The gravitational constants in English and metric systems (32 ft/sec^2 and 9.8 m/sec^2, respectively) are also explained. The following fomulas are given, together with derivations and verbal explanations.

1. $S = v*T$,

where S is distance, $v*$ is average speed, and T is time.

2. $S = vT$, for constant speed, v.
3. $a = (v - v_0)/T$,

where a is acceleration, v is final speed, and v_0 is initial speed.

4. $v = v_0 + aT$
5. $v* = (v_0 + v)/2$

6. $v* = v_0 + 1/2(aT)$
7. $S = v_0 T + 1/2(aT^2)$
8. $v^2 - v_0{}^2 = 2aS$

Equations are also given for the special case where the body starts from rest, that is, where $v_0 = 0$:

9. $v = aT$
10. $S = 1/2(aT^2)$
11. $v^2 = 2aS$.

Note that the symbol v is used both for constant speed and for final speed in uniformly accelerated motion. In other respects, the symbolism is unambiguous. The English-language text preceding the introduction of each group of equations above specifies the condition (e.g., constant acceleration, constant speed) under which the equation holds.

The material we have just described occupies the second through the tenth pages of Taffel's Chapter 5; the remainder of the chapter, which we shall not consider, is devoted to relative motion, graphical analysis of motion, and motion of falling bodies. The text and formulas are illustrated by seven sample problems, worked out step by step. These are followed by 15 questions and 25 problems. The two subjects whose behavior we analyze here read the text, answered the questions, and worked the problems in order.

The whole empirical and formal content of Taffel's Chapter 5 is modest, for it can be summed up in the 11 equations listed earlier. Even these are not independent, for they can all be derived from the three relations: (1) $S = v*T$, (4) $v = v_0 + aT$, and (5) $v* = (v_0 + v)/2$. (To solve the problems, the student must also know the value of g, the gravitational constant.) Without specifying precisely what a "thing" is, we may say that mastery of this chapter requires the student to learn not more than about ten "things." If this chapter is typical of the whole text, then a one-year physics course calls for the mastery of about 300 "things." Again, if this course is typical of high school courses, a student carrying four courses might be expected, during a school year, to learn more than 1,000 but less than 2,000 "things." We may compare these crude estimates with the estimate made by Chase and Simon (1973) that a chess master spends ten years or more learning about 50,000 chess patterns which he can recognize on a chess board. By way of further comparison, a Japanese elementary school child learns to read and write 200 to 300 ideograms each year, and to associate with each the meanings and "readings" (pronunciations) it can have in different contexts.

SOLUTION TIMES AND PATHS

As mentioned earlier, our data were obtained from two subjects, one quite expert in working problems of this kind, although without recent practice, the other having fair skill in algebra but essentially new to the subject of kinematics. Our

TABLE 13.1
Number of Words, Time, and Rate Used in
Solving 19 Physics Problems

Problem Number	S1			S2		
	Number of Words	Time in Seconds	Words per Minute	Number of Words	Time in Seconds	Words per Minute
3	54	16	203	100	85	70
5	120	54	133	270	233	70
6	102	36	170	167	163	60
7	100	36	167	176	169	62
8	60	19	189	208	184	68
9	100	43	140	285	240	71
10	82	28	176	[a]	[a]	[a]
11	116	52	134	700[b]	513[b]	82[b]
12	50	26	115	63	48	79
13	149	79	113	591	560	63
16	351[c]	152[c]	139[c]	341	246	83
17	106	50	127	597	545	66
18	116	40	174	[a]	[a]	[a]
19	142	45	189	271	195	83
20	141	55	153	312	260	72
21	197	80	148	138	120	69
23	67	25	160	311	295	63
24	258	110	141	514	555	56
25	87	35	150	137	135	61

[a]Protocol incomplete.
[b]Minimum time – first part of solution lost from tape.
[c]Does not include checking time, which took 107 seconds, 212 words.

expert subject, $S1$, and our novice, $S2$, each worked the 25 problems at the end of Taffel's Chapter 5 under standard thinking-aloud instructions, using paper and pencil freely. $S2$ referred to the textbook when she needed to find or recall a relevant equation, but she made fewer and fewer such references as she proceeded and none at all in handling the last six or eight problems. $S1$ did not refer to the textbook. The subjects' protocols for 19 of the 25 problems are analyzed here. Problems 1, 2, 4, 14, and 15, which dealt with relative motion, are omitted, as is Problem 22, which was more complex than the others (involving a pair of moving bodies instead of only one). Problem 22 is discussed in a later section.

Times and Protocol Lengths

Table 13.1 shows, for each subject, the total number of words in each protocol, the time in seconds required to solve each problem, and the average rate of speech in words per minute. It can be seen that $S1$ solved some of the problems in less than half a minute and required only 2.5 minutes for the hardest (Problem 16). Only four of these problems took him more than 1 minute. There was a small upward trend in his solution times from beginning to end of the sequence, but it must be remembered that the subjects solved the problems in the order in which they appeared in the textbook and that the problems had been arranged by the author so as to increase in difficulty. Hence, difficulty is confounded with practice. $S2$, the novice took on average about four times as long per problem as $S1$. Her solution times ranged from about 1 minute to over 9 minutes (Problem 24). While all of $S1$'s solutions were correct, $S2$ arrived at incorrect answers for two problems, both of which involved arithmetic errors.

$S1$ produced on average about 160 words per minute. His average rate of speech was slightly higher on the easy problems and slightly lower on the hard ones. After allowance is made for differences in problem difficulty, there appears to be no trend in his rate of verbalization over the course of the problem-solving session. $S2$'s speech was less than half as fast as $S1$'s, averging about 70 words per minute, and the number of words in her protocols averaged about twice the number of those in $S1$'s.

Characteristics of the Protocols

Figures 13.1 and 13.2 exhibit the protocols of these subjects on Problem 19. These protocols illustrate quite clearly the characteristic differences between the verbalizations of the two subjects and can be regarded as reasonably typical of the protocols for the other problems in the set. First, however, the similarities: Both subjects begin by reading the problem aloud, as they were instructed to do. They then evoke (or sometimes, in the case of $S2$, look up) appropriate equations to describe the physics of the situation, and then they solve the equations to find the unknown quantities. They answer the two questions — about average speed and duration — in the order in which they were asked.

---

1. A bullet leaves the muzzle of a gun at a speed of 400 meters per second.
2. The length of the gun barrel is half a meter.
3. Assuming that the bullet is uniformly accelerated,
4. what is the average speed within the barrel?
5. Well, obviously one half of 400 is 200 meters per second.
6. Ah . . . How long was the bullet in the gun after it was fired?
7. If the average speed was 200 meters per second,
8. and the barrel is half of a meter,
9. then it would be 100 . . . one . . . wait a while . . .
10. The average velocity is 200 meters per second,
11. and the length is half a meter . . .
12. Yeh, then . . . ah . . . it's a half meter,
13. and it's 200 meters per second,
14. then it would have to be one four-hundreth of a second.

FIG. 13.1   Protocol of $S1$ on Problem 19.

1. A bullet leaves the muzzle of a gun at a speed of 40 meters per second.
2. V-zero equals 40, no, 400 meters per second.
3. The length of the gun barrel was uniformly accelerated,
5. what is its average speed inside the barrel?
6. Its average speed inside the barrel was from zero plus . . . to 400 . . .
7. Um . . . average velocity times the time it was there,
8. time divided by two.
9. Its average velocity was 200 meters per second.
10. Assuming that the bullet was uniformly accelerated, what is the
    average speed inside the barrel?
11. Its average speed was 200 meters per second.
12. That's got to be right.
13. The average speed is speed, is the speed, is the v-zero, which was zero,
14. plus v, which was the other, divided by 2. . .
15. Why divided by two?
16, The average of the two speeds, right?
17. Or 200 meters per second.
18. There's something wrong with that; maybe that's what I did something
    wrong with on the other one. Maybe I should have taken a square or
    something. I'll go back and look at it in a minute.
19. How long was the bullet in the gun after it was fired?
20. How long was the bullet in the gun?
21. All right. The time.
22. If s equals vt,
23. t equals the distance divided by the average speed,
24. equals 200 meters. . .
25. No, point 5 divided by 200 meters.
26. So let's worry about that.
27. Point 5 by 200 is 002.5.
28. Time equals .002.25 seconds.
29. Clearly, something is wrong with Problem 18. Let's go back and
    do that again based on one of the sample problems.

FIG. 13.2   Protocol of $S2$ on Problem 19.

There are also important differences between the two protocols, the most obvious being the typical two-to-one ratio of their lengths. After reading through the first question (Lines 1–4), $S1$ simply calculates the average speed (Line 5), without mentioning the formula he has evoked from memory and is applying. He then reads the second question (Line 6), and again carries out the calculation without mentioning the formula ($v^* = S/T$) he is using. He does mention the values of the givens (Lines 7–8), and then repeats them (Lines 9–11) before carrying out the computation successfully (Lines 12–14). Even though the formulas are not mentioned explicitly, it is entirely clear from the computations that they are Equation 5 (specialized for $v_0 = 0$) and Equation 1 (transformed to solve for T in terms of S and v^*). $S2$, on the other hand, writes down the first given (Line 2) as she reads the problem (Lines 1–5), making a correction in a reading error as she goes. She then states explicitly the formula she is going to use (Lines 6–8), and applies it (Line 9). Next, she checks her result

(Lines 10–17) – in particular, the correctness of the formula she used. Now she interrupts herself (Line 18) to comment on a possible mistake in the previous problem. She reads the second question (Line 19), repeats it (Line 20), evokes an appropriate formula (Lines 21–22), transforms the formula to make T the dependent variable (Line 23), substitutes numerical values for the givens in the formula (Lines 24–25), and carries out the numerical computation (Lines 26–27). (The answer, although incorrect as verbalized, is correct on the worksheet.)

While a single verbalization covers $S1$'s evoking a formula, putting it in the appropriate form, and substituting the numerical values for the independent variables, each of these three steps is verbalized separately by $S2$. This may merely reflect a difference in the subjects' programs of verbalization. On the other hand, it may represent an automation of successive steps in $S1$'s program that results in the individual steps' being no longer available for verbalization. If the latter interpretation is adopted, then $S1$'s program calls for combining information from the problem statement with knowledge of physical laws at the earliest possible moment, by instantiating the laws with the given values of variables as soon as the former are evoked from long-term memory. Instantiation appears to be less automatic in $S2$'s program: more time elapses before information from the two different sources are brought together, and in some protocols, formulas are produced in literal form without being immediately instantiated.

In $S1$'s protocols, almost all of the verbalizations are directly descriptive of the calculations he is making. There are relatively few verbalizations of plans, or other "metastatements" about the process. These occur mainly in protocols for the problems that took him 50 seconds or more. In Problem 19, for example, $S1$'s only metacomment is "Wait a while" (Line 9). $S2$, on the other hand, makes a number of such comments: "That's got to be right" (Line 12), "Why divided by 2? The average of the two speeds, right?" (Lines 15–16), "There's something wrong with that" (Line 18), and "So let's worry about that" (Line 26). In the last six problems (Problems 19–21, 23–25) $S2$ averages about five metacomments per problem, while $S1$ averages only one per problem.

The contents of the two subjects' metacomments are similar – observations that a mistake has been made; a comment on the physical meaning of an equation; the question, "What do we know?" (i.e., what are the givens, or what formulas are available?); statements of plan or intent (e.g., "Let's just clear fractions"), evaluations (e.g., "Is that right?"), and a few others. $S2$ expresses uncertainty fairly often about the steps or calculations she has taken, $S1$ very rarely.

Solution Paths

We observed in the previous section that the basic structures of the two protocols are quite similar. Immediately after reading the problem, they evoke an equation from long-term memory. The equation is instantiated by substituting in it quantities that are given in the problem statement, and it is then solved. This process is repeated (usually two or three times) until values have been found for the unknowns mentioned in the problem statement. This is the same basic structure as reported by Bhaskar and Simon (1977) in their studies of a subject solving physics problems. The fundamental cycle can be described as:

FIND EQUATION
INSTANTIATE EQUATION
SOLVE EQUATION

The scheme may be applied repetitively or recursively — that is, if values for all the independent variables in an equation are not known, a new equation may be found in one of the unknowns, instantiated, and solved.

Although both subjects used this scheme, they often retrieved different equations from long-term memory to find the same unknowns. The 19 problems called for the values of 32 unknowns to be found. In 19 of these 32 cases, $S1$ and $S2$ used essentially the same sequence of equations (solution path) to solve for an unknown; in 13 cases, they used different paths (see Table 13.2, Columns 3 and 5).

The most frequent difference (nine cases) was that $S1$ used Equation 5 followed by Equation 1 to solve for S, while $S2$ used Equation 7 or its specialization, Equation 10. The converse difference did not occur even once. Nor did $S1$ on any occasion use Equation 7, although he did use Equation 10 in five problems. $S2$, on the other hand, used Equation 7 eight times and Equation 10 seven times.[1]

The other principal difference between the two subjects (three cases) was that $S2$ used Equation 8 or 11 and $S1$ did not. In fact, $S1$ reported that he was unfamiliar with Equations 8 and 11, and he was willing to accept them as correct only after he had rederived them. Notice that these equations have no obvious direct physical interpretation.

A Production System

A rather close simulation of the behavior of both subjects — in particular, of their successful solution paths — can be obtained within the framework of a common program structure. The simulation attempts to account for the sequence in which required equations are retrieved from long-term memory and solved. The differences between $S1$ and $S2$ are to be explained by rather modest differences in the way in which equations are cued by information in the problem and retrieved from long-term memory.

---

[1]Table 2 shows only successful solution paths. $S2$, especially, actually made a number of false starts and corrections in solving most of the problems. However, the aim we set ourselves was to study the knowledge demands made on the student in solving this type of physics problem. The analysis in this and the following section reflects the way each of the subjects met these demands.

TABLE 13.2
Comparison of Solution Paths for Subjects
and Simulations by Problem Type

Problem Type Given	Find	Prob. No.	S1 Protocol	Simulation	S2 Protocol	Simulation
V_0AT	VS	5	V4-S7	V4-V*5-S1	V4-S7	V4-S7
		8	V4-V*5-S1	V4-V*5-S1	V4-S7	V4-S7
		9	V4-V*5-S1	V4-V*5-S1	V4-S7	V4-S7
		10	V4-V*5-S1	V4-V*5-S1	V4-S7	V4-S7
V_0AT	SV	11	V4-S7	V4-V*5-S1	V4-S7	V4-S7
V_0AT	S	12	S7	V4-V*5-S1	S7	S7
		20	V4-V*5-S1	V4-V*5-S1	S7	S7
		21	V4-V*5-S1	V4-V*5-S1	S7	S7
V_0VT	S	23	V*5-S1	A4-V*5-S1	A4-S7	A4-S7
		25	V*5-S1	A4-V*5-S1	V*5-S1	A4-S7
V_0VT	AS	7	A4-V*5-S1	A4-V*5-S1	A4-S7	A4-S7
		17	A4-V*5-S1	A4-V*5-S1	A4-S7	A4-S7
V_0VA	TS	6	T4-V*5-S1	T4-V*5-S1	T4-S7	T4-S7
		18	T4-V*5-S1	T4-V*5-S1	T4-V*5-S1	T4-S7
V_0VS	AT	24	a	V*5-T1-A4	A8-T7	A8-T7
V_0VS	V*T	19	V*5-T1	V*5-T1	V*5-T1	A8-T7-V*5
V_0AS	VT	16	T7-V4	T7-V4	V8-T7	T7-V8
V_0ST	V*V	13	A7-V4-V*5	V*1-A7-V4	A7-V8-V*5	A7-V8-V*5
ST	V*	3	V*1	V*1	V*1	V*1

Key: Letter is variable to be solved for; number is equation type used; e.g., V4 means "Equation 4 was used to solve for V."

Variables: A, acceleration; S, distance; T, time; V_0, initial velocity; V, terminal velocity; V*, average velocity.

Equation Type	Equivalent equations, pp. 326–327
1	1, 2 $S = V*T, S = VT$ (constant speed)
4	3, 4, 9 $A = (V - V_0)/T, V = V_0 + AT, V = AT$ (where $V_0 = 0$)
5	5 $V* = (V_0 + V)/2$
7	7, 10 $S = V_0T + 1/2(AT^2), S = 1/2(AT^2)$ (where $V_0 = 0$)
8	8, 11 $V^2 - V_0^2 = 2AS, V^2 = 2AS$ (where $V_0 = 0$)

[a] Anomalous solution. See text.

The simulations take the form of simple *production systems.* A production system (Newell & Simon, 1972) is a program consisting of an ordered set, or list, of *productions.* Each production consists of a *condition* part and an *action* part. The rules for the operation of the system are these: (a) the productions are arranged in linear order, and the conditions of each one are tested in turn; (b) if, upon testing, the conditions of a production are found to be satisfied, the action part of that production is executed; (c) after execution of a production,

TABLE 13.3
Production System for $S1$

		SUBJECT $S1$	
Prod.	Ind. Vars.	Dep. Var.	Equation
P1	vv_0T	a	$a = (v - v_0)/T$
P2	$v*T$	S	$S = v*T$
P3	$Sv*$	T	$T = S/v*$
P4	vv_0a	T	$T = (v - v_0)/a$
P5	v_0v	$v*$	$v* = (v_0 + v)/2$
P6	v_0aT	v	$v = v_0 + aT$
P7	ST	$v*$	$v* = S/T$
P8	v_0aS	T	$T = (-v_0 + (v_0^2 + 2aS)^{1/2})/a$
P9	Sv_0T	a	$a = 2(S - v_0T)/T^2$
P10	v_0aT	S	$S = v_0T + .5aT^2$

TABLE 13.4
Production System for $S2$

		Subject $S2$	
Prod.	Ind. Vars.	Dep. Var.	Equation
P1	$Sv*$	T	$T = S/v*$
P2	v_0aS	T	$T = (-v_0 + (v_0^2 + 2aS)^{1/2})/a$
P3	aSv_0	v	$v = (v_0^2 + 2aS)^{1/2}$
P4	v_0aT	v	$v = v_0 + aT$
P5	$v*T$	S	$S = v*T$
P6	v_0aT	S	$S = v_0T + .5aT^2$
P7	vv_0T	a	$a = (v - v_0)/T$
P8	vv_0S	a	$a = (v^2 - v_0^2)/2S$
P9	vv_0a	T	$T = (v - v_0)/a$
P10	v_0v	$v*$	$v* = (v_0 + v)/2$
P11	Sv_0T	a	$a = 2(S - v_0T)/T^2$
P12	ST	$v*$	$v* = S/T$

the testing process resumes, beginning with the first production on the list.

In the production systems under consideration, the conditions are the presence or absence of particular variables in an equation. Associated with each of the kinematics formulas is the name of its dependent variable and the list of its independent variables. As each problem is being solved, lists are kept, for that problem, of the variables whose values are known and of the variables whose values are wanted. Tests can then be performed to determine whether the values of any of the independent or dependent variables in the formula are known or whether they are wanted. Clearly, a particular formula *can* be solved only if the values of all independent variables are known; generally, there is a *reason* to solve the formula only if the value of the dependent variable is wanted. The tests used in the production systems for $S1$ and $S2$ are based on these considerations. To be specific:

1. The condition for $S1$'s productions is that the values of all independent variables be known. If they are, the action part of the production is executed — that is, the equation is solved for the dependent variable.

2. The conditions for $S2$'s productions are that (a) the dependent variable of the production's formula be on the "wanted" list, and (b) the values of all its independent variables be known. If both conditions are met, the action part of the production is executed. If the first condition is met but not the second, then the name of the first independent variable whose value is unknown is placed on the "wanted list," but the production is not executed.

The production systems for $S1$ and $S2$ also differ in having different orderings of the productions. In all other respects they are identical. The lists of productions of the two systems are shown in Tables 13.3 and 13.4.

The production systems (P) are even simpler than the lists suggest. In $S1$'s production system, only four distinct equations appear: Equations 1, 4, 5 and 7 of our original set, together with the equations obtained by permuting independent and dependent variables in these. Thus, P1, P4, and P6 correspond to Equation 4; P2, P3, and P7 to Equation 1; P5 to Equation 5; and P3, P9, and P10 to Equation 7. They are listed separately for simplicity in writing the system, and no psychological significance should be attached to this format. Moreover, $S1$ actually used only Equation 10 instead of the more general Equation 7, but P8, P9, and P10 have been kept in the general form to avoid having to express the condition, $v_0 = 0$, in the production system. In the same way, $S2$'s 12 productions correspond to only five distinct equations: P1, P5, and P12 to Equation 1; P2, P6, and P11 to Equation 7; P3 and P8 to Equation 8; P4, P7, and P9 to Equation 4; and P10 to Equation 5. P3 and P8 appear in her protocols only in the special case of Equation 11 (i.e., the special case where $v_0 = 0$).

Table 2 compares the subjects' paths with the paths used by the simulation programs on each of the 19 problems. There is an extremely close correspondence. $S1$ uses Equation 10 instead of Equations 5 and 1 to solve for S in Problems 5, 11, and 12. (These are the only problems involving both vertical motion and v_0 = 0, which may be the cues that divert $S1$ to this path.) In Problems 23 and 25, the simulation, but not $S1$, computes the value of a, which is not called for by the problem statement. In Problem 24, $S1$ performs complex manipulations using Equations 10 and 9 to find the time, and then applies Equation 9, as does his simulation, to find the acceleration. (See p. 338 for a fuller discussion of his solution of this problem.) In Problem 13, $S1$ solves for a and v first, then for $v*$, while the simulation reverses the order (thereby following the order in which they are asked in the problem text). In this problem, $S1$ also uses $v*5$ instead of $v*1$, which can be found directly from the givens. In the case of $S2$, the match between simulation program and human protocol is even closer, the paths differing only for Problems 18, 19, and 25. In Problem 18, $S2$ uses Equations 5 and 1, instead of her customary Equation 10, to solve for S. In Problem 19, she solves first for v^*, then uses Equation 1 to solve for T, while the simulation solves successively for a, T, and v^*.

In Problem 25, $S2$ also solves first for v^* and then applies Equation 1; the simulation first finds a so that it can use Equation 7 to find S. The only other difference is that in Problem 16 the simulation reverses the requested order in finding the dependent variables.

The production systems, therefore, appear to capture very well the processes the two subjects are using to solve these 19 problems. What do they tell us about the nature of skill and expertness? There are two ways to characterize the differences between the two systems. First, $S1$'s system represents a "working forward" strategy while $S2$'s represents a "working backward" strategy. That is to say, $S1$ operates from the givens in the problem, solving successively the equations that can be solved with these givens, without much attention at the outset to the particular variables that the problem statement asks him to evaluate. Only in Problem 16, which took him the longest time to solve, and Problem 24, the second longest, does $S1$ make any comments that can be interpreted as means—ends analysis. In the course of solving Problem 16, he remarks, "No, what am I doing. I'm finding . . . ah" . . . "No, I don't want the T; where are we now?". . . "So we have to find the time first." And while solving Problem 24 he says, "And what do we know? What we know is the final velocity." $S2$, on the other hand, evokes equations in which the desired quantitites are dependent variables, and if not all the independent variables in these are known, sets up subgoals to solve for them.

Viewed in this way, $S2$'s behavior seems to be more goal directed than $S1$'s — at first blush a surprising result. However, this phenomenon has also been observed in subjects working thermodynamics problems (Bhaskar & Simon, 1977; see also Marples, 1974). When the problem is very easy, the expert knows that he can solve it simply by solving equations as he comes to them, so to speak. When the problem is harder his behavior becomes more purposeful and is guided by a means—ends analysis of the goals he is seeking to reach. Thus, the more "primitive" approach of $S1$ is to be attributed to his confidence that forward search will lead quite directly to a solution of the problem and will not generate a large and inefficient search. This confidence is based on his experience with the problem domain.

A Comment on Physical Intuition

Physicists and engineers often refer to "physical intuition" as an essential component of skill in solving physics problems. Sometimes solving a problem with the help of physical intuition is contrasted with solving it "simply by plugging in the formulas." The facts that the idea of physical intuition is somewhat elusive and that is has not been defined operationally do not mean that the phenomenon underlying it is unimportant to problem-solving skill. We would like to venture here an interpretation of physical intuition in information-processing terms and provide some evidence that $S1$ made important use of it.

Physical intuition might be interpreted in the following way: When a physical situation is described in words, a person may construct a perspicuous representation of that situation in memory. By a perspicuous representation, we mean one that represents explicitly the main direct connections, especially causal connections, of the components of the situation. For example, in a statics problem involving a ladder leaning against a wall, the representation might be an associational structure with nodes for the ladder, the wall, the floor, and the points of contact between the ladder and the wall and the ladder and the floor. The force of gravity acting on the ladder would be associated with the ladder, and the forces at the points of contact would be associated with those points. Once this schema had been constructed in memory, it would be a straightforward matter to construct the equations of equilibrium for the situation. In fact, Novak (1976) has built a computer program for understanding statics problems stated in natural language that proceeds in exactly this way: First it constructs a schema representing the essential relations in the situation, then it sets up equations corresponding to this representation. In our present terminology, we would say that the program exhibits physical intuition.

We claim that $S1$ used physical intuition in solving our kinematics problems; that is, he first translated the English prose of the problem statements into physical representations, then used those representations to select and instantiate the appropriate equations. The representations reflected his causal view of uniformly accelerated motion, a view that can be summed up in two statements: (1) A distance is traversed in uniform motion by the cumulation of equal unit distances incremented over successive unit time intervals, and (2) a velocity is acquired, in uniform acceleration, by the cumulation of equal unit velocities incremented over successive unit time intervals. In this representation, velocity is measured by the unit distances traversed in unit times of Statement 1, while acceleration is measured by the unit velocities of Statement 2.[2]

---

[2]We have modeled these two statements on Galileo's definitions of uniform motion ("one in which the distances traversed by the moving particle during any equal intervals of time, are themselves equal.") and uniform acceleration ("A motion is said to be uniformly accelerated, when starting from rest, it acquires, during equal time-intervals, equal increments of speed.") in *Dialogues Concerning Two New Sciences,* translated by Henry Crew and Alfonso de Salvio, Evanston: Northwestern University Press, 1939, pp. 154 and 162, respectively. Since Galileo was *deriving,* for the first time, the kinematic laws of uniform motion and acceleration, he was striving in these pages to infer a mathematical description from a physical one; hence, these definitions and the passages surrounding them may plausibly be taken as indicating Galileo's physical representation of the situation. Galileo uses this physical representation to derive the equations that we have labeled Equations 2 and 9. He then proceeds, still working from the physical representation, to derive Equation 1, where average velocity is given by the definitional Equation 5 (*ibid.,* pp. 173–174), and finally (*ibid.,* pp. 174–175) the celebrated Equation 10.

What is the empirical basis for claiming that $S1$ used a physical representation of the sort just described instead of going directly from the problem statements to the equations? The evidence is far from conclusive, and we will have to let the reader decide whether he finds it persuasive. First, we have the fact, already noted, that $S1$ generally calculates distance from Equation 1 rather than from Equation 10, even though this choice requires him first to solve Equation 5, and sometimes Equation 9. To be sure, $S1$ does use Equation 10 in Problems 5, 11, 12, 13 and 16, but in three of these five cases (Problems 5, 13, and 16), he is not satisfied with his answer until he checks it, or tries to check it, using the other path. Thus, in Problem 5, after using Equation 10 to find the distance traversed by a rolling ball, he says: "That seems like a lot . . . ah, oh, in 4 seconds, sure, its final velocity was 12 meters per second so half of that is 6 meters per second and 4 seconds is 24. So that figures." Here he uses the known final velocity to find the average velocity, and the average velocity and the known time to check the distance. In Problem 11, $S1$ actually begins by using Equation 9 to find final velocity from time and acceleration, but then (for no reason that can be discerned from the protocol) he shifts to Equation 10. He does not, however, check his answer. In Problem 13, after using Equation 10 to find the acceleration from the time and distance, then the final velocity and average velocity (4 meters per second), he concludes with: "I should have known that since it went down 12 meters in 3 seconds." In Problem 16, the distance and acceleration are given, and the time is called for. After using Equation 10 to solve the problem, $S1$ says, "Another way to do that would have been to say it goes down 88.2 meters . . . . oh, no, I couldn't do that without first solving for the time, so that's ok." That is, he tries to check his calculation with Equation 1 but discovers that neither the time nor the average velocity is given. Problem 24 provides a striking example of checking. This is the only problem in which distance and terminal velocity are given, while acceleration and time are to be found. $S1$ first evokes Equation 9, to solve for a, but realizes that T is not given ("Oh, no, that's not quite as easy as that"). He then evokes Equation 10, but again observes that he has two unknowns. Reviewing what is given, he notes that he can eliminate a from Equation 10 by using Equation 9. He thereby obtains $S = \frac{1}{2} vT$, pauses, and says, "Oh, of course. The distance is one half times the velocity — the terminal velocity — times the time."

There are *no* problems in which $S1$ proceeds in the opposite direction — that is, in which he uses Equation 1 to find the distance, and then checks his result with Equation 10. We conclude that the former equation has some priority over the latter, and we attribute this priority to the fact that Equations 1 and 9 (and Equation 4, which is the generalization of the latter) derive directly from the hypothesized physical representation. We would also (and still more speculatively) attribute $S1$'s assurance that he is using the correct equations to the fact that he is not simply recalling them from memory, but is either generating them from the physical representation or at least using the latter to check his recall. When $S1$ uses an equation that is not based directly on the physical representation

(Equation 10), he exhibits no such assurance and usually feels obliged to check his result.

There are only two comparable paragraphs in $S2$'s protocols, in spite of her much more frequent use of Equations 7 and 10, where she checks using the other path. These occur in Problems 5 and 17. In Problem 18, she does the reverse: She uses Equation 10 to check a result derived by the more intuitive path. Hence, there is little evidence that $S2$ used a physical representation as the source of her equations or to check her results.

Our confidence in this explanation of $S1$'s superior performance is buttressed by evidence for the use of such physical representations in the literature. In particular, Paige and Simon (1966), who presented their subjects with algebra problems that corresponded to physically unrealizable situations, found that many of the subjects unintentionally transformed the problems into similar but physically realizable forms.

A MORE DIFFICULT PROBLEM

The 22nd problem at the end of Taffel's Chapter 5 is one of the more difficult ones. It reads:

> At the moment car A is starting from rest and accelerating at 4m/sec^2, car B passes it, moving at a constant speed of 28m/sec. How long will it take car A to catch up with car B?

The problem refers to two moments in time, which we will call t_0 and t_1, where t_0 is the time when car A starts from rest just as car B passes it, and t_1 is the time when car A catches up with car B. During the interval $T = t_1 - t_0$, the two cars travel the distance, S. That the two cars travel the same distance, S, in the same time, T, must be inferred by the problem solver from the language of the problem statement.

There are a number of ways to solve this problem, three of which are reasonably direct:

1. Remembering that T and S are the same for both cars, we have from the first sentence, together with Equation 10, $S = \frac{1}{2}(4T^2)$. From the second sentence, together with Equation 2, we have $S = 28T$. Eliminating S between these two equations, we solve $2T^2 = 28T$ for T, obtaining $T = 14$.

2. Starting with the two equations from the previous solution, we solve the second for $T = S/28$, and we substitute this value in the first, obtaining $S = 2(S/28)^2$. Substituting the solution, $S = 392$, in the second equation, we again obtain $T = 14$.

3. The average speed, v^*, of car A over T must be the same as the average speed of car B, which is 28. But $v^* = (v_0 + v)/2$. Since $v_0 = 0$, it follows that the terminal velocity of car A is twice its average velocity, or 56. Using the equation

$v = 56 = 4T$, we immediately obtain $T = 14$. This third path is the one that rests most directly on physical intuition, as we have defined that term.

Performance of $S1$ on Problem 22

The experienced subject used the first of these methods to solve Problem 22. His protocol is so brief we quote it in full:

[Reads problem]
1. Ah well, that's a little trickier.
2. Ah, car A goes a distance of $\frac{1}{2}aT^2$,
3. where acceleration is 4 meters per second.
4. So it's . . . ah . . . $2T^2$ is the distance it goes.
5. And the other car goes a distance of 28 meters per second times T,
6. so 28 times T . . .
7. and so $2T^2 = 28T$
8. Which says that $T = 14$.
9. what . . . seconds, I guess.
10. Ah, so we will assume that that will catch up in 14 seconds.
11. Now, let's see if that makes any sense.
12. In 14 seconds that car would be . . . ah . . . going at a velocity of
13. . . . ah . . . whatever 14 times 4 is
14. which is 56.
15. So it would have gone . . . um . . . ah . . . at an average velocity of one-half that
16. or 28,
17. which is right to catch up with the other one.

Thus, $S1$ spoke 84 words while solving the problem by the first of the three solution paths described above. He then spoke 56 words while checking his result by the third solution path. Although he used Equation 10 in solving the problem, we see that he checked his result by the third path, giving us additional evidence for his reliance on a physical representation. The protocol provides no clues as to how he chose his steps. In lines 2 through 4 he simply translates the facts about car A into an equation, and in lines 5 and 6, the facts about car B. He then equates the two distances, in line 7, and solves the resulting equation.

On the basis of the information he uses, but without explicit support from the language of the protocol, we can infer that he must have used processes such as the following:

1. He generated some kind of problem representation that incorporated the starting time, t_0, and location, s_0, and the terminal time, t_1, and location, s_1, thus defining the time interval, T, and distance, S.

2. Mention of the constant acceleration of car A evoked from his long-term memory Equation 10, $S = \frac{1}{2}(aT^2)$.

3. Similarly, mention of the constant speed of car B evoked from his long-term memory Equation 2, $S = vT$.

4. He noticed that both of the equations had the same dependent variable, S, and he set the two equations equal.

5. He noticed that the new equation contained only the single variable T, and he solved for it.

In this whole sequence, perhaps the most sophisticated processes are those involved in interpreting key terms in the original problem statement. The first sentence of the problem as given is of the form:

At the moment when X is occurring, Y is occurring,

where X is a pair of events involving car A, and Y a pair of events involving car B. The sentence asserts that all these events took place at one time, t_0: $v(A,t_0) = 0$, $a(A,t_0) = 4$, $v(B,t_0) = 28$, and B passes A. This last condition may be expressed algebraically by the assertion that cars A and B are in the same location at time t_0: $s(A,t_0) = s(B,t_0) = s_0$. The "how long" of the second sentence implies a time interval, T, and hence a second point in time, t_1, at which car A "catches up" with car B. The parser must be clever enough to know that the latter phrase means that the two cars have the same location at that time: $s(A,t_1) = s(B,t_1)$. Furthermore, from the fact that cars A and B have the same locations at times t_0 and t_1, he must infer that they have gone the same distance, $S = s_1 - s_0$, during the time interval, $T = t_1 - t_0$. Once these translations had been accomplished, a fairly straightforward set of "noticing" processes would be capable of evoking the appropriate equations.

$S1$'s processing scheme for Problem 22 involves only slight elaboration of the scheme he used in solving the simpler problems. The main components of this scheme are (1) parsing capabilities powerful enough to handle such phrases as "at the moment," and "catch up"; (2) capabilities for creating a semantic representation of a physical situation and for drawing inferences (e.g., that the times and distances are equal for the two cars); (3) capabilities for evoking physical relations (equations) from long-term memory (LTM), cued by suitable words or phrases in the text; and (4) capabilities for solving simultaneous equations. Again, there is no evidence in the protocol that the subject planned the path he took — and the brevity of the protocol argues against any elaborate planning effort. A simple set of productions could produce such a path without planning.

Performance of $S2$ on Problem 22

$S2$'s protocol for Problem 22 extends over 18 minutes until the problem is solved and contains about 1,200 words, encoded into some 150 statements. The protocol divides neatly into five major episodes. The first episode (Lines 0–42), which took about 6:15 minutes, was occupied with reading the problem, translating its content into algebraic equations, making some inferences from the semantic representation of the problem, and evoking some physics equations from LTM. The second episode (Lines 43–78), which took about 3:30 minutes, is occupied with rereading the problem statement and summarizing the information that was generated in the previous episode. No new information is produced in the second episode. The third episode (Lines 79–109, 3:30 minutes) begins with $S2$ setting some fairly specific goals and then pursuing them. Up to this point, she has failed to evoke one of the physics equations essential for solving the problem (Equation 10). This failure is consistent with the production system we have postulated for $S2$, for the problem statement does not ask for a value for S, the dependent variable in Equation 10. The formula is finally evoked from LTM (Line 92), and equations adequate for solving the problem are set up. The equations are judged to be "too complicated," and $S2$ abandons this plan. The brief fourth episode (Lines 110–117, 1 minute) involves an unsuccessful effort to execute an infeasible plan. In the fifth and final episode (Lines 118–150, 4:30 minutes), $S2$ returns to the plan of the third episode. This time she is not deterred by the complexity of the resulting expressions and solves the problem.

The second of the three solution paths was employed. Ignoring, for the moment, $S2$'s search activities, the solution path itself is longer than that of the expert subject. For car A, $S2$ uses the formula, $S = \frac{1}{2}(aT^2)$, substituting 4 for a on the basis of problem statement. For car B, she uses $S = vT$, where $v = 28$ is also given in the problem statement. From the semantics of the problem, $S2$ has deduced that the S's and the T's in the two equations are equal. Next she solves the second equation for $T = S/v$, and substitutes this value in the first, obtaining $S = 2(S/28)^2$. She then solves this equation for S and, substituting the value in the second equation, finds $T = 14$, the desired answer.

As with the simpler problems, $S2$ is much more meticulous than $S1$ in mentioning and writing down in algebraic notation all of the facts mentioned in the problem statement (e.g., in Lines 2–16 of her protocol). By Line 19, however, she has constructed a representation of the situation that permits her to infer that the times and distances are the same for the two cars. In Lines 24–32, she deliberately evokes physics formulas that may be relevant to the problem, recalling Equations 2 and 9, but not the crucial Equation 10. These formulas are not evoked, however, as translations of particular statements about cars A and B but as general laws of physics — for example, "We know that distance equals velocity times time," which is true only for the constant velocity of car B or the unknown average velocity of car A.

These steps have taken $S2$ more than 6 minutes. She takes the next 3:30 minutes to summarize and recopy this information. In the next 1:30 minutes, $S2$ arrives at a solution plan and evokes the missing formula, Equation 10. The rest of the protocol consists of attempts, first unsuccessful then successful, to carry out this plan.

Both subjects, very early in their search, retrieve from memory a physical law to describe the motions of each of the two cars. For $S1$, the laws are Equations 10 and 2, whose simultaneous solution leads immediately to the solution of the problem. $S2$, however, (Line 27) retrieves Equation 9, $v = aT$, instead of Equation 10, $S = \frac{1}{2}(aT^2)$, to describe the motion of car A, but Equations 9 and 2 cannot be solved simultaneously because they have more than two unknowns (S, v, and $v*$). $S2$ notices this almost immediately (Line 34) but does not then evoke Equation 10. That equation, which involves the variable S is evoked only after $S2$ notices (Line 87) that the problem can be solved as well in terms of S as in terms of T. She then puts S on the "want list." The planning episode, Lines 79–94, is so crucial to the solution effort that it is reproduced here:

79. Now, we have some things that relate these;
80. we ought to be able to get one in terms of the other.
81. If . . . the . . . We know the velocity and that seems to be sort of crucial.
82. So, lets see if we can relate those two.
83. So the distance . . .
84. Let's see, no here, time or . . .
85. time equals distance over velocity.
86. And since it's the time we want to find . . .
87. Oh well, it doesn't really matter.
88. So let's say the distance equals the distance for B,
89. or distance, it doesn't matter for either of them since they're equal,
90. distance for B equals 28 times the time.
91. And what do we know about the distance in terms of the other?
92. S also equals one half of the acceleration times the time squared
93. or one half of the acceleration, which is 2,
94. times T squared.

The context makes it reasonably clear that the "relate these" of Line 79 refers to time and distance. The goal of relating time and distance for car B evokes Equation 2, and the goal of relating them for car A evokes Equation 10. $S2$ now has all of the information she needs to solve the problem. She is not confident of this, however, for she engages in two brief episodes (Lines 95–98 and 110–117) where she attempts to use relations in terms of velocity.

$S2$ employs the second solution strategy. This strategy follows from the method she uses for solving simultaneous equations: Solve the first equation for one variable in terms of the other; then substitute that value in the second equation and solve it. The alternative, setting the right-hand sides of the two equations equal to each other, does not appear to be in her repertoire.

Problem 22 is more complex than the others we have considered because it requires the solution of two simultaneous equations. Nevertheless, the performance of both subjects on this problem, and the differences in their ways of attacking it, are quite similar to their performances and the differences between them on the simpler problems. $S2$'s difficulties on Problem 22 were exacerbated by her failure to evoke Equation 10 promptly and by her temporary abandonment of the correct path because of its complexity. Nearly 10 minutes elapsed before a plan of attack was formulated — a delay related to the fact that $S2$ did not regard S as a "wanted" variable, and hence she did not evoke Equation 10.

IMPLICATIONS FOR LEARNING

We can extract from this experiment two kinds of information that have implications for learning. First, we can see if there was any significant change in the behavior of either subject over the sequence of problems. Since $S1$ was already experienced in these kinds of problems, we would not expect much change in his approach, but we might expect $S2$'s behavior to resemble $S1$'s more closely on the later problems than on the earlier ones. A second implication for learning might be derived from the comparison of the two subjects' styles. What was it that $S2$ had *not* learned that would have facilitated her solving the problems? Is there anything we can say about the learning method she used (i.e., studying the chapter of the textbook) that would account for what she had learned and for what she failed to learn?

Progressive Changes in Behavior

There were no striking changes in the behavior of either subject from the earlier problems to the later ones. This is shown by the fact that a single production system can be written for each subject that predicts behavior quite well for the entire sequence of problems. Nor does $S1$'s advantage over $S2$ in solution times appear to decline over the sequence, as we might expect if $S2$ were learning rapidly.

On the other hand, $S2$'s learning may be obscured by the fact that later problems are, on average, more difficult than the earlier ones (for both subjects) and of more varied types. Three of the four problems $S1$ found most difficult were the only problems of their type (the fourth, Problem 21, was the one where he started with English instead of metric units). These same three problems were also difficult for $S2$.

There is one clear piece of evidence of learning in $S2$'s behavior and one that is more speculative. First of all, on a number of the earlier problems, she had to refer back to the textbook to find the appropriate equations or to verify them. This dependence on the textbook disappeared fairly rapidly. The information was gradually transferred to, and became available from, long-term memory. The more subtle change was that, on two occasions, $S2$ used different methods of solving two problems of the same type. Although Problems 6 and 18 are identical in structure (v_0, a, and v given, T and S unknown), $S2$ uses Equation 10 to solve Problem 6, but finds distance in terms of average velocity in Problem 18. The same shift occurs from Problem 23 to 25 (v_0, v, and T given, S unknown).

Hence, in two of the later problems (Problems 18 and 25), $S2$ uses the path more closely related to physical intuition, where earlier she had used the other path.

We should not be surprised that other clear evidence of learning has not been discovered in the protocols. Even in a restricted task domain, working some two dozen problems does not represent an enormous amount of practice of the requisite skills. In domains of motor skill (playing the piano, riding a bicycle) we would not be astonished if this much practice yielded only modest gains.

Gaps in Skill

No single factor accounts for $S1$'s greater skill in solving these kinematics problems. $S2$ takes each step in her solutions more slowly than $S1$, frequently expressing lack of confidence that she is on the right track. She takes a considerable amount of time summarizing and recapitulating the information she obtains. When she evokes a formula, she does not always substitute into it immediately the values of the variables given in the problem statement. She is less skilled and sure than $S1$ in both algebraic and arithmetic manipulation, and makes more arithmetic mistakes. Because of her lack of confidence, she sometimes abandons a solution attempt when she is on the right path.

Differences of these kinds might well account for the full difference in skill between the two subjects, but we have adduced evidence that another factor, too is involved. If $S1$'s approach to these problems may be characterized as "physical," $S2$'s is "algebraic." There is evidence, though less decisive than we should like, that $S1$ generally moves from the problem statement to a representation of the physical situation, and from that representation to a set of equations. Most of our evidence for this claim is indirect − principally, the fact that $S1$'s solution paths lie close to simple physical representations of the phenomena.

When we say that $S2$'s techniques are "algebraic," we mean that she appears to go rather directly, in the manner of the production system with which we simulated her behavior, from the problem statements to the equations required to solve them. By studying the textbook chapter and the illustrative problems, $S2$ learned the algebra of kinematics, including the necessary equations for solving kinematics problems, but she was only beginning to learn the physics − how to represent complex kinematics situations. The textbook seems to have been more successful in teaching equations than in inducing a high level of physical intuition.

CONCLUSION

In this study we have undertaken a detailed analysis of the task of solving simple kinematics problems. We have sought to describe not only the explicit knowledge of physical laws that the student must acquire but also the way those laws must be organized and "indexed" in memory in order to provide a basis for problem-solving skills in this domain.

The physics content of the problems, which test about one week's work in a standard high school or college physics course, is quite limited, amounting to only about three or four laws and a few consequences that are derivable rather directly from them. Yet physics is not usually regarded as an easy school subject. What does the student need to learn besides the bare laws themselves? One approach to answering this question is to compare and contrast highly skilled performance on the problems with the performance of someone who is just beginning the study of physics.

Using this strategy, we have examined the protocols of two subjects working physics problems under thinking-aloud instructions. The two subjects, one an expert and one a novice, spanned a wide range of skill in both physics and algebra. We have constructed production systems that provide a first-approximation theory of the processes the subjects were using in solving these problems, and we have studied in detail both the differences between the processes of the two subjects and the deviations of each from this first-approximation theory.

The production systems that describe the behavior of the two subjects are quite similar in basic structure. The condition sides of the productions test whether the values of the independent and dependent variables in each of the physical laws are known, and they trigger the action of solving the corresponding equations for the dependent variables when the appropriate conditions are met. The conditions induce a "working forward" strategy in the expert, and a "working backward" strategy in the novice.

Much of the difference in skill between the two subjects can be explained in terms of a generalized "practice effect." The skilled subject has had vastly more experience in the kinds of algebraic and arithmetic manipulations required for solving problems of these kinds. This difference in experience shows up as both difference in a variety of skills and difference in confidence.

We believe that we have also identified a more important difference that may be labeled "physical intuition." To assert that an advantage in physical intuition accounts for the superior ability of physicists to solve physics problems should occasion no surprise. Physicists and teachers of physics have been saying that for years. What we hope to have contributed in this study is a reasonably operational definition of what consitutes physical intuition and an indication of how it enters into the solution of physics problems.

Some clear research tasks lie ahead. We must find more reliable means of detecting the presence or absence of physical intuition in problem-solving behavior. We suspect that skilled subjects will provide fuller and more revealing protocols if we give them more difficult problems than the ones used here, and that is a direction in which we intend to move.

As a clearer picture of the nature of physical intuition emerges, it will become feasible to address some pedagogical issues. What kinds of experiences encourage the growth of physical intuition? How easy is it to learn to take the step from a physical representation of a problem to equations for solving it, and what training will facilitate that step? Is high skill in a subject such as physics attainable purely with algebraic skills and without cultivating physical intuition? How can we diagnose a deficiency in physical intuition when a high level of algebraic skill is present? These questions seem to us to be central to facilitating development and instruction in school subjects that are concerned with understanding the physical world.

ACKNOWLEDGMENTS

This research was supported by Research Grant MH-07722 from the National Institute of Mental Health.

REFERENCES

Bhaskar, R. *Problem solving in semantically rich domains.* Unpublished Ph.D. dissertation, Carnegie–Mellon University, 1977.

Bhaskar, R., & Simon, H. A. Problem solving in semantically rich domains: An example from engineering thermodynamics. *Cognitive Science,* 1977, *1,* 192–215.

Bobrow, D. G. Natural language input for a computer problem-solving system. In M. Minsky (Ed.), *Semantic information processing.* Cambridge, Mass.: MIT Press, 1968.

Brown, J. S., & Burton, R. R. Multiple representations of knowledge for tutorial reasoning. In D. G. Bobrow & A. Collins (Eds.), *Representation and understanding: Studies in cognitive science.* New York: Academic Press, 1975.

Bundy, A. Analyzing mathematical proofs. In P. Winston (Ed.), *Proceedings of the Fourth International Joint Conference on Artificial Intelligence.* Cambridge, Mass.: MIT Press, 1975.

Bundy, A., Luger, G., Stone, M., & Welham, R. MECHO: Year One. In J. M. Brady (Ed.), *Proceedings of the Second AISB Conference.* Edinburgh, Scotland, Department of Artificial Intelligence, University of Edinburgh, 1977.

Chase, W. G., & Simon, H. A. Perception in chess. *Cognitive Psychology,* 1973, *4,* 55–81.

Gagné, R. M. Learning and proficiency in mathematics. *Mathematics Teacher,* 1963, *56,* 620–626.

Greeno, J. G. Indefinite goals in well-structured problems. *Psychological Review,* 1976, *83,* 479–491.

Greeno, J. G. Process of understanding in problem solving. In N. J. Castellan, D. B. Pisoni, & G. R. Potts (Eds.), *Cognitive theory* (Vol. 2). Hillsdale, N.J.: Lawrence Erlbaum Associates, 1977.

Hinsley, D. A., Hayes, J. R., & Simon, H. A. From words to equations: Meaning and representation in algebra word problems. In M. A. Just & P. Carpenter (Eds.), *Cognitive processes in comprehension.* Hillsdale, N. J.: Lawrence Erlbaum Associates, 1977.

Klahr, D., & Wallace, J. G. *Cognitive development: An information-processing view.* Hillsdale, N. J.: Lawrence Erlbaum Associates, 1976.

Larkin, J. *Human problem solving in physica, I: Global features of an information-processing model.* (Working Paper), Group in Science and Mathematics Education, University of California, Berkeley, 1976.

Marples, D. L. *Argument and technique in the solution of problems in mechanics and electricity.* (CUED/C-EDUC/TR1), Department of Engineering, University of Cambridge, England, 1974.

Newell, A., & Simon, H. A. *Human problem solving.* Englewood Cliffs, N.J.: Prentice-Hall, 1972.

Novak, G. S. *Computer understanding of physics problems stated in natural language.* Austin, Tex.: Department of Computer Sciences, The University of Texas (Technical Report NL-30), March 1976.

Paige, J. M., & Simon, H. A. Cognitive processes in solving algebra word problems. In B. Kleinmuntz (Ed.), *Problem solving: Research, method, and theory.* New York: Wiley, 1966.

Taffel, A. *Physics: Its methods and meanings.* Boston: Allyn & Bacon, 1973.

14

Representing Knowledge Development

Gordon H. Bower
Stanford University

My task is to evaluate critically the chapters by Katherine Nelson, Lee Gregg, Steven Kosslyn, and Dorothea and Herbert Simon. The chapters are interesting, informative, and contain much that is praiseworthy. I have relatively few criticisms, most of which are very minor. I hope the contributors will take my remarks in the understanding of my assigned role here.

COMMENTARY ON NELSON'S CHAPTER

Nelson has chosen a good issue to investigate — the child's developing knowledge of everyday events. She probes for this knowledge by asking children to tell her what happens at lunchtime at their day care center and during similar routines. She then examines the sequential character of the child's descriptions of the activities.

I found Nelson's paper, particularly the opening remarks, full of very interesting theoretical questions and distinctions, but somewhat short on useful methods for collecting valid data to decide these questions. I can agree with most of what she says. Yes, of course, the knowledge a child acquires about routine daily activities serves as a background against which he learns to talk about those activities and learns to refer to objects and characteristics of such situations in their absence. And yes, many of these activities have a prototypic serial order to them. And yes, we can readily believe that older or more experienced children will have learned more about the actions, conditions, and objects involved in particular activities. In proving this point, it was unfortunate that in

349

Study II Nelson confounded age with time in residence at the day care center; nonetheless, I am willing to accept her conclusion that children who have been at the center longer know more about its lunchtime routines.

However, all these conclusions would have come as no surprise either to William James or John B. Watson, to mention a few of our august forefathers. The main difference between Nelson and, say, John B. Watson is in their vocabularies. Watson, of course, used the language of stimulus–response habit sequences to talk about routines, whereas Nelson uses the vocabulary of "scripts" that have variable slots that can be instantiated with details of a specific situation.

It is therapeutic to pause on occasion to ask what we have bought in switching to the frame or script formulations and away from the habit sequence vocabulary. I believe the main advantages of frames or scripts are their abstractness, the notions of variable slots, semantic constraints on what are acceptable fillers, and the passing along of variable bindings from one slot to the next in the frame. To put it concretely, it is difficult to state in $S–R$ terms the metarule that in a restaurant scene, for example, the food you eat is usually the same food you ordered as well as the food you pay for. It is not clear when children learn such constraints — Nelson's MacDonald's interviews are silent on the point — but I suppose that appropriate test probes might elicit such information, even from 4-year-old children.

Let me discuss methods for studying scripts. Nelson has chosen to assess children's knowledge of scripts by the interview technique. She asks, "What happens when you eat at MacDonald's?," and follows that with general, then more specific probes. Finally she tabulates common responses and reports commonalty measures. There are several problems with this methodology. The first major problem is that little children do not know how to talk very well; they cannot always plan a lengthy recitation so that it all comes out straight. A second problem is that in normal conversation, even with a child, the answer you get to a question depends very much on what your listener assumes you want. Thus, when I ask you to "Describe what happens at a typical dinner," you will try to make *general* statements rather than instantiating specific details of specific events. If generalities are asked for, then that is what you get from a comprehending adult — you will not often get details of specific instances. This conversational rule might explain the absence of detail in Nelson's children's descriptions of the central event of eating, such as the type of food they ate, how they ate it, and so on. Such details may be deleted because they vary a lot, so that no instance defines the class of lunches. Notice, however, that hamburgers are mentioned for MacDonald's, where such food is invariable. Similarly pizzas and ice cream would be named for pizza parlors and ice cream parlors.

A problem with the free description technique is that the experimenter must rely on order of mention of events as the main indicator of serial knowledge in memory. But order of mention is neither a necessary nor a sufficient condition for inferring a temporally ordered memory structure. Consider some counterexamples. A baseball game unfolds in time. Yet if you read newspaper accounts of games — or listen to people describe a game they have seen — they almost never describe the events of the game inning by inning. They are more likely to mention events in their order of importance in determining the outcome. The sportswriter deliberately renders selected highlights, although his data base — his memory record, if you will — is a temporally ordered set of events. As another counterexample, people's knowledge of their house or apartment is not temporally organized, but if they are asked to describe their house, as did Linde and Labov (1975), people give a temporally ordered tour around the rooms of the house, usually starting with entering the front door. In this case, order of mention depends on spatial contiguity of the objects, as well as where the narrator begins his tour and how he proceeds through the house. Such examples only emphasize that order of mention of actions in a free description is neither necessary nor sufficient evidence for conclusions about a temporal-serial memory structure.

Another hazard of the verbal description method is that a child may name an action or event without fully understanding its proper role in the social act. For instance, a child may mention "Daddy gives money to MacDonald's lady," and may place this act in the correct temporal position. Yet the child may understand nothing of the significance of the giving of money. He may not know that it is an exchange, a fulfillment of an obligation under an implicit social contract, that the amount of money depends on the food ordered, and so on. All of these are testable bits of knowledge. Any of them might be missing even though the child can describe the event of "giving money." The point is that one must be cautious not to attribute more knowledge to children than they have.

There are other ways to probe for knowledge of an event sequence besides free description. One way is to use forced-choice recognition testing. This can be used for identifying likely *objects* or props in a script ("Is your day care lunch more likely to include milk or coke?"); for identifying the *sequence* of canonical events ("Do you nap before or after you eat?"); and for identifying *actors* and their standard *roles* in the scene ("Who's likely to call you to day care lunch, the teacher or your mother?"). Such questions could elicit considerable information that a child has stored about lunch at the day care center. Nelson's "specific probing" technique comes close to such forced-recognition methods.

What do we do with the information so obtained? How do we decide which information, elicited by what means, is in the "lunch script," versus what is ancillary and can be reconstructed from specific instantiations of the general script? This seems to be a nearly unanswerable question. Of the several indexes possible — free description, probed recall, recognition, and enactment — there is no good argument for claiming that information gained by one method is in the memory script whereas the remaining knowledge revealed by a more sensitive method is not in the script. When different retrieval methods provide slightly different answers, we must assume that the methods differ in their ability to tap into the memory that is there as well as differing in the way they get children to talk about what they know.

Having noted some alternative methods for studying scripts, I end with a few cautions, because it is not clear that scripts will solve all our problems regarding the representation of actions. First, it is not clear in Nelson's paper or in Schank and Abelson's (1977) book at what level of abstraction a memory script is to be described. For example, suppose a text is about someone going to visit a particular cardiologist. How do I describe that in memory? Is it an instance of the "visit cardiologist" script, or the "visit doctor" script (including clinical psychologists), or the "visit professional" script (including lawyers), or the "visit a person" script, or a "go to location X and talk to person Y" script? It's all right to say that these are connected in a subset hierarchy and that properties true about scripts at one level are also true about subordinate scripts in the tree; but when we fill in the slots of the new memory structure set up to encode the visit to the cardiologist, from which scripts (and at which levels) are copy tokens pulled?

A second problem is that it is not clear how many contextual variations are stored under one script header. Schank and Abelson (1977) introduce the notion of different tracks through a class of scripts. Thus, I have tracks for dining at MacDonalds, at a summer camp, a cafeteria, a church picnic, a Moroccan bazaar, and so on to the limits of my experience. The place itself tells me which track to call up from memory. But if this is so, then my knowledge is beginning to sound just like a vast collection of specific memories about eating occasions, with a context-dependent specification of roles, props, reasons, typical foods, and action sequences. Where is the conceptual economy of the general script formalism? Another tough problem is to see how context modulates and alters details of a script. To take an example, Nelson had her subjects playact a script in a toy-world of MacDonalds with dolls. How does the toy-ness of that pretend world get passed along as a context to modulate this instantiation of the child's real world restaurant script? The child expects the hamburgers to be plastic and without smell; he doesn't expect to pay real money, and so on. The issue is how we permit a context like "toy world" selectively to cancel certain aspects or expectations of the script but not others.

Despite these reservations, I find the script idea attractive, and I believe Nelson has made some fine, initial explorations into probing for action—knowledge in children. I wish her well with her further efforts.

COMMENTARY ON GREGG'S CHAPTER

Gregg's chapter concerns the child's learning of spatial concepts and the development of exocentric representations. His paper was not available to me when these remarks were prepared, so I have only my memory of his speech to rely on. I generally thought that Gregg's task domain was an interesting one, full of possibilities for research. He has 4- to 5-year-old children learning to guide a toy turtle to a specific destination by remote commands (button presses that rotate the turtle clockwise or counterclockwise, or move it forward). The task requires the child to place himself "on the turtle's head," taking its perspective when deciding whether to move it left or right. Presumably, the child could carry out the instructions if he or she was there in place of the turtle; the problem is therefore one of mapping the turtle's spatial layout onto a set of buttons.

A puzzling result from the first study is that the initial orientation of the turtle with respect to the child produced no differences in the percentage of problems solved without errors. We are left to wonder why. Perhaps it is simply because the task of taking the turtle's perspective is equally difficult regardless of the turtle's orientation with respect to the child. Or perhaps the null result came about because the children inserted extra loops and amusing maneuvers into the turtle manipulations (which were counted as "errors"), and having such fun was more rewarding than getting the turtle directly to its stated goal. The low level of "correct performance" in the first experiments suggests such an interpretation. Later experiments, introducing the horn as an explicit error signal, shaped the children's behavior somewhat more toward the experimenter's criterion of "good behavior."

It would have been informative to have an error analysis of the protocols rather than a report of overall success percentages. I would like to see a breakdown of errors by the type of move, number of steps from beginning to end in the solution sequence, and so on. I suspect that many "errors" were caused by "overshooting," by the child is turning the turtle farther in one direction than the straightline path to the goal. These analytic measures were not reported in Gregg's chapter.

Putting colored earmuffs corresponding to the color of the button on the button on the turtle's head was an ingenious method of converting the problem of perspective orientation into one of color matching. The child merely has to note which ear color is closer to the goal (if the turtle's head is pointed 90° or 270° away from the goal) and press the button of that color to orient the turtle correctly. This "redundant cue" training did not transfer to the task without the earmuff cues. Specific transfer effects really cannot be assessed in this design, however, because there is no control group (one not receiving the color-cue training), and there is a general practice effect across the entire experiment.

Gregg emphasized in his chapter that he was reporting preliminary observations from pilot studies. This is an accurate assessment of the reliability of his findings. Nonetheless, I believe he has developed an interesting task with which he and his colleagues will be able to design experiments to study reliably children's developing spatial perspective abilities. We can wish him well with his continuing investigations in this domain.

COMMENTS ON KOSSLYN'S CHAPTER

I liked Kosslyn's chapter because it is highly organized and well written, and the arguments are laid out in an orderly fashion. I believe that his reasearch provides most impressive evidence regarding the characteristics of our sensory information store and the processes that operate upon it. He is also to be commended for developing an explicit simulation model that appears to capture the major qualitative trends of his data. The existence of a concrete model serves as a good target for focusing scientific efforts; it also eases the job of a commentator, since the bolder and more definite the target, the easier it is to pick away at. Having given proper priority to my very favorable impressions of Kosslyn's paper, I mention a few reservations.

The paper may be divided into four sections. First are some general remarks about how to proceed in theoretical research. Second is a review of Kosslyn's experimental findings on critical issues surrounding the representation of sensory information in memory. Third is the computer simulation model. Fourth are some experiments on children's handling of sensory information.

First, I simply did not understand the reference to teleology and its relevance to developmental psychology; I do not see how final goal states can be a reasonable explanation of cognitive development. Specifically, I do not believe that a child's knowledge of adult cognitive processes is what causes him to develop them; instead, a lot of social modeling and interactive learning in an educational environment would appear to be largely responsible.

Second, laying down in advance and following a "decision tree" regarding critical issues in theory development (as Kosslyn advocates) is nice if and when you can manage it. But, alas, very little scientific research that I know of proceeds with such surefooted mowing down of thoughtful alternatives. My impression is that we mostly bumble and bungle along, thrashing about for some new idea or experiment to keep ourselves busy and out of mischief. I suspect Kosslyn's decision tree is, in fact, a reconstruction of a poorly ordered research history, done sometime after the fact and after considerable research had shown that his four issues were indeed of primary importance. But only he can evaluate the truth of that.

In the second section of his paper, Kosslyn adduces evidence for the view that mental imagery is not epiphenomenal but contains real information. Let us concede at the outset that organisms — people among them — store descriptions of sensory information, of patterns, and that this includes spatial measures such as the approximate size of familiar objects and the size and location of parts relative to the whole object (e.g., the size and location of the nose relative to the whole human face). We may suppose that this normative size and location information is attached directly to the concept nodes in memory networks that represent common objects such as rabbits, collies, and German shepherd's ears. It is an interesting intellectual exercise to see how much of Kosslyn's data can be handled by a processor working over such a semantic network, where imagery is not essentially involved (Pylyshyn, 1973). On this theory, the internal TV is tuned on simply for the amusement of the executive monitor but it has no real function. (Although I don't believe this thesis [i.e., I think Kosslyn is right], the Devil's Advocate role helps to clarify critical from noncritical experiments. Kosslyn and I have played out this scenario several times before to sharpen his arguments.)

A first impression is that one cannot think of how the results could have come out other than they did, given the way Kosslyn's basic experiments were run. Kosslyn induces his subjects to engage in an elaborate game of pretense or role playing. They play a perceptual game of "as if." Consider, for example, his investigation of the visual angle of the "mind's eye." Kosslyn says to his subject: "Suppose there's a cow standing over by the wall. Now, walk up to it until it fills your whole visual field, then stop. Okay, fine. Now suppose there's a skunk over there. Walk up to it until it fills your field," and so on. If you're a compliant subject, how can you possibly act sensibly on such instructions? Only by accessing your stored metric information about lengths of cows (say they're 6 ft long), and then walking up to the wall until you can just barely see a six-foot length of wall within a foveal ring. You play the same charade for skunks, elephants, and the like. Of course, when Kosslyn plots the distance you stop from the wall, it will increase linearly with the length of the animal. Yet, you never had to image anything to do the job. You would give the same data if Kosslyn told you to "image" a mythical object called a "Glunk" with only the information that it was 10 ft long.

Kosslyn answers this objection by noting that we assume a sensory magnitude component when we suppose the subject can judge a six-foot length on the wall. In other words, my objection begs the very abilities it presumes to question.

Next, consider Kosslyn's data that the time needed to scan from one object to another in an image is a function of the objects' physical distance. If you read Kosslyn's instructions carefully, they make it clear that the person is not simply to say whether the second object is in the picture; rather, he is to "scan over" to it and push the button after he arrives. The obvious demand characteristic of such instructions is that the subject should output times that are linearly related to the stored distance between the two objects. You would get the same data if I simply told you to output a response time proportional to the time it takes to drive from any point to another. But is it necessary to assume imagery is involved? Kosslyn could have the subject change the size of the "subjective map" or the speed of the "scanner," but this should simply result in a linear transformation of the response times. As an incidental comment, I suppose Kosslyn is aware that the time required to shift the gaze from one spot to another in physical space is determined by the latency of a saccad, which is nearly constant and independent of the physical distance between points (within limits).

Kosslyn would reply in three ways. First, I again beg the question of magnitude information when I assume a subject can (mysteriously) output an analog reaction time proportional to a distance. Second, several of his distance experiments did not instruct the subject so explicitly on scanning, so the compliance with demand characteristics should be less troublesome. Third, a map with 10 or so objects in it has 45 interpoint distances. It is inconceivable that subjects would compute, store, and use all such interpoint distances to guide their later reaction times. One needs a simpler representation of a map and something like a "scanner" to get Kosslyn's results. I become more convinced he is right.

Having examined some of the experimental evidence Kosslyn presents, let us turn to the simulation model of image generation that he and Schwartz have worked out. I found it a most intriguing model, well worth careful study. First, I like their idea of a visual short-term memory, where an image needs to be continually refreshed from long-term memory or it will fade out. This concept allows them to specify storage capacity in terms of the number of holdable chunks, where chunks may be objects or parts of objects. This clearly implies a tradeoff between the number of objects and the amount of detail that can be held active at one time in visual short-term memory. What Kosslyn does not elaborate on here are the conditions under which the processing of external stimuli will interfere with material in visual short-term memory. Experiments by Brooks (1968), Byrne (1975), Kroll (1975), and Segal and Fusella (1970) are clearly relevant to this issue of modality-specific interference, but it is not obvious how Kosslyn's model would deal with these differing results. That is something requiring further development.

I liked Kosslyn's way of representing perceptual information in terms of polar coordinates, the (R, Θ) pairs for points on the contours of an object. Although he doesn't mention it, I suppose one really has to store only the coordinates of inflection points, since these convey the most information about shape; a simple point connector can then fill in straight lines between the inflection points to draw a reasonable contour (see Attneave, 1954). As Kosslyn notes, the (R, Θ) format makes it easy to expand or contract images or to rotate them in the picture plane. What this representation lacks, of course, is the third dimension in which real objects exist. That requires another Θ value for each point. The model knows only a flat, two-dimensional world, whereas a real brain knows about projective geometry, knows how to relate an object's image size to its distance away in space, knows how to rotate an image in the depth plane, knows about occlusion, foregrounding, haze cues to depth, and so on. But again, these are issues for further development of the model.

One objection to the computer model is that it does not address itself to one topic that has concerned imagery researchers for the past 10 years: Why does mental imagery improve memory? Why are pictures remembered better than words? Why are concrete words or sentences remembered better than abstract words or sentences? These are the issues Paivio (1971), myself, and many others have been concerned with. In his chapter, Kosslyn does not show how his model helps to clarify such issues. One way to augment the model to handle the benefits of imagery in paired-associateds learning is to assume that a semantic relation between two concrete concepts can be displayed on the internal TV screen and that this interactive scene can be stored in memory as a new data file. Thus, for the pair **DOG—HAT**, the system might store an image of a **DOG** wearing a **HAT**. A similar idea has been in the imagery and learning literature for 10 years. The problem is to deduce from that view the hypotheses needed to handle the myriad of findings in this area. For example, how would it explain the fact that paired-associates learning is helped by interactive imagery but not by imaging noninteracting objects standing side by side (see Bower, 1970)? Of course, the preliminary report of a new model should not be seriously faulted for the topics not immediately covered and explained by it. Perhaps a fairer attitude is to wait and see what develops from Kosslyn's active theoretical program.

I found Kosslyn's speculations at the end of his chapter interesting and worth pursuing. I agree with his conjecture that if we repeatedly query a subject's perceptual store (e.g., "Does a Volkswagen have ventwings?"), he will soon store the answer verbally. Perhaps this is a model of how children convert perceptual knowledge into verbal codes. I believe that people make such conversions only when someone explicitly asks for the implicit information. That is, I do not believe that children sit around spontaneously formulating propositions about their experience. They may be taught how to question others as well as themselves, but that would seem to be a kind of metaknowledge that I suspect most of us rarely use.

Having offered these criticisms of Kosslyn's paper, let me end by emphasizing again my highly positive reaction to his research and theoretical program. It is bold and imaginative. I believe my Devil's Advocacy has not really damaged his case. Kosslyn infers (properly, I believe) that the cumulative weight of his evidence supports his theoretical position. His theory also leads to several important developmental questions, as he illustrates at the end of his chapter. These developmental questions provide a rich lode to be mined by researchers in future years.

COMMENTS ON THE CHAPTER BY DOROTHEA AND HERBERT SIMON

In their paper on solving physics problems, the Simons characterize the performances of two problem solvers of quite different talents, and they indicate the similarities, as well as differences, in their approaches to problem solving. Specifically, they use production systems to model the sequences of equations the two subjects use while solving 19 problems involving the laws of motion. The subjects think aloud as they work. The protocols are then analyzed by content to decide which equation the subject is thinking of. The edited protocols are then reported in the Simons' Table 13.2, which contains the final data, comparing the solution paths of the two subjects to the authors' simulations.

My first comment is that there seem to be very few errors indeed, very little search, and few false starts that required backing up. The subjects seemed to have gone straight through the problems, varying greatly in the time they took to reach the solution. Because there are so few mistakes, one wonders how much we should be impressed by the correspondence between the production system model and the data. If the problems so constrain behavior that all the subject can do is plug into one formula or sequence of formulas, then it takes no strong scientific theory to predict that he will usually do just that. I could not tell how much uncertainty there was regarding the successful solution path for a given type of problem. Are there really more than two or three ways to get to most solutions? Once a theorist notices how someone characteristically handles problems of a given type, then he simply predicts that the subject will be consistent with later problems of that type. This does not seem to be a major theoretical accomplishment.

What parts of the problem-solving process are not modeled by the Simons' production system models? First, they have clearly ignored the language input part, the parsing device that identified variable names, relations among variables, and so on. Moreover, the model treats the problem formally, in terms of abstract variables only. I suspect that this is unrealistic. Studies of logical reasoning (with syllogisms) have repeatedly found that subjects are very much affected by the way the premises are stated as well as by the content of the premises. Logically equivalent paraphrases of the premises are not psychologically equivalent. Similar influences can be expected when novices solve kinematics problems. One aspect of the expert's talent probably is his ability to extract a relevant formal description from the specific contents of the problem.

A second problem is that the simulation does not predict the few mistakes there are — the incorrect substitutions, false starts, and subjects' detection of their false starts. For instance, the model for $S2$, the slower subject, cannot calculate something and then say "Oh no, that's not what I want." But their protocols probably include many such boo-boos. The simulation does not predict the ubiquitous checking and rechecking of the answers that both subjects show, nor does it deal with $S2$'s rehearsal and summarizing of what is known and what is wanted for the problem.

Because the model does not deal with these issues or with memory searching, it does not predict the difficulty of the various problems or the time required to solve each. The solution time is not simply related to the number of equations evoked in the solution path.

As the Simons point out, the production system models provide a slightly misleading characterization of the relative skills of the expert and novice problem solvers. The model of the novice, $S2$, uses careful means—ends analyses for goal-directed planning, whereas the model of the expert, $S1$, "blindly" calculates new quantities from the givens, hoping to stumble on the desired variable. As a result, $S2$ often has fewer equations in her solution path than $S1$ has in his. She appears to be more efficient and planful, in the eyes of the model. The slack was taken up informally when the Simons claimed that the real differences were, first, that the expert calculates more swiftly and more confidently than the novice, and second, that the expert has better "physical intuitions" than the novice, thus helping him select the right equations. The Simons' data provide only exceedingly indirect evidence that the expert uses physical models. They also do not make clear how a model of the physical situation would call the production system to evoke appropriate equations. That interfacing would be interesting to see, but that is not what the chapter is about. One would like to have a generator of physics situations (like Kosslyn's procedures) that will turn on its TV screen and draw an internal model of the relevant variables and physical interrelationships described by the problem.

I have a few questions about production systems as models of psychological processes. A first question is this: Given a small sample of someone's behavior on a short list of kinematics problems (or any other kind), can any reasonably consistent behavior be reasonably well modeled by some production system? In other words, does the fact that the Simons developed a production system from each subject's solution path lend credibility to the production system method of theorizing? Second, would it not be proper to test a production system model by predicting what the subject will do on a new set of problems, either equivalent paraphrases of the prior problems or concatenations (embeddings) of them? Third, production system models are deterministic and therefore falsified by a single misprediction. If we use a criterion of falsifiability to advance our theories, will not all production system models quickly become rejected corpses along the roadsides of scientific progress? This reaction of mine probably reflects a fundamental difference in preference for deterministic versus probabilistic models.

I close my comments on the Simon and Simon paper by noting that they use the "thinking aloud" method for collecting data. At issue is whether such introspections validly report cognitive processes. Simon and Simon view their subjects' introspective reports as veridical indicators of when a production (equation) has been evoked and/or is being applied. They believe that the verbal report either precedes or occurs coincidentally with the theoretical process their simulation theory is about, namely, noticing the current conditions, evoking equations from memory, substituting values for variables, or performing the arithmetic operations. However, it may be the case that most problem-solving gymnastics occur outside of consciousness, so that only products of cognitive operations are available for report, and even these self-reports lag considerably behind, describing only those decisions that occurred several seconds previously.

I have recently been reading the literature on the accuracy (or rather inaccuracy!) of self-reports. I was particularly impressed by a paper by Nisbett and Wilson (1977) entitled "Telling more than we can know: Verbal reports on mental processes." They systematically marshall evidence for the view that people are often not aware of what they are doing, of how they have changed, of what is causing their actions, of what stimuli are controlling their feelings and behaviors. The main occasions when they happen to guess their controlling variables correctly is when the alternatives are few and conspicuous and when there is a cultural belief or causal schema which says that people's behavior in situations of type X are often reflections of this or that controlling variable.

Consider just a few examples of non-rule-governed behaviors in which introspections about causal events are false and misleading. Latané and Darley (1970) found that the biggest single variable inhibiting helping behavior from bystanders to a potential disaster (e.g., an epileptic seizure, a sickness, a robbery) was how many other bystanders heard or saw the same scene and remained passive. Yet, if you ask subjects who have been through the experiment, they almost never report that it was the presence of that passive audience that inhibited their helping. You get the same discounting from people who simply imagine the bystander apathy situation: They always underestimate the impact of social pressure. Another example: As part of an apparent consumer survey, women in a department store were asked to indicate their preference among many pairs of nylon stockings. It happened that the biggest factor in the entire experiment was the left-right positioning of the alternative (counterbalanced across types of stockings); the stocking presented on the subject's right was preferred almost four to one over that presented to her left, regardless of what it was. Yet, no subject identified position of the alternative stockings as the controlling variable. In fact, when asked that question directly, after having been shown the four-to-one preference, the women thought the questioner was crazy. Their causal schema supposed that people prefer stockings for their quality, texture, sheer appearance, and so on, not because of their left-right presentation position.

Simon and Simon may accede to these remarks about the inaccuracy of causal attributions in self-reports, but they would reply that the remarks are irrelevant to the manner in which they are using self-reports in their work. They use the person's report only as an indicator of which equation is in the current focus of attention, and they are not concerned here with modeling the subject's beliefs about what is causing different equations to come to mind in the order they do. In other words, they ascribe no causal validity to any attributions their subjects might have given, so the criticism simply does not apply to their work. This is probably correct in this instance.

FINAL COMMENTS

Before closing I want to share some thoughts with you about our popular conceptions of scientific criticism. This is the first time I have assumed the role of public discussant; I have found it a most disagreeable job. I dislike the role of examining someone's prized writing, looking for possible flaws or things to take issue with or disagree about. It is particularly distressing to do this with work of the quality of that by Nelson, Gregg, Kosslyn, and Simon and Simon. I have not enjoyed doing this hatchet job.

Why are critics enjoined to do this? It is the popular belief that Science and Truth (with capital S and T) are best advanced by the fine polishing of rough ideas before the hoary, deliberate sandblastings delivered by intellectual adversaries. This belief underlies the popular scientific debating style of challenging, questioning, probing, and seeking to find the weakest spot in someone's argument.

However, as I grow older and more mellow, I have become increasingly disenchanted with that adversarial view. It leads to devastating criticisms that are terribly destructive of the spirit, self-esteem, and enthusiasm of the parties involved as well as the onlookers. First and foremost, scientists are human beings whose productive work requires sincere praise and encouragement from peers in order for them to maintain enthusiasm for their scientific pursuits. Nothing kills our enthusiasm and joy in our work more than receiving a steady diet of nitpicking criticisms and put-downs. I believe it is much more beneficial to support one another and encourage one another's best efforts. From my perspective, what is good about a conference like this one is that it brings together a community of scholars, many of whom have been friends for years, and who respect and support one another. We depend on one another, not only for intellectual stimulation, but also for emotional support and reinforcement.

This is why the role of critic is so nihilistic and life denying. I propose that in the future we dispense with the critic and replace him or her with a Grand Celebrator, a Herald, a Cheerleader, who leaps up to proclaim the depth and originality of the participant's ideas and findings. Such a hornblower would surely make all of us — participants as well as onlookers — feel a lot better about ourselves and the professional life in which we toil.

To right the wrongs in just a small way, I thank the participants for the achivements of the intellect that have brought their work together in this volume. I thank them for sharing with us their new perspectives and insights into the topics. I have been impressed and inspired by the ideas, speculations, and new experiments reported here. We celebrate their achievements. They should feel good about themselves for what their dedication and work have contributed to knowledge.

REFERENCES

Attneave, F. Some informational aspects of visual perception. *Psychological Review,* 1954, *61,* 183–193.

Bower, G. H. Imagery as a relational organizer in associative learning. *Journal of Verbal Learning and Verbal Behavior,* 1970, *9,* 529–533.

Brooks, L. R. Spatial and verbal components of the act of recall. *Canadian Journal of Psychology,* 1968, *22,* 349–368.

Byrne, B. Item concreteness vs. spatial organization as predictors of visual imagery. *Memory and Cognition,* 1974, *2,* 53–59.

Kroll, N. E. A. Visual short-term memory. In D. Deutsch & J. A. Deutsch (Eds.), *Short-term memory.* New York: Academic Press, 1975.

Latané, B., & Darley, J. M. *The unresponsive bystander: Why doesn't he help?* New York: Appleton-Century-Crofts, 1970.

Linde, C., & Labov, W. Spatial networks as a site for the study of language and thought. *Language,* 1975, *51,* 924–939.

Nisbett, R. E., & Wilson, T. D. Telling more than we know: Verbal reports on mental processes. *Psychological Review,* 1977, *84,* 231–259.

Paivio, A. *Imagery and verbal processes.* New York: Holt, Rinehart & Winston, 1971.

Pylshyn, Z. W. What the mind's eye tells the mind's brain: A critique of mental imagery. *Psychological Bulletin,* 1973, *80,* 1–24.

Schank, R., & Abelson, R. *Scripts, plans, goals, and understanding.* Hillsdale, N.J.: Lawrence Erlbaum Associates, 1977.

Segal, S. J., & Fusella, V. Influence of imaged pictures and sounds on detection of visual and auditory signals. *Journal of Experimental Psychology,* 1970, *83,* 458–464.

Author Index

Numbers in italic indicate the pages on which the complete reference appears

A

Abelson, R. P., 256, 257, 260, 270, *273,* 352, *362*
Abrahamson, A., 155, 156, 178, *179*
Acredolo, L. P., 24, *31*
Ahr, P. R., 164, 165, 175, 176, *179*
Allen, T. W., 117, *148*
Ames, E. W., 21, *31*
Ammon, P., 52, *70*
Anderson, J. R., 296, *321*
Anderson, R. C., 178, *180*
Angelev, J., 117, *148*
Arlin, P. K., 63, *67*
Attneave, F., 356, *362*

B

Baddeley, A. D., 80, *95*
Ball, T. M., 297, 308, *322*
Banerji, R., 130, *149*
Baron, J., 75, *95*
Barratt, B. B., 117, *147*
Bates, E., 50, 60, *67*
Baylor, G. W., 295, *321*
Beale, I. L., 281, *289*
Beck, I. L., 16, *34*
Beckwith, M., 214, *240*
Bellugi, U., 146, *148*

Belmont, J. M., 9, 11, *32,* 74, *96*
Bemesderfer, M. E., 312, 320, *322*
Bever, T. G., 49, 50, 51, *67,* 305, *321*
Bhaskar, R., 326, 332, 336, *347*
Biemiller, A., 45, *67*
Bigi, L., 99, *105*
Bloom, L. M., 276, *289*
Bobrow, D. G., 326, *347*
Bovet, M., 12, *33,* 40, 45, 61, *69*
Bower, G. H., 296, 315, *321, 357, 362*
Bower, T. G. H., 55, 58, *67*
Boychuk, L., 45, *67*
Boyes-Braem, P., 145, *149*
Braine, M., 133, 146, *148*
Brainerd, C. J., 111, 117, 118, *148,* 171, 173,
174, 176, 177, *179,* 240, *240*
Bransford, J. D., 14, *31*
Brener, R., 76, *95*
Brian, C. R., 314, *321*
Broadbent, D. E., 85, *95*
Bronner, A. F., 51, *67*
Brooks, L. R., 356, *362*
Brown, A. L., 3, 6, 7, 8, 11, 12, 13, 14, 16,
19, 20, 27, 28, 31, *32,* 34, 35, 73, 87, 88,
95
Brown, J. S., 326, *347*
Brown, R., 146, *148*
Bruner, J. S., 21, 22, *34,* 44, *67,* 292, *321*
Bryant, P. E., 45, *67*
Buchanan, M., 80, *95*

Bucher, B., 45, *67*
Bundy, A., 326, *347*
Burke, D., 17, *33,* 74, *96*
Burton, R. R., 326, *347*
Butterfield, E. C., 9, 11, *32,* 74, *96*
Byrne, B., 356, *362*
Byrnes, M. A., 183, *211*

C

Campione, J. C., 11, 16, 20, *32, 35,* 87, *95*
Campos, J. J., 58, *69*
Carpenter, P. A., 119, *148*
Carroll, J. B., 75, *96*
Carson, M. T., 155, 156, 178, *179*
Case, R., 44, 45, 48, 50, 51, 53, 58, 62, *67,*
    68, 75, *96,* 117, 118, *148*
Cazden, C., 146, *148*
Charlesworth, W. R., 183, *211*
Chase, W. G., 81, 82, 84, 85, 90, *96,* 327,
    347
Chi, M. T. H., 4, 7, 13, 17, *32,* 58, 68, 74,
    76, 77, 79, *96*
Chiesi, H. L., 81, *96*
Chomsky, C., 53, *68*
Church, J., 255, 256, *273*
Chzhi-tsin, B., 21, 22, *35*
Cole, M., 27, *33*
Collings, A. M., 316, 319, *321*
Conrad, C., 300, *322*
Cook, T. W., 183, *211*
Corballis, M. C., 281, *289*
Craik, F. I. M., 5, *33*

D

Daehler, M. A., 23, *33*
Dale, L., 48, *68*
Dale, L. G., 110, 111, *148*
Daneman, M., 50, 53, *68*
Darley, J. M., 360, *362*
Day, J. D., 19, *32*
Day, M. C., 21, 25, *33*
DeAvila, E., 48, *68*
DeForest, M., 25, *34*
Dempster, F. N., 58, *68,* 75, 76, 80, *96*
Diaz, S., 48, *68*
Donaldson, M., 164, *179*
Drozdal, J. G., 25, *33*
Dulit, E., 110, *148*

E

Egan, D. E., 183, *211*
Egeland, B., 25, *33*
Eggleston, V. H., 178, *180,* 214, 239, *241*
Eisenstadt, M., 81, *96*
Eriksen, C. W., 294, *322*
Ernst, G. W., 130, *149,* 286, *290*

F

Fabian, V., 51, 53, *68*
Faddis, C., 278, *290*
Farley, A. M., 295, *322*
Farnham-Diggory, S., 276, *290*
Feinstein, K. J., 312, 320, *322*
Fergunson, C., 239, *240*
Fischer, K. W., 58, *70,* 99, *105*
Fischer, W., 58, *69*
Fitch, J. P., 24, *34*
Flavell, E. R., 99, *105*
Flavell, J. H., 5, 6, 13, 24, 25, *33, 34, 35,* 87,
    96, 98, 99, 103, 104, *105,* 147, *148,* 291,
    322
Franks, J. J., 14, *31*
Friedrichs, A. G., 87, *96,* 103, *105*
Fusella, V., 356, *362*

G

Gagné, R. M., 40, *68,* 183, *212,* 283, *290,*
    326, *347*
Gallistel, C. R., 213, 218, 219, 226, 233, *240*
Gamlin, P., 52, *70*
Garner, W. R., 294, *322*
Gast, H., 216, 236, *240*
Gelman, R., 40, 45, *68,* 178, *179,* 213, 218,
    219, 224, 226, 233, 236, *240, 241*
Gentner, D. R., 15, *34*
Gibson, E. J., 21, *33,* 144, *148*
Gibson, F. J., 40, *68*
Ginsburg, H., 216, 217, *240*
Glass, A. L., 315, *321*
Globerson, T., 48, *68*
Goodenough, F. L., 314, *321*
Goodson, B. D., 51, *68*
Gordon, F. R., 25, *33*
Gray, W. D., 145, *149*
Greenfield, P. M., 51, *68,* 292, *321*
Greeno, J. G., 11, 18, *33,* 130, *148* 183, 191,
    211, 212, 326, *347*

Gregg, L. W., 276, 278, *290*
Grieve, R., 163, 165, 167, 173, 177, *180*

H

Hake, H. W., 294, *322*
Halford, G. S., 40, 46, *68, 69*
Harris, P. L., 23, *33*
Havassy, B., 48, *68*
Hayes, J. R., 16, *33* 186, *212*, 326, *347*
Heart, W., 51, *67*
Hegion, A. G., 24, *34*
Hester, M., 278, *290*
Hinsley, D. A., 326, *347*
Hirst, W., 59, *70*
Hormann, A., 183, *212*
Hoyt, J. D., 87, *96*, 103, *105*
Hughes, M., 163, 165, 167, 173, 177, *180*
Hunt, J. McV., 55, *70*
Huttenlocher, J., 17, *33*, 74, *96*, 287, *290*

I

Inhelder, B., 12, *33*, 40, 45, *69*, 109, 110,
    111, 113, 117, 119, 121, *148, 149*, 152,
    153, 154, 159, 162, 177, *179*, 283, *290*,
    292, *322*
Isen, A. M., 157, 158, 160, 161, 162, 175,
    176, 177, *179*
Istomina, Z. M., 15, 24, 28, 30, *33, 35*

J

Jackson, E., 58, *69*
Jackson, S., 110, 111, *148*
Johnson, D. M., 145, *149*
Johnson, L. J., 145, *149*
Just, M. A., 119, *148*

K

Kagan, J., 314, *322*
Kaplan, E., 276, *290*
Kaprove, B. H., 24, *34*
Kareev, Y., 81, *96*
Kaszor, P., 171, 173, 174, 176, 177, *179*
Kelley, J., 304, *323*

Klahr, D., 8, 9, 11, 12, 13, 26, 39, 40,
    45, *69*, 99, 104, *105*, 111, 119, *148*, 152,
    154, 159, 164, *179*, 188, 211, *212*, 214,
    241, 325, *347*
Klix, F., 183, *212*
Knobloch, H., 50, *69*
Kobasigawa, A., 24, *33*
Kosslyn, S. M., 292, 294, 295, 297, 298, 299,
    301, 304, 306, 308, 309, 311, 312, 317,
    319, 320, *322*
Kreutzer, M. A., 25, *33*, 87, *96*
Kroll, N. E. A., 356, *362*
Kuhn, D., 12, *33*, 117, *148*
Kuhn, T., 110, *148*
Kurland, M., 45, 50, 52, *68, 69*

L

Labov, W., 351, *362*
Lakatos, I., 243, *251*
Langendoen, D. T., 50, *67*
Langer, J., 45, *70*
Larkin, J., 326, *347*
Latané, B., 360, *362*
Latz, E., 21, *35*
Lawton, S. C., 19, *32*
Lea, G., 296, *322*
Lee, L. C., 111, *148*
Lefebvre, M., 45, *69*
Lemkin, J., 314, *322*
Lempers, J. D., 99, *105*
Leonard, C., 25, *33*, 87, *96*
Leung, E. H. L., 99, *105*
Levy, V. M., Jr., 25, *35*, 87, *96*
Liben, L. S., 102, *105*
Liebert, D. E., 117, *149*
Liebert, R. M., 117, *149*
Lindauer, B. K., 102, *105*
Linde, C., 351, *362*
Little, S., 304, *323*
Lockhart, R. S., 5, *33*
Loughlin, K. A., 23, *33*
Lovell, K., 110, 111, *148*
Lowe, G. M., 51, *67*
Luger, G., 326, *347*
Luria, A. R., 146, *148*, 230, *241*
Lyon, D., 74, 77, *96*

M

MacDonald, C., 44, *69*
Mackworth, N. H., 21, 22, *34*

Mal'tseva, K. P., 15, *35*
Mandler, J. M., 25, *34*
Maratsos, M. P., 270, *273*
Markman, E., 168, 169, 173, 177, 178, *179, 180*
Markman, E. M., 13, *34,* 87, *96*
Marples, D. L., 326, 336, *347*
Martorano, S. C., 111, *148*
Masur, B., 23, *35*
Maurer, D., 21, *34*
McGarrigle, J., 163, 165, 167, 173, 177, *180*
McLanahan, A. G., 158, 165, 166, 169, 170, *180*
McLaughlin, G. H., 44, *69*
McNemar, Q., 52, *69*
Meacham, J. A., 27, *34*
Menninger, K., 217, *241*
Merkin, S., 237, *241*
Mervis, C. B., 145, *149*
Miller, G. A., 61, *69,* 76, *96*
Miller, P. H., 99, *105*
Moran, T. P., 295, *322*
Murphy, G. L., 312, 320, *322*
Murphy, M. D., 28, *34,* 87, *95*

N

Nadolny, T., 23, *35*
Neimark, E. D., 111, *148*
Neisser, U., 59, *70,* 183, *212*
Nelson, K., 19, *34,* 257, *273,* 276, *290*
Nelson, K. E., 317, *322*
Neves, D. A., 183, 211, *212*
Newell, A., 119, *148,* 182, 286, *290,* 292, 305, *322,* 333, *348*
Nisbett, R. E., 360, *362*
Nitsch, K. W., 14, *31*
Noelting, G., 38, 39, 60, 63, *69*
Norman, D. A., 15, *34*
Noton, D., 22, *34*
Novak, G. S., 326, 337, *348*

O

Oakley, D. D., 20, *35*
Olsen, M. G., 24, *31*
Olson, D. R., 22, *34*
Olver, R. R., 292, *321*

P

Paige, J. M., 326, 339, *348*
Paivio, A., 357, *362*
Papert, S., 275, *290*
Paris, S. G., 102, *105*
Parkinson, G. M., 48, *69*
Pasamanick, B., 50, *69*
Pascual-Leone, J., 37, 44, 45, 48, 55, 61, *70*
Peterson, J., 183, *212*
Piaget, J., 37, 39, 40, 44, *70,* 109, 110, 111, 113, 117, 119, 121, *148, 149,* 152, 153, 154, 159, 162, 164, 177, *179, 180,* 183, 189, 208, *212,* 240, *241,* 283, *290,* 292, *322*
Pick, A. D., 146, *149*
Pick, H. L., 24, *31*
Pick, H. L., Jr., 146, *149*
Pinard, A., 45, *69*
Platt, J. R., 294, *322*
Pomerantz, J. R., 295, *322*
Popper, K. R., 294, *322*
Portnuff, W., 51, *68*
Posner, M. I., 48, *70*
Presson, C. C., 287, *290*
Pufall, P. B., 145, *149*
Pushkina, A. G., 22, *34*
Pylyshyn, Z. W., 295, 296, *322,* 355, *362*

Q

Quillian, M. R., 316, 319, *321*

R

Reed, S. K., 130, *149*
Reese, H. W., 145, 146, *149*
Reinfeld, F. 81, *96*
Reiser, B. J., 297, 308, *322*
Reitman, J. S., 81, 84, 85, *96*
Resnick, L. B., 16, *34*
Restle, F., 214, *240*
Rheingold, H. L., 99, *105*
Ricciuti, H. N., 145, *149*
Riley, C. A., 157, 158, 160, 161, 162, 175, 176, 177, *179*
Ripps, L. J., 300, 311, *323*
Ritter, K., 24, *34, 35*
Rochford, M., 45, *67*
Rosch, E., 145, *149,* 155, *180*

Rosenthal, T. L., 47, *71*
Ruff, H. A., 21, *34*
Ryan, S. M., 24, *34*

S

Salapetek, P., 21, *34*
Samokhvalova, V. I., 15, *35*
Scardamalia, M., 44, 47, 48, *70*
Schaeffer, B., 99, 102, *105,* 178, *180,* 214, 239, *241*
Schank, R. C., 256, 257, 260, 270, *273,* 352, *362*
Schneider, R. E., 45, *67*
Scott, J. L., 178, *180,* 214, 239, *241*
Scribner, S., 27, *33*
Segal, S. J., 356, *362*
Seibert, J., 168, 169, 173, 177, 178, *180*
Serlin, R., 48, *68*
Shanks, B., 133, 146, *148*
Shaw, R. E., 145, *149*
Shimberg, H. E., 51, *67*
Shipley, E., 164, *180*
Shoben, E. J., 300, 311, *323*
Shwartz, S. P., 309, 311, *322*
Siegler, R. S., 8, 9, 11, 26, *33, 34,* 45, *70,* 111, 112, 118, 120, 121, 122, 130, 133, 137, 138, 140, 143, *148, 149,* 188, 195, 210, *212,* 285, *290*
Silfen, C. K., 21, *31*
Simon, H. A., 37, 38, 48, 58, *70,* 76, 81, 82, 84, 85, 90, *96,* 119, *148,* 182, 183, 186, 187, 188, 189, 191, 193, 195, *212,* 286, *290, 295, 323,* 326, 327, 332, 333, 336, 339, *347, 348*
Sinclair, H., 12, *33* 40, 45, *69*
Slobin, D. I., 50, *70,* 276, *290*
Smedslund, J., 317, *323*
Smiley, S. S., 6, 8, 19, 20, *32, 34*
Smirnov, A. A., 15, *35*
Smith, E. C., Jr., 183, *212*
Smith, E. E., 300, 311, *323*
Smith, J., 45, 48, *69*
Smock, C. D., 40, *69*
Snow, C., 239, *240*
Spelke, E., 59, *70*
Spilich, G., 81, *96*
Spitz, H., 183, *211*
Stark, L., 22, *34*
Starr, A. S., 76, *96*
Stechler, G., 21, *35*

Steinberg, E. R., 178, *180*
Stevens, A. L., 15, *34*
Stone, M., 326, *347*
Strauss, S., 45, *70*
Suchman, R. G., 314, *323*
Suci, G. J., 52, *70*
Sullivan, E. V., 45, *70*
Sydow, H., 183, *212*

T

Taffel, A., 325, *348*
Tarakanov, V. V., 21, 22, *35*
Thomas, E. L., 22, *35*
Thompson, N., 80, *95*
Tomlinson-Keasey, C., 111, *149*
Townsend, M. A. R., 19, *32*
Trabasso, T., 157, 158, 160, 161, 162, 175, 176, 177, *179,* 314, *323*
Tucker, M. F., 224, 233, 236, *240*
Tucker, T., 157, 158, 160, 161, 162, 175, 176, 177, *179*

U

Uzgiris, I. C., 55, *70*

V

Vago, S., 111, 119, 120, 133, *149*
Voss, J. F., 81, *96*
Vurpillot, E., 22, *35*
Vygotsky, L. S., 15, *35*

W

Wales, R. J., 164, *179*
Wallace, J. G., 39, 40, 45, *69,* 99, 104, *105,* 111, 119, *148,* 152, 154, 159, 164, *179,* 211, 214, *241,* 325, *347*
Wambold, C., 9, *32,* 74, *96*
Watson, J. S., 55, *70*
Watson, M. W., 58, *70*
Webb, R. A., 23, *35*
Weber, R. J., 304, *323*
Weir, M. W., 145, *149*
Welham, R., 326, *347*
Wellman, H. M., 8, 13, 24, *33, 35*

Werner, H., 276, *290*
White, B. L., 58 *70*
White, S. H., 62, *71*
Wilkinson, A., 153, 154, 159, 168, 173, 174, *180*
Wilson, T. D., 360, *362*
Winer, G. A., 173, 174, *180*
Winograd, T., 13, *35*
Wohlwill, J. F., 156, 157, 159, 169, 173, 174, *180*
Woods, W. A., 13, *35*
Worthen, D., 20, *35*

Y

Youniss, J., 164, 165, 175, 176, *179*
Yussen, S. R., 25, *35*, 87, *96*

Z

Zimmerman, B. J., 47, *71*
Zinchenko, V. F., 21, 22, *35*

Subject Index

A

Attentional capacity, 58–59

B

Baby biographies, 255–56
Backward extrapolation strategy, 291
Balance scale task, 9, 11–12, 109–147, 195, 245–246
Basic events, 259

C

Chess, 80–92, 102
Chunking, 9, 44, 76, 81, 83–87, 289, 297
Class inclusion, 151–179, 244–245
  decision rules for, 154, 175–177
Cognitive development, general theory of, 99–100
Cognitive maps, 276, 282–284, 287–289
Computer simulation, 37–38, 188–197, 203, 246–247, 250, 332–338, 357–359
Conservation,
  of number, 240
  of volume, 285
  of the whole, 153, 159

Counting, 9, 213–240, 246–249
  array size, 248–249
  memory load, 60–61
  principles of, 9, 213–218, 221–240, 246, 248–249
    Abstraction principle, 215–216, 221, 236–237
    Cardinal principle, 215, 224, 231–233, 239–240
    One-One principle, 214–215, 218, 223–224, 226–230, 239–240
    Order invariance principle, 216–217, 221–222, 237–238
    Stable ordering principle, 215, 231

D

Developmental tractibility, 8, 98

E

Ecological validity, 7–8, 27, 99
Encoding, 118, 137–142, 144–146, 156–159, 245–246
Error patterns, 9, 228–230, 353, 358
Experience, 39, 40, 45, 51, 100–102
Experimenter effects, 267–268

F

Field independence, 118
Frames, 51, 257, 286–287, 289

G

General Problem Solver (GPS), 286

I

Imagery, 291–321, 354–357
  adult processing model of, 292–295
  computer simulation of, 306–312, 356–357
  development of, 304–306
  as epiphenomenon, 295–301, 354
  generation of, 304
  as memory aid, 311–312, 356–357
  representational development hypothesis,
    292, 315–320
  retrieval of, 301–304
  as spatial entity, 297–303, 355–356
  teleological approach to, 291–292,
    313–320, 354
  and verbal code, 357
Instructional relevance, 10–11, 98–99
Intelligence, 244, 251
Intuition, 145–146, 152–153
  physical, 338–339, 345–347, 359

L

Language, 133, 146, 151, 164–172
  interpreting questions, 151, 164–166
Learning, 15–16, 61–62, 144
  how to learn, 15–16
  perceptual, 144
Left-right discrimination, 275–276, 281–282
Linguistic categories,
  development of, 168–169, 174–175, 260,
    265–266, 270
    class nouns, 168–169
    collective nouns, 168–169
    comparatives, 174–175
    definite articles, 265, 270
    deictic referents, 270
    indefinite articles, 266
    mediational deficiency, 146
    misunderstanding of instructions, 133
    pronouns, 270
    temporal order terms, 260, 270
Logical operations, development of, 151–154

M

Main idea, extraction of, 18–20, 25–26, 272
Maturation, 98,
Means-ends analysis, 182, 286, 337, 359
Memory, 4–7, 9–10, 16–17, 22–26, 28–30,
    40, 44–48, 50–51, 60–61, 73–76, 78,
    80–92, 94–98, 100–103, 145, 255–256,
    273, 309–310, 350–351, 356
  capacity, see short-term
  constant capacity hypothesis, 78, 84
  for everyday events, 255–256, 350–351
  interaction of capacity, knowledge, and
    strategies, 73–76
  and knowledge, 74–75, 80–92, 100–103
  long-term (LTM), 256
    visual LTM, 309–310
  mediation deficiencies, 5, 10
  mnemonic strategies, 5, 9, 22–26, 28,
    73–74, 94–98, 102, 104
  on nonstrategic tasks, 6–7
  production deficiencies, 5, 10
  short-term (STM), 40, 44–48, 50–51,
    60–61, 75–76, 80, 83, 100–101, 145
    visual STM, 309, 356
  span, see short-term
  voluntary, 24, 28–30
  weaknesses in the literature, 16–17
  working, see short-term
Mental rotation, 287–288
Metacognitive development, 12–17, 28–30,
    87–94, 98, 103–104
  metamemory, 12, 28–30, 87–94
    knowledge and, 87–94
  self-interrogation, 13–17, 98
  self-regulation, 13–17, 98
Modeling, 50

N

Natural language, 49–51, 53, 255–256
  childrens', 49–51, 255–256
  computer simulation of, 53
Novice/expert performance, 13–14, 98,
    328–332, 335–345, 357–359

O

Operations, development of, 60–63

P

Perceptual parsing, 313–314
Perceptual set hypothesis, 156–157
Perspective-taking, 282–283, 287–288, 353
Physics, 325–361
Practice effects, 346
Problem-solving, 15–16, 119–120, 122–132, 145–146, 181–183, 247–249, 332, 336–338
  application of, 249
  "common sense" reasoning, 181–182
  debugging, 15–16
  ethological study of, 183
  in physics, 332, 336–338
  rule-governedness, 145–146
  rules, 119–120, 122–132, 247
  strategies, 101, 152, 159, 173, 177, 187, 189, 191–195, 206
    addition, 152, 159, 173, 177
    evolution of, 38–39, 40, 44–45
    goal recursion, 191–194
    rote, 195, 206
    subtraction, 152, 159, 177
Production systems, *see* Computer simulation
Projection of shadows task, 121
Protocols, 29–30, 207, 260, 329–330, 340, 343
  value of self-reports, 351, 359–360

Q

Quantification, 159–161, 172–174
  and comparison, 174–175

R

Representation of knowledge, 289, 312–316, 345
  exocentric representation, 289, 352
  perceptual knowledge, 313–315
  propositional knowledge, 312, 316
  spatial representation, 275–289
Reversibility, 153–154, 159
Rule assessment methodology, 111–116, 119–122

S

Scientific reasoning, 110–111, 116–119, 132–142
  ability to learn, 116–117, 132–142
Scripts, 256–273, 349–352
  abstraction, degree of, 352
  enactive, 259–260
  of everyday events, 350–351
  implicit structure of, 269–270
  skeletal, 257, 271
  slots within, 256, 269
Soviet studies, 15, 24, 27–30, 230
Stages, Piagetian,
  concrete operational stage, 37–48
  formal operational stage, 63, 109–147, 285
  post-formal operational stage, 63
  preoperational stage, 49–54
  sensorimotor stage, 54–58
Stimulus-response habit sequences, 246, 350
Symbols, learning of, 276

T

Task analysis, 8–12, 244, 246, 285–289
Tasks, facilitating, 61–62
Task selection criteria, 18, 98–99
Theory development, 354
Tower of Hanoi, 183–186, 190–191, 203–205, 250
  minimum solution path, 186
  move types, 186, 190–191, 203–205
  problem types, 186, 191
Training studies, 10–12, 132–142
Turtle, 275–278, 353

V

Vertical décalage, 65
Visual scanning, 21–22, 25–26, 99

W

What develops?, 17, 20, 26, 31, 64, 104, 146, 177–179, 209–211, 238–240, 244, 272–273